A Journey Through The New Testament

The Story of Christ and how He Developed the Church

Elmer L. Towns

Harcourt Brace *Custom Publishers*
Harcourt Brace College Publishers
Fort Worth Philadelphia San Diego New York Orlando
Austin San Antonio Toronto Montreal London Sydney Tokyo

Custom Publisher   Virginia Colbourn
Senior Production Administrator   Sue Dunaway

A Historical Survey of the New Testament:
What the New Testament is all About

Printed in the United States of America

0-15-505476-7

TABLE OF CONTENTS

INTRODUCTION

The content of this book casts a long shadow over the rest of history, because it tells of the coming of Jesus Christ into the world, the establishment of His church, and the consummation of the age. Therefore, *What the New Testament Is All About* is a study of what history is all about.

There are many ways to approach the New Testament, i.e., a book-by-book study (survey), a synopsis of its doctrines and accomplishments, or a historical study. This book approaches the New Testament by a historical development integrating the impact of people, events, and contemporary history in the Roman world with the plan that God in heaven is working among men.

When approaching history, one could follow many theories. Some see history as a cycle where people struggle from hardship to prosperity, then become lax so that they lose their attainment and plummet back into the captivity of adversity. People seem to continually go through this cycle. Historians also interpret history as a struggle between good and evil, sometimes called a Jewish view of history. Then, some people see it through the evolutionary eyes of the progress of individuals from the alleged embryonic beginnings of the cavemen to the advancement of modern society. However, when we study civilization like Abraham in Ur of the Caldees we realize that history began at a high level – in the Garden of Eden. This volume approaches history through the study of "great men" who were history makers of the New Testament and altered the life of all those who followed them.

I have chosen to interpret the New Testament through the influence of great individuals as they impacted society or, in some cases, destroyed the quality of life in their times. These people are integrated with the ongoing story of history.

What the New Testament Is All About gives us insight into today's life, for the spiritual level of society is always measured by the quality of its leadership. Whether that leader was Jesus Christ in His human influence or His redemptive supernatural work on Calvary, He changes history so that He becomes the ultimate history maker. After studying the Apostles and those around them, I interpret the world today in light of what these great men have done to build churches and influence pastors today.

I believe the average American is not interested in dusty history stories. They want to know people, and the people of God want to examine God's people, so I have revealed these New Testament people as they were. I believe you will find the people of the New Testament are fascinating because they are like us in many ways. They rose above their circumstances to do exploits, and they left behind principles by which we can live our lives and hopefully accomplish the type of results they accomplished. Therefore, as we study these people who had the same desires as us, the same family problems, and the same frustrations, we see that in difficult circumstances, with inadequate means, facing insurmountable obstacles, they rose above their problems to conquer the world for Jesus Christ. They became history makers and their lives are worthy of our study.

This book is more than a collection of historical data about the people of the New Testament. It attempts to analyze the spiritual principles that have made these people great, then apply the principles to our twenty-first century life. Watch the practical applications at the end of each chapter of how the lives of New Testament heroes can impact modern people.

A book like this is never the product of a single individual. This one is inspired by those who have influenced my life directly. I thank Rev. Buck Hatch, Professor of Bible at Columbia Bible College, who gave me the historical insights of the prophets and of how prophecy impacts the New Testament. Also, I recognize Jimmy Breland, my Sunday school teacher who challenged me and my classmates by saying, "I am going to teach you the whole Bible" and as juniors we learned the pattern of the whole Bible. I recognize the work of Dr. Douglas Porter on this manuscript. During his seminary days, he lived in my home and we developed more than a teacher-student relationship. We became friends and shared the same philosophy of history. Doug was my graduate assistant, helping in the research, typing, the narrative from the classnotes. We thought through many of these issues together. Mrs. Cindy Spear edited and typeset the manuscript and Mrs. Christine Norton provided the artwork for the cover.

Special recognition is given to Henrietta Mears, author of *What the Bible Is All About,* who was one of the greatest Bible teachers in this century. Her students left her singles Sunday school class at First Presbyterian Church in Hollywood, California, and went out to serve Christ around the world. Her book, *What the Bible Is All About,* gave inspiration to the title *What the New Testament Is All About.*

For all of the problems, omissions, and inadequacies of the text, I must take full responsibility. May you the reader come to know Jesus Christ and bow at the foot of the Cross as you study the life of Jesus Christ and learn *what the New Testament is all about.*

Sincerely yours in Christ,

Elmer Towns

CHAPTER 1

ZACHARIAS AND ELISABETH: THE BIRTH OF A SON

Luke 1:5-80

It was the best of times. It was the worst of times... Eighteen hundred years after the birth of Jesus Christ an English author would use those words to describe the times in which He lived. But the phrase "best of times" well summarized the outlook of the aging priest Zacharias the morning he prepared for a very special day – a day of sacrifice in an honored position which any priest would long to fulfill. It was a dream come true, a once-in-a-lifetime opportunity. But it was also the "worst of times" because the Jews were a captive people in their own land, to the oppressive Roman government. No Davidic successor was on the throne and there was no prophet with a word from God, "Thus saith the Lord."

As Zacharias walked through Jerusalem that morning, he may have wished for the return of their glorious nation and freedom. It was the year 4 B.C. and a Roman garrison sat next to the temple to remind rebellious Jews of the vicious military might of the Roman Army. The Romans had conquered the land of the Jews in 63 B.C., but the Romans were not the initial cause of the problems that Zacharias felt that morning. They were the most recent of the four empires that had dominated their known world for the past few centuries.

Babylon under Nebuchadnezzar had captured and destroyed Jerusalem and its walls in August 586 B.C. Judah's last king, Zedekiah, saw his own sons killed before his eyes were put out. The remaining Jews were marched to Babylon (modern Iraq) and remained in captivity for seventy years.

The Jews returned from Babylon when Cyrus, the Persian Ruler decreed they could return to Jerusalem in 536 B.C. This second world empire allowed the Jews to rebuild their towns; they provided a lucrative tax base. Persian rulers gave the nation a degree of liberty, even recognizing the high priest as a civil authority subject to the governor of Syria.

Persia fell to the third world empire, Greece and its leader Alexander the Great. Even then the Jews were still well treated by the world ruler of that day. When Alexander arrived at Jerusalem, the Jewish high priest went out to him and explained how Daniel the prophet had predicted the Greeks would rule the world. Alexander was so impressed that he spared Jerusalem.

As Zacharias walked through the city of Jerusalem, the influence of

Greece still permeated the society. Greek was the official language and European ethnics from Greece and Rome still influenced business, government, and had even influenced the traditional Hebrew Bible.

The Jews in Alexandria, Egypt, had translated the pure language of Hebrew and of God into the Greek language (the Septuagint) in 285 B.C.

The time had come for Zacharias to enter Israel's most sacred room, the holy of holies in the temple. This was an honor not every priest enjoyed. For many years now he had seen other priests pass beyond the veil and wondered if the honor would ever be afforded to him. Now it was his turn. He would make his way to the place where God had promised to meet His people. There Zacharias would pray for the nation. He sensed the sacredness of the place and felt assured his prayer would be answered. Perhaps that is why he secretly planned to offer another prayer of a more personal nature in the moments he spent beyond the veil.

I.   Good Times and Bad Times at Home

Zacharias was concerned about a personal problem affecting both him and his wife Elisabeth. Although they had been married for many years, they still did not have a child. Both he and his wife wanted children, but Elisabeth was barren. They had both prayed about it before, many times, but still there was no child. Zacharias dealt with the problem by concentrating his energies on his work. His dedication to work had earned him the respect of his coworkers and was no doubt a factor leading to his selection for this special honor that was about to be his, but still he wanted a son. Soon he would retire from active service as a priest and he wanted an heir to carry on the family name.

Elisabeth had not been as fortunate as her husband in dealing with their problem. Nothing could be worse for a couple in those days to live together as husband and wife for several years and not have children. Children were considered an evidence of God's blessing upon a marriage. Not having children was interpreted as a sign of God's dissatisfaction with the wife or couple. Even though she knew she was righteous before God, probably surpassed her neighbors in the keeping of the law, she also knew most of her neighbors suspected there was something wrong in the life of this couple who still did not have children after so many years. More than anything else in the world, they longed for a son. Not only would an heir fulfill their longing and be a sign of God's blessing, it would serve as God's rebuke to their suspicious neighbors, confirming that Elisabeth was indeed righteous and honorable.

II.   Good Times and Bad Times in Government

As Zacharias considered the honor that would be his in praying for the nation, he realized there were problems in his world much larger than the barrenness of his wife. The past four centuries had been one of political turmoil impacting his nation greatly. Although he now lived in a time characterized by what later historians would call *Pax Romanas,* "the Roman peace," this priest knew it was a fragile peace at best. Even as he entered the temple to pray, he knew his nation was only moments away from a potential conflict with the mightiest nation on earth.

Four hundred years earlier, that nation would have been Persia. They ruled the world then and continued to do so until conquered by the Greeks in 334 B.C. Zacharias remembered the Greek empire break-up impacting Israel to a greater extent. First the land was ruled by Syria from Damascus, then Egypt (323-198 B.C.). During the Egyptian control of Israel, a large number of Jews moved to Egypt. Then Judaea was conquered by Antiochus III in 198 B.C. and annexed to Syria. The Holy Land was divided into five provinces: Galilee, Samaria, Judaea, Trachonitis, and Peraea. Initially, the Jews were still allowed to live under their own laws and continued to be ruled by the high priest and a council of elders. But Syria tended to interfere with the affairs of the temple and priesthood from time to time.

Finally, in 171 B.C., Antiochus IV Epiphanes plundered Jerusalem, killed many of the residents, and profaned the temple. On December 25, 168 B.C., he erected an altar to Jupiter in the temple, offered a sow upon the altar, and commanded the Jews to eat pork. Even though these actions were recognized as the fulfillment of Daniel's "little horn" prophecy (Dan. 8:9ff.), the people were horrified. The excesses of Antiochus sparked a popular and patriotic revolt among the people. The revolt was begun by a priest named Mattathias Maccabee. His motivation was an apparent genuine concern for the holiness of God. He led a band of Zealots into a campaign to free Israel and restore the worship of the temple in accordance with the law of Moses. He himself did little more than rally enthusiasm. His son and successor, Judas Maccabaeus, regained possession of Jerusalem and purified and rededicated the temple. This purification of the temple is still celebrated by Jews each December and is the only religious celebration of the Jews which has a historic background outside of the Old Testament (cf. John 10:22). The Maccabean Revolt was one of the most heroic in all history, but it failed to achieve a lasting victory against the Imperial power of Rome. Judas was killed in battle but was succeeded by his brother Jonathan. Although they maintained control of a few major centers for some time, Rome soon conquered and reigned over Palestine again. For some time the Zealots continued as an underground group of freedom fighters, but they never again posed a serious threat to Rome. The civil war in Judaea came to an end with the conquest of Judaea and Jerusalem by Pompey in 63 B.C. Although John Hyrcanus was given a nominal leadership role, the real ruler of Judaea was Antipater. In 47 B.C., he was formally made procurator of Judaea by Julius Caesar. In that role, he made his son Herod governor of Galilee. But Rome was not without its own civil problems. News of the assassination of Caesar resulted in another outbreak of disorder in Judaea. For his own security, Herod went to Rome. While there, he was appointed King of the Jews. Two years later (38 B.C.), he married the granddaughter of John Hyrcanus and appointed the Maccabean Aristobulus III high priest.

Although everything seemed to be settled on the surface, Zacharias knew of the turbulence building in the land. Some Zealots in the land were not prepared to accept an Idumean Roman puppet as a Jewish king. In sporadic uprisings, Jews were usually slaughtered. To Zacharias, "it was the worst of times." His people were slaves to Rome. As he walked through Jerusalem he saw Roman soldiers everywhere, a symbol of their oppression. The money that was donated to Jehovah bore the image of Caesar. From inside the temple courtyard, Zacharias could see the standard of the Plaetorium flying in the breeze.

III. Good Times and Bad Times in the Temple

For approximately 400 years no prophet had stood before the people as a spokesman for God. Four hundred years earlier, the prophet Malachi spoke God's message (Mal. 1:1). He rebuked the growing coldness of men's hearts and formalism of their worship. He warned the priests themselves they were among those most guilty of contributing to this national sin. "For the lips of a priest should keep knowledge, and people should seek the law from his mouth; For he is the messenger of the LORD of hosts. But you have departed from the way; You have caused many to stumble at the law. You have corrupted the covenant of Levi" (Mal. 2:7-8). Despite the pleas of Malachi, the only response of the religious establishment was to bury the record of his prophecy in a book containing the writings of eleven other lesser known prophets. Evaluating the situation from the perspective of four hundred years later, Zacharias could only conclude the situation of Malachi's day had gone from bad to worse. None of the events of the past four hundred years caused the people to heed the warning of Malachi. The Jews lived and died in a changing world without a fresh visitation from God. Inevitably the religion of Israel experienced changes during this time. The Babylonian captivity seemed to have cured Israel of her tendency toward idolatry, but it also resulted in the establishing of synagogues in every center where there were Jews. The synagogue was vastly different from the temple. Some have called the synagogue (i.e. assembly of teaching) a symbol of defeat, in opposition to the temple which was a symbol of victory. Israel met God in the temple between the seraphim when they brought a blood sacrifice, but they retreated to the synagogue to learn and reinforce their sectarian identity. The Jews built synagogues everywhere to hear the Old Testament Scriptures read to them during those years when no prophets thundered, "Thus saith the Lord." The vital faith of Israel became increasingly institutionalized.

Another "fly in the ointment" irritated old Zacharias – it was the rival religion of the Samaritans located on Mount Gerizin, thirty miles to the north of Jerusalem. They claimed an Old Testament heritage with rival sacrifices, a rival priesthood, and rival holy days. Zacharias thought of them as half-breeds, without Jewish blood running in their veins, even though the Samaritans claimed perpetuity from the ancient fathers. The Samaritans were established when Israel was in captivity (586-536 B.C.). By the end of the Persian rule of Palestine, the Samaritans had a well-established pattern of worship and had built their own temple. The racial and religious tensions between the Jews and the Samaritans had grown to the point that Jews now avoided all dealings with Samaritans. Even those who traveled between Galilee and Jerusalem went out of their way to avoid even passing through Samaritan territory.

Both Zacharias and his wife Elisabeth were literate and well read. Whereas in the Old Testament God's people were mostly illiterate, during the inter-testament period they became a reading people. That helped preserve

Jewish identity (through the synagogue) while other cultures disappeared. The Jewish colony in Alexandria had translated the Septuagint (LXX), a Greek translation of the Old Testament from the original Hebrew language (285 B.C.). This action sharply divided faithful Jews. Many felt the language of God was Hebrew and everyone should learn to read the sacred text as God originally gave it. Jews living outside of Palestine were generally looked down on because they preferred and used the Greek translation over the Hebrew version used in the temple.

Religious literature was written and revered in the synagogue until the traditions, comments, and interpretations recorded in the Talmud, Midrashim, and Kabbala were considered as authoritative as the Scriptures they commented upon. As the priests tended to become more rationalistic in their approach to the Scriptures, they alienated many of the common people who identified with stories of men who met angels and experienced miracles. Sects formed within Judaism as various theological systems became prominent. Before long, not only the priests were teaching the Scriptures, but the Pharisees, one of the most popular sects to arise within Judaism, became a popular instrument to teach the law. While the Sadducees, the rationalistic party that denied the supernatural, still controlled the Sanhedrin, a number of prominent Pharisees had seats on this governing body.

The Pharisees or Sadducees influenced the popular opinion of the multitudes by teaching in the synagogues while the priests ministered to the people in the temple. While all Jewish males (Deut. 16:16) still made pilgrimages to Jerusalem to worship God, they developed their understanding of God and His world in the synagogue. Many of these synagogues were large and very beautiful even in contrast to the temple itself. The synagogues were built by prosperous businessmen and foreign money in modern cities, whereas the temple was rebuilt many centuries earlier by a struggling group of immigrant Jews who had returned to Jerusalem. That was beginning to change. As a gesture of good will to the Jews, Herod had begun a major restoration of the temple which amounted to the building of a third temple.

IV. The End of God's Silence

For four hundred years, God did not speak to His people. They had the biblical record of what He had already said, but it was increasingly ignored. But one would be wrong to assume that God had abandoned His people. Jehovah had been silent, but He was about to speak as loudly and clearly as He would ever speak to any people. "God, who at various times and in various ways spoke in time past to the fathers by the prophets, has in these last days spoken to us by His Son, whom he has appointed heir of all things, through whom also he made the worlds" (Heb. 1:1-2).

The priests had been grouped into thirteen divisions. Temple duties passed each month from division to division. This practice had been going on for years and was almost taken for granted. Still, for a righteous and faithful priest like Zacharias, it was an honor to be the one that ministered in the temple. Some priests served the Lord a lifetime and never led in sacrificing to God. No doubt Zacharias felt a special closeness to God as his time came to pray at the altar of incense. Though there was much to pray for pertaining to the nation, he would not forget the ache of his own heart and that of his wife Elisabeth. Zacharias asked God for a son even though they were too old to parent a child. He may have even thought prayer made at that place could not be refused by God. But Zacharias did not think God would send an angel to confirm His answer. "Do not be afraid, Zacharias, for your prayer is heard; and your wife Elisabeth will bear you a son, and you shall call his name John," the angel announced to the terrified priest (Luke 1:13). God's special messenger went on to explain how the birth of this son would bring rejoicing beyond the immediate family because he would be set apart from birth as a Nazirite, a man with a special mission in life. This son who would be named John would be the forerunner of the Messiah who had been promised in the prophecy of Malachi.

THREEFOLD CHARACTERISTIC OF A NAZIRITE

1. Not eat of fruit of the vine.
2. Not to come near a dead body.
3. Not to cut his hair.

Perhaps Zacharias had been praying too long to accept this dramatic answer to his prayers. Zacharias listened, but what he heard was too incredible to be easily believed. "How shall I know this?" he asked. "For I am an old man, and my wife is well advanced in years" (Luke 1:18).

Only then did the angel identify himself by name. Zacharias learned he was speaking with Gabriel, the same angel who had told Daniel about many of the events of the last four hundred years. This angel had come to Zacharias direct from the presence of God with a message from God. But if Zacharias needed a sign before he could believe this good news, Gabriel would oblige. "You will be mute and not able to speak until the day these things take place, because you did not believe my words which will be fulfilled in their own time" (Luke 1:20).

Even if Zacharias hurried to finish his duties in the temple, the meeting with Gabriel had taken up time and he was behind schedule. Those waiting for him outside noticed it was taking him considerably longer to perform his duties than was usual. But when Zacharias exited the temple unable to speak, the people realized what had happened in the temple was anything but usual. "They perceived that he had seen a vision in the temple, for he beckoned to them and remained speechless" (Luke 1:22).

Although he could not speak, he could still see and hear. In the months following, he watched his wife and saw the evidence that the angel's prophecy was coming to pass. He heard his wife as she marvelled privately that she was finally about to become a mother. He understood when his wife chose to stay out of public view fearing the possibility of a miscarriage and the personal humiliation that might follow in that event. Unable to speak, he could communicate at least to his wife some of what had happened in the temple that day.

Six months into her term, a relative of Elisabeth came from Nazareth to visit her. Mary, a young girl in her mid-teens, had learned of Elisabeth's pregnancy from an angel, the same angel who had appeared to Zacharias in the temple seven months earlier. Mary too was expecting a son, even though she was not married and had not been involved physically with a man. Mary stayed with Elisabeth for three months. These two expectant mothers rejoiced with each other as they talked about the honor that was theirs to give birth to two special babies. Together they counted the months, then the weeks, and then finally the days. Mary had to return to Nazareth before Elisabeth gave birth, but she left knowing it would not be long. "Now Elisabeth's full time came for her to be delivered, and she brought forth a son" (Luke 1:57).

The birth of a son was an event worth celebrating in the life of Zacharias and Elisabeth. That sleeping child in the arms of his mother was a silent rebuke to those who had suspected their relationship with God and a public confirmation of what they knew to be true privately, that God was pleased with their righteous life style. But these parents realized their son would do more than just bring joy to their home. He would turn his nation back to God in preparation for the Messiah.

Eight days after his birth, John was brought by his parents to be circumcised as required in the law of Moses. It was customary to announce the name of the child at his circumcision. The most natural thing to do was name a son after his father or some other close male relative. But Elisabeth insisted this son would be called John, not named Zacharias after his father. Friends and family members who had come together on this occasion tried to dissuade her from this strange urge to chose a name outside the family. It took the intervention of Zacharias himself to convince them he was in accord with the naming of his son John. He secured a writing tablet and wrote so all could see, "His name is John" (Luke 1:63). And no sooner had he written those word that he found himself once again able to speak. This act of obedient faith by Zacharias healed him.

V.   The End of Zacharias' Silence

For four hundred years, Israel had not heard a word from God. For almost ten months, his friends had not heard a word from Zacharias. Now they would hear from both. Not only could Zacharias speak, he was filled with the Holy Spirit and could prophesy. And on the occasion of his son's circumcision, he did just that.

When Zacharias prophesied over the birth of his son John, he called his son "the prophet of the Highest" (Luke 1:76). But the emphasis of his prophecy focused upon another one he called "the Dayspring from on High" (Luke 1:78). It was to be characteristic of the life and ministry of John that he, "a bright and shining light," should ever be dimmed in contrast with his cousin, who was the Light of the World (John 8:12; 9:5).

The word *Dayspring* is a translation of the Greek word *anatole* literally meaning "a rising of light" or "sunrise." The place of the dayspring was the point along the eastern horizon at which the sun rose (cf. Job 38:12). By implication, the term came to mean the east, i.e. the direction of the sunrise (cf. Matt. 2:1). It was used by Zacharias metaphorically of Christ, the one through whom the true Light shone not only to Israel, but to all the world.

This particular sunrise is unique. This dayspring is described as being "from on high" (*ex hupsos*). The word *hupsos* refers not only to height but to the idea of being raised to a high or exalted state (cf. James 1:9). It is closely related to the adjective *hupsistos* used when describing John as the prophet "of the Highest" (Luke 1:76). The implication from the use of this particular term in this context is that this was uniquely a divinely appointed or exalted sunrise.

The appearance of the Dayspring from on High on the horizon of human history was not without its effect. Its shining is the light to reveal our sin. Its warmth is the source to revitalize us in our sorrow. Its beacon redirects our steps. But the ultimate effect of its appearance is the redemption of our soul.

THE DAYSPRING FROM ON HIGH

It reveals our sin.
It revitalizes us in our sorrow.
It redirects our steps.
It redeems our souls.

Those who witnessed the events surrounding the birth and naming of John, and those who heard the reports, knew there was something special about this boy. "And all those who heard them kept them in their hearts, saying, What kind of child will this be?" (Luke 1:66).

But this boy had more than the love of his parents and support of his community as he began life. "The hand of the Lord was with him" (Luke 1:66). "So the child grew and became strong in spirit, and was in the deserts till the day of his manifestation to Israel" (Luke 1:80).

Conclusion

Sometimes in the Christian life, God's silence may be deafening. A believer may pray for weeks, months, or even years for something without receiving a definite answer from God. There are many reasons why God may not answer one's prayer and some of these have no relationship at all to the presence or absence of sin in one's life. Sometimes it may only be a matter of timing. God may intend to give the believer what is requested, but not until later when it better fits into God's plan and program for that believer. In the interim, it is important that one continues in faith and not allow doubt to unconsciously replace belief as apparently what happened in Zacharias' experience.

CHAPTER 2

JOSEPH AND MARY:
THE SUPERNATURAL BIRTH OF
GOD'S SON

Matthew 1:18–2:23; Luke 2:1-52; John 1:14

*S*ixty miles north of the temple where Zacharias learned of the impending birth of his son, another couple met often in Nazareth to share their dreams of the life they planned to spend together. Joseph had worked hard to establish his reputation as a carpenter in that Galilean community and was now ready to take a wife and begin a family. Prenuptial arrangements had been made and within the year, Joseph would be married to Mary, the young daughter of Heli. This young couple was planning and dreaming about their future. Nazareth was not the kind of place where dreams come easy. Like many of the other communities in Galilee, Nazareth was often visited by the unwelcome Roman soldiers sent to keep the peace in this trouble spot of the Roman Empire. The residents of this town resented the intrusion of the Romans into their lives and determined to make life miserable for those who dared march down their streets. Nazareth was on the trade route between Damascus and Egypt. Travelers of the world trudged wearily down its main street and stopped to drink at the one well in town. It was common for families to litter the streets with garbage that might otherwise have found its way to the compost pile. Littering their street was great fun for the residents – a safe way to express their anger toward the Romans – but when the soldiers left, the garbage remained. To those living outside the city limits, Nazareth was known simply as "the city of garbage."

I.   Dreaming Great Dreams in an Unlikely City

A. The Dream of a Couple in Love. Still, Nazareth was the home of this couple very much in love. They had been raised to believe anything was possible. From their earliest childhood, both Mary and Joseph had been taught they belonged to a special people, God's people. Not only were they Jews, but they belonged to the tribe of Judah, a family which God had designated as the ruling tribe and family of the nation. The blood of King David flowed in their veins. As Joseph repaired the broken wheel of a Roman chariot, he knew in his heart that under different circumstances he would be recognized as the son of a king rather than servant of a Herod. At times it may have seemed hard to wait out the period of their betrothal as Joseph and Mary anticipated married life together. Still, both Joseph and Mary knew they were expected to live by the moral code taught them by their parents and were disciplined in their relationships with each other. There was never any doubt in their minds that this was certainly the best way to prepare for what was anticipated as a happy life together. Much still had to be accomplished before they would be recognized as husband and wife. But Mary quickly learned that her dreams were not to be fulfilled quite as she expected when her thoughts were interrupted one day by a visit of an angel.

B. *Shattered Dreams and an Angel from God.* Gabriel, an angel used by God, brought a special message for Mary, but she had no way of recognizing him as such. Few people ever saw an angel. The popular ideas about death suggested most people would not see an angel until one came to take the living to the place of the dead. It is understandable that the presence of Gabriel scared this young bride-to-be. "Do not be afraid, Mary," Gabriel called out. "For you have found favor with God. And behold, you will conceive in your womb and bring forth a Son, and shall call His name Jesus" (Luke 1:30-31). This messenger from God went on to explain that her son would someday sit on the throne of David and reign forever as king of Israel. This message was overwhelming to Mary. Moments before, she had dreamed of being the wife of a carpenter and living a comfortable life as the mother of his children. Now she was being told she would be the mother of the Messiah.

"How can this be, since I do not know a man?" she asked (Luke 1:34). Gabriel explained a man would not be involved in the birth of this son. God Himself would be the Father of this unique child. He would "be called the Son of God" (Luke 1:35) meaning the child would have the same divine nature as His Father. The prophet Isaiah had foretold of a virgin birth of a son (Isa. 7:14), but Mary must have found it hard to believe *she* would be the one to fulfill that prophecy. Gabriel knew Mary would have had difficulty believing what he told her, so he told her about Elisabeth. Mary knew Elisabeth could not have children, but according to the angel, this barren relative was now six months pregnant. She began to understand how both of these miracles would be possible as the angel reminded her, "For with God nothing will be impossible" (Luke 1:37). God was offering her a unique opportunity to give birth to His Son. No other woman in history had or would have this privilege and responsibility. But what about her dreams with Joseph, the man she loved and looked forward to marrying? How would she explain this to him? Would he understand? This meant her life would never be the same, nor would her marriage be what she had hoped and thought it might be some day. Before her lay two options; the offer of God or the dreams she shared with the man she loved. It was time for her to make a decision. "Behold the maidservant of the Lord! Let it be to me according to your word," she responded (Luke 1:38). Above all else, Mary was prepared to yield her life to God's will.

C. *Elisabeth and the Celebration of a New Dream.* There were still a lot of unanswered questions, but no sooner than had she agreed to be available to God, the angel left. Where would she turn for answers. As she considered the matter, she remembered what Gabriel had told her about Elisabeth. Her elderly aunt too was involved in what only could be described as a miracle. Quickly she packed her things and raced off to the home of her relative. Mary arrived in the home of Elisabeth three months before the birth of John the Baptist, but already the unborn child was sensitive to spiritual things and responded to the voice of Mary, the expectant mother of the Son of God, by leaping in his mother's womb.

Elisabeth too was aware of the significance of Mary's role as the mother of the Son of God and being filled with the Holy Spirit began to speak. When Elisabeth spoke, she uttered the first of four psalms recorded in the Gospel of Luke. Each of these four statements takes the form of Old Testament poetry, but is found in the pages of the New Testament. While most Old Testament psalms are found in the Book of Psalms, there were exceptions to this rule. Perhaps the two most notable Old Testament exceptions are the song of Hannah (1 Sam. 2:1-10) and the prayer of Habakkuk (Hab. 3:1-19).

THE PSALMS OF LUKE

The Song of Elisabeth (1:42-45)
The Magnificant of Mary (1:46-55)
The Benedictus of Zacharias (1:68-79)
The Nunc Dimittus of Simeon (2:29-32)

In her song, Elisabeth confirmed the essence of the angel's prophecy. She identified Mary as "the mother of my Lord" (Luke 1:43) acknowledging the character of the child then growing in Mary's womb. She further assured Mary "there will be a fulfillment of those things which were told her from the Lord" (Luke 1:45). In the Old Testament, a matter was said to be confirmed with the testimony of at least two witnesses. When Mary heard Elisabeth restate the essence of Gabriel's statement, she could believe she was indeed a part of something unique which God was doing. Her response was that of celebration and worship directed to the Lord. While Mary in her song recognizes future generations "will call me blessed" in the sense of being privileged (Luke 1:48), she also identified God as her Savior (Luke 1:47) suggesting she was not unique from the rest of humanity (there was no immaculate conception) in that she also needed to trust in the redemptive work her son would accomplish on Calvary.

D. Joseph's Dream and a Night Wedding. Mary and Elisabeth had probably not seen each other in some time, and it was customary for expectant mothers to be surrounded by female friends and relatives in the latter stages of their pregnancies. This no doubt contributed to Mary's prolonged visit to the home of Elisabeth and Zacharias. Whether Mary remained until the actual birth of John or left just prior to it is unclear in Scripture, but the visit lasted some three months. By the time she returned to her home in Nazareth, she was already three months pregnant. It would not be long before Joseph would notice a change in Mary's physical appearance. Prior to the appearance of Gabriel to Mary, Joseph had already agreed to take Mary as his wife. According to the custom of that day and culture, the couple were in a state of betrothal to each other. Normally, this period lasted about a year and gave the couple time to get to know each other better and prepare for the adjustments of married life. It was similar to the contemporary western custom of engagement in that a commitment to marry each other was present, but it differed in that a betrothal could not be broken without a formal writ of divorce.

When it became obvious to Joseph that Mary was pregnant, and he knew the child was not his because of his disciplined relationship with Mary, he could only conclude Mary had been involved physically with another man. Under the circumstances, he had the option of having Mary publicly stoned to death for adultery (Deut. 22:23-24) or arranging a quiet divorce (Deut. 22:25-27; 24:1-4). As he considered these options, he was inclined to avoid any further embarrassment and divorce Mary. While Joseph was considering this matter, he too received a visit from an angel. After four hundred years of silence from God, this was the third of four angelic appearances within a year and a half. Each time the angel appeared, he began his statement with the words, "Do not be afraid," then identified a spiritual principle which when understood was designed to help individuals overcome their natural fears.

DO NOT BE AFRAID

God is answering your prayer (Luke 1:13)
You have found favor with God (Luke 1:30)
God is at work in this situation (Matt. 1:20)
God has provided a Savior (Luke 2:10-11)

This angel appeared to Joseph in a dream and encouraged Joseph "to take to you Mary your wife" (Matt. 1:20). Joseph was told the child's name would be Jesus which means "Jehovah saves." This child would be so named because "He will save His people from their sins" (Matt. 1:21). The angel assured Joseph of Mary's moral purity by reminding him of the Immanuel prophecy of Isaiah (cf. Isa. 7:14; Matt. 1:22-23). Joseph was immediately responsive to the Lord's instruction in the dream. Being aroused from his sleep, he took immediate steps to take Mary as his wife. Prior to talking with the angel, marriage was not an option he had considered. Once he understood what God was doing in Mary's life, he agreed it was best to share his married life with a wife who was totally yielded to God, even if it meant something different than their dreams. Also, Joseph's understanding of what God was doing meant he would remain disciplined in his sexual relations with his wife until the miracle child was born. When that child was born, the son would be named Jesus after His Heavenly Father Jehovah.

II. The Birth of a King in the City of a King

A. *Moving to a New Home.* The sudden marriage of Joseph and Mary and the growing physical evidence of Mary's condition no doubt was enough to get the neighbors talking. Premarital sexual activity was not as acceptable then as it has become in some segments of today's permissive society. Joseph and Mary must have both noticed the difference in the way people began treating them.

Although Joseph probably built a home and established a business in Nazareth, the suspicion of his neighbors made his hometown anything but a desirable place to live. The garbage in the streets was nothing compared to the garbage he perceived in the minds of his neighbors. The solution to this growing problem came in an imperial edict from Rome. "And it came to pass in those days that a decree went out from Caesar Augustus that all the world should be registered" (Luke 2:1). This registration of the Roman empire meant a move for Joseph and Mary. It was customary in Israel and Egypt to return to one's hometown or ancestral city for this census. Because both Joseph and Mary were descendants of King David, this meant they would go to the city of Bethlehem in Judea. Traveling along the normal route a Galilean would take would involve a journey of about seventy miles. Apparently the young couple intended not only to visit Bethlehem and register for the census, but to remain in that city to live. Some Bible teachers believe they intended to move there and begin their new life together in a new city. This is indicated by the fact that they were still in Bethlehem forty days after the birth of Jesus and were living in a house in Bethlehem when the Magi came to worship Jesus as King of the Jews. The visit of the Magi may have occurred up to two years after the birth of Jesus.

Joseph and Mary may have seen such a move as the wisest course of action. Living in Bethlehem would help them escape the suspicion of their neighbors, bring them closer to Jerusalem which was the focus of their faith in God, and provide a better community environment in which to raise a family. Also, both Joseph and Mary would have been aware of the biblical prophecy which identified the Messiah as coming from Bethlehem (Micah 5:2).

B. The Birth of Jesus. By the time the couple had made the necessary arrangements for the move, Mary was very near the end of her term. When they arrived in the city of Bethlehem, they discovered the city was overcrowded with others who had also come to be counted. Bethlehem was so crowded, the best lodging Joseph could find for his expectant wife was a cave in which livestock was kept. The custom in those days was to build homes near caves when possible and use the cave as a stable. The visitor to Bethlehem today can visit The Church of the Nativity which is located over a cave which church officials claim to be the actual birthplace of Jesus.

When Jesus was born, his parents improvisation turned the stable into a nursery. He was wrapped in bands which wound around him (swaddling cloths) and placed in a soft bed of grasses in a manger which was usually used to feed the livestock when they could not graze the pasture land surrounding the city. Despite the fact both Joseph and Mary knew the supernatural significance of this birth, it must have seemed a strange way for the Son of God to enter the world. The casual observer of this birth would have seen nothing different beyond the unusual place in with the child was born, but almost a century later, one of that child's future disciples would describe His birth with the words, "And the Word became flesh and dwelt among us" (John 1:14).

C. The Angels Worship. While others might not realize what was happening in that Bethlehem stable, it did not escape heaven's notice. Shortly after the birth of Jesus, an angel appeared to a group of shepherds watching their flocks on the hills outside the city of Bethlehem. As soon as he announced the birth of the Christ child to the shepherds, that angel was accompanied by a multitude of angels praising God for what had just taken place. This was the first of several angelic multitudes which would be associated with Christ during His life and ministry.

D. *The Shepherds Worship.* A group of shepherds on the hills surrounding Bethlehem was the first to learn of Jesus' birth. Some wonder why God chose to tell shepherds first about Jesus' birth. Several reasons may be suggested. First, Jesus was described as a shepherd (cf. 1 Peter 5:4) and in that sense a kinship existed between them. Also, Jesus was the Son of David (cf. Matt. 1:1) the shepherd boy who had often met with God in communion on those same hills. Third, Jesus was the Lamb of God (cf. John 1:29) and shepherds would know how to rejoice in the birth of a lamb. A fourth reason the shepherds may have been the first to know was that like the shepherds, Jesus would be despised and rejected by other classes of men (cf. Isa. 53:3; Gen. 46:44).

WHY WERE THE SHEPHERDS THE FIRST TO KNOW?

Because the baby was a Shepherd.
Because the baby was the son of David.
Because the baby was the Lamb of God.
Because the baby would be despised and rejected.

After learning of the birth of the Messiah, these shepherds quickly made their way to the stable to worship. Once they saw that what the angel had told them was true, they began telling others what had happened. While most who heard the shepherds that evening simply wondered about their report of the appearance of angels, the testimony of the shepherds held special significance for the child's mother (Luke 2:19).

E. *The Worship of Prophets.* Under Jewish law, certain religious responsibilities were incumbent upon the parents of a firstborn son. Eight days after the birth of Jesus, he was circumcised and formally named Jesus. The act of circumcision was a Jewish ritual which brought Jesus under the law. Forty days after his birth, Jesus was presented to the Lord in the temple (cf. Luke 2:22; Ex. 13:2, 12, 15). The sacrifice of two birds offered by Jesus' parents at this time suggests they were from the poorest class of society (cf. Lev. 12:8).

While in the temple, the young family had an unusual encounter with two godly persons who were known in the temple. The first was a prophet named Simeon who had received a special witness of the Holy Spirit that he would not die before he saw the one through whom God would bring redemption to the nation. On the day Joseph and his family made their way to the temple, Simeon was directed by the Holy Spirit to go to the temple. When he met the young family, he took Jesus in his arms and began worshiping God. He recognized this child represented the salvation of God not only for the Jews, but also for the Gentiles (Luke 2:29-32). Although Isaiah had included the Gentiles in his messianic prophecy, few Jews understood the Messiah would have a ministry beyond the nation itself. Simeon's prayer to God has been called *Nunc Dimittis* meaning "now die" because it was a prayer to die now that God had fulfilled

His promise. The second person to worship God in the temple in celebration of the Messiah was a very old but spiritually alert woman named Anna. Anna had been a widow for eighty-four years and had been married for seven years prior. She was probably well over one hundred years old the day she saw Jesus. She not only thanked God for the opportunity of seeing Jesus, she told others whom she knew were looking for the Messiah about Him. It is interesting to note Anna was of the tribe of Asher, a tribe which was blessed with abundance even to providing food for kings (Gen. 49:20). This member of the tribe had often denied herself through fasting and was rewarded with meeting the King of Kings.

F. The Worship of Rulers. Some time later, Jesus was worshiped by a group of eastern rulers known as the Magi. These men may not have been kings themselves, but certainly possessed enough influence to be regarded as king-makers in their society. They probably belonged to a particular caste of people given to the study of astrology and other "sciences" of the day. The appearance of a "star" in the heavens had been interpreted by them as an indication of the birth of the King of the Jews.

While most evangelical Bible teachers believe the star which appeared in the east was a miraculous sign placed in the sky by God, a number of alternatives have been suggested. About A.D. 200, one of the church fathers, Origin, suggested the possibility that the Christmas star may have been a comet. According to the Chinese scholar Ma Tuan-lin, what was later named Halley's Comet appeared on August 25, 7 B.C., and was observed for sixty-three days as it passed through several constellations in the sky. A second natural explanation is that of the conjunction of Saturn and Jupiter in the constellation of Pisces first proposed by Johannes Kepler. He observed this phenomenon on December 17, 1603, and suggested this may have occurred as a forerunner of the Christmas star. Later astronomers have confirmed a conjunction of these planets did occur in 7 B.C. on at least three occasions, including October 3 which was the Jewish Day of Atonement that year. While these signs occurred around the estimated time of Christ's birth (c. 8-4 B.C.), the Bethlehem star led the Magi from Jerusalem to a specific home in Bethlehem, suggesting it was something more than a comet or conjunction of planets (Matt. 2:9). The Magi interpreted the star as a sign or an announcement of the birth of "the King of the Jews" (Matt. 2:2). In their search for this king, they naturally went to the historic Jewish capital of Jerusalem. When they began asking where the newborn king was, they hit a sore spot with Herod who had taken the title "King of the Jews" to himself. Other historical records report that Herod was engaged in a messianic controversy about 6 B.C. with the Pharisees. The dispute came to the point that the Pharisees predicted the early death of Herod because he had taken a messianic title to himself. Herod responded by having the leaders of the Pharisees arrested and executed. In light of this, the appearance of an educated and influential caste of people from another country who were looking for this Messiah posed a threat to the security of his throne. As the rumors spread throughout Jerusalem, the whole city felt uneasy wondering how this tyrant would respond.

Herod consulted with "all the chief priests and scribes of the people" (Matt. 2:4) to learn where the Messiah was to be born. This group probably included all those who had recently held the office of High Priest as well as the heads of each of the twenty-four courses of priests and perhaps some of the leading scribes. Most of these individuals would have been Sadducees who tended to deny the miraculous, rather than Pharisees with whom Herod had his earlier dispute. Although Sadducees did not believe the supernatural nature of the Old Testament Scriptures nor accept them as their final authority in matters of faith and practice, they did know them and were able to identify Bethlehem as the birthplace of the Messiah (Matt. 2:5; cf. Mic. 5:2). Herod reported this information to the Magi and encouraged them to bring him a report of the exact location of the newborn king when they found him.

When the Magi came to the home of the family in Bethlehem, they worshiped Jesus and presented Him with gifts of gold, frankincense and myrrh. Because three gifts were presented, it has been traditionally thought three men were present. Actually, the Bible does not identify the number present. It is reasonable to assume more than three men may have made the journey.

G. Exile in Egypt. The Magi anticipated returning to Jerusalem to share their discovery with Herod, but after being warned by God in a dream not to return to Jerusalem, "they departed for their own country another way" (Matt. 2:12). Probably they went along the south shore of the Dead Sea rather than by the route that would have taken them to Jerusalem. Some Bible teachers have observed the response of the Magi as typical of everyone's reaction who comes to worship Jesus. No one can worship Jesus without being different. They go home another way.

The Magi were not the only ones warned to leave Bethlehem. Once again an angel appeared to Joseph in a dream urging him to take Mary and Jesus to Egypt. Joseph was told Herod would try to destroy the child. Quickly Joseph gathered what was needed and he and his family made their way to Egypt that very night. Probably the family made their way to the city of Alexandria which at that time was home to over one million Jews. They remained there until they heard of Herod's death. Herod did try to destroy the child. When he realized he had been tricked by the Magi, he issued a decree that every male child aged two and under in the greater Bethlehem area should be killed. This type of decree is characteristic of the man Flavius Josephus called "the most cruel tyrant who ever ascended the throne." Based on the known size of Bethlehem at that time, the slaughter of the innocents probably involved the execution of less than two dozen children and was one of Herod's lessor evils.

H. Back to Nazareth. When Joseph learned of Herod's death, he and his family made plans to return home as instructed by an angel in a dream. Probably they intended to return to Bethlehem, but changed their minds when they learned of the rule of Archelaus in the place of his father. When the Jews mourned the victims of Herod rather than the death of Herod, Archelaus began his rule by sending his troops into Jerusalem, including the temple area. An estimated three thousand people were killed in one day alone. After the riots which accompanied the Feast of Tabernacles that year, another two thousand men were arrested and crucified. No doubt Joseph would have heard these and other similar reports as he neared Bethlehem, located just five miles south of Jerusalem. Wisely he chose to relocate his family back in Nazareth where he knew many of the people and could rebuild his carpentry business.

III. A Son about His Father's Business

A. *The Childhood of Jesus.* Apart from his brief exile in Egypt, there is no indication that Jesus' childhood differed much from that of other children. Joseph and Mary had other children in time and Jesus learned to relate to these and other children in the town. Legendary accounts of Jesus' childhood exist which suggest Jesus performed miracles involving other children with whom he played, but the New Testament identifies the changing of water to wine as the first miracle of Jesus (cf. John 2:11). He probably joined other boys his age in the Synagogue School of Nazareth where he would be taught the Scriptures and basic skills such as reading, writing, and arithmetic. "And the Child grew and became strong in spirit, filled with wisdom; and the grace of God was upon Him" (Luke 2:40).

B. *The Journey to Jerusalem.* The only further record we have of Jesus' childhood is the account of a visit to Jerusalem during the Passover season. His family went to Jerusalem for passover annually. When Jesus was twelve, He remained in the city without His parents knowledge. They began the trip back to Nazareth, thinking he was along. Three days past before they found Him in the temple. While the teachers with whom He was meeting were impressed by His understanding of the law, His parents had been concerned for His welfare. When they finally found Him, Mary rebuked Him admitting both she and Joseph had been worried about Him. He responded, "Did you not know that I must be about My Father's business?" (Luke 1:49).

C. *The Maturing of Jesus.* While Jesus had an understanding of who He was and what His mission in life would be at a very early age, He remained subject to His parents for another eighteen years before he began His public ministry. He was approximately thirty years old when he was baptized (Luke 3:23). During that time, "Jesus increased in wisdom and stature, and in favor with God and men" (Luke 2:52). While someday He would be about His Heavenly Father's business, as a teenager and young adult, Jesus learned the business of his adopted earthly father Joseph and probably worked as an apprentice in the carpenter's shop.

Conclusion

Sometimes God's plan for one's life is not the same as that which might be planned by the individual involved; it's better. Yielding one's dreams and goals in life to something else is difficult, especially when the long-term benefits of the alternate plan are not readily apparent. Mary's and Joseph's decision to abandon their worthy dreams to be available to God and accept His plan for their life demonstrated their willingness not only to dream dreams, but also allow God to redirect their steps as they began working to fulfill those dreams. "A man's heart plans his way, but the LORD directs his steps" (Prov. 16:9). This fundamental principle of planning needs to be a part of the decision-making and problem-solving process in every believer's life.

CHAPTER 3

JOHN THE BAPTIST:

CALLING A NATION BACK TO GOD

Matthew 3:1–4:11; Mark 1:1–4:13; John 2:6-13

The Roman empire produced a number of influential political leaders such as Caesar, Mark Anthony, and Herod, but one of the most influential men in the Near East was an unlikely prophet named John the Baptist (technically, his description was not an adjective but a verb, i.e., "the baptizer") who attracted multitudes to hear him preach in the wilderness around the Jordan River. He was not known for his influence in political circles yet at least one politician of his day feared him greatly. Neither did John have connections in the Jewish temple, but leading members of Israel's religious community joined the crowds by the river Jordan to listen to him and learn more about him. He claimed to be nobody particularly important, but his message from the Lord was the most important message announced to the masses. The common people identified him with prophets like Elijah and Jeremiah. Some even thought of him as the promised Messiah. Yet in spite of his undeniable popularity, John the Baptist continued to insist he was merely a forerunner of One who was much greater. Yet Jesus said, "Among those born of women there has not risen one greater than John the Baptist" (Matt. 11:11).

John began his ministry when a number of prominent historical leaders held a degree of political power in the region (Luke 3:1-2). Rome was in its fifteenth year of being ruled by its second Caesar, Tiberius. Tiberius began his reign as a coregent in A.D. 11 or A.D. 13, and assumed full control in A.D. 14. Therefore, the fifteenth year of his reign could be as early as A.D. 25 or as late as A.D. 28, depending upon which year Luke considered Tiberius' reign as beginning.

In A.D. 6, Archelaus was disposed by Augustus. He then established the office of procurator. This title was used to identify the governor of a minor province. By the time John began preaching, five men had held this office and had responsibility for governing Judea, Samaria, and Idumaea. The fifth procurator of this region was Pontius Pilate, a man who would forever be remembered for one decision he made while holding this office. Herod Antipas was still the tetrarch of Galilee. This Herod was the son of Herod the Great and a Samaritan woman. The word "tetrarch" means "a ruler of a fourth part." In this office, he ruled over the region of Galilee and Peraea. Because his father was Herod, his mother a Samaritan, and his office represented the authority of Rome, the people of Galilee had three reasons why they hated Antipas.

Philip was tetrarch of Iturea and Trachonitis, two regions north and northeast of Palestine proper. This Philip was the half-brother of Antipas and Archelaus, and was probably the best of the lot. The city of Caesarea Philippi was named in his honor. Philip ruled this region until his death in A.D. 34.

Lysanias ruled over Abilene, a minor province in the same region as Iturea and Trachonitis. Josephus identified a person named Lysanias who ruled over Chaleis and Abilene's tetrarch and was killed by Mark Anthony at the instigation of Cleopatra about A.D. 36. Some writers have identified these two Lysaniases as being the same individual and therefore conclude Luke was inaccurate in his historical facts. But inscriptions have been found which confirm the existence of a later Lysanias of the time identified by Luke, probably a descendant of the one mentioned by Josephus.

In Jerusalem, both Annas and Caiaphas were recognized as high priests. Annas had been appointed high priest in A.D. 6 or A.D. 7 by the Roman government, but was deposed by another governor in A.D. 15. In A.D. 18, yet another governor appointed Caiaphas Joseph as high priest. He held this office until A.D. 36. Because the office of High Priest was a hereditary office in the Old Testament, the Jews continued to recognize Annas even after he had been formally deposed. As a result, while there was only one official high priest, there were two in the minds of the people. Both of these men held trial over Jesus in the early morning of His crucifixion (see John 18:12-14).

I.   John: The Man Sent from God

A. His Call as a Prophet. At a time when these men ruled the world politically, "the word of God came to John the son of Zacharias in the wilderness" (Luke 3:2). Some teachers believe he may have been involved or associated with the Jewish "monastery" of Quran. This is the place where the Dead Sea Scrolls were found in the twentieth century. It is called the Quran Community. John may have been trained there as a child or perhaps used the facility for his own private meditation. The Quran Community is located near the place where John baptized Jesus. Those associated with the desert community practiced baptism by water immersion and held to a strict observance of the law.

John was probably 30 years old at the time he began preaching because that was the age a Levite began his active ministry. He appeared out of the wilderness and began proclaiming his message from God to the people. He began his ministry with a clear sense of his calling as one sent from God to proclaim the message of God and prepare the way for the Messiah. The expression "the word of God came to John" may mean he had a direct revelation from God or that in his meditation of God's Word (i.e., Isa. 40 or Mal. 3 in particular), the Holy Spirit made it clear that this Scripture described the ministry in which God wanted him to be engaged.

B. His Commission as a Preacher. Regardless of how God called John to preach, it is obvious John identified his commission closely with the prophetic statements made concerning the forerunner of the Messiah by Isaiah and

Malachi. At John's birth, his father Zacharias had prophesied, "And you, child, will be called the prophet of the Highest; for you will go before the face of the Lord to prepare His ways" (Luke 1:76). In this sense, John had his commission as a preacher from his birth. Yet in another sense, this commission became real to him during his years of preparation in the deserts until "the day of his manifestation to Israel" (Luke 1:80). John viewed his commission from God as threefold. First, he was to call individuals to turn from their sins using the act of baptism to symbolize their repentance (Matt. 3:2; Luke 3:3). Secondly, he was to call his nation back to God in preparation for the coming of the Messiah (Matt. 3:3; Mark 1:2-3; Luke 3:4-6). Finally he was to bear witness of the True Light – the Messiah – and identify Him to the nation (John 1:8).

C. His Conduct as a Person. The success of John's popular appeal was at least in part due to the consistency of his life with his message. He had no other authenticating signs or miracles to draw people to himself. Neither did he invest time in building social relations with influential people. When the people came to see John in the wilderness, they saw authenticity which was rare in the religious leaders of that day. So popular was John's appeal that three centuries later, Judeo-Christian sects still existed which identified John as their chief prophet.

John lived a very simple lifestyle. His clothing was made of camel's hair and tied together with a simple strip of tanned hide. His diet consisted of locusts, a grasshopper type of insect common in the region, and wild honey he found in his wandering. These two items were probably not the sole elements of his diet but suggest he ate what he could scrounge from his environment. The Bible's description of John suggests he was content to live in poverty rather than amass wealth or seek a position that could have been his as a popular religious leader.

From his birth, John lived in accordance with the vow of a Nazirite. This vow was observed in keeping three symbols. First, he could not cut his hair with a razor. Secondly, John would not touch a dead body, human or otherwise. Also, the Nazirite restricted his diet, refusing to eat grapes or corn or any food or drink derived from these items (Num. 6:2-8). The symbolism of this vow served as a reminder to the Nazirite and others that God had set that individual apart for some special service.

II. John: His Message Spoken for God

A. His Message in its Principle Objective. In keeping with the prophecy of Isaiah, the principle objective communicated in John's message was that of building "the highway of holiness" in the wilderness (cf. Isa. 40:3-5). The custom in those days was to prepare for a monarch's visit by building a highway of the best class upon which the king would make his journey to the city. The building of this highway normally involved filling in valleys, leveling mountains and hills, straightening crooked places which were small hills and valleys that might otherwise go unnoticed, and smoothing rough places which were the more dangerous parts of the trip such as winding trails along the edges of steep cliffs. When this highway was completed, the king would then make his way to the city and bring with him his blessing upon the city. Isaiah used this practice to illustrate the purpose of John's ministry. As a forerunner of the King of Israel, he was to mobilize the people to prepare the highway upon which the King would come with His blessing. John was not preparing a physical highway such as a modern interstate, but rather a spiritual highway which was repentance and godly living that is necessary to obtain the blessing of God. The usual activities involved in building a king's highway have spiritual application in the life of the believer. Christians need to fill in the valleys of defeat with the fullness of the Holy Spirit (Eph. 5:18). They need to bring low the mountains and hills of unbelief with the faith of God (Mark 11:22-24). The crooked places suggest the need to deal completely with little sins which might otherwise be tolerated by the believer (2 Chron. 7:14). Also, the rough places in one's relationships need to be made smooth so as not to hinder one's relationship with God (cf. 1 Peter 3:7). When this is done in the life of a believer, "the glory of the Lord shall be revealed" (Isa. 40:5) suggesting the spiritual blessing of revival.

B. *His Message in Its Practical Application.* John did not limit his preaching to ambiguous platitudes but rather made specific practical applications to various classes of people who gathered to hear him preach. When he addressed the hypocritical religious establishment of his day, he warned them to produce "fruits worthy of repentance" rather that depending upon their spiritual heritage (Luke 3:8). To the popular masses he spoke specifically of sharing what they had with those who were less fortunate, even if it meant giving away a used coat or sharing a little food (Luke 3:11). He told the tax collectors of his day to stop extorting money from the poor (Luke 3:13). He instructed soldiers not to use their position to intimidate and abuse others (Luke 3:14). Even the political leaders of his day did not escape John's pointed remarks. When Herod married his sister-in-law Herodias, John rebuked the powerful ruler for his incest (Luke 3:19). For John the Baptist, building the highway of holiness meant specific repentance and no one was exempt.

C. *His Message in Its Prophetic Outlook.* John's personal integrity and unusual directness in preaching God's Word made him stand out in his age as unique from other religious teachers. Soon people began wondering if he was not the Messiah himself. John consistently denied this, claiming he was only a forerunner of the Messiah. John's view of the Messiah differed from the popular notion of most people. He saw the Messiah not so much as a political leader or a military savior, but as One who would baptize with the Holy Spirit and with fire (Luke 3:16). Many Bible teachers believe this refers to a twofold aspect of Christ's ministry. The first is that of baptizing believers with the Holy Spirit into His body, the church (cf. 1 Cor. 12:13). The second is that of the final judgment of unbelievers in the Lake of Fire (cf. Luke 3:17; Rev. 20:14-15). John held the Messiah in such high regard he claimed he was not worthy to loosen His sandal strap (Mark 1:7). Loosening sandal straps was a task designated for the lowest servant of the household.

III.   Jesus: The Messiah Sent from God

A. *His Identification and Baptism.* The climax of John's ministry was when he introduced the Messiah to the nation. John did so by reluctantly baptizing Him, thus marking the beginning of Jesus' public ministry. When Jesus appeared as part of a group of others desiring to be baptized, John immediately recognized who He was and refused. "I have need to be baptized by You, and are You coming to me?" he asked (Matt. 3:14). Those whom John baptized were baptized as an act of repentance for sin. Because Jesus was without sin, He had no reason to repent and be baptized.

Jesus did not dispute John's understanding of His character, but asked to be baptized because "it is fitting for us to fulfill all righteousness" (Matt. 3:15). When the disciples of John were baptized publicly, they were confessing that they were turning from their sin and committing themselves to serve God. While Jesus did not need to turn from sin, He used the opportunity to be baptized by John as a public statement of His commitment to do the will of His Father. On this basis, John agreed to baptize Jesus.

B. His Anointing of the Holy Spirit. The baptism of Jesus was so unique that John the Baptist remembered it for some time and retold its story to his disciples. As Jesus ascended out of the water, He was anointed by the Holy Spirit as the Spirit of God descended like a dove upon Him (Matt. 3:17). This was the first of three such utterances of God during the public ministry of Jesus.

THREE TIMES GOD SPOKE ALOUD

• At the Baptism of Jesus
• On the Mount of Transfiguration
• At the Beginning of Jesus' Final Week

The baptism of Jesus at the hands of John the Baptist marked the beginning of Jesus' public ministry. In addition to being physically baptized in water on that occasion, Jesus was also anointed with the Holy Spirit. The anointing of the Holy Spirit in Scripture is a spiritual experience which designates and empowers an individual for specific service for God. Although Jesus was God, He was not prepared to minister without this anointing. It became the foundation of his public ministry (Luke 4:18). If Jesus needed to be yielded to the Holy Spirit to serve God, it is even more necessary for His disciples to be spiritually prepared for ministry in the same way.

C. His Victory over Satan. Bible teachers do not agree on exactly when the temptation of Christ by Satan took place apart from the fact it followed Jesus' baptism by John. Some believe it occurred immediately following the baptism of Jesus. They note that each of the synoptic gospels (Matthew, Mark and Luke) describe Jesus' forty-day fast in the wilderness and subsequent temptation by Satan immediately following their account of His baptism by John. Others argue the fast and temptation of Christ did not occur until later, following the events of a week described in John 1:19–2:22 (see chapter four). They note these details are ignored by the other gospel writers and suggest they fall into place at this point. Because none of the gospel accounts give us the full biographical details of the life of Christ, conservative Bible teachers sometimes disagree over the exact timing of certain minor details of Christ's life.

Early in the first year of His public ministry, Jesus spent forty days in prayer and fasting in the wilderness. While this was not a common practice, neither was it unheard of or without biblical precedent. Both Moses and Elijah spent similar time with God at Mount Sinai (cf. Ex. 24:13; 1 Kings 19:8) and later Saul of Tarsus did the same immediately following his conversion (cf. Gal. 1:17). Later in His ministry, Jesus' success and popularity meant He would not be able to spend such an extended period of time alone with God.

As this period came to a close, Satan himself appeared to tempt Jesus. In his appeal to the Lord, Satan tempted Jesus in each of the three areas in which every person is tempted. Although Jesus was God and could not by nature sin (James 1:13), the temptations were nevertheless very real. Jesus overcame the temptation of Satan by relying on God's Word rather than upon Himself. Three times Jesus answered Satan, "It is written" (Matt. 4:4, 7, 10). In doing so, Jesus gave His disciples a pattern to follow in their struggles with temptation.

HOW SATAN TEMPTED JESUS	
1 John 2:15-17	*Matt. 4:1-11*
Lust of the Flesh	Stones to Bread
Lust of the Eyes	Glory of Kingdoms
Pride of Life	Prove Deity with a Miracle

Jesus' victory over Satan in the wilderness was not the last time the two would engage in spiritual conflict. Later, Satan would use a natural storm and even one of Jesus' closest disciples to attempt to destroy or sidetrack Jesus from His messianic work. Ultimately, the Cross itself was Jesus' most intense battle with Satan. But at the beginning of His ministry, in the wilderness, He overcame Satan and his attack at its most basic level, the temptation to do wrong. In at least one sense, Jesus' victory over Satan in the wilderness marked the beginning of the end for that fallen angel.

Conclusion

Just as John the Baptist was "sent from God...to bear witness of the Light" (John 1:6-7), believers today are the lamps through which that Light may be communicated to others (cf. Matt. 5:14). Like John, believers today need to be faithful witnesses that others may be attracted to the Light of the World who is Jesus. Jesus urged His disciples, "Let your light so shine before men, that they may see your good works and glorify your Father in heaven" (Matt. 5:16).

CHAPTER 4

JOHN AND ANDREW:

THEIR FIRST WEEK WITH JESUS

John 1:15–2:12

Sometimes things happen in a person's life that make such a significant impression that they remain clear in one's memory years later. People remember significant political events as they affect their life or important days in the experience of their family such as a wedding day or birth of a child. Others remember important dates in their career advancement or tragic and dramatic events which altered the course of their lives. More than sixty-five years after John the apostle met Jesus, he could remember the vivid details of that first week. According to a tradition of the early church, John wrote the fourth gospel at the request of church leaders who saw a need for another account of the life of Christ. Accordingly, John is said to have fasted three days with Andrew. At the conclusion of this period, John began writing the gospel occasionally consulting with Andrew to insure he remembered the details correctly. Of course, John was inspired by the Holy Spirit as he wrote so that his gospel is the very Word of God (2 Peter 1:21), but it is interesting to note the personal touch and details included in the fourth gospel which the other writers overlooked.

Unlike the other gospel writers, John had the advantage of having not only been with Jesus, but of also having witnessed the outworking of the gospel in the lives of so many in the early years of the church. Writing toward the end of the first century, he was particularly impressed with two truths about Christ which he emphasized in his gospel. First, Christ had to be understood in the context of eternity (John 1:1-3). Secondly, Christ had to be understood in the context of the time of which He ministered. As he meditated on this theme, John was impressed again by the first week he met the Eternal God in Human Flesh, remembering not only the days, but sometimes even the very hour.

Thursday: The Day John Responded to the Sanhedrin

The first day of that momentous week was Thursday, the day John the Baptist was interviewed by members of the Sanhedrin at Bethabara (John 1:19-28). Had John the Baptist wanted to gather his own following and declare himself the Messiah, he certainly had opportunity to do so on several occasions.

He was clearly the most popular preacher of his day, and his influence would last centuries beyond his death. Both John and Andrew recognized something unique about John the Baptist and committed themselves as his disciples (John 1:35). They might have been willing themselves to have followed John as their Messiah had he asked them to do so, but he made no such request.

John and Andrew were fishermen by trade, sons of the two men who had founded a successful partnership that had brought a measure of wealth to both families. Archaeologists have uncovered a pew in the ruins of a synagogue in Capernaum bearing the family name Zebedee. This pew could have belonged to the father of James and John who was a leader in the community. Apparently John was not always rich. He was born in Bethsaida, a poor community on the northern flood plain of the Sea of Galilee, but the family later moved to the luxurious city of Capernaum as the fishing business prospered (Mark 1:19-20). According to a Franciscan tradition, the business was so prosperous that Zebedee also bought a house in Jerusalem where he established a franchise of his fishing business which provided fish for many of the city's prominent religious leaders including the high priest. This may have been how John first met and got to know many of the Jewish leaders in Jerusalem who later tried and condemned Jesus (John 18:12-14). John and Andrew may have first heard of John the Baptist's ministry as they transported fish from Galilee to Jerusalem.

John the apostle describes in his gospel the occasion of Jewish leaders questioning John the Baptist. First, they asked him if he were the Messiah (John 1:19). What an opportunity! If this popular wilderness preacher would make such a claim, it appeared some of the most important religious leaders of the day were willing to support him. But the wilderness prophet was unmoved by the temptation and simply confessed he was not. Then they asked if he were Elijah (John 1:21) appearing in fulfillment of the prophecy of Malachi (Mal. 4:5). Again he denied it. Then he was asked if he was the prophet like Moses who was also to appear (John 1:21; cf. Deut. 18:15). While many Bible teachers believe this prophet is a reference to the Messiah, these Jewish leaders were apparently open to an alternate view. Again he denied it.

The committee from the Sanhedrin was confused to say the least. If John was not any of these significant people, why was he gathering a following in the wilderness and calling people to repent and be baptized. But John was not interested in defending himself or justifying his actions. What was important was not himself but another standing among them of whom they were completely ignorant. "It is He who, coming after me, is preferred before me, whose sandal strap I am not worthy to loose," he declared (John 1:27).

Friday: The Day John Identified Jesus as the Lamb

John and Andrew must have been impressed by this unknown stranger in their midst of whom their religious mentor had such high regard. John remembers and writes, "the next day" (John 1:29). But they did not have to wait long before they and everyone else who cared to listen heard John identify Jesus as the Messiah. "Behold! The Lamb of God who takes away the sin of the world!" he declared (John 1:29). The Baptist used the image of the Passover lamb to identify Jesus and His primary work of taking away the sin of the world (cf. Isa. 53). The Greek word *airon* translated "takes away" has the idea of taking something up and carrying it away and in that sense destroying it. It refers to the means whereby Jesus took away sin by bearing it in His own body (1 Peter 2:24) and thus removed it as far as the east is from the west (Ps. 103:12). The tense of this verb is perfect, suggesting John the Baptist saw Jesus as already taking away sin even before the Cross. Also, the word John used for sin is singular, suggesting Jesus deals with the root problem rather than individual sins which are symptoms of the greater problem of a sin nature. Throughout the Scriptures, sin is "taken away" in some sense at least ten times.

WHEN DOES THE LAMB OF GOD TAKE AWAY SIN

Before the foundation of the world (Rev. 13:8)
At the fall of man in the Garden (Gen. 3:15)
With the offering of a sacrifice (Gen. 4:7)
On the Day of Atonement (Lev. 16:34)
At a time of national repentance (2 Chron. 7:14)
During the public ministry of Jesus (John 1:29)
On the cross of Calvary (1 Peter 2:24)
At the conversion of a believer (Rom. 6:6)
At the return of Christ (Rom. 8:18-23)
At the end of Christ's Kingdom (Rev. 20:15; 21:8)

As part of his testimony as to the nature of Jesus, John the apostle concluded, "And I have seen and testified that this is the Son of God" (John 1:34). He was the first of many to recognize Jesus as the Son of God. The Hebraism "son of" meant of the same nature and character as the father. To call someone "the Son of God" is to recognize the nature and character of God in that person. It is one of Christ's titles which suggest His deity.

Saturday: The Day John and Andrew Became Disciples

This was not the last time John the Baptist so identified Jesus. The very next day (John 1:34), the last of the prophets saw Jesus in a less public context, and while watching Jesus walk by repeated the phrase, "Behold the Lamb of God!" (John 1:36). John and Andrew were close enough to hear the Baptist repeat the phrase and wanted to learn more. They began following Jesus at a distance to see where He was staying so they could get their other questions answered. "Then Jesus turned, and seeing them following, said to them, 'What do you seek?'" (John 1:38). When the two disciples responded they wanted to know where Jesus lived, He responded, "Come and see."

The expression "come and see" was often used by Rabbis to invite their disciples to engage in study together, a call to discipleship. Jesus had not yet established his ministry of gathering followers, so the decision of these two to become Jesus' first disciples was especially courageous. In trusting Jesus, they were following someone who was publicly unknown and untested. Further, to follow Jesus meant leaving their first teacher, John the Baptist (John 1:35).

John was not only the most popular preacher of the day, but may also have been the most popular leader of the people at that time. In trusting Jesus, these two men were leaving the apparent security associated with following popular John and accepting the apparent insecurity of associating with the obscure Jesus. No wonder that years later, they not only remembered the day they met Jesus, but recalled the very hour they made that momentous decision (John 1:39), the tenth hour of the day, approximately mid-afternoon Roman time (4:00 p.m.).

John and Andrew spent the day talking with Jesus. They had heard John the Baptist preach about the coming Messiah, and the longer they talked with Jesus, the more they became convinced Jesus was that Messiah. John the Baptist had called Jesus "the Lamb of God" (John 1:36), but by the time Andrew found his brother Peter the next day, he had another name for Jesus. "We have found the Messiah!" he exclaimed (John 1:41).

Sunday: The Day Peter and James Became Disciples

Andrew not only became one of the first two disciples, he was also the first to influence someone else to follow Jesus (John 1:41). When he learned about Jesus, and had spent some time with Him, Andrew's life was changed, and he could not wait to tell his brother Peter.

Because Andrew's own decision to follow Jesus may have involved a struggle on his part, he may have determined to make it easy for others to come to Christ. The Greek verb *heuriskei* translated "found" (John 1:41) implies Andrew had to search before he succeeded in finding his brother Simon. Galileans tended to be eager to follow flamboyant new leaders and no doubt many had come to see John the Baptist in hopes the prophet would lead a rebellion against Rome. Simon Peter was probably "lost in the crowd" when Andrew began his search for him.

Finally, Andrew found his brother only to discover he did not share the same enthusiasm over finding the Messiah. While the Scriptures do not tell the words Simon actually spoke, they do suggest he was not eager to respond. The Greek word *eqaqev* translated "brought" (John 1:42) implies constraint was used on the one being brought because he is unwilling. The emphasis of this term is perhaps better expressed in the translation, "He dragged him to Jesus." Reluctantly, Simon Peter agreed to meet Andrew's Messiah. It was a meeting that would forever change his life.

One of the first things Jesus did when he met Simon was change his name. Jesus realized how out of character the name Simon (from the Hebrew "Simeon" meaning "listener") really was. Peter was not a listener but a talker, an impulsive leader. John uses the Greek word *emblepsas* translated "looked" (John 1:42) which refers to the penetrating stare of Jesus that looked "right through" Simon to see who he really was. It was the same look Jesus would give Peter more than three years later as he swore he never knew Jesus. On that occasion the disciple was overcome with conviction which led to a night of bitter weeping (Luke 22:61-62). Seeing what others might have missed, Jesus renamed Simon, Cephas or Peter meaning "a stone."

A number of things were involved in that name change. First, as the giving of names is an expression of sovereignty, Jesus was subtly telling Simon it was not enough that he came to meet Andrew's Messiah. Jesus had to be Peter's Messiah also, and further, he had the right to be so declared because he had the right of naming, i.e. ultimate control. Second, Jesus was telling Peter that He would transform him. The name Cephas is Aramaic, meaning "rock." That is also the meaning of the Greek name Peter. Peter, who if he resembled a rock at all was little more than sandstone, was being told he could become a building stone in the temple Jesus would build (1 Peter 2:5). By calling him Cephas, Jesus was challenging Peter to live up to the stability of that name.

Andrew was probably not the only one to bring a new disciple into the fold that day. Because the Scripture records Andrew found Peter "first," many Bible teachers believe John found James second and brought him to Jesus later the same day. While Scripture is silent on the subject, James may have later worked with his brother John to eventually convince their mother to follow Jesus. She is later identified with a group of widows who followed Jesus which may have been a philanthropic organization of widows which supported the ministry of Christ (Mark 15:40-41).

Monday: Philip and Nathanael Became Disciples

The following day (John 1:43), Philip became the next disciple Jesus called to follow him. He was probably the fifth to actually become His disciple. He may have known the four fishermen who had begun following Jesus on the previous day as he was from Bethsaida, the home town of Peter and Andrew. Philip responded positively to Jesus' invitation, "Follow me" (John 1:43) and became a committed disciple.

Philip's first expression of Jesus was the fullest initial expression by any of the twelve disciples. Philip described Jesus as "Him, of whom Moses in the law, and the prophets, wrote, Jesus of Nazareth, the son of Joseph" (John 1:45). The description itself almost forces one to the conclusion Philip had spent time with Jesus, perhaps discussing how Jesus was the fulfillment of prophecies or types recorded in the Old Testament.

Because Philip had an analytical mind, it is not surprising that he had his friend analyze Jesus Christ (John 1:43-46). The mention of going to Cana for a wedding in that city (John 2:1-2) may have prompted his memory and reminded him of a friend from Cana who was a member of a prominent family in that city. Philip soon followed the example of Andrew and John in bringing another to Jesus.

Most Bible teachers agree Nathanael is the disciple identified as Bartholomew on each of the listings of the twelve disciples. The name Bartholomew is not a first name but rather a surname which identifies a man to his father. Literally it means "son of Tolmai" or "son of Ptolemy." The church fathers differed in their exact interpretation of what the name meant, but agreed Bartholomew was a man of regal descent. Jerome thought the name should be identified with Talmai king of Geshur (2 Sam. 3:3). Talmai's daughter "Maacah" was one of David's wives and Absalom's mother. Others suggested Bartholomew was related to the Ptolemies which once ruled the land of Egypt. Nathanael is generally thought to be his first name because (1) Nathanael was apparently one of the disciples (John 21:2), (2) his name never appears on the official listing, and (3) Bartholomew is never mentioned formally outside the listings of the disciples by his surname (cf. Matt. 10:3). Some believe he is identified on the official list by his last name to avoid confusion with Matthew. Both Nathanael and Matthew mean "gift of God."

When Philip first approached Nathanael about Jesus, Nathanael did not appear very impressed with Jesus. He was from Cana (John 21:2), a city that tended to attract the "upper crust" of society. It would have been the sort of place someone like Bartholomew would want to live, especially if the legends about his royal blood were true. As a result, he had a bias against the town of Nazareth, widely known as the city of garbage.

Philip was convinced Jesus was the Messiah and believed his friend could also be convinced if he had the correct data. He told his friend that Jesus fulfilled the predictions in the Old Testament and invited him to come and meet Jesus for himself. When Jesus met Nathanael, He said, "Behold, an Israelite indeed, in whom is no deceit!" (John 1:47). There is no reason to doubt this was an accurate appraisal of the inner character of Nathanael. When Nathanael asked how Jesus knew him, the Lord said He had seen Philip finding and talking to Nathanael under the fig tree (John 1:48). Nathanael was in fact under a fig tree when Philip found him. The fig tree was a symbol of peace and a place of meditation. When Israel was at peace, men had time to sit under their fig trees and meditate on the Word of God. Because of its shape, the fig tree was an ideal place for shade and relaxation. Some commentators have concluded from Jesus' later remarks to Nathanael that he had been meditating on Genesis 28, the account of Jacob's ladder. Nathanael then used two important messianic titles for Christ from the second psalm, "Son of God" and "the King of Israel" (John 1:49; cf. Psalms 2:6-7). This may suggest Nathanael had been meditating on that passage also.

THE FIRST DISCIPLES OF JESUS

1. *Andrew* – The First Called Disciple (first disciple of Jesus named)
2. *John* – The Youngest Disciple (probably 17 or 18 years old)
3. *Peter* – The Primary Disciple (his name appears first in the lists)
4. *James* – The Silent Disciple (no record of his ever speaking)
5. *Philip* – The Analytical Disciple (portrayed as analyzing situations)
6. *Nathanael* – The Sincere Disciple (he came to Jesus without guile)

When Nathanael addressed Jesus by two Old Testament messianic titles, Jesus realized Nathanael had doubted His deity but now believed (John 1:50). He told Nathanael he would see Jesus as a ladder between heaven and earth, with angels going up and down upon Christ. This was the fulfillment of the type associated with Jacob's ladder (Gen. 28:12ff). What this actually meant to Nathanael has been described by various commentators in four different ways. First, it could mean Nathanael would come to understand Jesus to be the only ladder to heaven providing salvation to the world. A second interpretation suggests Nathanael would witness the ascension of Christ. Some believe a third view that means Christ will send angels to receive dead saints and bring them to heaven at death. A fourth view related this statement to the second coming of Christ in glory with his angels. However Nathanael actually understood Christ's words, they were the means of strengthening his initial faith in God.

Wednesday: The Wedding in Cana of Galilee

The last day of that memorable week was identified, "and the third day" (John 2:1). This was the day Jesus and His band of six disciples attended a wedding celebration in Cana of Galilee (John 2:1-12). Tuesday would have been spent travelling to Cana so they would be there for the wedding. Although the Bible does not identify the specific days of the week in these seven days, it was customary for Wednesday to be the wedding day. That is the basis for the designation of the days used in this account. Although wedding celebrations usually lasted up to a week, the Greek word *gamos* translated "wedding" (John 2:1) is singular rather than plural and may reflect the poverty of the family giving the feast, suggesting a single celebration on the day of the wedding rather than the usual extended celebration. Also, they ran out of wine because they were too poor to buy extra.

When Jesus arrived at the wedding, his mother was already present. He and His six disciples were welcome and were invited to join in the celebration. Hospitality was important to a Jew, and it is highly unlikely anyone would ever be turned away from a wedding. Unfortunately, this open door policy toward uninvited guests meant it was difficult to plan accordingly.

Most commentaries believe the bride involved in this wedding was a female relative of Jesus and as a result, Mary was fulfilling her family obligation and helping cater the meal. This would explain why she learned of this problem before others and turned to her Son for help. Why did she tell Jesus about the problem? There are various answers: (1) she wanted Jesus to purchase more wine, (2) to perform a miracle, (3) to leave with six extra appetites, or (4) preach a sermon. But the felt need at the wedding became the focus for the beginning of Jesus' ministry through miracles.

Jesus instructed the servants to fill six water pots with water. Each of these pots would hold twenty to thirty gallons so this must have involved some effort to accomplish the task. Then He instructed them to draw more water from the well and take it to the master of the feast. When the servants did this, somewhere between the well and the head table, the water became wine. This miracle was a means of Jesus manifesting His glory and so impressed His disciples that they began to believe in Him (John 2:11).

This miracle has been the focus of controversy and debate among Christians for years. The Bible speaks of two kinds of wine including alcoholic, usually referred to as the adder's sting (cf. Prov. 23:31-32), and sweet wines, nonalcoholic fruit juices (cf. Ps. 104:15). Some Christians claim Jesus created alcoholic wine noting the use of the verb *methusthosin* translated "have well drunk" (John 2:10). This verb is often used in Greek literature to identify intoxication. But this verse describes they had a lot of wine, but could taste the superior wine Jesus created. They were not intoxicated. Other reasons why it is more likely the wine used here was a sweet wine are that a marriage festival was a family affair and not the kind of place alcoholic beverages would be served, and it was close to the beginning of Passover (2:12-13). Jews were prohibited from using leaven (the source of fermentation) during the season.

Some Bible teachers believe this miracle was a symbolic announcement that the old Jewish order was passing to be replaced by a new expression of faith in God. Jesus had the servants fill the six water pots associated with the Jewish rite of purification. The Old Testament legal system failed to meet the need of the hour. He then called for more water to be drawn from the well which became the best wine at the feast. Whether or not Jesus intended to show the emptiness of Jewish law in performing this miracle, it certainly caused Andrew and John to come to that realization. This was the climax of the most important week of their lives and a significant milestone in their pilgrimage of faith. At the beginning of that week, they were listening to one of the greatest of the prophets instructing representatives of the decaying old Jewish order that One standing among them was so great the He would take away the sin of the world. By the end of that week, they had begun to see for themselves the very glory of God manifested in the One they had come to trust as their Messiah. They had begun an exciting relationship with God in human flesh.

Conclusion

From the very beginning, the most effective means of spreading the gospel has involved people who know about Jesus telling people who don't know about Jesus. God has given everyone a sphere of influence and part of the stewardship of the resources God has entrusted to believers involves using one's influence to persuade others to follow Jesus as Messiah. Some believers like John the Baptist have a large sphere of influence and could be used by God to attract many to personal salvation in Christ. Others can be a faithful witness to members of their own family like Andrew, or to friends, neighbors or associates, like Philip. When Christians are faithful in their stewardship of this resource, they and others they have influenced for Christ enter into a deeper celebration of life in worship to God.

CHAPTER 5

NICODEMUS: A PASSOVER

TO REMEMBER

John 2:11-3:36

℘assover was an important time of the year for every Jewish family. It was an annual reminder of how God delivered the nation from Egypt and the oppression of Pharoah. In one sense, it was the anniversary of their nation's birth. At Passover, people were reminded how God liberated a nation of slaves and sent them on their way to a promised land that flowed with milk and honey.

Even to this day, Passover is observed by faithful Jews in every part of the world. Normally, the Jewish celebration of Passover falls near the Christian celebration of Easter. As Jewish families gather around the world to carry on a ritual now more than three thousand years old, they gather around the table and eat the bitter herbs, unleavened bread, and other prepared foods. In the course of the meal, children ask questions and parents anwer them. Prayers are offered and songs are sung. Usually the meal concludes with the expression of a heart-felt desire, "Next year in Jerusalem." To celebrate Passover in Jerusalem is an honor most Jews can only dream about in the world today. That dream has a better chance of becoming a reality for those living in the land. Most Jewish men would make an attempt to get to Jerusalem for Passover if it were at all possible (Deut. 16:16). Jesus was brought to Jerusalem as a child for Passover. Now in His public ministry, He took time out annually to celebrate Passover in Jerusalem.

While each Passover season Jesus spent in Jerusalem was memorable, His visit in 26 A.D. near the beginning of His public ministry was particularly so. He quickly attracted the attention of the leaders in the town by disrupting the economic trade in the temple. During that Passover, Jesus also met with one of the more prominent leaders in the community. After Passover, Jesus remained in the region with His disciples and carried on a rather successful outreach among the people of Judea.

I.   A New Look for a Revered Temple (John 2:13-25)

When Jesus arrived in the city of Jerusalem, He would have joined the crowds on their way to the temple to pray and offer sacrifices. This temple was built by the remnant who returned to Jerusalem after the Babylonian captivity, but at the time was being transformed into a much more majestic site. This renovation really amounted to rebuilding a new temple on the site of the old. It had begun in 20 B.C. and at this point had been going on for forty-six years (John 2:20). This identification by the Jews that construction had been going on for forty-six years is another historical reference to Jesus' age being thirty at the time. He was born in 4 B.C. The temple was not completed until A.D. 63, just seven years before it was destroyed by Roman soldiers. Even while it was still under construction, it was considered one of the most beautiful buildings in the city. But when Jesus arrived at the temple site, the thing that appeared most obvious was a crowd of businessmen exchanging money and selling animals which could be used for sacrifices. This was a necessary service provided at the temple by businessmen to assist worshipers. Many who came to Jerusalem from great distances did not bring a sacrifice with them but rather chose to buy one when they arrived in the city. Also, the official Roman coins most foreign Jews used in their daily business was inscribed with claims of the deity of Caesar, something that was offensive to the faithful Jew. As a result, a number of businessmen provided a service by exchanging funds to temple currency and selling animals for sacrifices. The practice had been going on for years, and no one seemed to mind.

When Jesus entered the temple area, He began driving the traders out. He braided a whip and drove out herds of sheep and oxen. He took the trays of money used by the exchangers and poured them out. Turning to those who sold doves He ordered, "Take these things away! Do not make My Father's house a house of merchandise!" (John 2:16). These actions were recognized by His disciples as consistent with a messianic prophecy concerning the Messiah's zeal for the house of God (John 2:17; Ps. 69:9), but they could not be understood by the religious hierarchy who had rented the space to the businessmen.

As noted above, the business being conducted in the temple was necessary and was designed to assist people in worshiping God. But it was also very profitable. Sometimes profit margins have a way of distracting even the most committed businessman from his original purpose. Although the practice itself was not wrong, the place and manner in which it was being done was very wrong. The temple was divided into four courts, the outer court being the Court of the Gentiles. This was the only part of the temple in which a Gentile convert to Judaism could come to pray. Perhaps because of the renovations underway at the time, this was also the place these businessmen had set up shop. As a result, their commercial activities made it practically impossible for a Gentile to come and meditate upon the things of God. Also, because of their monopoly on the market, there is some evidence their prices and rates of exchange were highly inflated. What had begun to help people worship God had actually become a hindrance to worship. They had turned the place of prayer into a den of thieves.

Jesus' actions on this occasion led to His first of many confrontations with the religious establishment of Jerusalem. The Jews also knew Jesus' actions were consistent with messianic prophecy, but they also were well aware of many who around that time tried to establish a messianic following. While they may have secretly wanted Messiah to bring an end to Roman involvement in temple affairs, they were more cautious than others in committing their support to every popular self-proclaimed leader. They asked Jesus for a sign, i.e., a miracle that would authenticate His apparent claim to be the Messiah. Jesus offered the sign of the resurrection. He resounded, "Destroy this temple (referring to His own body), and in three days I will raise it up" (John 2:19). But the Jewish leaders missed the whole point. They thought He was claiming He could rebuild in only three days a temple which had already been forty-six years in construction. Not until after the resurrection did His own disciples come to understand the true significance of what He said (John 2:22). If the religious establishment was reluctant to follow Jesus, the masses were not. Jesus did perform a number of miracles and "many believed in His name when they saw the signs which He did" (John 2:23). But Jesus was not fooled by their apparent commitment to His cause. He knew the inner nature of man and realized He could not build a ministry on their shaky commitment (John 2:24).

II.   A New Life for a Respected Man (John 3:1-21)

Not all of the Jewish leaders in the city were quick to rule out Jesus as the possible Messiah. One of the more prominent Pharisees in the city was a man named Nicodemus (John 3:1). According to the Talmud, he was one of the four richest men in Jerusalem and became known later as a follower of Jesus. He was probably a lay member of the Sanhedrin, the governing body of the Jews in religious and cultural matters. Other historical sources suggest he was a member of the same aristocratic family which furnished Aristobulus with his ambassador to Pompey in 63 B.C. His son appears to have been the man who eventually negotiated the terms of surrender of the Roman garrison in Jerusalem in the struggle prior to the city's final destruction in A.D. 70.

Nicodemus recognized the authenticating nature of Jesus' miracles and was interested in learning more about His message. He arranged a night meeting with Jesus probably because the crowds surrounding Jesus during the day made it virtually impossible for such a meeting to occur at any other time. John's use of plural verbs in his account of this meeting between Jesus and Nicodemus has led some Bible teachers to conclude Nicodemus was the spokesman for a small group within the Sanhedrin which were sympathetic toward Jesus (cf. John 3:2, 7, 10-12). This was probably not a meeting of only two men as many assume, but rather a conference involving a number of Jewish leaders who came with Nicodemus. Some of Jesus' disciples may have been present at the time.

Nicodemus came quickly to the point. "Rabbi, we know that You are a teacher come from God; for no one can do these signs that You do unless God is with him" (John 3:2). When Nicodemus expressed the belief Jesus was an authentic teacher from God, Jesus applied His ability to know people (John 2:21) to the situation. Jesus pointed out Nicodemus' need. "Most assuredly, I say to you, unless one is born again, he cannot see the kingdom of God," He explained (John 3:3).

The Greek verb *idein* translated "see" (John 3:3) implies more than mere physical sight. It includes the idea of actively participating in that which is seen (cf. John 8:51; Rev. 18:7). The Jews believed part of the suffering of hell was that a person could see into heaven where they could not live (cf. Luke 16:31).

Jesus explained no one could participate in the bliss of heaven without first being born again from above (cf. John 3:5).

The expression "born again" has been widely used in evangelical circles to describe the change which takes place in the life of the believer at conversion. The Greek word *anothen* may be translated "from the top" (Matt. 27:51), "from above" (John 3:31), "from the beginning" (Luke 1:3), or "again" (Gal. 4:9). Although Nicodemus apparently understood in this contest that Jesus was speaking about a second birth, this rebirth could also be described as being "born from above," i.e., "of God," as it is identified in other places in John's writings (cf. John 1:13; 3:31; 19:11, 23; 1 John 3:9; 5:18).

In response to Nicodemus' questions, Jesus explained the nature of the new birth and how it could be accomplished. First, He explained the new birth was spiritual and produced spiritual life just as the first birth was physical and produced physical life (John 3:6). Secondly, He emphasized the sovereignty of the Holy Spirit in this new birth suggesting some elements of the experience may be beyond his understanding at that time (John 3:8). Third, He gently reminded Nicodemus there was an Old Testament foundation to this teaching and encouraged him to accept their collective witness (John 3:11; cf. Jer. 31:33; Ezek. 36:26-28; Ps. 143:10-11). Finally, He identified the basis of the new birth in His own redemptive sacrifice for sin (John 3:14-15).

In his summary of what Jesus taught about the new birth to Nicodemus, John penned what is probably the best known and most loved verse in all of Scripture, John 3:16. It has been called many things including "the greatest verse in the Bible." The following chart suggests several reasons why this description may be accurate.

JOHN 3:16 - THE GREATEST VERSE IN THE BIBLE

For God   The Greatest Being
so   The Greatest Degree
loved   The Greatest Affection
the world   The Greatest Object of Love
that He gave   The Greatest Act
His only   The Greatest Treasure
begotten   The Greatest Relationship
Son,   The Greatest Gift
that whoever   The Greatest Company
believes   The Greatest Trust
in Him   The Greatest Object of Faith
should not perish   The Greatest Deliverance
but have   The Greatest Assurance
everlasting   The Greatest Promise
life.   The Greatest Blessing

III.   A New Liberty for Religious People (John 3:22-26)

Jesus and His disciples probably did not return to Galilee immediately following the Passover season, but rather may have remained in the region of

Judea. During this time, the disciples likely left from time to time to attend to business and domestic matters and joined Jesus in His preaching mission whenever possible. Also, some of those who would be eventually identified among the twelve had not yet met Jesus and others who would not remain faithful may have been involved in ministry at this time (John 6:66). During this preaching mission in Judea Jesus may have met and enlisted the only one of His twelve disciples who did not have Galilean roots, Judas Iscariot.

Like John the Baptist and other religious leaders of that day, Jesus used baptism as a symbol of a disciple's conversion to the movement. John the Baptist was still actively involved in ministry but had relocated to the Samaritan village of Aenon near Salim. John's disciples were involved in a controversy with the Jewish establishment over the ritualistic practice of purification. This may have been a factor in the Baptist's decision to relocate the base of his ministry. Jesus' success in gathering disciples soon came to the attention of some of John the Baptist's disciples, and they took the matter to their leader.

John's disciples may have hoped he would do something to discourage others from following Jesus, but the Baptist responded exactly the opposite. He acknowledged any success in ministry could only come from God and reminded his disciples of his previous statements concerning the Messiah. On numerous occasions, John had denied he was the Messiah and would only agree he was the forerunner of the Messiah. Just as the friend of a bridegroom rejoices at the bridegroom's wedding, he explained, so he would rejoice in the popularity of Jesus was the Messiah. Rather than work to reverse the trend of people turning to Jesus rather than to him, John the Baptist encouraged it. "He must increase, but I must decrease," John confessed (John 3:30).

John the Baptist was content to remain the humble servant of God and encourage others to recognize Jesus as the honored Son of God. His belief that Jesus was the Son of God was based on several reasons. First was His divine origin. Although Jesus came into this world as a baby in Bethlehem, His real origin was in heaven rather than on earth (John 3:31). Second was His divine testimony. Jesus' teaching had a certain character that certified itself as being from God (John 3:33). Third was His divine authority. Jesus spoke God's words (John 3:34) and God had given Him authority over all things (John 3:35).

The message Jesus proclaimed was too important to be hindered by unnecessary disputes between those who were on the same side. Eternal destinies hung on one's response to the message, and the kind of infighting John's disciples may have been encouraging would only have resulted in some making the wrong response. "He who believes in the Son has everlasting life; and he who does not believe the Son shall not see life, but the wrath of God abides on him" (John 3:36). John the Baptist continued to rejoice in Jesus' success even though Jesus eventually gathered more disciples than him.

Conclusion

When Jesus met with Nicodemus, the most important thing they needed to talk about was the necessity of the new birth. This was likely a constant theme in Jesus' preaching and teaching during the Judea mission. Jesus emphasized it because it is foundational in the Christian life. The new birth is still the most important matter an individual must address today. Just as Jesus reminded Nicodemus, people today should not marvel at the claim of Jesus, "You must be born again" (John 3:7).

CHAPTER 6

THE SAMARITAN WOMAN:

A REVIVAL AT SHECHEM

John 4:1-42

*D*espite the continued success of Jesus' ministry in Judea, a couple of things were happening that suggested it was a good time to move on. The first was the very success of His mission. Jesus was becoming so popular that the Pharisees had been told Jesus had baptized more people than even John the Baptist (John 4:1). Jesus may have actually baptized only a few of the many who followed him. Most who were baptized under His ministry were actually baptized by his disciples (John 4:2).

The second factor which may have influenced His decision was John the Baptist's arrest. On a journey to Rome, Herod Antipas got to know his sister-in-law Herodias and decided to marry her even though it violated Jewish incest laws and was considered offensive by many of those over whom he ruled. John was not intimidated by Herod's political power and openly rebuked the ruler for his sin (Matt. 14:4). A part of Herod secretly admired John for his courageous stand, but he was certainly not about to mend his ways. He had John the Baptist arrested and placed in the prison at Machaerus located on the east side of the Dead Sea. Later, Herod had John beheaded upon the request of his wife Herodius and her daughter Salome.

While these recent events may have influenced Jesus' decision to leave Judea, Jesus was also aware of God's timing in His life and was sensitive to the leading of the Holy Spirit (Luke 4:14). He had experienced success in His ministry in Judea in part because of John the Baptist's faithfulness in preparing the way. More recently, John had been preparing the way in Samaria and Jesus must have realized the time had come for the harvest of souls to begin in that region. When He made His decision to return to Galilee, He refused to bypass Samaria as was the custom of the legalistic Jew, but rather determined to pass through the heart of that region.

I. The Samaritan Woman: A Candidate for Repentance (John 4:5-26)

As Jesus passed through the region of Samaria, He and His disciples stopped near a well outside the city of Sychar to rest on their journey during the hottest part of the day. While the general area where Jesus stopped is easily identified, the exact location of the city is disputed among Bible teachers. Some believe Sychar was located at the city of El-Ascar at the foot of Mt. Ebal and near what is believed to be Jacob's well. This city has been called Sychar in the past and was probably a fair sized city at the time. Other Bible teachers believe the city "called Sychar" was really Shechem which is in the same general area. Those who hold this view suggest *Sychar* was a popular corruption of the name Shechem. The name *Sychar* may be derived from the word *shecker* meaning "falsehood" or *sheckar* meaning "liquor." The Jews who hated the Samaritans may have called many cities *Sychar* meaning "city of liars" or "city of drunks."

Both of the above named cities were located near the site of a plot of ground which Jacob gave Joseph, at the base of Mount Ebal. While Jesus rested by a well, His disciples went into the city to purchase some food. While they were gone, Jesus met and ministered to an unlikely woman who came from the city to draw water at the communal well. This woman was the opposite in many respects from the religious leaders Jesus had met earlier in Jerusalem. The author John compares the two to show that Jesus ministered at both ends of the social spectrum.

NICODEMUS AND THE SAMARITAN WOMAN	
Nicodemus (John 3:1-15)	*The Samaritan Woman (John 4:7-26)*
A Man with a Name	An Unnamed Woman
A Good Reputation	A Bad Reputation
A Wealthy Man	A Poor Woman
He Came to Jesus	Jesus Came to Her
Outstanding in Society	An Outcast of Society
A Jew	A Samaritan
Religious (Morally Upright)	Worldly (Immoral)
No Immediate Response Recorded	Immediately Told Her City
Jesus was Blunt	Jesus was Tactful
Began with Spiritual Things	Began with Physical Things

As soon as Jesus asked the woman for water she identified Him as a Jew. Often the thing that betrays one's ethnic background is a subtle accent he may overlook himself. When Jesus asked for a drink of water, He probably said, "teni lischechoth." Making the same request, a Samaritan man would have pronounced the expression "teni lisechoth."

Jesus' request for water surprised the woman for a number of reasons. First, Jewish men did not customary speak to women publicly. Second, ethnic prejudice between Jews and Samaritans was so strong a Jew would have no dealings with a Samaritan (John 4:9). Beyond this, a Jew would never share the same drinking utensil with a Samaritan – and Jesus obviously had no cup of His own (John 4:11). According to rabbinical teaching, "to eat bread with a Samaritan was like eating swine's flesh." Beyond these reasons, the woman may have thought Jesus would realize she was an outcast of her own city which was probably why she came to the well by herself rather than with a group of women from the city. Being used to verbal abuses, she found it surprising that Jesus treated her kindly.

Jesus was not interested in expressing ethnic slurs or keeping His distance from people who needed what He had to offer. Rather than try to explain His actions, He chose to speak to her about the gift of God using the image of a spring of refreshing water to illustrate this gift. At first, the woman did not understand what Jesus was trying to say. He went on to explain, "Whoever drinks of the water that I shall give him will become in him a fountain of water springing up into everlasting life" (John 4:14). But she was not yet able to receive this gift of God. Although she herself did not realize it, Jesus knew she had to confront another problem in her life before she could enjoy God's gift of eternal life. He pointedly drew attention to her problem by asking her to call her husband. The request drew attention to an area of her life the woman would rather not discuss. "I have no husband," was her direct response (John 4:17). While her answer was legally correct, she was avoiding the real issue. She had been married five times and was at the time living an immoral lifestyle with a man to whom she was not legally married. By responding to Jesus with her non-committal answer, she may have hoped they could avoid discussing a painful area of her life.

But that was not to be the case. Although Jesus did not want to bring her unnecessary pain, He knew she could not experience the fullness of the gift of God until she first repented of sin in her life. Jesus did not condemn her for her actions of the past but did force her to face them. When she did not offer any further explanation, He told her exactly what her marital status had been and was (John 4:18).

She wanted to worship God and asked Jesus directly who was right in their approach to worship (John 4:20). God had told Moses that worship should be centralized in the law (Deut. 12) and that was the source of a major dispute between the Jews and the Samaritans. The Jews taught that place was the temple in Jerusalem. The Samaritans held the place was their temple on Mt. Gerizim. Now that the Samaritan woman was ready to worship God, she wanted to know where.

Jesus explained the place of worship was not as important as the spirit and integrity of worship. "God is Spirit, and those who worship Him must worship in spirit and truth," He explained (John 4:24). The longer she listened to Jesus, the more He sounded like the Messiah she and others were anticipating. "I know that Messiah is coming," she confessed. "When He comes, He will tell us all things" (John 4:25).

When she mentioned this to Jesus, she became the first person to hear Jesus identify Himself as the Messiah. "I who speak to you am He," Jesus acknowledged (John 4:26). In her enthusiasm over this discovery, she left her water pot and raced back to the city.

II. The Disciples: The Communicators of Revival (John 4:27-38)

One of the ironies in the events of that day was that the disciples who had been effective communicators of revival in Judea failed to recognize the potential for ministry in Samaria. They had been in the city and purchased their supplies without noticing the people who would become the focus of Jesus' ministry for the next two days. When they returned to the well to find Jesus talking with a Samaritan woman, they wondered why He would do so but were "too polite" to ask what was going on (John 4:27).

While the woman returned to her city, Jesus took time to explain a few principles of ministry to His disciples. Although they offered Him food, He was no longer hungry. Doing the will of His Father had a rejuvenating effect on Him physically much as ministering through one's spiritual gift affects the Christian today (John 4:32, 34). His disciples needed to learn that spiritual ministry in the lives of others was more important than taking care of their own physical needs.

Not only did the disciples need to understand the priority of ministry, they needed to learn the principle of readiness for God's timing related to ministry. "Do you not say, 'There are still four months and then comes the harvest'? Behold, I say to you, lift up your eyes and look at the fields, for they are already white for harvest" (John 4:35). Jesus and His disciples were returning from the Passover in April, four months before the grain in the field would be harvested. But Jesus knew the time had come for a harvest of souls. Some Bible teachers believe Jesus may have applied this statement about "fields white for harvest" to a group of Samaritan men making their way toward Him from the city. Samaritan men wear white turbans and would have looked literally like "white fields" as they came to see Jesus.

Jesus also needed to teach His disciples the principle of rejoicing together over a harvest for eternity. Perhaps He knew their ethnic attitudes toward the Samaritans would hinder them in ministry and cause them to fail to appreciate what God was going to do among the people of the city. He reminded them the harvest of souls for eternity was greater than a mere harvest of grain from the fields. In a harvest for eternity, "both he who sows and he who reaps may rejoice together" (John 4:36).

The fourth principle of ministry Jesus needed to teach His disciples was that ministry is what God does *through* a person rather than what a person does for God. The success in ministry His disciples might experience was not the result of their own labor exclusively. "I sent you to reap that for which you have not labored; others have labored, and you have entered into their labors," He explained (John 4:38). The Christian who understands this principle of ministry is eager to work together with others to accomplish ministry objectives.

III. The Samaritan Woman: A Carrier of Revival (John 4:39-42)

God had prepared this city, and the woman Jesus met at the well became a carrier of revival to the city. Samaritans were descendants of pagan colonists from Mesopotamia who had adopted the worship of Jehovah as a sort of tribal deity (2 Kings 17:24ff., 2 Chron. 30:6, 10; 34:9). During the Babylonian captivity, they intermarried with the Jews who remained in the land. Sanballat built them a temple of their own on Mt. Gerizim. They established their worship of God in accordance with the principles of the Pentateuch. Although their temple had been destroyed in 129 B.C. by the Maccabean leader John Hyrcanus, they continued to worship on the mountain. Even in the last part of the twentieth century, faithful Samaritans continue to offer blood sacrifices to God on Mt. Gerizim.

Not only had their religious and cultural heritage helped to prepare them for the ministry of Jesus, John the Baptist had ministered in the region and had probably awakened the interest of many Samaritans in the fulfillment of many messianic prophecies recorded in their own Pentateuch. In her conversation with Jesus, the woman at the well indicated this expectation when she noted, "I know that Messiah is coming" (John 4:25). While many of His own people, the Jews, were unwilling to accept Jesus as their Messiah, many in this Samaritan city eagerly anticipated His coming.

When the woman returned to her city, she invited others to come and meet the One she believed to be the Messiah. "Come, see a Man who told me all things that I ever did. Could this be the Christ?" she asked (John 4:29). Her simple testimony of what Jesus meant in her life impacted others who were also looking for the Messiah. They too wanted to meet the One who had changed this woman's life. Quickly they went out of the city and headed toward the well, eager to meet Jesus before He continued on His journey.

The testimony of the woman became the catalyst to awaken the inner spiritual longings of many residents of the city. Not only did they go to the well to meet Jesus, they urged Him to remain in the city and teach them more. As a result of Jesus' willingness to devote two days to ministry among them, many others came to believe in Him as Messiah (John 4:41). The Bible identifies two groups of Samaritans who responded to Jesus during His brief ministry in Samaria. The first were those who were looking for the Messiah and believed immediately upon the testimony of the Samaritan woman (John 4:39). The second group only came to faith in Him as Messiah after they had spent some time with Jesus and considered His message more thoroughly (John 4:42). As a result of His ministry among them, the Samaritans of that city came to understand the breadth of Jesus' redemptive work and identified Him as "the Savior of the world" (John 4:42).

The day after Jesus left that Samaritan city, that woman returned to the well where she had met Jesus. As she lowered her water pot to draw water from Jacob's well, she remembered what Jesus had promised about "a fountain of water springing up into everlasting life" (John 4:14). The city did not look much different physically than it had a few days earlier and the climate was still hot and dry, but much had changed. While they still came to the well to draw water to drink, many in that city had experienced that fountain of water springing up within them. For the first time in her life there was a fullness where only days earlier there had been a void. She still did not enjoy drawing water in the heat of the day, but the memory of that meeting at the well and the change that had begun to take effect in her life and the lives of so many others somehow made it all worthwhile. As she brought her full water pot up out of the well, she wondered if she would ever meet her Messiah again. Perhaps not in this life, but certainly in the eternal life which was now hers.

Conclusion

It is possible for believers today to miss opportunities to effectively minister for Christ because personal prejudice may blind their eyes to real needs. The disciples had experienced a very successful ministry in Judea, but when they came to Samaria, they apparently let their personal feelings for that ethnic group hinder their spiritual desire to tell others about the Messiah. Fortunately, Jesus not only overcame the natural tendency of the Jews to hate the Samaritans, but was willing to spend time to help a Samaritan overcome her hatred for Jewish men and thereby effectively reach that village. When believers today are prepared to set aside their ethnic prejudice, they can become effective in helping members of other people groups come to recognize Jesus as "the Christ, the Savior of the world" (John 4:42).

CHAPTER 7

JESUS OF NAZARETH:
A PROPHET WITHOUT HONOR
AT HOME

Matthew 4:13-17; Mark 1:14; Luke 4:14-31; John 4:46-50

After Jesus had enjoyed a successful ministry in both Judea and Samaria, He returned to Galilee where He was generally received because of what people had seen Him do in Jerusalem. He knew, however, that ministering in His home region would be difficult in that prophets tended to be rejected at home (John 4:44). That proved to be true in Jesus' case. While He was extremely popular most places He went, when He returned to His hometown of Nazareth, He was soundly rejected. Still, Jesus had an effective ministry in Galilee.

The providence of Galilee was one of five provinces in the area. It was so named after the major body of fresh water at its eastern boundary, the Sea of Galilee (meaning "circle"). This lake was also known by a number of other names including Tiberias and Chinnereth (meaning "harp"). The lake was also called Gennesaret which means "garden of princes" or "garden of abundance." This was the name of a fertile plain at the north end of the lake. More recently, this lake has been called Pickleville Lake (English) or Tarichaean (Greek) because many of the fish caught in it are preserved in the area. As recently as 1937, 276 tons of fish were caught in this body of water.

The population of Galilee was probably about 3,000,000 at the time Christ ministered in the region. Many of these inhabitants had Gentile roots and the region became known as "Galilee of the Gentiles." The principle industries of the region were fishing and agriculture. Galilean farm crops included various kinds of grain and fruit including both grapes and figs.

When Jesus returned to Galilee for ministry. He engaged in a strategy which initially involved preaching in the synagogues. Later He preached in open areas. Since the Babylonian captivity, synagogues were established as cultural centers of the Jews, where they gathered to study the Scriptures and engaged in a wide variety of activities. They became so popular among the Jews that it is estimated that in the city of Jerusalem alone there were between 360 and 480 synagogues.

The message Jesus began preaching in His early ministry in Galilee was simple and direct, "Repent, for the kingdom of heaven is at hand" (Matt. 4:17).

This was the same message John the Baptist had been preaching before his imprisonment. As Jesus began His ministry in Galilee, His popularity grew so rapidly that some Bible teachers identify this phase of His ministry as "the year of popularity." This was a typical Galilean response. A number of messianic movements had begun in Galilee and found a significant following with relative ease. One factor which many have contributed to this phenomenon was the visible presence of Rome in their midst. Roman soldiers regularly marched through their streets and tax collectors from Rome were everywhere. Not only was the fishing industry on Galilee a major source of tax revenues, a great deal of trade to and from other places passed through this region and was taxed accordingly. Many Galileans were always prepared to follow any leader who brought hope of once and for all disposing of Rome. For many Jews, this dream and deep desire was the core of their messianic expectation.

I.   The Reception of His Miracle in Cana (John 4:46-50)

The first recorded miracle of Jesus upon His return to Galilee was the healing of a nobleman's son. Jesus healed the boy without going to Capernaum where the miracle took place, by simply assuring the father the miracle had taken place and sending him on his way. Because of its similarity with a later healing by Jesus in Capernaum, some Bible teachers confuse these two events. However, a closer look at the biblical accounts also reveals a number of differences between these two miracles.

TWO HEALINGS IN CAPERNAUM	
John 4:46-50	*Matt. 8:5-13, Luke 7:1-10*
Jesus in Cana	Jesus in Capernaum
Approached by a Courtier	Approached by a Centurion
Son is healed	Servant is healed
Jesus invited to home	Jesus asked to speak a word
Jesus comments on unbelief	Jesus comments on great faith
Early in Galilean ministry	Later in Galilean ministry

The Greek term *basilikos* used to describe this nobleman was normally used to identify those related to the king by blood or office. This man was probably a high ranking officer associated with Herod Antipas. (On the night before Jesus' crucifixion, Herod himself met Jesus hoping to witness a miracle [Luke 23:8]. The healing of an associate's son may have been the event that first introduced Herod to the miraculous ministry of Jesus.)

Although this nobleman may have been very familiar with the diplomacy involved in making requests of others, his request to Jesus for his son's healing was not a formal request for favors but rather a desperate father's pleading. The Greek word *paidion* translated "child" (John 4:49) is a term of endearment similar to the expression "my little boy." In his official capacity, this man may have been involved in resolving many problems for others, but was suddenly confronted with a problem he could not handle in his own family. In desperation he appealed to Jesus to do what he as a father could not. Jesus assured the man his son was healed and sent him on his way home (John 4:50). In faith, the nobleman made his way back to Capernaum. He was not surprised when a servant later told him his son was healed. When they compared notes they confirmed the healing occurred at the exact hour he had been talking with Jesus (John 4:52).

This was the first recorded example of "household salvation" in the New Testament. Typical of others, the father "himself believed (first), and his whole household" (John 4:53). Sometimes this is called "Oikos Evangelism" because the Greek word for "household" is *oikos*. In the New Testament, this happened when an influential member of a household, usually the male head of the household, believed in Jesus and became instrumental in leading others in his sphere of influence (i.e., the household which included both family members and servants) to make a similar commitment to Christ. Some individuals have confused this principle to argue an entire family can be saved by the faith of one member of that family. However, in the New Testament, a Christian in the household led others to make their own individual decision for Christ as the Christian used his or her influence and shared his or her faith with others.

II.   The Rejection of His Mandate in Nazareth (Luke 4:16-31)

After this second miracle in Cana of Galilee, Jesus returned to his childhood home of Nazareth. He had been raised in the community and was widely known among His friends and relatives, but the reception He may have received among them was not extended to His ministry. As was His custom, Jesus attended the synagogue on the Sabbath, perhaps in the company of His younger half-brothers who may have still been living in the town. As a visiting rabbi, Jesus was spotted in the synagogue in Nazareth. Because they had heard of Jesus' ministry success in other places, an invitation was extended to their native son to minister among them. While it is difficult to know what they might have expected from Jesus, they were not prepared for what they received that morning. He took the scroll of Isaiah offered Him and began reading at the appointed place (Isa. 61:1-2). When He finished reading the brief text, He returned the scroll to the attendant of the synagogue and took His seat to begin teaching the lesson. "Today this Scripture is fulfilled in your hearing," he began (Luke 4:21). Initially, those who heard Him speak marveled at the way words seemed to flow from the mouth of Jesus. They began to understand why vast multitudes gathered in other places to hear this man speak. What they could not understand was how the son of the community carpenter had become such an eloquent speaker. Still they were proud of Jesus and felt good as He began His sermon. Some of those present remembered Him as a child playing with their own children and had their own special memories. Others may have attended the synagogue school with Him and recalled how they studied together under a particular rabbi. Still others may not have known Him as a child, but still felt special knowing He had grown up in their town. But as Jesus continued His message, those attitudes began to change.

Jesus continued His message that morning by addressing the matter of miracles. He knew that many of His listeners were secretly hoping He would display His miraculous power in some significant way in Nazareth, but He also knew that would not be done. As He preached, He reminded His audience of two other Galilean prophets of a former age, Elijah and Elisha. Both of these men were remembered for their miracles, but a closer look at their miracles revealed they ministered not to the Jew but the Gentiles. Elijah ministered to a widow not in Israel but Zaraphath during the three years of drought at the beginning of his ministry. Similarly, Elisha did not heal any of Israel's lepers but rather a Gentile military leader, Naaman the Syrian.

Nothing Jesus said was new to them. They were no doubt familiar with the ministries of these two great prophets. But the reminder that Elisha helped a Gentile military leader irked them. They hated the presence of the Roman occupation army and Jesus' apparent willingness to heal the son of one of Herod's officials and refuse to do miracles in His own hometown of Nazareth. To them it sounded like He was collaborating with the enemy. What might be an acceptable attitude of a prophet who had ministered centuries before was not an acceptable attitude of one of their own, one who had been raised with their children and educated in their school. Those who moments before marveled at the words of Jesus now hated Him with an intense passion.

So intense was their feeling of anger toward Jesus that they thrust Him out of town. There was a steep cliff on one of the hills nearby and the mob "led Him to the brow" (Luke 4:29). They intended to kill Him by throwing Him over the cliff but Jesus escaped. He managed to work His way through the crowd and left them frustrated on their attempt to destroy Him. This was the first of several recorded attempts on His life during His public ministry. This was not the last time Jesus would visit His hometown, but His ministry was never received by those with whom He grew up. On His final visit to Nazareth, the people did not try to kill Him but only a few sick people were healed (Mark 6:5). Jesus was limited in his ability to perform any significant miracle because of the people's unbelief (Mark 6:6; Matt. 13:58). Jesus' rejection in Nazareth extended to members of His own family. Later some of His own brothers expressed their unbelief (John 7:3-5) and on at least one occasion suggested Jesus was mentally incompetent (Matt. 12:46-50; Mark 3:31-35; Luke 8:19-21). Not until Jesus was raised from the dead did He see members of His own family come to trust Him as Messiah. Later, His half-brother James wrote an epistle of the New Testament.

III.   The Return of His Ministry in Capernaum (Matt. 4:13-16)

Following His initial rejection in Nazareth, Jesus moved to Capernaum making that city on the northwest shore of the Lake of Galilee his home base of ministry. He and His disciples had been in Capernaum for a brief visit prior to going to Jerusalem for Passover (John 2:12). Several of those who were commissioned as His apostles lived and worked in or near this city before they met Jesus. Now this city would have a more prominent role in His ministry.

Jesus' choice of Capernaum as the base for His ministry was consistent with Isaiah's prophecy concerning the shining of a great light in the area (cf. Isa. 8:23–9:2). Light was one of the symbols of the Messiah and one which Jesus Himself would use to explain His uniqueness to others. Capernaum was a principle city in the region and the logical choice for a ministry base. It was one of the more affluent cities in the region and became the desired home of important government officials. Although it was the site of many of Jesus' greatest miracles, and many people from the area followed Him, the city itself did not repent. Today, all that is left of the city is the ruins of a first century synagogue which was probably built over the very spot where Jesus often sat to teach the Scriptures.

Conclusion

As stewards of the resources entrusted to them by God, Christians need to learn from the example of Jesus and invest themselves and their resources in areas which produce the greatest fruit. When Jesus developed His own personal ministry strategy, He chose to devote the greater part of His time in more fruitful areas while not neglecting other important ministry opportunities. He visited His hometown of Nazareth on at least two occasions even though there were few results, but much of His ministry was among the multitudes and inner group of disciples which were more promising fields of service. His move to Capernaum was symbolic of this priority in His personal ministry strategy as this town was more central to both His disciples' homes and those of the crowds.

CHAPTER 8

SIMON PETER:
THE DAY HE BROUGHT JESUS HOME

Matthew 8:14-17; 9:1-8; Mark 1:21–2:12; Luke 4:31-5:26

What a morning! Jesus had been asked to teach the lesson at the synagogue, but no one could have anticipated what actually happened. As was becoming the custom, the crowds thronged Him; even the synagogue itself was packed. The way Jesus taught, and the things He said that the other visiting rabbis and scribes of the law seemed to lack, exuded a certain air of authority. But the message was not what made the great impression that day. It was the interruption! Usually, people were polite and endured the lesson, even if they disagreed with the teacher or thought the message was particularly boring. But that morning, the person people were saying was demon possessed showed for the service. Suddenly without warning he started calling Jesus "the Holy One of God" (Mark 1:24).

If that was not strange enough, Jesus' response was most unusual. When He told the man to be quiet, it was as though He didn't want him telling some secret. And when He spoke, Jesus spoke beyond the man and talked directly to the demon. A few moments later, the man came back to his senses as the demon left. As Jesus and His disciples left the synagogue that day, they could hear bits of conversation as they passed by various groups. "What is this? What new doctrine is this? For with authority He commands even the unclean spirits, and they obey him?" (Mark 1:27).

Obviously Jesus of Nazareth was going to be talked about for a while. He was certainly among the most popular men of the region and the events of that morning were sure to spread quickly. But even in his wildest imagination, Simon Peter was highly unlikely to have guessed what would happen the day he brought Jesus home.

I. Jesus: Offering Help to Hurting People (Matt. 8:14-17; Mark 1:29-3; Luke 4:38-41)

Actually, it wasn't a good day for Peter to bring Jesus home. His mother-in-law was there and had come down with some kind of serious fever which confined her to bed. She would not be impressed with her son-in-law when she heard the voices of guests in the home and was not able to get out of bed to be hospitable. Apparently not until they got to the house did the issue of

Peter's sick mother-in-law come to Jesus' attention. When He saw her, He was ready to deal with her problem immediately. He dealt directly and severely with the fever while dealing tenderly with Peter's mother-in-law. When Luke recorded that Jesus "rebuked the fever" (Luke 4:39), it must have struck the doctor as an unusual medical treatment. The Greek word he used to describe Jesus' rebuke of the fever was *epitimao,* the same word used to describe the way Jesus rebuked a storm at sea (Luke 8:24) and the demon which had possessed the man in the synagogue that morning (Mark 1:25). This word does not, however, imply any critical attitude involved in the rebuke. The rebuke was directed at the fever, not Peter's mother-in-law's poor hygiene or unhealthy lifestyle. Jesus chose not to be critical of people while helping them with their problem. Each of the three synoptic gospels (Matthew, Mark, and Luke) record this particular miracle, but each account reveals only part of the total picture. In treating Simon Peter's mother-in-law, Jesus first stood over her much as a doctor with a good bedside manner might stand over a suffering patient (Luke 4:39). Then, reaching down to her, he touched her hand (Matt. 8:15). Only then did the fever actually leave her. But even when the immediate problem was resolved, Jesus was not through with the woman. Lovingly He took her by the hand and lifted her up, restoring her to her former place of service (Mark 1:31). Her healing and restoration was complete and because of what Jesus had done in her life, she was eager to minister to others including Jesus Himself.

II.   Jesus: Offering Hope to Hopeless People (Matt. 9:1-8; Mark 1:35-39; 2:1-12; Luke 5:17-26)

Before the day was through, the whole town was at Simon Peter's door. Word had spread that Jesus was there, and everybody knew that meant hope for the hopeless. Some may have come that evening with a "hope so" kind of faith in Jesus' ability, not really sure He would be able to deal with their specific problem. But when Peter saw the multitude at his home that evening, he should have had no doubts concerning what Jesus could do for others, after seeing Jesus cast out a demon in the synagogue that morning and later healing his mother-in-law. In allowing his home to be a center for Jesus' healing ministry, Peter had a unique ministry which like most ministries was born out of his problems.

The next morning Peter discovered a second principle of an effective ministry. Not only does an effective ministry to others grow out of one's experience with Christ, it must be bathed in prayer. Peter may not have realized it at the time, but years later he told young John Mark about that occasion at his home. "Now in the morning, having risen up a great while before daylight, He (Jesus) went out and departed to a solitary place; and there he prayed" (Mark 1:35). The words almost sound like Peter recalling what he later noticed as a habit of prayer in Jesus' life. Not only must an outreach ministry of hope be bathed in prayer, it must be built upon a spiritual strategy of power and encounter. Jesus understood He should not try to do everything during His earthly ministry, so He limited Himself in His labors and made major ministry decisions in times of prayer with His heavenly Father. That morning when

Peter finally found Jesus, he tried unsuccessfully to get Jesus back to Capernaum. "Everyone is looking for you," the disciples insisted (Mark 1:37). But Jesus could not be swayed from His commitment by the popularity of the crowds. "Let us go into the next towns, that I may preach there also, because for this purpose I have come forth," He responded (Mark 1:38). He had a passion for ministry and was wholeheartedly committed to that goal. But Peter still needed to learn some important lessons before he too would be a part of an outreach ministry offering hope to those who felt hopeless. Although Jesus apparently wanted Peter to travel with him throughout Galilee ("Let us," Mark 1:38), only Jesus was engaged in ministry in Galilee ("he preached," Mark 1:39). Something held Peter back from the place of usefulness. Perhaps he was just too comfortable in his nice home in Capernaum. Perhaps the thought of traveling with an itinerant teacher lacked appeal.

After this tour of Galilean towns, Jesus returned to Capernaum and spent time at Peter's house. On one of these later occasions, word spread through town that Jesus was back. Again the crowds surrounded Peter's house. Among those present that day were Pharisees and scribes who were teachers of the law (Luke 5:17). They apparently had come from various towns and villages from all over Galilee to see for themselves and analyze Jesus' teaching more closely. To have a rabbi in one's home was an honor which would be coveted by any Jew. But as Peter looked out over the crowded room, he saw not one but a group of the areas' most prominent religious leaders in his own home. Perhaps he began to swell with pride. To think that religious leaders would come to his house to hear his friend teach the Scriptures! Then, in Peter's moment of glory the roof collapsed on his dreams. First there was a faint scratching sound. Bits and pieces of dirt were falling over those in the room. The one time Peter is likely to have rabbis in his home and the roof begins to crumble! Four men were deliberately breaking up the roof. They removed the ceiling tiles used over the roof in the homes. The hole continued to grow. Then the four men began lowering something through the hole. It was a palette containing a crippled man sick of the palsy. This crippled man had a genuine need that only Jesus could meet.

Peter was about to learn another important lesson in reaching out to others with hope and would realize that following Jesus meant certain sacrifices.The servants and somewhat secure income of a fishing business would no longer be available to Peter, and he would follow Jesus with eleven other men, never quite sure where the next meal would come from or where they would sleep at night.

FOUR PRINCIPLES FOR AN EFFECTIVE MINISTRY

- Born out of Personal Problems
- Bathed in Prevailing Prayer
- Built upon a Prior Purpose
- Bearing a Private Price

What Peter saw Jesus do in his home that afternoon was beginning to make an impression. When the paralytic man was presented to Jesus, Jesus did not heal the man but forgave his sins. Peter must have heard the scribes muttering to themselves, "Why does this Man speak blasphemies like this? Who can forgive sins but God alone?" (Mark 2:7). But Peter also saw the way Jesus responded to this murmuring. "Which is easier to say," He asked, "Your sins are forgiven you" or "Arise, take up your bed and walk?" (Mark 2:9). The answer is obvious. Healing is an external miracle, forgiveness of sin is internal. Because only God knew for sure if one's sins were forgiven, any one could make such a promise knowing no one could prove Him wrong. But as soon as someone told a lame man to walk, that person's credibility would be exposed. When Jesus was sure everyone had got the point of what He was saying, He turned to the man and said, "I say to you, arise, take up your bed and go to your house" (Mark 2:11). And the man did exactly that. The outward miracle would authenticate Jesus and demonstrate His power to forgive sins. No wonder those present that day left confessing, "We never saw anything like this!" (Mark 3:12). While the unusual miracle did not secure an immediate response from Peter, it likely helped him see Jesus in a different way. He knew Jesus was a religious teacher and a worker of miracles, but had he considered Him as the forgiver of sins? Peter knew he himself had sin in his life he could not deal with and may have been intimidated by Jesus' response to the man who had been let down through the roof.

III. Jesus: Offering Honor to a Humbled Follower (Luke 5:1-11)

Although the fishing business of Jonas and Zebedee was a growing commercial enterprise, some nights even the best fishermen get skunked. That is exactly what had happened to the four fishermen the night before Jesus came walking by the shore. The crowds still followed Jesus and on this occasion they forced Jesus into the water. Peter and Andrew, James and John had been out all night fishing but without success. All they had as a result of their night's labor were nets that needed to be cleaned and mended. That is what they were doing when Jesus spotted the boat and recognized the owners.

The boat was just what Jesus needed to help him keep the masses at a distance so He could teach all. So Jesus used Peter's boat. Peter apparently didn't mind taking the boat out a bit from shore and letting Jesus use it. Jesus taught sitting in the boat as it rocked gently in the shallow waves. As Peter heard Jesus' message, there was no question in his mind why the multitude had latched on to this particular rabbi. There was a power in all he said that, if it were possible, seemed to surpass the power evident when he healed the sick and cast out demons. It almost seemed as though the very words Jesus uttered were impregnated with life itself. Peter had come to the place where he addressed Jesus as "Master" (Luke 5:5).

The Greek word *epistates* only occurs in the Gospel of Luke and is only used by the disciples to address Jesus. It was a term one used to address a religious teacher when the title rabbi did not express everything one wanted to say (cf. Luke 5:5, 8:24, 45; 9:33, 49; 17:13). Literally it meant chief, commander, leader, or overseer. It denoted the absolute authority of the one so addressed, but that authority was limited to the master's area of specialty. It is related to one of the many titles for the pastor of a local church in the New

Testament, bishop (1 Tim. 3:1). When one called another master using this word *epistates*, he was acknowledging the supremacy of that person as a religious teacher. Peter was prepared to acknowledge Jesus' supremacy as a religious teacher just as he might have considered himself a master fisherman.

After teaching the multitudes, Jesus encouraged Peter to launch out into deeper water and let down his net for a catch (Luke 5:4). Peter knew there were good reasons why that was not a good idea and was tired enough to say so. He, the master fisherman, had been on the lake all night and had come away empty. Every man who fished those waters knew fish came to the surface during the cool nights and stayed in the deeper waters during the warm days. That is why they worked nights to catch fish. But maybe there was a better way to show Jesus what a bad idea He had. Peter agreed to throw in one net (Luke 5:5) probably expecting to be able to pull it back into the boat with a comment like, "See, I told you so." But that is not exactly what happened. No sooner had the net been thrown into the water than it was filled with a large school of fish. It was so full that the net actually began to break. James and John were called out to help and responded quickly. As the net was emptied, the boats were so full of fish they began to take on water, and still there seemed to be no end to the fish. And then Peter remembered. The people in his home had never seen anything like Jesus forgiving sin either. Suddenly it must have dawned on him. Jesus was more than a rabbi. He was even more than the best rabbi, the Master. He was the One the Old Testament prophets called Lord or Jehovah, the personal God who delighted in forgiving sin. And as he realized who Jesus was, he was also deeply conscious of what he was. He found himself on his knees before Jesus crying out in fear, "Depart from me, for I am a sinful man, O Lord!" (Luke 5:8). The new term was *Lord,* one who was his possessor, as a rich person owned a slave. From henceforth, Jesus would be Peter's owner. Peter would be the slave. But there was nothing to fear from Jesus. He turned to Peter and encouraged him. "Do not be afraid. From now on you will catch men" (Luke 5:10). This time, Peter and the others would rise to the challenge of personal discipleship. "So when they had brought their boats to land, they forsook all and followed Him" (Luke 5:11). From this moment on, Peter would no longer split his energies between fishing and following Jesus. Peter would be a dedicated disciple.

Conclusion

Sometimes it takes time for a believer to develop the kind of relationship with Jesus that recognizes Him as one's personal Lord. When believers come to a deeper and richer understanding of who Jesus is, it is important that they respond with a commitment similar to that of Peter. First, knowing who Jesus is helps people better understand themselves (Luke 5:8). Based on that realization, a second thing happens to believers. They begin to understand the new nature of their relationship with Jesus (Luke 5:11). Third, when they are prepared to recognize Jesus as their possessor, Jesus is willing to entrust them with ministry (Luke 5:10).

CHAPTER 9

MATTHEW: CELEBRATING A
NEW RELATIONSHIP WITH GOD

Matthew 8:2-4; 9:9-17; Mark 1:40-45; 2:13-22; Luke 5:12-16, 27-39

*J*esus was getting very close to formally appointing twelve disciples to be with Him and be the focus of His ministry both to and through them (Matt. 10:1; Mark 3:14). Before that could be done, there were still a few more things to do. He would not place His ministry on hold until He could get better organized. Instead, He used His ministry to reach those who would become a part of His worldwide strategy.

As Jesus' ministry began to take on a character of its own, it soon became obvious that it would differ significantly from the many other sects of Judaism which appealed to people of that day. While each sect had their own distinctives, they were remarkably the same in that they called people to serve God out of a sense of guilt and duty. But this was never Jesus' appeal. He taught people to celebrate a new relationship with God.

Those who met Jesus shared their newfound faith in the Messiah with friends and family members out of the overflow of a new experience. His first miracle in Cana of Galilee enabled the celebration of a new home to continue. When Jesus met with individuals, whether they were respected Jewish leaders or despised Samaritan outcasts, He offered them a "faith relationship" with God which could become the basis of their celebration. People were beginning to worship God again from their hearts as they came into contact with Jesus. Their lives were changed. What had begun would continue, and the very church Jesus would establish would be one which celebrated a new relationship with God.

Several incidents in the ministry of Jesus which occurred during His final phase of gathering the twelve disciples highlight His emphasis on celebration. Each of them suggest reasons why people then and now celebrate the fulfillment of physical needs met in their life through a relationship with God (Matt. 8:2-4; Mark 1:40-45; Luke 5:12-16). Others celebrated the forgiveness of sins they found in a relationship with the only One who can forgive sins (Matt. 9:9-13; Mark 2:13-17; Luke 5:27-32). Still others celebrated the rich fellowship and communion they could experience with God (Matt. 9:14-17; Mark 2:18-22; Luke 5:33-39).

I. A Celebration of Fulfillment (Matt. 8:2-4; Mark 1:40-45; Luke 5:12-16)

One of the many who found fulfillment in a relationship with Jesus during His public ministry was a leper who was healed by Him about the time the four fishermen began following Jesus as full-time disciples. Though this man's name remains unknown, his story was recorded in each of the synoptic gospels, perhaps because his experience with Jesus was so typical of others who were made complete in a new relationship.

Leprosy was more than a disease, it became a lifestyle to the victim. Under Mosaic law, the leper was banished from his home and city and required to warn others he came in contact with of his physical condition. While some types of leprosy are not contagious, all were considered ceremonially unclean. Once a person was diagnosed as a leper, he would be required to call out, "Unclean, unclean" whenever he saw someone approaching him. Obviously, no one would touch a leper lest he would also become ceremonially unclean. He would have to be cleansed for that touch.

The condition of leprosy would normally last the rest of one's natural life. Adjusting to the physical effects of the disease was not the only adjustment the leper had to make. Because of the necessity to isolate the leper from others, being diagnosed a leper normally meant leaving close friends and family members. Also, in fulfilling his responsibility to warn others of his condition, the leper would feed his already depressed self-image with the negative reminder he was ceremonially unclean.

While under the law of Moses provision was made to restore a cleansed leper back into society, it was seldom if ever used. Before the ministry of Jesus, the only two recorded cases of a leper being healed were those of Miriam and Namaan the Syrian. If a leper were healed, the priest would probably have to look up what to do before he began the process of confirming the healing and integrating the man back into society.

Despite all of this, one man in the advanced stages of the disease believed Jesus could help. Perhaps he had heard of or met others healed by Jesus and became convinced he could also heal leprosy. Although no one had been healed of this disease before, he was willing to be the first.

He was willing, but was Jesus? There was a great difference between being able to heal and being willing to heal. When he had the opportunity to meet Jesus in a deserted place one day, he determined to find out once and for all. Humbly begging Jesus, the man expressed both his faith and request, "If You are willing, You can make me clean" (Mark 1:40).

Jesus answered the man in such an incredible way no one could ever again doubt His willingness to assist those in need again. "Then Jesus, moved with compassion, stretched out His hand and touched him" (Mark 1:41).

Jesus touched the leper! Since the day the man had been diagnosed a leper, he had not felt the loving touch of a single individual. People had been quick to see his physical disease and slow to recognize his emotional needs. As Jesus touched him, He also talked to Him. "I am willing; be cleansed," He said (Mark 1:41). No sooner had He spoken the words than the man was completely healed.

Jesus reminded the man of his responsibility under the law to submit to an examination by the priest and urged him to do so quickly. The man left, but not to see a priest. He wanted to talk to people, people with whom he had been unable to talk for many years now, and he wanted to tell them what Jesus had done for Him. He was the first of many lepers who would be healed under the ministry of Jesus and leave celebrating the physical, emotional, social, and spiritual fulfillment they found in a new relationship with Him.

II.   A Celebration of Forgiveness (Matt. 9:9-13; Mark 2:13-17; Luke 5:27-32)

The healing of this leper and the decision of men like the sons of Zebedee and Jonas to leave their business to follow Jesus only served to add to Jesus' growing popularity. As people heard others sharing their experiences with Jesus, they would make an effort to go and see Jesus for themselves. Whether they were rich or poor, prominent in religion and society or merely children did not matter; it seemed like everybody wanted to see Jesus and was making some effort to do so. In all Israel, this attitude applied to every class of people with only one possible exception, the tax collectors.

Like others in their society, the tax collectors were very much aware of what was happening under the ministry of Jesus. Also, like others they experienced that inner emptiness that other things did not seem to fill. As they collected taxes and conducted their business affairs, they could see the difference in others and realized Jesus had done something for them. Many of them may have come to the place where they believed He could do it for them also, but there was still a problem.

A tax collector worked for Rome, and in Galilee, Rome was the enemy. Because most of them were Jews, they were generally considered traitors who had sold out to the occupying army. They used Roman soldiers to enforce their demands if people refused to pay. That only confirmed the suspicions of the people. They had learned to compensate by inflating the tax rate and keeping the profit. This meant the tax collector was usually very wealthy, but was still hated by his neighbors. They were considered the most outrageous of sinners and were refused admission to the synagogue. Even if a tax collector wanted to meet Jesus, any thinking man believed the Rabbi would have nothing to do with him. The best course of action in the minds of most was to save the embarrassment and not even try.

But unlike other religious leaders of His day, Jesus was not prepared to cut off any group of people from His ministry. If there were reasons why they felt uncomfortable approaching Him, He would approach them. He did it by calling one of their own into His growing band of disciples.

Matthew was probably the oldest of the twelve men who became Jesus' disciples and may also have been the best educated. He had exceptional business skills and used them in the conducting of his own tax business as well as in dealing with local businessmen, property owners, and traveling merchants. Because of the nature of his business and requirements of the job in that region, likely he was fluent in Hebrew, Aramaic, Latin, and Greek. Some

Bible teachers believe Matthew may have taken shorthand notes of Jesus' discourses which later became the basis of the first gospel.

Matthew's collection office was on the shore of the Sea of Galilee. Here he calculated the proper tax on each fisherman. He no doubt had many dealings with the sons of Jona and Zebedee long before he began following Jesus as a disciple. Also the road from Damascus to Jerusalem passed Capernaum, so he probably collected taxes from those traveling this road.

When Jesus called Matthew to follow him, this tax collector responded immediately. Jesus' appeal was direct and to the point, the shortest call to discipleship ever made by Jesus, "Follow Me" (Matt. 9:9). As an experienced businessman, Matthew was willing and able to make an immediate and meaningful decision.

One of the first things Matthew did as a disciple of Christ was to host a banquet in Jesus' honor. Prior to meeting Jesus, he had no doubt attended and conducted many such dinners. At these dinners, friends would be invited to come meet and honor visiting dignitaries or high-ranking officials. Matthew did for Jesus what he had done for others he wanted to honor. He prepared a dinner and invited others to celebrate with him the new relationship he had with Jesus. In doing so, he brought Jesus into a gathering of tax collectors.

Not everyone thought it was a good idea for Jesus to attend the banquet, but Jesus was present just the same. When the Pharisees murmured about Jesus associating with the publicans and sinners, He quoted one of the popular sayings of the day, "Those who are well have no need of a physician" (Matt. 9:12). This is the only statement found in classical Greek literature that Jesus is known to have quoted. To this He added, "I did not come to call the righteous, but sinners, to repentance" (Matt. 9:13). Because that was His ministry objective, that banquet was the very place Jesus should have been. He reminded His critics that God was more concerned with the spirit of religion than forms associated with it (cf. Hosea. 6:6).

We do not know the immediate results of that banquet in terms of how many tax collectors discovered the forgiveness of sins. But there was at least one significant long-term result of Matthew's decision to follow Jesus. Some time later, Matthew's former employer, a chief tax collector named Zacchaeus, went out of his way to meet Jesus as He passed through Jericho (Luke 19:1-10). Zacchaeus must have marveled at the change in Matthew's life and wondered about the One who could draw such a strong commitment from the successful businessman. Matthew's obedience to Jesus' call to discipleship may have been one of the major factors in Zacchaeus later being able to celebrate the forgiveness of sin which he too discovered in a new relationship with Jesus.

III.　A Celebration of Fellowship (Matt. 9:14-17; Mark 2:18-22; Luke 5:33-39)

The Pharisees were not the only ones who began to criticize Jesus' ministry. Before long the disciples of John the Baptist came to question Jesus about His disciples' lack of fasting (Matt. 9:14). Both the Pharisees and John's disciples fasted on a regular basis as a spiritual discipline, but Jesus' disciples were better known for their feasting rather than fasting. Some Bible teachers believe the question may have been prompted by Jesus' and His disciples' appearance at Matthew's banquet on what some Jews regarded a fast day. Under Mosaic law, fasting was practiced one day annually, Yom Kippur (Lev. 16:29; 23:27), but by the time of Jesus' public ministry, Pharisees prided themselves that they fasted twice a week, usually Monday or Tuesday and Thursday. While Jesus did not oppose the practice of fasting and instructed His disciples on the correct way to fast, He did not impose the practice upon those who followed Him. He recognized the time would come when they too would fast, but that time was not then. He defended His disciples' actions, reminding the critics one does not fast at a wedding celebration, rather they eat and enjoy themselves. So Jesus' disciples did not fast, but celebrated the presence of the Bridegroom in their midst.

The celebration of fellowship with Jesus was an integral part of what it meant to be one of Jesus' disciples. The two primary reasons Jesus chose twelve disciples were "that they might be with Him and that He might send them out to preach" (Mark 3:14). A disciple was one who first spent time with Jesus celebrating a close and intimate relationship with God. Only then was a disciple involved in a ministry of communicating what he had learned to others.

After a night of prayer, Jesus chose twelve very different kinds of men to follow Him as His disciples. Each of them had their own unique gifts and abilities to contribute to help shape the overall character of the group. During the time they spent with Jesus, they would became the focus of His attention. None of them were perfect and some were less perfect than others. They were not chosen because of who they were as much as who they would become. Much of Jesus' earthly ministry was wrapped up in training the twelve. When it was over, one of them would destroy himself. The other eleven would change the world.

THE TWELVE APOSTLES OF THE LAMB

Simon Peter - The Apostle of Hope
Andrew - The Apostle of Introduction
John - The Apostle of Love
James - The Apostle of Witness
Philip - The Apostle of Spiritual Growth
Nathanael Bartholomew - The Apostle of Spiritual Perception
Matthew - The Apostle of Hospitality
Thomas - The Apostle of Faith
James the Less - The Apostle of Second Place
Simon the Zealot - The Apostle of God and Country
Judas Thaddaeus Lebbaeus - The Apostle of Intimate Christianity
Judas Iscariot - The Apostle of Honor

Jesus also called these men apostles (Matt. 10:2). The Greek word *apostolos* was a technical term referring to a messenger who had been commissioned with special authority. In the New Testament, this special authority was evident in what was called "the signs of the apostle" (2 Cor.

12:12) which probably included the supernatural power to validate their message (cf. Matt. 10:1). The office of the apostle included foundational gifts to validate their ministry and write the Scriptures by inspiration of the Holy Spirit. Their signs are no longer evident among Christians today, just as there are no apostles living today (a criteria to be an apostle was to have seen Jesus in the flesh, cf. Acts 1:22). Apparently Jesus never intended any succession of the office of apostle.

Who were these apostles who spent so much time with Jesus? They are identified four times in Scripture as a group and each listing differs from the others slightly. Because Matthew lists the twelve disciples in pairs, some have concluded these were the pairs who worked together in ministry. While it was common for the disciples to work in pairs, they were not always involved in ministry by the same pairs listed in Matthew. Matthew pairs Peter with his brother Andrew, and John with his brother James; yet the Book of Acts suggests Peter and John worked together as a pair.

GROUPING THE TWELVE	
Matthew 10:2-5	*Mark 3:16-19*
Simon Peter	*Simon Peter*
Andrew	*James of Zebedee*
James of Zebedee	*John*
John	*Andrew*
Philip	Philip
Bartholomew	Bartholomew
Thomas	Matthew
Matthew the Publican	Thomas
James of Alphaeus	*James of Alphaeus*
Lebbaeus Thaddaeus	*Thaddaeus*
Simon the Canaanite	*Simon the Canaanite*
Judas Iscariot	*Judas Iscariot*
Luke 6:14-16	*Acts 1:13*
Simon Peter	Peter
Andrew	James
James	John
John	Andrew
Philip	*Philip*
Bartholomew	*Thomas*
Matthew	*Bartholomew*
Thomas	*Matthew*
James of Alphaeus	James of Alphaeus
Simon Zelotes	Simon Zelotes
Judas of James	Judas of James
Judas Iscariot	Judas Iscariot

The different listings of the twelve disciples more likely reveal something of the organizational structure that existed within the group itself. They were apparently divided into three groups of four disciples each. While none of the lists place the disciples in the same order, in every list, the first, fifth and ninth disciple is always the same. Some Bible teachers interpret this to mean Peter led the first group, Philip led the second group and James of Alphaeus led the last group. Although Jesus was the leader of the larger group, He apparently delegated His leadership to these three men who led subgroups. Also, the twelve seem to be grouped on the basis of their closeness to Christ, Peter's group being the "inner circle" and the group led by James the Less being the most distant. These men were among the first to learn a new approach to religion, that of celebrating one's relationship with God. As one began to consider it, there was much to celebrate. A relationship with God was the means of personal fulfillment for many people. Others thought of that relationship primarily in terms of the forgiveness of sin. Everyone could celebrate it in the context of their fellowship with Jesus. Years later, one of the twelve wrote to those who did not have the opportunity he had to live with Jesus so they too could hear his witness and enjoy that fellowship and celebrate (1 John 1:3-4).

Conclusion

One of the privileges Christians enjoy in their relationship with God is that of worship. Worship is a celebration of who God is and what He has done in, through, and for the worshiper. Sometimes, people worship God because of a personal fulfillment they have found in a new relationship with God, similar to that of lepers cleansed by Jesus. Others are overwhelmed by a sense of forgiveness like that experienced by Matthew when he began his new life in Christ. Still others celebrate God in worship in response to their ongoing experience of fellowship with God. Regardless of the reason, it is good to obey one of the Scripture's final commands, "Worship God" (Rev. 22:9).

CHAPTER 10

THE SANHEDRIN:

THE BATTLE FOR THE SABBATH

Matt. 12:1-14; Mark 2:23–3:6, 13-19; Luke 6:1-16; John 5:1-47

When spring came to the Holy Land in A.D. 28, perhaps many minds centered on and questioned the growing popularity of Jesus of Nazareth and His ministry of miracles and teaching in Galilee. There had been many self-proclaimed "messiahs" from the region ruled by Herod. The region was not as respectable as Judea, the area around Jerusalem. By the time "the deliverers" and their crusade reached Jerusalem, they tended to fade. If the glaring examination of the Jews didn't wither them, the iron fist of Rome crushed them. Among many of Israel's religious thinkers and leaders, the question was being asked, "Would Jesus come to Jerusalem?" A second Passover season approached in the ministry of Jesus. He again made His way to Jerusalem as was commanded all Jewish males (Deut. 16:16). While His ministry style did not involve looking for controversy, that was what He had experienced to some degree a year earlier when He cleared the Court of the Gentiles and drove the money makers out of the temple. Since that time, Jesus had gone from obscurity to become one of the nation's most popular religious leaders. He was not part of the Sanhedrin, nor was He certified by any element of the religious establishment, but the crowds followed Him and listened closely to what He said. He must have known He would be watched closely as He moved about the city.

Once again, a visit to Jerusalem for Passover would result in Jesus being found in the midst of controversy. This time the observance of the Sabbath rather than the cleansing of the temple concerned the religious leaders of the city. They had a holy regard for the Sabbath and defined their loyalty by an endless list of rules and regulations governing how one should observe this weekly day of rest. Jesus was concerned with ministry and would meet a person's needs on the Sabbath as readily as He would on any other day of the week.

What seems like such an insignificant issue to those outside of the culture of that day was in reality a deeply rooted religious conviction. Built on the biblical principle of honoring every seventh day as a day of rest, fifteen hundred years of tradition had turned one of ten significant laws of God into the single most important ritual of the Jewish religion apart from possibly that of circumcision. Laws existed governing specific acts on the Sabbath that if broken could result in death to the offending party. While the religious establishment opposed Jesus' ministry for many reasons, His attitude toward their Sabbath was what so filled them with anger that they seriously considered killing Him (John 5:16).

I.   Jesus Healing by the Pool of Bethesda (John 5:1-15)

As Jesus entered the city on that Sabbath, He passed through the Sheep Gate in the north wall of the city. This gate was so named because it was the one most commonly used to herd sheep through as they were brought to the temple for sacrifice. He was probably coming from Bethany on the east side of the Mount of Olives. As He made His way through the city street toward the temple, He passed by the Pool of Bethesda, a large rectangular pool where sacrificial animals were usually washed on their way to the temple. But the animals were not the only ones gathering around that particular pool.

The waters of Bethesda were widely believed to have a special curative power under certain circumstances, and as a result many sick gathered around the side of the pool. Typically, a couple hundred people would be waiting for the appropriate time to enter the deep pool, but during a feast season like Passover, that number would swell to three thousand or more. People believed that an angel troubled the water from time to time and the first one to enter the water after that happened would be completely healed of his infirmity. Although no record exists of anyone ever being healed by the waters and the proposed means of healing was inconsistent with biblical teaching concerning how God heals, the multitudes came hoping for a miracle. God did not heal by an unseen angel or by some perceived curative waters, but God would heal by the Son of God who made a lame man walk.

While many were by the pool as Jesus passed by, one man in particular caught His attention. Thirty-eight years earlier, he had been involved in something he should not have done and as a consequence, he had acquired a serious physical condition. When Jesus looked at the man, He knew instinctively he had been by the pool a long time and went to the man to offer assistance. As he approached, the sick man, He asked, "Do you want to be made well?" (John 5:6).

Jesus asked the question to determine if the man had given up hope for a miracle or if it was still his desire to be healed. The Greek verb *theleis* used in this context means not only "do you wish" but also "are you still earnestly desiring" to be made well. Jesus knew that when some people are sick for a long time, they sometimes become so accustomed to the illness that they may no longer care if they are healed or not. This man's response suggests his hope had deteriorated. Rather than answer the questions directly, he suggested a number of excuses why he had not yet been healed.

THE SICK EXCUSES BY THE SICK MAN AT THE POOL

I have no man – depending on people!
to put me into the pool – depending on places!
when the water is stirred up – depending on conditions!
but while I am coming – depending on self-effort!
another steps down before me – blaming others!

Jesus was not interested in excuses, He wanted to help. He knew none of the excuses given by the man were sufficient to prevent the man from enjoying a healthy lifestyle. Jesus told the man to pick up his bed and walk, and that is exactly what the man did. Like others before him who had been healed by Jesus, this man had much to celebrate. But if he thought all his problems were behind him, he was about to find out differently very soon. As the healed man passed through the city carrying his bed, he was spotted by a group of religious leaders. Immediately they confronted him with his actions. "It is the Sabbath," they reminded him. "It is not lawful for you to carry your bed" (John 5:10).

Suddenly the man's rejoicing turned to terror. Carrying one's bed on the Sabbath day was punishable by stoning, and if there was ever a time and place that sentence was likely to be carried out it was in Jerusalem during Passover. Defensively he explained he had been healed and the man who healed him told him to carry his bed. The religious leaders wanted to know who it was that would counsel a man to violate the Sabbath laws. The man did not know, he had not thought to ask the name of his Healer. Later, when he discovered His name was Jesus, he quickly passed that information on to the Jews.

II.   Jesus Teaching in the Court of the Temple (John 5:16-47)

When Jesus learned the Jews had been offended by His actions, He did not try to defend Himself. Instead He argued He did not have to defend Himself because of who He was. Jesus made the strongest statement of His deity that He had made to that date. "Therefore the Jews sought all the more to kill Him, because He not only broke the Sabbath, but also said that God was His Father, making Himself equal with God" (John 5:18).

Jesus claimed to be equal with God in three areas. First, He was equal with God in nature. When He called God His Father, He was claiming He and God had the same nature (John 5:17). Secondly, Jesus claimed to be equal with God in power. Like the Father, Jesus claimed to have power to give life (John 5:21). Finally, Jesus claimed to be equal with God in authority. Both He and the Father had authority to judge and continue receiving honor (John 5:22-23).

His claim to equality with God was not some philosophical reasoning divorced from practical application. Rather it was the basis for three distinct acts He would accomplish to demonstrate His authority. As He continued His discourse on this occasion, Jesus noted (1) all life was in His hands (John 5:25-26), (2) all judgment was in His hands (John 5:27), and (3) all resurrection was in His hands (John 5:28-29).

Jesus' very direct statements about His deity would be blasphemous if they could not be demonstrated true. Although it is logical to expect God to claim to be God, it is not logical to believe everyone who claims to be God or even believes he is God unless he can demonstrate the accuracy of his claims. Under Jewish law, a matter could be authenticated by as few as two witnesses (Num. 35:30; Deut. 17:6). As Jesus concluded this discourse, He identified four witnesses whose testimonies were consistent with His own claims.

FOUR WITNESSES TO THE DEITY OF JESUS

John the Baptist (John 5:33-35)
The Messianic Works of Jesus (John 5:36)
The Witness of the Father (John 5:37-38)
The Witness of the Scriptures (John 5:39-47)

III.   Jesus Eating in the Fields of Grain (Matt. 12:1-8; Mark 2:23-28; Luke 6:1-5)

A week later, Jesus again found Himself in a dispute over His lack of observing the Sabbath. This particular conflict can be dated in two ways from Luke's account of the event (Luke 6:1-5). The fact the fields had grain which was ripe or nearly ripe but not yet harvested suggests a date in late spring. Also, Luke uses an unusual expression to identify this Sabbath calling it literally "the second-first Sabbath." This expression identifies the Sabbath as the second following the first which is Passover, much like some Christian churches which use a liturgical calendar might speak of the fourth Sunday following Easter or Pentecost.

Although some roads connected cities throughout the land, many people traveled along worn paths through fields to get from one place to another. If they got hungry on their journey, they would often grab a handful of grain from the field they were passing through like a camper today might pick berries along a wilderness trail.

The practice was not considered theft unless the individual was using some instrument to actually harvest grain that was not his. Many farmers followed the guidelines of the law in leaving the corners of their fields uncut to encourage the poor to glean in their fields.

But once again, what was an acceptable practice six days a week was not acceptable on the Sabbath under Jewish law. The official limit on plucking heads of grain and rubbing away the chaff to eat the seed was set at three heads. That was hardly enough to satisfy anyone's appetite if they were really hungry. It is not surprising therefore that Jesus and His disciples surpassed the official limit when they picked and ate grain while passing through a field. When spotted by a group of Pharisees, they immediately accused Him of working on the Sabbath.

Jesus was not intimidated by the charge of the Pharisees. While He was apparently not eating, He realized His disciples were not trying to be offensive but rather simply trying to satisfy their hunger. He argued their actions could be justified on the basis of five arguments. First, David himself had eaten the shewbread on one occasion to satisfy his hunger (Matt. 12:4). Secondly, the laws regarding the temple require priests to break their Sabbath laws (Matt. 12:5). Also, the prophet Hosea had emphasized God wanted worship from the heart rather than meaningless observance of a form (Matt. 12:7). Jesus' fourth argument pointed to the fact God had made the Sabbath for man's enjoyment (Mark 2:27). Finally, Jesus argued He was free from their Sabbath laws because He was the Lord of the Sabbath (Luke 6:5). In a later dispute with

Jewish leaders over the observance of the Sabbath, Jesus noted they themselves violated the Sabbath by insisting on the circumcision of male children on the eighth day after birth, even if that day happened to be a Sabbath (cf. John 7:20-24).

When Jesus responded to the Pharisees, He chose not to defend the infraction of the Sabbath law but rather addressed the spirit of the alleged offence. It was one thing to honor the Sabbath but it was something entirely different to be placed under a burden of a thousand rules and regulations. While the law clearly forbid working on the Sabbath, no one needed to or was expected to fuss over eating a few handfuls of grain. The Pharisees themselves recognized the tremendous burden of rabbinical law concerning the Sabbath and were aware of the many technical "exceptions" to these rules which they could use as they needed them. The really amazing thing about the various conflicts Jesus had with the religious establishment over the Sabbath is that He had the patience to answer their questions and reason with them.

IV.   Jesus Healing in the Synagogue of the Jews (Matt. 12:9-14; Mark 3:1-6, 13-19; Luke 6:6-16)

Some time later, Jesus again came into conflict with the Pharisees for healing a man on the Sabbath. As Jesus taught in a local synagogue, a man with a withered right hand was present in the meeting. Although the man may not have been drawing attention to himself intentionally, he soon became the focus of attention in the meeting. A group of scribes and Pharisees saw him and began watching to see what Jesus would do. Jesus also saw him and understood what was going on in the minds of His critics.

Jesus determined to involve His critics in the healing He was about to perform to help them understand why it was the right thing to do. He had the man stand in the midst of the crowd so that those who had not already noticed him would see what was about to happen.

Then turning to the scribes and Pharisees, Jesus asked them a number of moral questions about activities that might be performed on the Sabbath in accordance with the law. Under other circumstances, these were exactly the kind of theological discussions the scribes and Pharisees would have delighted to engage in. The scribes were the copiers of the law and as such had accumulated a great knowledge of the details of the law and its moral implications. The Pharisees prided themselves on their careful study and exposition of the law to the masses. But when Jesus invited their response to a series of reasonable questions, they refused to answer. They had already made up their mind that what Jesus was about to do was wrong and they did not wish to discuss any other alternative explanation of His actions.

Jesus was grieved at the evidence of their hardened attitude. Unable to help them at the moment, He returned to the need of the man with the withered hand. He told the man to stretch out his hand and the man did (Luke 6:10). Once again Jesus healed a man on the Sabbath and once again a group of Pharisees who were exposed to the miracle were enraged.

That would not be Jesus' last conflict with the religious establishment over observing the Sabbath. Later they would excommunicate a man because he would not condemn Jesus after He had healed him on a Sabbath (John 9:34). On another occasion, the ruler of a synagogue rebuked people who came to Jesus on the Sabbath to be healed (Luke 13:14). On yet another occasion, Jesus healed a man of dropsy while He was being entertained in the home of a ruler of Pharisees (Luke 14:4).

Jesus would not be bound by religious and cultural traditions which hindered His ministry potential. There was much to be done and little time in which to do it. Everywhere He looked He saw hurting people desperately needing someone to help them, but he could only be in one place at one time. The time had come to appoint His disciples and train them to assist Him in ministry. After spending a night in prayer (Luke 6:12-13), He called aside twelve special men and began to teach them as the multitudes listened.

Conclusion

Like the man by the pool, some Christians tend to lose hope as they wait on God for a response to a particular problem in their life. Rather, they should increase in hope as they approach God's time for resolving that problem. Also, Christians today need to be careful not to allow the traditions associated with their Christian heritage to hinder their understanding and appreciation of Jesus' ministry in their own life or the lives of others around them. Because Jesus is God, He is free to work whenever and however He determines and is limited in His creativity only by His own consistency with the laws by which He has chosen to govern His world. People should be very careful about adding to these laws in an attempt to restrict God from working in the manner He intends, because of their own preconceptions.

CHAPTER 11

THE DISCIPLES:
THE TRAINING OF THE TWELVE

Matthew 5:1–7:29

When Jesus saw the masses of people who followed Him, His heart filled with compassion for them. Later He expressed His impression of the crowds to His disciples, noting they were like scattered sheep without a shepherd. He knew they were hurting and that the time to minister to their needs had come, but He Himself could only do so much. Much more could be accomplished in the long term if He took time to train others in ministry, thereby multiplying His own ministry to the masses. After spending a night in prayer, He called aside twelve out of the larger number of disciples who had been following Him (see chapter nine). These twelve men would be the focus of His attention during much of the next two years as He prepared them to continue what He had begun. After He gathered them on the mountain, Jesus taught (Matt. 7:28-29) them what has come to be known as the Sermon on the Mount (Matt. 5:1-2). Some Bible teachers refer to this sermon as Jesus' ordination message to His disciples. Others describe it as His first staff meeting.

Certain dispensationalists maintain the Sermon on the Mount is kingdom truth, i.e. for the coming thousand-year millennium and does not apply to the church age. They maintain Jesus offered the earthly kingdom of heaven to His listeners, but when later they rejected it (Matt. 11:20) He finally offered the present heavenlies, church, and its Great Commission. They point out that this sermon emphasizes certain Jewish themes such as bringing a sacrifice (Matt. 5:23) and opposition to disfiguring one's form when praying (Matt. 6:16). They also point out the continuation of Old Testament commands such as maiming oneself (Matt 5:29-30). However, Jesus is teaching principles for living as a disciple, and principles are: (1) transcultural, (2) timeless, and (3) must be applied to every situation. The Sermon on the Mount was taught by Jesus to His disciples, probably in the presence of a larger group of people. The message of the sermon was directed primarily toward those who had been called into a new relationship with Jesus as disciples. He builds on the Old Testament and gives new meaning to their walk with God. In it Jesus described seven essential principles or lessons which a disciple of Jesus must learn to be most effective in Christian service. These principles are foundational in the life and ministry of the disciple.

SEVEN ESSENTIALS FOR DISCIPLESHIP

Character: What is your emotional adjustment?
Authority: What is your reason for service?
Inner Life: What is your motivation?
Priority: What governs your choices?
Compassion: What is your attitude toward people?
Discipline: How will you control your actions?
Discernment: How will you apply these principles?

I.   The Extraordinary Character of a Disciple

Jesus began by addressing the inner character of a disciple. He identified nine specific character traits in what has become known as the Beatitudes.

A. An Extraordinary Character Defined. Jesus used the Greek word *makarioi* which is translated "blessed" nine times to describe the inner fulfillment and motive of one who possessed the character He wanted in His followers. Jesus clearly expected all His disciples to develop this character, and intended for them to develop these characteristics. In identifying nine specific traits, He was not identifying options but rather essentials. The disciple who possessed all characteristics, in essence had one – he was Christlike. This person cannot help but be highly motivated to serve and have an effective ministry.

The first trait is identified by the phrase "poor in spirit" (Matt. 5:3). The Greek word *ptochoi* refers to extreme poverty so that one's only hope of survival is found in begging. Jesus did not use this expression to teach His disciples to beg for money as was wrongly interpreted by some priests in the dark ages. They were to ask or "beg" from God because all things come from Him. Jesus used the expression "poor in spirit" to emphasize that the disciple must come to the place where he totally depends upon God for everything. Next, Jesus identified brokenness as an essential trait of the disciple. The Greek word *penthountes* translated "mourn" is used in the Septuagint to identify both mourning for the dead and mourning for the sins and sorrows of others. In light of Jesus' emphasis on love as the essential mark of a disciple (cf. John 13:35), He likely intended to emphasize the need to be broken over sin in one's life and its effect on others. Meekness was the third essential identified by Jesus. By this He meant there would be times a disciple would have to be willing to set aside his legitimate rights and privileges in order to accomplish something that would bring greater glory to God. Rather than viewing it as an evidence of weakness, Jesus saw meekness as an evidence of inner strength. Moses, one of Israel's greatest leaders, was said to be the meekest man in all the earth.

The fourth character trait is identified by the expression "hunger and thirst for righteousness" (Matt. 5:6). The disciple must have a strong desire for personal holiness if he is to have a lasting and effective ministry. Of the twelve whom Jesus call as His disciples, the only one who did not have a ministry in the early church was the one who failed to learn this lesson. Judas Iscariot failed because he lacked financial integrity. The disciples also needed to be merciful in their dealings with others (Matt. 5:7). A merciful person looks at the consequences of sin in the life of another with empathy and has a desire to do something to help. Because mercy finds its fullest expression in God, Jesus wanted His disciples to learn how to treat others the way God treated them.

The next trait is purity of heart (Matt. 5:8). In the Jewish mind, the heart was the center of one's personality and moral self-perception. It included the intellect, emotions, and will. When Jesus called for purity of heart, He was referring to personal holiness which affected their innermost being rather than the external standards of holiness adopted by Jewish sects such as the Pharisees. The holiness which was to characterize His disciples was to be of such a nature that they would serve with pure rather than ulterior motives.

The seventh character trait of a disciple is revealed in the descriptive term "peacemaker" (Matt. 5:9). While this expression may refer to a ministry of helping people build relationships with each other, it goes beyond this to the most basic relationship of all. Later, the apostle Paul explained the preaching of the gospel in terms of "the ministry of reconciliation" (2 Cor. 5:18). One of the disciple's greatest sources of happiness and inner fulfillment is in introducing others to Jesus and seeing them trust Him as Lord and Savior.

A disciple must also be characterized by loyalty to the principles of righteousness. Opposition would be inevitable in the service of Jesus and His disciples needed to be able to endure persecution "for righteousness sake" (Matt. 5:10). This meant they needed to (1) know what was right, (2) be prepared to do what was right, and (3) be prepared to keep doing what was right in the face of opposition. The final character trait emphasized was loyalty to Jesus. The Person of Christ is the heart of Christianity. Throughout history, the church has always waned to her effectiveness as she wavered in her loyalty to Jesus. According to the traditions of the early church, only John died of natural causes. The other ten disciples were all martyred for their faith in and faithfulness to Jesus. Although John escaped death, he too spent time in prison for his faithfulness to Jesus.

B. An Extraordinary Character Developed. The most effective ministry many Christians engage in comes naturally out of the overflow of a full relationship with God. Jesus knew His disciples would accomplish their task if they served out of a condition of blessedness. He used three pictures to describe the ministry which would naturally flow from the kind of character He wanted His disciples to develop.

The first of these pictures was salt. Just as salt is useless if its savoring ability is lost, so His disciples would "be thrown out and trampled under foot by men" if they failed to be salt (Matt. 5:13). Salt is used to preserve the quality of something by preventing decay. Jesus saw His disciples being the preserving influence of righteousness in a decaying world of sin.

The second picture Jesus used to describe the ministry of a disciple was light. His disciples were to "let your light so shine before men, that they may see your good works and glorify your Father in heaven" (Matt. 5:16). Many Bible teachers suggest Christians should have a two-fold ministry in the world. They as salt should work for social reform and as light work for saving their friends and relatives. Jesus also likened His disciples to a city. Throughout history, cities have been the center of the very life of any group of people. The Greeks built their entire system of democratic government around the city. Even in more agricultural societies the city is often the place to which farmers turn for their supplies. Jesus said, "A city that is set on a hill cannot be hidden" (Matt. 5:14). Because His disciples are the source of the gospel which is able to meet the most basic needs of humanity, they need to be in a place where they can reach out to others with help and others can reach out to them in their time of need.

II.   The Ultimate Authority of Disciple

A. The Principles of God. Sometimes Christians have conflicting views as to whether one should emphasize the development of inner character or adherence to an external standard. Jesus resolved this issue by emphasizing both. He may have realized some people would interpret His emphasis on inner character as an argument that one no longer needed to recognize the principles of the Old Testament Scriptures. Therefore, He clarified His position noting, "Do no think that I came to destroy the Law or the Prophets, I did not come to destroy but to fulfill" (Matt. 5:17). When Jesus taught, He did not offer an alternative to the Scriptures but rather a fulfillment of what was only partial in the Old Testament. In the obscure details of the Scriptures were a host of typical pictures and prophetic sayings which when properly understood clearly point to their fulfillment in Scripture. It is interesting to note how many times an expression such as "that it might be fulfilled which was written in the prophets" occurs in the written record of Jesus' life and ministry to describe some activity which He accomplished. This is particularly true in the gospel of Matthew, a gospel written to those who understood the Old Testament best.

B. The Proclamations of Christ. While Jesus supported the principles of the law, His own proclamations concerning personal holiness suggest he wanted His disciples to go beyond the mere ritualistic following of the external standard. He wanted them to have attitudes consistent with the law. If it is wrong to take someone's life, it is also wrong to hate that person or allow a broken relationship without making an effort to restore it (Matt. 5:21-26). If adultery is wrong because it breaks a marriage, so is a lustful attitude or divorce (Matt. 5:27-32). Rather than observing rules as to how one would take an oath, it is better to be characterized by integrity in your speech so people will believe you without an oath (Matt. 5:33-37). Rather than seeking a narrow justice, it is better to offer kindness in the face of injustice (Matt. 5:38-42). If it is right to love one's neighbor, it is also right to love one's enemy and in that way demonstrate how one differs from the world around them (Matt. 5:43-48). Jesus used the expression, "But I say to you" or some similar phrase nine times in this part of His sermon (Matt. 5:18, 20, 22, 26, 28, 32, 34, 39, 44). Other Bible teachers have noted the expression, "Thus saith the Lord." Jesus did not have to appeal to the Lord to give His statements divine authority because he is the Lord. Also, in each of these statements, Jesus contrasted the popular interpretation of some principle of the law with its real meaning and spirit. Not only does the disciple look to the principles of Scripture as his standard of faith and practice, he must understand them in the context of these proclamations of Jesus.

III.   The Secret Devotional Life of a Disciple

The life of a disciple begins with his relationship with God, and the relationship is intensely personal. Some of the Jews customarily performed their religious service in such a way as to attract attention to themselves. Jesus taught His disciples to serve God in secret and let God reward them in a public manner. This principle was specifically applied to three common religious practices.

A. *The Secret Life of Charity.* First, in giving alms to supply the needs of the poor, Jesus told His disciples not to attract attention to themselves. When people gave money to meet the needs of the poor, they could do so quietly or they could cause their coins to rattle loudly in a metal container so that they would draw attention to themselves. This practice became known as "sounding the trumpet" (cf. Matt. 6:2), because the container had a slot to receive money that looked like a trumpet. Jesus told His disciples to give secretly and not be concerned about what others may think about their giving. What they did for the poor was to be a matter between them and God alone.

B. *The Secret Life of Prayer.* Prayer was also something to do secretly. Some people do not pray unless they are observed by others (Matt. 6:5). While Jesus on other occasions emphasized the importance of corporate prayer and Himself prayed publicly on occasion, what He emphasized to His disciples was that their secret prayer life needed to be right before God. It is more important that one's private prayers influence God than one's public prayers impress others. In the course of His instructions concerning prayer, Jesus offered His disciples a pattern prayer which has become known over the years as "the Lord's Prayer" (Matt. 6:9-13). This prayer contains all of the essential elements one needs to have a deeper, more meaningful prayer life. Commenting on this prayer, St Augustine suggested, "When we pray rightly and properly, we ask for nothing else than what is contained in the Lord's Prayer." This prayer consists of seven specific requests, embryonically including everything a believer needs to live for God. This suggests prayer reflects one's inner character and will develop one's character as God hears and answers. The requests mentioned in this prayer remain a good model for one's private prayer life even today.

THE LORD'S PRAYER AS AN EXPRESSION OF CHARACTER

The worship of God – *Hallowed be your name*
The reign of God in your life – *Your kingdom come*
Yieldedness to God – *Your will be done*
Request for daily provision – *Give us this day our daily bread*
Cleansing – *Forgive us our debts*
Guidance – *Lead us not into temptation*
Protection – *Deliver us from evil*

C. *The Secret Life of Fasting.* Fasting was another discipline of the Christian life which Jesus emphasized. In light of the Pharisees' and John the Baptist's disciples' criticism over the lack of fasting on the part of Jesus' disciples, Jesus must have been tempted to encourage His disciples to make a public display of their fasting. But rather, He encouraged His disciples to wash their face and anoint themselves "so that you do not appear to men to be fasting, but to your Father who is in the secret place" (Matt. 6:16).

IV.   The Ultimate Priority of a Disciple

The ultimate priority of Jesus' disciples had to be the "the kingdom of God and His righteousness" (Matt. 6:33). This priority should govern every area of a Christian's life including his or her financial stewardship. Jesus understood the relationship between one's financial commitments and what was really important when He noted, "For where your treasure is, there your heart will be also" (Matt. 6:21). Also, when one is ultimately concerned about the kingdom of God and His righteousness, the other concerns of life which create anxiety can be left to God to resolve (Matt. 6:25-33). This matter of priority was greatly important because double-mindedness causes inner confusion and frustration. "No one can serve two masters; for either he will hate the one and love the other, or else he will be loyal to the one and despise the other" (Matt. 6:24). Jesus' disciples had to determine if they would serve God or be enslaved to money.

V.   The Compassionate Attitude of a Disciple

A fifth essential principle emphasized in Jesus' training of the twelve was the need for them to have a compassionate attitude toward others. Jesus had taught much about personal holiness, encouraging His disciples to have high personal ethical standards in their attitudes and behavior. He knew some tended to criticize others who did not share their convictions. Jesus taught his disciples not to be judgmental or critical toward the minor faults of others but rather to use the opportunity of noticing sin in the life of another to take a closer look at their own life. If disciples do this, they will find areas of their own life which need to be developed. In this way, the awareness of sin in the life of another leads disciples to love them rather than criticize them. Hence they will grow spiritually so that they can better minister to their needs (Matt. 7:1-5).

Some people have taken Jesus' instruction at this point as a justification for their own lack of discernment. However, within the context of the sermon this clearly is not what Jesus was teaching. He urged His disciples to be discerning in not giving the holy to dogs nor pearls to swine (Matt. 7:6). Later, He would instruct them to be "wise as serpents" but "harmless as doves." This is the balance Jesus sought in a disciple. Disciples should be very discerning in the Christian life, but their relations with others should reflect a compassionate, dove-life attitude toward them.

VI.   The Disciplined Lifestyle of a Disciple

Disciples' lifestyles are characterized by self-control – influencing their prayer life, their relations with others, and their moral behavior.

A.   Discipline in Prayer. Jesus described prayer as asking, seeking, and finding (Matt. 7:7). Each of these Greek verbs imply continuity. This means disciples must continue in a disciplined lifestyle of prayer even when the answers to prayer are not immediately evident. Just as a father gives good things to his son, disciples understand that their "Father who is in heaven (will) give good things to those who ask Him" (Matt. 7:11).

B. *Discipline in Relationships.* Understanding this truth concerning the nature of God should impact one's relationships with others. In what has come to be known as "the Golden Rule," Jesus emphasized the importance of treating others in a way consistent with how they wanted others to treat them (Matt. 7:12). Actually, this principle was not new with Jesus. It was the essence of what the Old Testament prophets had taught concerning relationships for many years.

C. *Discipline in Behavior.* Jesus taught the way of discipleship was narrow in contrast to the more popular broad "way that leads to destruction" (Matt. 7:13). Something that is acceptable for others may be unacceptable for a disciple. In some cases this is because certain behaviors are morally wrong. In other cases, activities which are not morally wrong in and of themselves will not be characteristic of disciple's behavior because they may tend to hinder his service for Christ.

VII.   The Consistent Discernment of a Disciple

As noted above, Jesus wanted His disciples to be discerning. As He concluded this sermon, He noted three particular areas in which a disciple would have to exercise this ability. The presence of false prophets, false profession, and false principles of life demanded their discernment if they would build successful lives and ministries.

A. *False Prophets.* Jesus warned that false prophets would arise as ravenous wolves among the sheep. These prophets would mask themselves "in sheep's clothing" so as not to be readily identifiable (Matt. 7:15). Some Bible teachers believe this reference to sheep's clothing means the false prophet looks like a member of the flock – one of the sheep. Others claim the sheep's clothing refers to the garment worn by the shepherd. When addressing this subject in his final message to the elders at Ephesus, Paul suggested both applications may be true. He foresaw a time when "savage wolves will come in among you, not sparing the flock" (Acts 20:29), but he also recognized a tendency would exist even among some good pastors to seek to establish their own following and produce similar results (Acts 20:30). There is only one sure way to discern between true and false prophets. "Therefore by their fruits you will know them" (Matt. 7:20).

B. *False Profession.* Jesus also warned His disciples to be discerning of false professions. "Not everyone who says to Me, 'Lord, Lord' shall enter the kingdom of heaven, but he who does the will of My Father in heaven," He explained (Matt. 7:21). Even though some might have abilities to cast out demons, their lawless approach to God revealed they did not have a genuine commitment to serve God in obedience to His revealed will.

C. *False Principles.* Jesus concluded this sermon with a parable of two men building their homes. The first man built his home on a rock, illustrative of those who would build their life and ministry on the principles of Jesus. This man's home survived the testing of the storm. The second man built his home on the sand, illustrative of those who built their life and ministry on false principles of life. This man's home was destroyed by the storm, suggesting the same would happen to the life and ministry of the disciple who failed to consistently apply the principles of this sermon. Those who heard Jesus instructing His disciples "were astonished at His teaching, for He taught them as one having authority, and not as the scribes" (Matt. 7:28-29). When scribes taught the law, they summarized the various opinions expressed in the commentaries. Jesus, however, went directly to the Scriptures and drew out principles the people could apply to life.

Conclusion

Just as the disciples needed to learn and apply these foundational principles of discipleship to become effective in ministry for Jesus, Christians today need to become all they can be for God before they can do all they would like to do for God. Only as one develops the character and commitments of a true disciple does that person have a foundation for continued ministry in the lives of others. Jesus dealt with these issues early in His relationship with the twelve just as believers today need to deal with these issues early in their Christian life.

CHAPTER 12

SIMON THE PHARISEE: A WITNESS OF FAITH AND UNBELIEF

Matthew 8:5-13; 11:2-30; Luke 7:1-50

s Jesus came down from the mountain with His band of disciples, there was still much to do before they could be sent out on their own to be involved in effective ministry. Jesus knew His disciples needed time to internalize the principles of discipleship He had taught them. Also, they needed to see Jesus Himself in ministry. Some disciples had been following Jesus for some time, but even they would begin to see Him in a new light as they looked to Him as their model for ministry. In the days to come, they would watch Him closely as He ministered to men of great influence and those otherwise overlooked by society.

I. The Healing of the Centurion's Servant (Matt. 8:5-13; Luke 7:1-10)

When Jesus returned to Capernaum, He was immediately approached by a popular centurion in town through the elders of the synagogue. Although most Jews in Galilee hated all Romans and anything to do with Rome, this centurion had done much to win the favor of the Jewish leaders in that town. In contrast to other Romans stationed in the region, this leader had a deep love for the people and land of Galilee. Among other demonstrations of his love for the Jews, he had built a synagogue. In the ruins of Capernaum, archaeologists have found the remains of a synagogue which gives evidence of Roman influence in its original construction and design, possibly the very one built by this centurion.

This man's servant was "lying at home paralyzed, dreadfully tormented" (Matt. 8:6) and apparently so sick he was "ready to die" (Luke 7:2). As Jesus heard the pleas of the Jewish elders who had come to Him as the centurion's ambassadors of goodwill, He agreed to go to the man's home to heal the servant. But when the centurion heard Jesus was coming, he felt unworthy of the honor of having Jesus in his home and sent a message. "I am unworthy that You should enter under my roof," he explained. "Therefore I did not even think myself worthy to come to You. But say the word, and my servant will be healed" (Luke 7:6-7).

The title "centurion" is a military term which was applied to a Roman officer who was responsible for one hundred soldiers. There were usually about sixty centurions in a Roman legion. His duties included leading his men in drill; inspecting their food, clothing, and arms; and commanding them in battle. One who held this office was well-experienced in both giving and receiving orders. This centurion applied his military frame of reference to the work of Jesus and determined the command would be accomplished if Jesus merely issued it.

Although this man probably had a pagan background, he evidenced a greater faith than many Jews. Perhaps his love for the people and land had led him to read their Scriptures. He may have reasoned, "If God could speak the world into existence, certainly Jesus, who apparently has power with God, could speak a healing for my servant." Also, as a Roman officer, he may have known the official who met Jesus on behalf of his son in Cana or have heard of the miracle which had resulted (see chapter seven).

Jesus honored this man's faith and healed the servant. Also, He used the occasion to warn the Jews of a trend that was beginning to develop and has since continued throughout history. Although Jesus came primarily to His own people, the Jews, He was rejected by them and found a warmer reception among the Gentiles. He explained many would be in the kingdom from other nations and some of the Jews themselves would be absent (Matt. 8:11-12).

II.   The Raising of the Widow's Son (Luke 7:11-17)

Shortly after that miracle, Jesus went to the city of Nain. This city was located southwest of the opposite end of the Sea of Galilee by three hills, Gilboa, Tabor, and Little Hermon. The name of the city literally means "beautiful" and under normal circumstances its name may well have described not only the physical setting but also the quality of life of its residence. But as Jesus entered the city, He met a woman on one of the saddest days of her life. She was leading a large crowd of mourners out of the city to bury her only son. Some time before, she had gone through the same motions to bury her husband. As Jesus saw the open coffin and crowd of mourners, Jesus was moved with compassion for the widow. Out of that compassion came a desire to do something to help. He spoke first to the widow, then to the corpse. When Jesus said, "Young man, I say to you, arise" (Luke 7:14), the body of the dead man was revitalized and he sat up and began to speak. Obviously this miracle made quite an impression. "Then fear came upon all, and they glorified God, saying, 'A great prophet has risen up among us'; and, 'God has visited His people.'" (Luke 7:16). Word of this miracle spread not only throughout the region of Galilee, but into Judea as well.

Some people have attempted to discount this miracle calling it a case of "premature burial," that the man being buried was not really dead. The Jews did not embalm the bodies of their dead and burials took place quickly after a person was pronounced dead, often the same day. While cases of premature burial are recorded throughout history, this was clearly not the case here. The Bible describes him as "a dead man" (Luke 7:12) and Jesus treated him as a dead man (Luke 7:14). Later, Jesus recalled this miracle, claiming "the dead are raised" (Luke 7:22). There can be little doubt that this man was really dead, or that he was really alive after Jesus raised him.

III.   The Wavering of the Prophet's Faith (Matt. 11:2-30; Luke 7:18-35)

Among those who heard of these and other miracles of Jesus was John the Baptist. No longer was this prophet engaged in an active preaching ministry to the masses. His direct preaching concerning Herod's incest had resulted in his arrest and imprisonment in the fortress of Machaerus. As a result, the man who had been used to open spaces and fresh air now was confined to a musty cell.

Machaerus was the southernmost fortress of Perea located about 3,800 feet above the Dead Sea. The fact that news of Jesus' ministry reached him that far south is an indication of the growing popularity of Jesus. John had his last communication with Jesus from that prison cell..

John's own personal experience was inconsistent with his anticipation of what was involved in the Messiah's coming. He had been convinced he was the forerunner of the Messiah, yet he found himself in prison. Also, he had been convinced Jesus was the Messiah, yet Jesus did not seem to be intervening to rid Israel of Rome, something most Jews believed the Messiah would do. As he found himself wondering about these important issues of life, he decided to put the question directly to Jesus. "Are You the Coming One, or do we look for another" (Luke 7:19).

When two of John's disciples reported this question to Jesus, He did not condemn John for wavering in his faith. He no doubt realized the circumstances John found himself in had left him depressed and that was probably the source of the question. Neither did Jesus answer the question directly. Had he done so, it is doubtful that would have resolved the issue for John. Jesus knew John needed encouragement more than he needed answers, and He responded in such a way as to provide the Baptizer with both.

The very hour John's disciples arrived, Jesus was involved in ministry to the masses. He continued meeting the needs of people and "cured many people of their infirmities, afflictions, and evil spirits; and to many who were blind He gave sight" (Luke 7:21). Then Jesus turned to John's disciples with a verbal answer to the question He had been asked. "Go and tell John the things you have seen and heard: that the blind see, the lame walk, the lepers are cleansed, the deaf hear, the dead are raised, the poor have the gospel preached to them. And blessed is he who is not offended because of Me" (Luke 7:22-23). One of the purposes of Jesus' miracles was to produce faith in those who saw and heard about them (John 20:31). Jesus knew when these two disciples reported enthusiastically what they had seen to John the Baptist, he would be encouraged out of the depression which had led to his questioning. Also, John would have recognized the character of Jesus' ministry was consistent with the Old Testament prophecies on which John had based much of his own ministry (Isa. 61:1). When John's disciples left to take their message to him, Jesus spoke to the masses, reminding them of the greatness of John's ministry. Many of those following Jesus had heard John in the wilderness and been baptized by him. They were attracted to him because of a special quality that marked him out as one of God's unique prophets. As John was now passing off the scene, Jesus knew there would be a tendency to redefine what John had been and done. People would use other reasons to explain why the crowds flocked to John, but they would only serve to obscure the charisma which had surrounded the prophet's ministry.

One of the explanations offered may have been to simply write John off as a raving mad man whose poor judgment had eventually cost him his life. Some Bible teachers believe Jesus' reference to "a reed shaken by the wind" (Luke 7:24) may have been an idiomatic reference to this false explanation. The opposite tendency of future generations would involve making John a respectable part of their heritage, but Jesus reminded the people that John did not dress the part of a member of the royal court (Luke 7:25). The only possible explanation for John was to recognize him as the greatest of the prophets (Luke 7:26-28).

While most of the people were prepared to recognize the uniqueness of both John and Jesus, the ministries of both of these men was largely rejected by some professionals including both the Pharisees and lawyers. They were distinct among other classes of people in that they had not been baptized by John. Because they rejected the ministry of the Messiah's forerunner, they now rejected the Messiah's ministry. Jesus could do little more than point out to them the inconsistency of their own behavior. They had rejected John as a demon because of his apparent antisocial behavior. Now they condemned Jesus for His involvement with people, accusing Him of being "a glutton and a winebibber, a friend of tax collectors and sinners" (Luke 7:34).

While the masses reponded positively to Jesus' minitsry, the sort of repentance that should have resulted in the cities where much of His ministry had been focused did not occur. The cities of Chorazin, Bethsaida, and Capernaum witnessed many significant miracles, yet this produced little discernible behavioral change in the people's lives. Jesus warned those cities in particular of the judgment that would come their way for rejecting His ministry, a judgment more severe than that of Sodom, Tyre, and Sidon, three cities which were judged by God in the Old Testament.

Even in judgment, there was hope for individuals living in those cities and elsewhere who would repent. Jesus invited people to come to Him for rest, "take My yoke upon you and learn from Me" (Matt. 11:29). The expression "take the yoke" was a rabbinical expression inviting individuals to become disciples in the school of the rabbi. Some Bible teachers mark this event as the turning point in Jesus' ministry. From this point, the Cross would become increasingly the focus of His ministry rather than His earlier emphasis on the kingdom.

IV.   The Anointing of the Messiah's Feet (Luke 7:36-50)

One witness of all that was happening was a Pharisee named Simon. He was present when Jesus performed miracles to encourage John's faith. Simon had heard Jesus' comments about the greatest of the prophets. No doubt Simon had also heard about the raising of the widow's son and may or may not have been familiar with the healing of the centurion's servant. Unlike many of the Pharisees who were already committed to destroy Jesus, Simon wanted to hear more. He extended an invitation to Jesus to come to his house for a meal, and the invitation was accepted.

Although Jesus came to Simon's home as a guest, a number of customary elements of hospitality were not extended to Jesus. Under normal circumstances, the guest would be greeted by the host with a kiss and a servant would wash the visitor's feet and anoint his head with oil. Perhaps because Simon was aware of the growing antagonism of many Pharisees toward Jesus, he was careful not to appear too receptive toward Him. Whether this was the case, Simon neglected his duties in this regard.

As was customary at such an occasion, the dining room in Simon's home became a public auditorium whenever an individual was being honored. Although one needed an invitation to eat at the table, anyone was welcome to come into the home and listen to what may be said. Among those who came to Simon's home that day was a woman who was known in the city by her poor reputation. She came to the home because she knew Jesus would be there, and she wanted to express her own feelings to Him in a symbolic way.

When she found Jesus, she saw that He, like herself, was really an unwelcome guest. Simon had invited Jesus to his home because he was impressed with His ministry as a prophet, but he was unwilling to welcome Him into his home as the Messiah. She came to the place Jesus was reclining and eating, bowed at His feet, and began washing them with her own tears and wiping them dry with her hair. Then she took the perfumed oil she had brought with her in an alabaster flask and began to anoint Jesus' feet. Because of the custom of that day to recline at a dinner table, this was done behind Jesus and may not have been noticed by many in the crowd until Jesus' feet were anointed with perfumed oil. But the woman's activity had not escaped the notice of Simon.

SIMON THE PHARISEE AND THE SINFUL WOMAN

No customary kiss for Jesus – Kissed His feet continually
No water to wash Jesus' feet – Washed them with her tears
No towel to dry Jesus' feet – Dried them with her hair
No anointing of Jesus' head – Anointed His feet with oil

Simon knew this woman's reputation and as a Pharisee had a high personal standard of righteousness and opposition toward sin in his own life and that of others. In his mind it was inconsistent that a righteous person would let a woman of that reputation even touch him. He reasoned, "This man, if He were a prophet, would know who and what manner of woman this is who is touching Him, for she is a sinner" (Luke 7:39). Although Simon's reasoning remained unspoken, Jesus perceived what was going on in his mind and decided to use that opportunity to teach everyone present an important spiritual lesson. Jesus told Simon a story about a man who was owed money by two others. "One owed five hundred denarii, and the other fifty" (Luke 7:41). Fifty denarii was equivalent to about two months wages. Five hundred denarii was equivalent to about twenty months wages. The man to whom the money was owed decided to forgive both debts. "Tell Me," Jesus asked, "which of them will love him more?" (Luke 7:42).

The answer was obvious to Simon as it would have been to the others present. "I suppose the one whom he forgave more," he responded (Luke 7:43). Jesus agreed with Simon's answer and immediately began making a rather direct application. This woman who was looked down upon as a sinner had fulfilled in the most humble way all of the social duties Simon had left unfulfilled in his responsibilities as a host. She had washed, kissed, and anointed His feet. Further, her response had not been motivated by social custom, but out of a heart full of love. She gave evidence of loving Jesus more than others loved Jesus, and as a result, her many sins were forgiven. When Jesus announced to the woman that her sins were forgiven, other invited guests at the table began to murmur, "Who is this who even forgives sins?" (Luke 7:49).

This was the second time Jesus publicly forgave an individual's sins in the presence of religious leaders (see chapter eight). They would have clearly understood the implications of this act. Because only God could forgive sins, to forgive the sins of another was to claim to be God. Although Simon had witnessed much of Jesus' ministry and had seen others express their faith in Him, it is unlikely he was prepared at this time to believe. Like so many in the cities which refused to repent, Simon apparently remained in his unbelief.

Conclusion

Just as Simon was a witness of faith and unbelief as expressed in the lives of those around him, there are many today who are quietly observing expressions of faith and unbelief in the lives of Christians around them as they consider their own response to Jesus. Many people who turn to Christ as Savior today do not do so primarily because they are attracted to His moral teachings. Rather, many turn to Jesus because they believe He can help them overcome the problems confronting them in life. In many cases, they have come to this conclusion because of the testimony they have witnessed in the lives of friends and relatives. Christians need to pause from time to time and ask themselves the question, "What are others seeing in my life that would lead them to faith or unbelief in their response to Christ?"

CHAPTER 13

JESUS OF NAZARETH:

A LONG DAY OF MINISTRY

Matthew 8:23-34; 9:18-34; 12:22–13:58; Mark 3:19–5:43; Luke 8:1-56

Shortly after the dinner in the home of Simon the Pharisee, probably during the summer of A.D. 28, Jesus toured Galilee again. He was accompanied on this ministry trip by a following which included both the twelve disciples and a group of women who had begun following Him and may have helped underwrite the cost of His ministry. During this tour, three things began to happen. First, Jesus began to encounter a growing hostility toward His ministry in Galilee. Second, He began to reveal more fully who He was. Third, the focus of Jesus' ministry increasingly turned to training the twelve.

One of this tour's unique features was the presence of women. Luke identifies three of these women by name and suggests there were others in the group (Luke 8:2-3). Mary Magdalene is described as one out of whom Jesus cast seven demons. Magdalene was located three miles north of Tiberius which was probably her home. Joanna is described as the wife of Herod's steward Chuza which suggests she was probably very wealthy. The Greek word *epitropos* used to describe Chuza refers to the financial manager of a ruler's personal estate. Apparently a number of people close to Herod were acquainted and to some degree involved in Jesus' ministry. The third woman named is Susanna about whom nothing more is said.

Luke describes this diverse group of women as having two things in common. First, they each had been recipients of Jesus' ministry in that they had been "healed of evil spirits and infirmities" (Luke 8:2). Second, they were women who wanted to help Jesus take his ministry to others and "provided for Him from their substance" (Luke 8:3). Their example illustrates a fundamental principle of stewardship. Those who have received from the Lord should give to Him out of a sense of gratitude for what He has done for them.

The first account of activity on this second tour of Galilee is a record of what has been called "The Long Day," because of all the activity described that happened in this one day. Some feel this day is minutely detailed to tell the reader how busy most of Jesus' days were. This day of ministry is recorded in greatest detail by Mark. It begins with Jesus in a home again in conflict with the scribes and Pharisees and concludes with Jesus raising the dead and healing blind men. Also, this must have been a significant day to Peter who was the eyewitness source that supplied details to Mark who wrote the second gospel. This was the first recorded day that Jesus called aside the three disciples who came to be known as "the inner circle." Also, it was a memorable day in that Jesus demonstrated His power in a variety of ways.

THE DAY OF THY POWER
Power in Doctrine
Power over Demons
Power over Danger
Power over Disease
Power over Death

I. Jesus Confronts Growing Opposition (Matt. 12:22-50; Mark 3:19-35; Luke 8:19-21)

This busy day was probably typical of how busy Jesus was in His three and a half years of ministry. As Jesus became increasingly more popular, there were more demands on His time, but He also attracted the attention of those opposed to his ministry. On this particular day, a group of Jesus' friends (Mark 3:21) and later His own family (Mark 3:31) came apparently hoping to take Him home and out of the public spotlight for a while. His friends had begun to think of Him as being "out of His mind" (Mark 3:21).

While the reason His family sought Him is not specifically mentioned, several possibilities have been suggested over the years. Some believe His family shared the view of His friends that He was mentally incompetent. Others suggest His family may have been concerned for His health, i.e. that the pressures of His ministry had resulted in His not eating right (cf. Mark 3:20). Another view suggests His family was concerned over His conflicts with the rabbis and wanted to protect Him from further confrontations (cf. Mark 3:22). Since His brothers did not accept Him as the Messiah until the resurrection (John 7:5), they may simply have wanted to stop what they viewed as an erring brother who might be spreading heresy.

The opposition from friends and family was accompanied by the growing opposition of the scribes and Pharisees. The scribes were the copiers of the Scriptures and other religious books. As a result of their work, they came to have a better understanding of the Scriptures than many religious leaders and became teachers of the law. Most scribes belonged to the sect of the Pharisees which were more conservative in their interpretation of Jewish law than the Sadducees. When they are mentioned in the gospels, they are almost always mentioned in connection with the Pharisees.

The fierce opposition of the scribes and Pharisees on this day was prompted by the apparent readiness of the people to recognize Jesus as the Messiah. As the people crowded around Jesus, "one was brought to Him who was demon-possessed, blind and mute" (Matt. 12:22). Jesus responded to this man's need by not only liberating him from the bondage of demon-possession, but also restoring his ability to see and speak. The demon was cast out and the man was healed. The crowd witnessing this miracle was amazed and began to ask, "Could this be the Son of David?" (Matt. 12:23).

This is apparently the first time the title "Son of David" was used by the people to identify Jesus. Although it is only used here tentatively – as a question – by the end of this day it was being affirmed (cf. Matt. 9:27). This title "Son of David" tends to emphasize one of Israel's highest ideals of the Messiah, that He was in the physical lineage and now in the spiritual lineage and therefore qualified to be King of Israel. When Nathaniel came to faith in Jesus as the Messiah, he confessed, "Rabbi, You are the Son of God! You are the King of Israel!" (John 1:49). While the Messiah is identified by many titles in the Old Testament, the Jews considered the Son of David to be among the greatest of these titles.

One of the chief objectives of Matthew's gospel appears to have been to identify Jesus as the "Son of David." His gospel was written primarily to the Jews and reflects a strong Jewish appeal. Some Bible teachers believe it may have been written shortly after Pentecost at a time when the church was largely Jewish and ministering almost exclusively in Jerusalem and Judea. He did not write a chronological biography of Jesus but rather a topical account selecting key events and teachings of Jesus which tend to reveal Him as either "the Son of David" or "the Son of Abraham" (cf. Matt. 1:1). While the title "Son of David" emphasized the Messiah's ministry to the Jews, the title "Son of Abraham" pointed back to the broader promise of God which extended beyond the nation, "In you all the families of the earth shall be blessed" (Gen. 12:3; cf. also Gen. 18:18; 22:18; 26:4; 28:14). The following chart suggests one way the first gospel may be outlined to show the relationship between these two titles of Christ.

MATTHEW'S PORTRAYAL OF JESUS	
Son of David	*Son of Abraham*
1:2-17	1:18-25
2:1-23	3:1-17
4:1-11	4:12-25
5:1 – 7:29	8:1–9:26
9:27 – 10:42	11:1-30
12:1-42	12:43-50
13:1-58	14:1-36
15:1 – 16:20	16:21-28
17:1-13	17:14-23
17:24 – 25:46	26:1–28:20

The apparent willingness of the people to ascribe this highest of the titles of the Messiah to Jesus irritated the scribes and Pharisees who by now were primarily opposed to Jesus and His ministry. They realized the crowds gathered around Jesus because they were attracted by His miracles. They concluded the best way to discourage the multitude from following Jesus would be to question the credibility of His miracles. The Pharisees believed in the reality of demons and the ability of God to release people from the bondage of demon-possession, but they were unwilling to believe God would so endorse the ministry of Jesus.

They suggested rather that Jesus was able to work signs including the casting out of demons by the power of Beelzebub (Matt. 12:24; Mark 3:22).

During the reign of Ahaziah, Baal-Zebub was the god of Ekron, a god in which Ahaziah himself placed some measure of faith (2 Kings 1:1-18). The name Beelzebub is a corruption of this title Baal-Zebub. The name Baal literally means "lord" or "master." The title "Zebub" probably referred to the "high house" or "high place" of Baal in its original Canaanite context, but was used by the Jews to identify dung and filth and the flies which gathered about them. The Hebrew has been translated, "The lord of the flies," which became a general title of the devil.

The Pharisees charged that Jesus was casting out demons by the power of the prince of demons was absurd. Jesus responded to this charge by asking, "How can Satan cast out Satan?" (Mark 3:23). He further explained, "And if Satan has risen up against himself, and is divided, he cannot stand but has an end" (Mark 3:26). Even in the ridiculous explanation offered by the scribes and Pharisees, they did not deny Jesus' ability to cast out demons. Jesus had effectively bound the devil and could cast out demons.

Not only was this explanation ridiculous from a logical point of view, it was spiritually dangerous. In this context Jesus spoke of "the unpardonable sin" (Matt. 12:31). Since that time, various ideas have been suggested as to what the unpardonable sin is, but Jesus suggested within this context that this sin was ascribing the miraculous power of Jesus to the ability of the devil. First, some believe the unpardonable sin could only be committed during the earthly ministry of Jesus. It was unpardonable because some refused to accept the overwhelming evidence of Jesus' miracles and ascribe them to Satan. This could only happen during the time of Jesus' life and public ministry. A second view believes it happens today because of unbelief. Since the unpardonable sin is against the Holy Spirit, some Bible teachers teach that those who do not believe refuse the drawing influence of the Holy Spirit.

In describing the effect of this sin, Jesus noted, "It will not be forgiven him, either in this age or in the age to come" (Matt. 12:32). St. Augustine and others since him have argued this means some sins can be forgiven in the next life if one dies in their sins. This idea is the basis for the Roman Catholic dogma of purgatory and the liberal idea of universal salvation. Actually, Jesus was saying the exact opposite, the unpardonable sin would not be forgiven "in the age to come." The clear teaching of the Scripture on the subject of forgiveness of sin is that only sin which is forgiven in this age will be forgiven in the age to come. Sin can only be forgiven when the blood of Christ is applied by faith (1 John 1:7).

The response of some of the scribes and Pharisees to Jesus' pointed comments was to request a sign. Obviously this was not a sincere request as they had just witnessed and rejected the casting out of a demon and healing of a man. Jesus offered what He called "the sign of the prophet Jonah." "For as Jonah was three days and three nights in the belly of the great fish, so will the Son of Man be three days and three nights in the heart of the earth" (Matt. 12:39-40). His resurrection from the dead was the ultimate sign revealing His true identity (cf. Rom. 1:4).

This passage of Scripture has been a center of three controversies. The first relates to the integrity of the Old Testament. Conservative Bible teachers often point to Jesus' comments about Jonah to support the view that the book of Jonah is historical and not merely a legend or myth. Those who tend to deny the miracles in Scripture are divided in their attempts to explain away the comments and activities of Jesus. Some claim Jesus was limited in knowledge and simply did not know better, but the biblical account of Jesus' life reveals He had greater insight than some are apparently willing to admit (cf. John 2:24-25). Others argue He was simply accommodating the view of others and did not want to challenge what was generally believed, but as a teacher of truth, Jesus often confronted and challenged widely held popular opinion.

The second controversy surrounding this passage relates to a matter of chronology in the life of Jesus. Each of the four Gospels was written with a different objective in mind. While each one documents certain details in the life of Jesus, it was left to students of His life to work out the details of chronology based upon what is recorded. Some conservative Bible teachers argue that the reference to the Son of Man being "three days and three nights in the heart of the earth" (Matt. 12:40) means Jesus must have been crucified on a Wednesday rather than a Friday as traditionally believed. According to this view, Jesus spent Thursday, Friday and Saturday in the tomb and rose on Sunday. The problem with this interpretation is twofold. First, if Jesus was crucified on a Wednesday, then He would have spent four nights in the grave (Wednesday, Thursday, Friday, and Saturday) rather than three as mentioned in the text. Second, the Jews counted any part of a day as a day so that a man buried Friday afternoon and raised Sunday morning would be thought of as having been in the grave three days (Friday, Saturday, and Sunday). There is no reason to doubt the traditional view that Jesus was crucified on "Good Friday." This view best fits with the biblical record of Jesus' final week..

The third issue raised in this passage relates to Jonah's experience in the belly of the whale. According to some Bible teachers, this passage teaches Jonah was dead when he was swallowed by the great fish, just as Jesus was dead when He was in the grave. Two statements in Jonah appear to support this view. First, Jonah claimed, "Out of the belly of Sheol I cried, and You heard my voice" (Jonah 2:2). Sheol refers to hell, the grave, or the deep. Second, Jonah also claimed, "Yet You have brought up my life from the pit" (Jonah 2:6). Those who believe Jonah died when swallowed by the great fish interpret this to mean he was brought back to life from the grave. Other Bible teachers disagree with this conclusion and argue Jesus only referred to Jonah because their experience would be similar, not the same. They point out that Jesus' statements can be understood in the context of Jonah's experience assuming he remained alive in the fish. In his own account of his experience, Jonah's description of his experience neither insists nor denies he was raised from the dead. Good conservative Bible teachers adopt different points of view on this minor issue of biblical interpretation. Both groups agree on the major issue that Jesus was raised from the dead.

Jesus concluded His remarks to the scribes and Pharisees on this day by warning them of the return of unclean spirits. Jesus claimed demons which were cast out of people wandered "through dry places, seeking rest" (Matt. 12:43). Unable to find the rest they long for, they will return to the person from which they were cast out. If they find that person "empty, swept, and put in order" (Matt. 13:44), he will not only return himself but will bring "with him seven other spirits more wicked than himself" (Matt. 12:45). While this has specific application to those out of whom demons are cast, Jesus' comments on repossession by demons may have been intended in this context to be applied directly to the nation of Israel. The Jews had struggled with idolatry until they returned from the Babylonian captivity. But they gave up idolatry only to be later bound by traditions and a legalistic attitude which resulted in their hard-heartedness and blindness toward the Messiah. Their latter state of legalism may have been worse than their former state because the spiritual blindness of idolatry grows out of rebellion rather than self-righteousness. God can bring a rebellious person to Himself easier than one blinded by his self-righteousness.

II. Jesus Communicates Principles in Parables (Matt. 13:1-53; Mark 4:1-34; Luke 8:4-18)

Although the religious leaders of Israel were becoming increasingly hostile toward Jesus, the people were still receptive to His teaching. On this long day, Jesus taught the people though using parables. Seven of the parables taught by Jesus on this day were recorded by Matthew where they are described as "the mysteries of the kingdom of heaven" (Matt. 13:11). Some Bible teachers interpret the prophetic significance of these parables to explain the trends characteristic of this age (see chapter forty-eight). Jesus often taught through parables which are described as an earthly story with a heavenly meaning. When teaching in this manner, Jesus illustrated great truths using common situations with which most people could identify. In many cultures even today, story-telling is an important and effective means of communicating truth. In stressing certain truths through parables on this day, Jesus apparently taught them in pairs. Eight of the recorded parables on the long day appear to be related.

PAIRS OF PARABLES

The Sower– The Seed
The Tares – The Dragnet
The Mustard Seed – The Leaven
The Hidden Treasure – The Pearl of Great Price

A. The Parable of the Sower. In the Parable of the Sower (Matt. 13:3-23; Mark 4:3-25; Luke 8:5-18), Jesus told of a man who scattered seed in his field and reported the different results from different soils. Four soil types are specifically identified in the parable. The first was the wayside which was the hard-packed soil of well-worn paths through the field. The second soil type was the very shallow earth over the rocks. The third soil type was where thorns grew which prevented good plants from producing fruit. The final soil type is simply described as "good ground" in that it provided all that was needed by the seed to encourage its growth and maturity.

Later Jesus explained the meaning of this parable in terms of the four different attitudes of people toward receiving the gospel. The seed is God's Word and people have different types of receptivity to it. The first represents those who hear the gospel without understanding and therefore do not respond. Just as the birds ate the seed on the paths, so "the wicked one comes and snatches away what is sown (the Scriptures) in his heart" (Matt. 13:19). The second soil type represents those who respond to the gospel initially with joy but stumble in the face of opposition because "he has no root in himself" (Matt. 13:21). The third soil type represents those who also have a positive response to the gospel initially, but "the cares of this world and the deceitfulness of riches choke the word, and he becomes unfruitful" (Matt. 13:22). The final soil type represents those who respond to the gospel and grow to produce fruit (Matt. 13:23). While three of the four soil types in this parable represent positive initial responses to the gospel, only one results in the maturing of the plant to produce fruit.

B. The Parable of the Seed. The parallel parable to the Parable of the Sower is the Parable of the Seed (Mark 4:26-29). In this parable, Jesus noted the growth of a seed into a mature plant without the understanding of the man who initially scattered the seed. The emphasis of this parable teaches the seed has life and can produce great results. Jesus wanted His disciples to have confidence in the message they would be preaching, knowing it would produce results when the harvest comes.

C. The Parable of the Tares. In the third parable, the Parable of the Tares (Matt. 13:24-30, 36-43), Jesus told of a man who sowed good seed in a field. Then while he slept, his enemy sowed "tares" in the same field. This was not discovered until both crops began to grow together. Rather than destroy the crop of tares immediately, the farmer thought it best to separate the crops during the harvest. At that time the tares would be destroyed and the wheat stored in the barn.

Jesus explained the source of tares was "the sons of the wicked one" which are sown by the devil (Matt. 13:38-39). Rather than deal with this problem as soon as it is discovered, Jesus has chosen to wait until the harvest at the end of the age. God will not judge every sin as soon as it is committed, but will exercise judgment in the future. At that time, those who are lawless and offensive to God will be judged, but the righteous will shine in the kingdom of their Father.

D. The Parable of the Dragnet. The Parable of the Dragnet (Matt. 13:47-52) also communicated this same truth. The dragnet caught all that swam in its path, but not all it caught was desirable. On the beach, the fishermen would sort their catch keeping the good fish for themselves or to sell in the market and casting away the bad, i.e. inedible fish, driftwood, etc. Jesus warned there would be a similar sorting or judgment of people at the end of the age (Matt. 13:49).

E. The Parable of the Mustard Seed. In the Parable of the Mustard Seed (Matt. 13:31-32; Mark 4:30-32), Jesus reminded His listeners of a phenomenon most could personally relate to. When a man planted his vegetable garden, the smallest seed he would plant would be the mustard seed. Other seeds were smaller than the mustard seed but they were not commonly used, so the mustard seed came to be known as "the least of all the seeds" (Matt. 13:32). Yet in that vegetable garden, the mustard would likely be the largest plant. In the Middle East, mustard normally grows two to four feet high and will sometimes reach a height of twelve feet. It begins to look more like a tree than a herb and is large enough to contain the birds nests. This parable illustrates the outward growth of the kingdom during this age.

   F. The Parable of the Leaven. The parallel Parable of the Leaven (Matt. 13:33-35) is also a story of growth. A woman would use only a small quantity of yeast to yield a large quantity of bread. The yeast caused the dough to rise. In this case, the woman began with three measures of meal which could be two to five pecks. As the yeast permeated this dough, it would produce an immense quantity of bread. As the Parable of the Mustard Seed illustrates the external growth of the kingdom in this age, the Parable of the Leaven illustrates the internal growth of the kingdom during the same period.

   G. The Parable of the Hidden Treasure. Jesus also told a parable of a man finding a treasure buried in a field (Matt. 13:44). In ancient times, people often divided their riches and invested in business, purchased jewels, or buried it in a safe place. Sometimes a treasure would be so well hidden, a man might forget where he had put it. Later, someone might discover this treasure and claim it for himself if it was found in his field. Even today, archaeologists have stumbled across hidden "pots of wealth" while digging in the ruins of ancient cities. When the man in this parable discovered the treasure, he arranged to buy the field so he could claim the treasure for himself.

   H. The Parable of the Pearl of Great Price. The parallel Parable of the Pearl of Great Price (Matt. 13:45-46) told the story of a pearl merchant who discovered one pearl of greater value than all others. Because he wanted the pearl, he liquidated his assets to raise the funds necessary to make the purchase. These two parables reveal two ways people come to recognize the value of the kingdom. Some discover it by accident like the man finding treasure in the field. Others discover it as they seek it out like the pearl merchant finding the valuable pearl.

III.   Jesus Controls Natural Circumstances (Matt. 8:23-34; Mark 4:35-5:20; Luke 8:22-39)

   Since it was a long day, Jesus decided to cross the Sea of Galilee probably to get some rest from the busy day of ministry. He and his disciples got into a boat and began across the lake. But as they pulled out from shore, they could see many people getting in boats and crossing with them (Mark 4:36). Obviously the crowd intended to follow, so Jesus apparently decided to get His rest during the journey. He placed His head on the leather covered seat normally used by the helmsman of the boat and fell asleep. Jesus must have often slept during His years of ministry, this is the only reference in the gospels to Christ sleeping. While He slept, a storm broke out on the Sea of Galilee. This lake is located 696 feet below sea level and surrounded by high mountains. The cool dry winds falling from these slopes naturally resulted in sudden and violent thunderstorms. The storm which broke out while Jesus slept was so violent the disciples who knew the lake well were not sure they would survive it.

When the disciples discovered Jesus asleep in the boat, they woke Him up and accused Him of apathy. They probably were not expecting Jesus to perform a miracle but may have thought He could help bail water. But Jesus was not interested in bailing water. He "rebuked the wind and said to the sea, 'Peace, be still!' And the wind ceased and there was a great calm" (Mark 4:39). The disciples and those in the other boats who witnessed this miracle, were again amazed at this demonstration of God's power.

After miraculously calming the storm, Jesus asked His disciples why they had been so fearful. One of the chief lessons Jesus taught His disciples during their time together was the need to trust God in all things. Despite the fact they had seen many miracles and could believe God to some degree, they failed the testing of their faith in an emergency situation. Jesus said, "O you of little faith" (Matt. 8:26). This is a phrase used only by Jesus that, (1) evaluated the trust of people in God and measured faith in a relative condition, "little," and (2) was a rebuke from an omniscient God who knew their hearts.

When they came to shore, they landed at a small village named Khersa. Seven miles inland was the larger city called Gadara. Because of the close proximity of these two cities, this area was referred to as the region of the Gadarenes or the Gerasenes depending on one's perspective. Some Bible teachers believe the disciples had not intended to go to Khersa, but arrived there because the storm had blown them off course. Just outside this village Jesus encountered the worst case of demon possession recorded in the gospels. This case is considered the worst case because of the number of demons involved. When asked to identify himself, the demon called himself "Legion; for we are many" (Mark 5:9). Legion was a military term to describe a whole regiment of the Roman army. Two demon-possessed men were identified by Matthew (Matt. 8:28-34) in this incident because the gospel of Matthew was written to the Jews who needed two witnesses to verify a testimony (cf. Deut. 17:6). Mark only describes one demonic man, probably the most severe, "no one could bind him, not even with chains" (Mark 5:3).

When Jesus cast out the demons from the men, the evil spirits requested and were granted permission to enter a herd of swine. When they entered into the two thousand pigs, the pigs stampeded down a steep hill into the sea. The question is sometimes asked, "Why did Jesus destroy the pigs?" This question has been answered in various ways. Some teachers argue it was wrong for Jews to be raising pigs in the first place, but this was a Gentile area, and it is not clear that the owners of the pigs were Jews. Another view suggests Jesus had just proven Himself to be El Elyon, the Possessor of Heaven and Earth in the calming of the sea, so the pigs really belonged to Him and He should be free to do as He pleased with them. A third view stresses the value of a man's soul was far greater than the price of pigs. A fourth argument explains that the demons, not Jesus, destroyed the pigs.

When the owners of the pigs heard the report of what had happened, they came to check things out for themselves. They found the man who had been demon possessed "sitting and clothed and in his right mind" (Mark 5:15). The men were fearful first of the power of Jesus to change lives, and second, because of their financial loss. "Then they began to plead with Him to depart from their region" (Mark 5:17).

Jesus had come to Gadara for rest, but He was sent away and had to recross the Sea of Galilee. As Jesus reentered the boat to leave, the men who had been delivered of the demons asked to join his band of disciples. Jesus refused to let them come but rather urged them, "Go home to your friends, and tell them what great things the Lord has done for you, and how He has had compassion on you" (Mark 5:19). This was not Jesus' normal advice to those He healed, but He realized the area needed a witness He would not be able to provide. Also, as these men were probably Gentiles and therefore were not under Jewish law, they did not have to present themselves to the priest to verify their healing.

IV.   Jesus Comforts People in Need (Matt. 9:18-34; Mark 5:21-43; Luke 8:40-56)

Again Jesus and His disciples crossed the sea and came to Capernaum. When He arrived back in Capernaum, the city that served as His home base of ministry, He was spotted by Jairus, one of the local synagogue rulers. The name Jairus means "the Lord has enlightened." The meaning of his name appears to have also been the experience of this man. At a time when the religious leaders of the Jews was growing increasingly more hostile toward Jesus, Jairus recognized in Jesus hope for a hopeless situation.

When Jairus left his home that evening, his daughter was extremely sick. Without his knowledge, she apparently died just after he began searching for Jesus. When Jairus found Jesus, he began to plead with Him to come and heal his daughter. He stressed the urgency of the situation. Jesus and His disciples began following Jairus through the city streets to his home.

But Jairus was not the only one who realized Jesus was back in town. Soon the crowds began to gather around Him. In the midst of the pushing and shoving crowd, there was another woman who faced an apparently hopeless situation and believed Jesus may be able to help her. For a dozen years, she had been bleeding. She had sought medical attention, but her problem only grew worse. According to Jewish law, she would have been ceremonially unclean and experienced social isolation and permanent defilement. She apparently understood something of the law because she thought she could be healed if she touched the hem of Jesus' garment. Many teach that her faith was in the superstition of touching, rather than in the person of Jesus. The outer fringe of Jesus' robe would be that part which indicated his loyalty to the law. Somehow she was able to push through the crowd and get close enough to reach out and touch the hem and she was immediately healed of her condition. Then Jesus stopped and asked, "Who touched My clothes?" (Mark 5:30). His disciples thought it was a ridiculous question to ask because the crowd had been pushing and shoving Jesus, He had been "touched" by many people. But Jesus had sensed "that power had gone out of Him" (Mark 5:30) and wanted to identify the one who had touched Him. The woman was scared. Perhaps she realized she had been ceremonially unclean under Jewish law and feared the consequences of touching a rabbi's robe, especially that part which represented His loyalty to the law. She confessed what she had done only to be encouraged by Jesus and commended for her faith.

Why did Jesus force an obviously shy woman to make public confession of her healing? Her prolonged illness and the mistreatment she must have experienced over the past decade or so must have left her with a very low view of herself and reluctance to be noted publicly. Jesus may have done this for three reasons. First, He wanted to encourage her, "only believe" (Mark 5:36), just as a pastor may encourage a new Christian to make a public profession of faith by walking an aisle during an invitation or being baptized. Second, Jesus wanted to make sure she understood that it was her faith and not the touch that had healed her, "Daughter, your faith has made you well" (Mark 5:34). Third, He may have wanted to encourage Jairus' faith. Jairus knew the urgency of the situation at home and was probably becoming increasingly concerned as the crowd hindered their progress in getting to his home. Just after this incident, Jarius himself would receive news of his daughter's death. He would be encouraged in his hopeless situation as he saw Jesus help another in her hopeless situation.

When Jesus arrived at the home of Jairus, He took the girl's parents and three of His disciples into the room where her body was lying. "Then He took the child by the hand, and said to her, 'Talitha, cumi,' which is translated, 'Little girl, I say to you, arise,'" (Mark 5:41). The expression *Talitha cumi* is Aramaic and probably reflects the actual words Jesus spoke as He raised this 12-year-old girl to life. Once again those who were aware of this miracle were amazed. Jesus instructed the girl's parents to feed her as He and His disciples made their way out of the home.

It had been a long day of ministry, but it was not quite over yet. As He reached the street, He was approached by two blind men asking for help. What the people had asked that morning they were now affirming. "Son of David, have mercy on us!" they asked (Matt. 9:27). Jesus healed the men and told them not to tell anyone. But the men were so thrilled at what Jesus had done, they could not help but "spread the news about Him in all that country" (Matt. 9:31).

Conclusion

This long day in the ministry of Jesus was probably not unique but rather typical of many busy days throughout His ministry. A similar long day is recorded on the Tuesday prior to His crucifixion. The New Testament also portrays the Lord today involved in constant long days of ministry. "Therefore He is also able to save to the uttermost those who come to God through Him, since He always lives to make intercession for them" (Heb. 7:25). Jesus' personal commitment to and involvement in ministry ought to encourage believers today and also motivate Christians in their own involvement in ministry.

▰▰▰▰▰▰▰▰▰▰▰▰▰▰▰▰

CHAPTER 14

THE TWELVE:

AN OPPORTUNITY TO MINISTER

Matthew 9:35–11:1; 13:54–14:12; Mark 6:1-32; Luke 9:1-10

Throughout the autumn of A.D. 28, Jesus continued traveling from city to city throughout Galilee teaching in various synagogues and healing those who came to Him. As He ministered to the multitudes, He was once again impressed with the great need that existed. When Jesus looked at the hurting multitudes, He began thinking of them as a harassed flock of sheep desperately in need of a shepherd. He had thought of them that way before, but this time something could be done about it.

The growing popularity of Jesus suggested the time had come for Jesus to multiply His ministry through His disciples. It was time to send them out to put in practice what they had learned in principle. They still had much to learn, but they could learn with on-the-job-training. They had watched Jesus minister victoriously to the multitudes. Perhaps, they longed for the day they could take a larger role in such dramatic aspects of His ministry such as healing and casting out demons.

But before Jesus could send out the twelve, He knew they needed to be reminded of another potential ministry scenario. It was one thing to serve faithfully when surrounded by vast multitudes of enthusiastic followers, but it was another thing to face rejection. Jesus knew His disciples needed to learn the lesson of hardness and that just telling them probably would not be enough. Rather, Jesus allowed them to see His faithfulness in the midst of rejection.

With His disciples, Jesus returned for the last time to the town He had called home for so many years. He had been to Nazareth earlier in His ministry, and they had tried to kill Him. As was His custom on the Sabbath, He attended the synagogue with His disciples. The ruler of the synagogue could not ignore the fact that one of Israel's most popular teachers was present in the service, so in spite of the commotion that had taken place on a former visit, Jesus was allowed to teach. Jesus taught in the same manner as He did in other places (Matt. 13:54; Mark 6:2). He may have even preached a message His disciples had often heard preached to other crowds. And as He spoke, the crowd was amazed at His evident wisdom and wondered if the gossip they had heard of Him could be true.

"Is this not the carpenter's son?" wondered some of the old timers present

(Matt. 13:55). Although most Bible teachers believe Joseph, Mary's husband, died prior to the beginning of Jesus' public ministry, some among the oldest generation in Nazareth would always remember Jesus as "Joseph's boy." Others recalled that Jesus Himself had been a carpenter among them (Mark 6:3). As it was customary among the Jews for every father to teach his son a trade, Joseph likely had taught his sons his own trade. The Greek word *tekton* translated "carpenter" is the word from which the English word "architect" is derived and could also be translated "builder." As a result, some Bible teachers believe Jesus worked in the construction industry, perhaps building houses prior to His public ministry. The second century Samaritan Christian writer and martyr Justin Martyr taught Jesus that made ploughs and ox-yokes.

One reason the crowd at Nazareth was reluctant to respond to Jesus' teaching as others had was due to the presence of Jesus' family. His brothers James, Joses (or Joseph), Simon, and Judas (Judah) still lived in Nazareth. Jesus' sisters who remain unnamed in Scripture also lived in that town. A tradition of the church suggests their names were Assia and Lydia, but it is unlikely that this last Gentile name would have been chosen by a Jewish family in Israel. Every indication in Scripture suggests the family of Jesus did not accept Him as the Messiah until after His resurrection (John 7:4).

This time the people did not try to kill Jesus, they largely ignored Him. Although a few were healed during His stay in Nazareth, once again, "He did not do many mighty works there because of their unbelief" (Matt. 13:58).

I. The Final Preparation of the Disciples' Ministry (Matt. 9:35–10:42; Mark 6:1-11; Luke 9:1-5)

As Jesus left Nazareth, He continued preaching in the various towns and villages in the area. As the multitudes appeared in the different places, His shepherd's heart was moved. He perceived them as weary or harassed sheep, "scattered, like sheep having no shepherd" (Matt. 9:36). Soon, He would do something to alleviate that situation; He would send out His disciples to minister to them. But first, Jesus would prepare His disciples with one final briefing before commissioning them for a short-term assignment.

This briefing began with a call to prayer. "The harvest truly is plentiful, but the laborers are few. Therefore pray the Lord of the harvest to send out laborers into His harvest" (Matt. 9:37-38). Jesus' statement may have brought back memories of two days in Samaria when Jesus first spoke of a plentiful harvest. Soon, each of them would have their own days of fruitful ministry to remember.

Jesus gathered His disciples to Himself and transferred to them the power to perform miraculous signs including the ability to cast out demons and heal all kinds of sickness and disease (Matt. 10:1). Two different Greek words are used here to describe the condition of those who would be healed under their ministry. The Greek word *malakal* denotes the idea of softness and was used to identify a disease or debility. The Greek word *nosos* is related to the Latin verb *nocere* meaning "to injure" and was also widely used to identify wounds associated with accidents. Perhaps the two words are used together here to suggest the disciples' ability to heal people of disease regardless of whether their sickness had an internal or external cause. As Jesus sent His disciples out, He directed them to restrict their ministry to Jewish villages, avoiding both areas with high concentrations of Gentiles and the cities of Samaria (Matt. 10:5). This was not because Jesus was opposed to preaching the gospel to non-Jews but because He knew the disciples needed to concentrate their efforts on receptive groups to be effective in this short ministry assignment. The essence of their message was to be the same which had been proclaimed by John the Baptist and Jesus, "The kingdom of heaven is at hand" (Matt. 10:7). Their ministry would be authenticated by signs and wonders which may have included such signs as healing the sick, cleansing lepers, raising the dead, and casting out demons (Matt. 10:8). Their ministry would be very much like that they had witnessed Jesus performing.

Their ministry would not be financially underwritten prior to their departure and there was no promise their basic needs would be met. When they came to a city, they would face either a warm reception or a cool rejection. If they were received, they would stay and accept the hospitality offered them. If they were not welcomed, they would leave that city or home and "shake off the dust from your feet" (Matt. 10:14). This practice of shaking the dust from one's feet was practiced by Jews as they left a Gentile area to return to Israel. They viewed the dust of the Gentiles as defiling and would shake it off their sandals so that they might be pure again. If the disciples came to a Jewish village which rejected their ministry, they were to treat that village as though it were a Gentile city and continue in ministry in another place. They traveled from place to place aware that God would later deal with those who mistreated them in any way.

Jesus warned the twelve they were about to enter a hostile territory but suggested two ways in which a hostile reaction may be avoided. First, they were to exercise the wisdom of serpents which neither draws attention to themselves nor unnecessarily confronts danger until they have accomplished their objective. Second, they were to be "harmless as doves" which means they should be careful not to give their enemies any reason for hostility. However, even when the disciples followed this advice, there would be times when they would face opposition. When called upon to account for themselves, the disciples were not to worry about what to say but let God put the right words in their mouths as they needed them. When they were persecuted, they should move on to another city. Jesus reminded them there were many places to reach and that they would not finish the task before they were once again rejoined as a ministry team (Matt. 10:23). "A disciple is not above his teacher, nor a servant above his master," Jesus reminded His disciples. If Jesus faced opposition and was accused of being in league with the devil, how could they expect to encounter anything less? But they had nothing to fear, "for there is nothing covered that will not be revealed, and hidden that will not be known" (Matt. 10:26). In light of that, they should be faithful in their confession of Jesus on the earth, knowing Jesus would more than make up for any inconvenience experienced when He confessed who they were in heaven.

Jesus taught much about the kingdom of God and the offer of inner peace, but the same principles when rejected would cause turmoil and be the source of conflict in the most basic relationships of life. He reminded His disciples of the need to love Him supremely above all else. The disciples' love for Christ should even surpass the strongest of natural bonds such as that which exists between parents and children. Motivated by that love, the disciples would willingly "take their cross" in the life of discipleship. They knew "he who loses his life for My sake will find it" (Matt. 10:39).

Jesus promised them God would see all that would occur during their ministry tour. The way people treated them would be assumed to be the way they would have treated Jesus had He come Himself. A tradition taught that individuals could earn rewards for hospitality extended to a prophet of God or a righteous man. Jesus extended that principle further and applied it to the ministry which they were about to begin. "And whoever gives one of these little ones only a cup of cold water in the name of a disciple, assuredly, I say to you, he shall by no means lose his reward" (Matt. 10:42).

II.   The Impact of Their Ministry on People (Matt. 11:1; 14:1-12; Mark 6:12-29; Luke 9:6-9)

After this briefing, Jesus sent His disciples to minister. Before this they were disciples (followers or learners), but after this they would be apostles (sent ones, Matt. 10:2). As they traveled, most likely they traveled in pairs, perhaps the pairs identified by Matthew in his listing of the twelve disciples (Matt. 10:2-4). "So they went out and preached that people should repent. And they cast out many demons, and anointed with oil many who were sick, and ➤aled them" (Mark 6:12-13). As they traveled everywhere preaching the gospel, word spread and the reputation of Jesus continued to grow. Although word of Jesus had reached the court of Herod earlier, the success of Jesus and His disciples in ministry was such that Herod himself was soon receiving reports of what was happening in Galilee over which he was the ruler.

Herod knew the tendency of the Galileans to follow messiahs and probably had officers in charge of spotting potential problems and monitoring them so that they did not get out of hand. A number of individuals who were a part of the royal court had already been sufficiently impressed by Jesus so much so that they turned to Him for help or assisted in underwriting the cost of His ministry. As the officers watched the ministry of Jesus from a distance, they recognized He posed no real threat to the security of Roman interests. If the followers of Jesus applied the principles He taught, they would more likely be an easier people to govern rather than a revolutionary mob. But a couple of things had happened that may have alerted the officers in charge to reconsider their earlier conclusion.

The first of these was the statement Jesus made to His disciples, "Do not think that I came to bring peace on earth. I did not come to bring peace but a sword" (Matt. 10:34). While these words meant one thing to the disciples to whom they were spoken, they meant trouble and a potential uprising among the people. This statement was followed by Jesus sending His disciples out on a mission to Jewish villages exclusively. Again, this was the sort of action that had been taken by earlier messianic leaders as they sought to gather a following to attack Rome. The fact that a suspected Jewish terrorist, Simon the Canaanite (Matt. 10:4), was known to be among the followers of Jesus only served to confirm the likelihood of a problem.

Herod received a full report on the situation. As he listened to his officers, he could not help but notice the similarities between the activities of Jesus and those of John the Baptist. Both appeared to be prophetic voices calling the Jews back to the faith of their fathers. Both included statements about the kingdom of God in their sermons. Both were perceived by some to be the Messiah for which the Jews longed, and both had gathered a large following among the populace while being rejected by the religious leaders who may have been easier to handle politically. Herod concluded, "This is John the Baptist; he is risen from the dead, and therefore these powers are at work in him" (Matt. 14:2).

The Romans were a deeply superstitious people and worshipped a wide variety of gods whom they believed had supreme power over areas of their life. If one of the gods determined something was to be so, nothing could be done to change it. The rise of Emperor worship and recognition of Caesar as a god may have been an effort to protect their ruler from the power of the gods by making him one of their equals. When they conquered a people who worshipped other gods, they were never certain what power those gods may actually have, so they allowed the people to continue worshipping their gods but insisted that they also recognize the deity of Caesar. The continued refusal of the Jews to do so made the power of their God even more threatening. As Herod attempted to understand the popularity of Jesus, his Roman way of thinking coupled with the guilt he felt over ordering the execution of John led him to conclude the Jewish God had raised John from the dead and given him supernatural powers. Herod may have feared the gods were out to get him. This may explain why Herod made no attempt to arrest Jesus despite the fact he longed to talk with Jesus and witness firsthand one of His miracles (cf. Luke 23:8).

Herod had arrested John the Baptist because the prophet had publicly rebuked him for marrying his brother's wife Herodias. He had hoped that imprisoning John may have silenced his ministry. Later, on his birthday, Herod had been tricked into ordering John's execution. "The king was sorry; nevertheless, because of the oaths and because of those who sat with him at the table, he commanded it" (Matt. 14:9). At the time, Herod had been willing to give his daughter Salome anything. As he heard the report of Jesus' growing popularity, he may have thought he had given her everything.

III.   The Impact of Their Ministry on the Preachers (Mark 6:30-32; Luke 9:10)

The people and politicians were not the only ones who were impacted by the disciples' ministry. Their own lives were also profoundly affected. When they returned to be with Jesus, they could not help but enthusiastically report all they had done. They shared with Jesus the insights they had learned and taught the people during this tour. As they one by one reported all that had happened,

Jesus listened. As He listened to His disciples' reports, Jesus may have perceived a problem or potential problem arising. "He took them and went aside privately into a deserted place belonging to the city called Bethsaida" (Luke 9:10). He knew the disciples needed to get away from the crowds so that they could spend time together, but the crowds themselves would prevent that from happening immediately.

Conclusion

When Jesus looks at the multitudes living in the tribes, towns, and cities of our world today, He still sees them as a harassed flock of sheep in need of shepherding. Jesus is still moved by the same compassion He felt for the Galileans and is sending His disciples today into ripe fields to gather the harvest. Like those first disciples who became apostles of Jesus, Christians today need to prepare themselves for the unique ministry God has in store for them.

CHAPTER 15

THE PEOPLE:
LOOKING FOR THE WRONG KIND
OF MESSIAH

Matthew 14:13-36; Mark 6:30-56; Luke 9:10-17; John 6:1-71

*J*esus' popularity had now grown to the point that the crowds were so constant He and His disciples found it difficult to find time even to eat together. Jesus used this situation to suggest taking time to get away from the crowds. He appealed to His disciples, "Come aside by yourselves to a deserted place and rest a while" (Mark 6:31). No doubt the idea of resting after completing a busy ministry tour would have been appealing. They agreed and got into a boat together to make their way across the Sea of Galilee to the city of Bethsaida Julias (Luke 9:10). The name "Bethsaida" means "house of catching" or "house of fish." Because of the meaning of the name, it is not surprising that more than one fishing village should bear the same name. The Bethsaida which was home to some of the disciples was on the west side of the Sea of Galilee near Capernaum in the territory ruled by Herod Antipas. Another Bethsaida was on the northeast shore of the Sea of Galilee located in the territory ruled by Herod Philip. Philip had enlarged and beautified this village and renamed it in honor of the daughter of Augustus, Julia. The actual community of Bethsaida Julias was located several miles from the shore, and a large grassy area existed between the shore and the city. This appears to be the region to which Jesus and His disciples journeyed. This was the first of four occasions when Jesus withdrew from the crowds to be alone with His disciples (*first* – Matt. 14:22; Mark 6:31; Luke 9:10; John 6:1; *second* – Matt. 15:21; Mark 7:24; *third* – Matt. 15:29; Mark 7:31; fourth – Matt. 16:5; Mark 8:13).

A number of reasons may have contributed to Jesus deciding to leave Galilee at this time. He may have learned that a report of His activities had been made to Herod Antipas and thought it wisest to live in a different district for a while. A second factor in the decision may have been an attempt to discourage fanatical elements in His own following from the kind of messianic revolution they appeared ready to conduct. Third, the growing hostility of the scribes and Pharisees in Galilee may have begun interfering with His ministry in that region. A more practical consideration may have been the climate of the region. Jesus was leaving the hot shores of Galilee to spend the summer months in the cool mountains to the north. Fifth, Jesus needed time alone with His disciples to continue preparing them for the ministry they would have after He returned to heaven. As Jesus and His disciples began the journey across the lake, many of the people who had been following Him guessed where they were going. They traveled around the lake to meet Jesus on the other side. Although He had wanted to get away from the crowds for a while, out of His compassion for the people, Jesus welcomed them and continued to minister to them. Because it was near Passover, the crowd may have grown as the Jews on their way to Jerusalem stopped and joined them for the day before continuing their journey south. As the day was coming to an end, the disciples looked forward to the crowd departing and their being able to get some needed rest. But Jesus was not yet prepared to send away the crowd. First, He would feed them.

I.   The Feeding of the Five Thousand (Matt. 14:15-21; Mark 6:35-44; Luke 9:12-17; John 6:5-13)

Apart from the Resurrection of Christ, the feeding of the five thousand is the only miracle which is recorded in all four gospels and the only miracle in the gospel of John which is recorded in any other gospel. This suggests it may have been one of the most memorable events in the public ministry of Jesus. Within a twenty-four hour period, the people were at first prepared to acclaim Him as their Messiah and, the next day to reject Him as the same. Between those two extreme reactions, Jesus spent time in prayer and walked on the Sea of Galilee in a storm to meet His disciples in a boat.

The feeding of the five thousand began with the disciples wanting Jesus to send the multitude away (Matt. 14:15; Mark 6:36; Luke 9:12). The region in which they were located was a deserted area and they knew the people would have to travel some distance to find food to eat. Jesus was also aware of this when He turned to Philip and asked, "Where shall we buy bread, that these may eat?" (John 6:5). Although He knew that He was about to perform a miracle, Jesus asked the question to test Philip (John 6:6). Philip estimated the cost of feeding the crowd at about 200 denarii. The denarius was a Roman coin which represented the normal day's wages for a common laborer of that day. The total amount referred to by Philip was probably worth $30 to $35. In terms of contemporary economics (1990), Philip estimated it would cost about $1.28 per head just to give them a little. Obviously, that option would not be sufficient to meet the need even if it were possible. We do not know if Jesus and the disciples had that much money available or if that much food was even available in nearby villages. Some Bible teachers believe both of these factors would have made Philip's proposal practically unachievable. Instead, Jesus chose to use the resources most readily available to Him.

Andrew reported, "There is a lad here who has five barley loaves and two small fish, but what are they among so many?" (John 6:9). Although Andrew was aware of the greatness of the need, he may have thought the obviously inadequate lunch of the boy may be part of the solution. His statement reveals he obviously did not see this as the complete solution. The Greek word *paidarion* used to identify the boy is a double diminutive emphasizing the boy's insignificance. The Greek word *opsaria* translated "small fish" is also a diminutive. Further, the designation of the bread as "barley loaves" suggests something that would not normally be offered to a guest. Barley was a grain normally fed to animals and sometimes given to an army under military discipline. Bread made from barley was "poor folk's food."

In feeding the five thousand, Jesus illustrated six principles which may be viewed as governing principles in doing the work of God. The first is the principle of order and organization. Jesus had all the men sit in an organized way on the grass, in groups of fifty and a hundred (Luke 9:14; Mark 6:40). Arranging the men in this way was a practical step that facilitated the feeding of the people. Christians would do well to begin a work for God by taking time first to organize and plan a strategy to accomplish the objective. The second principle of ministry illustrated by Jesus in this miracle is that of honoring God in everything. Although Jesus did not have much with which to feed the multitude, He paused to thank God before distributing the food. Third, this miracle illustrates the principle of the division of labor. He required the disciples to do what they could do, distribute the bread and fish, and then did what only Deity could do, multiply the resources. Also, the principle of availability and usability is illustrated in the performing of this miracle. Rather than looking for other resources, Jesus fed the multitudes with what was available. When God does something, He uses the most available resource at His disposal. Fifth, this miracle illustrates the principle of God's abundant supply. Five thousand hungry men were fed that day with those few loaves of bread and fish. Finally, Jesus was concerned with the conservation of results. After the multitude was fed, Jesus had His disciples gather the leftovers. Normally, the Jews carried a bottle-shaped basket with them when traveling. Each of the twelve men were able to fill their basket with leftovers.

PRINCIPLES GOVERNING THE WORK OF GOD

The principle of order and organization.
The principle of honoring God in everything.
The principle of the division of labor.
The principle of availability and usability.
The principle of God's abundant supply.
The principle of the conservation of results.

II. Jesus Walking on the Water in a Storm (Matt. 14:22-33; Mark 6:45-52; John 6:14-21)

The impact of this miracle triggered an undesirable response from the people. They were apparently prepared to reenact a Macabean-style revolution against Rome with Jesus as their King (John 6:15). The Galileans tended to be more willing to revolt against Rome than other Jews and this tendency was even stronger during Passover. From the way in which John describes what took place, it appears some in the crowd were already gathering support for the idea. Quickly Jesus got His disciples in the boat and sent them to Bethsaida in Galilee while He remained behind to deal with the crowd. When the disciples had gone out from shore, He slipped away into the mountains. This act successfully prevented the crowd from making Him their king and gave Jesus time to be alone and pray (John 6:15). Jesus fed the multitude late in the day, so likely the sun was setting by the time the disciples began to row their boat back to Galilee. The lake may have been calm and the disciples were no doubt tired, so they took their time crossing the lake. About three and a half miles into their journey, they were once again caught in the midst of a violent storm. It could not have come at a worse time. Not only were the men weary from the recent tour and the day of ministry with Jesus, the storm hit during the fourth watch, the darkest part of the night. Frantically they rowed struggling to keep the boat afloat as wave after wave crashed over the bow. Then, off in the distance, one of the men thought he saw something. Through the spray of the waves, the image became clearer and others saw it too. As it became obvious that many in the group could see the image, they became even more scared. They thought they were seeing a ghost, perhaps the Grim Reaper himself. But then they heard a voice. "Be of good cheer! It is I; do not be afraid," Jesus called out (Matt. 14:27). Men sometimes do strange things when they are very scared or very relieved; and Peter was either extremely scared that it was not really Jesus or extremely relieved that it was not the Grim Reaper. Whatever the reason, he called out, "Lord, if it is You, command me to come to You on the water" (Matt. 14:28). Jesus called Peter to come and "he walked on the water to go to Jesus" (Matt. 14:29).

The first few steps seemed to go well, but as he got within reach of Jesus, Peter realized what he was doing was not possible. He saw the waves splashing all around him and could feel the wind blowing spray into his face. Suddenly, fear returned and Peter felt the water on his knees. He was sinking. "Lord, save me!" he yelled as he began to go under (Matt. 14:30). Jesus immediately reached out and grabbed Peter and gently rebuked him for doubting. "O you of little faith, why did you doubt?" He asked (Matt. 14:31). When Jesus and Peter got into the boat, the wind stopped blowing. Bethsaida was in sight. As they rowed the boat to shore and beached it, the disciples sat amazed at what they had just witnessed. For some of them, it finally began to dawn. This really was the Son of God (Matt. 14:33).

III. Jesus Teaching on the Manna from Heaven (Matt. 14:34-46; Mark 6:53-56; John 6:22-71)

The next morning, the people realized Jesus was gone from them although the only boat missing was the one the disciples had used to cross the lake. They began to search for Jesus and eventually found Him across the lake in the synagogue at Capernaum (John 6:59). Although the Bible does not identify the day of the week, some Bible teachers believe this was another Sabbath in the ministry of Jesus. One reason for believing this is that the lesson to be read in the synagogue at the morning service on the Passover Sabbath was the lesson on manna. In light of the previous day's miraculous provision of bread, Jesus apparently chose that text as the basis of His remarks that day. He suggested those who had been seeking Him had the wrong reason. They wanted to follow Him because they had received physical benefits, "because you ate of the loaves and were filled" (John 6:26). Rather, they should seek Him because He had the seal of God upon Him (John 6:27). According to rabbinical teaching, the seal of God was "truth." This belief was based on a legend which claimed a scroll fell from heaven containing a three-lettered Hebrew word. These three Hebrew letters are first *aleph*, next *mem,* and the final *tau*. These letters of the Hebrew alphabet spell the word "truth." When Jesus claimed to have the seal of God upon Him, He was claiming His message was true for the beginning, middle, and end of life.

During the course of His lesson, the crowd twice referred to manna and asked Jesus to give it to them (John 6:31, 34). Many people believed Jeremiah had hidden the ark of the covenant and the Messiah would reveal Himself to the nation by producing the jar of hidden manna from the ark (cf. Rev. 2:17). Also, the rabbis taught the Messiah would cause manna to fall from heaven even as Moses had. Manna was also thought to be characteristic of the kingdom of God and giving manna at this time would confirm the time was right for the revolt they had tried to begin the day before. However, Jesus offered the people manna by introducing Himself as "the Bread of Life" from heaven (John 6:41, 48). Manna is one of several types of Christ in the Old Testament. In this discourse, Jesus identified several similarities and differences between the manna of Moses and the bread offered in Himself. While Jesus as the Bread of Life is similar to the manna in the wilderness, He is also superior in many respects. The following chart summarizes the Bible's teaching concerning the manna as a type of Christ.

MANNA AS A TYPE OF CHRIST

Both from Heaven
Both Individually Received
Both Accessible to All
Both Sweet and Pure
Both Gifts of God

Manna given through the mediation of Moses .Christ given directly.
Manna given temporarily. ....Christ given continuously.
Manna for Israel only. ....Christ for the whole world.
Manna sustained physical life   Christ sustains spiritual life
  until they died.. .... forever.

As Jesus taught the people that day, He not only explained how He was the true manna, or true bread, He talked to them about believing in Him. He noted they could receive Him because the Father drew men to Christ. As He taught about the work of God and response of men in the process of salvation, Jesus chose not to emphasize one aspect of this mystery over the other but suggested an order in salvation in which both the sovereignty of God and the will of man are involved. From the moment a person is confronted with the gospel until the day he begins eternity with God, Jesus outlined nine steps demonstrating clearly that salvation is of the Lord and man is personally responsible for his response to the gospel.

THE LOGICAL ORDER OF SALVATION IN JOHN 6:35-65

1. The Father draws sinners to Jesus by revealing Him as an attractive alternative to sin (6:44).
2. The sinner sees the gracious offer of the Father (6:40).
3. The sinner determines to trust the atoning work of Jesus for his salvation (6:40).
4. The Father gives the sinner to Jesus for the purpose of saving him (6:37).
5. The sinner evidences his heart desire for God by coming to Jesus (6:35, 65).
6. The sinner embraces Jesus by faith as Savior (6:35).
7. The disciple is embraced by Jesus never to be cast out or lost (6:37, 39).
8. The disciple enjoys a growing intimacy with Jesus during his life (6:54, 56).
9. All disciples will be raised by Jesus at the last day (6:39-40, 44, 54).

Most of those who had come to Capernaum that day to find Jesus were not interested in personal salvation from sin. They were looking for a political salvation for the Jewish nation from Rome. Although they had a messianic hope, it was a hope in a different kind of messiah than Jesus. When it became clear to them that following Jesus demanded a total spiritual commitment of their lives, they began to reevaluate their relationship to Him. Jesus did not alter His message to keep those who were wavering but rather emphasized that He knew some who were following Him really did not believe in Him. This thinned the ranks of the multitude substantially. "From that time many of His disciples went back and walked with Him no more" (John 6:66). They were only looking for an earthly kingdom. Not all who did not believe however departed on this occasion. At least one remained behind, Judas Iscariot. Jesus told His twelve disciples that even though He had chosen each of them, one of them was "a devil" (John 6:70). The Greek word *diablos* means "slanderous" and is a common title of Satan when accompanied by a definite article in the New Testament. Some Bible teachers believe this and other verses prove Judas was not really a man but rather the incarnation of a demon spirit. The word here however does not occur with a definite article in the Greek text and may have been used simply to mean "a slanderer." It is interesting to note that although Jesus warned the disciples of a traitor in their midst a year before the betrayal, they did not suspect Judas, even as he later left the Upper Room to betray Jesus (cf. John 13:29).

Conclusion

Sometimes even today people come to Jesus for the wrong reasons. Even some who consider themselves Christians identify with Jesus because of some blessing they perceive to be attached to Him, but fail to realize the full blessing of a personal relationship with Him. They may belong to a prestigious church for such benefits as making important business contacts, feeling like a part of their community or being allowed to marry in the church facility, but if they lack personal faith in Christ as Savior, they are missing out on the blessing of the abundant Christian life and the eternal benefits of heaven. Those who consider themselves Christians today should take time to be sure they are not like Judas Iscariot who identified with the disciples but never personally took the step of faith needed to trust Jesus as personal Savior.

CHAPTER 16

THE TWELVE:

BEHOLDING HIS GLORY

Matthew 15:1-17:13; Mark 7:1-9:13; Luke 9:18-36; John 7:1

Even though Jesus had successfully prevented the crowd from involving Him in a messianic revolution against Rome, it was still not safe for Him to be in certain parts of Israel. Had He marched to Jerusalem with those He fed, Rome would have wanted to arrest Him. As it was, Jerusalem was still unsafe because the religious leaders of the Jews were plotting against Him to kill Him (John 7:1). As a result, Jesus spent the better part of the year A.D. 29 outside Judea and away from Jerusalem. He ministered in other places. Apparently antagonism was so strong against Jesus among the scribes and Pharisees in Jerusalem that when He avoided Judea, a delegation was sent to confront Jesus in Galilee. The New Testament does not indicate how large this delegation was or how many of the estimated 6,000 Pharisees in Israel at that time were represented by the group.

On one particular occasion the Pharisees confronted Jesus over His failure and that of His disciples to wash their hands ceremonially before eating. They were using a small issue to make a larger point that Jesus broke the law. The ceremonial washing of one's hands before eating was part of the tradition or oral law of the Pharisees. They believed Moses had given Israel the written law in the Pentateuch, but had also given an oral law which was the basis of the traditions of the Jews. This law was thought to have been given to Joshua, who in turn gave it to the prophets, who passed it on to the "Men of the Great Synagogue" who were the traditional ancestors of the Pharisaic Party. This oral law was eventually recorded in the Mishna and the Talmud and thereby preserved in writing. By the time Jesus was engaged in a teaching ministry, these traditions of the Jews were actually held in a higher regard than the Law contained in Scripture. When the Pharisees confronted Jesus, calling on Him to explain why His disciples did not observe the ceremonial washing of hands when they ate (Matt. 15:2; Mark 7:5), Jesus turned the tables on them. In His opinion, it was the Pharisees and not His disciples who had a problem in this area. First, Jesus reminded the Pharisees of Isaiah's prophecy of a people honoring God with their lips but not having a heart for God (Isa. 29:13). Then He challenged the degree to which they honored their traditions even over the clearly revealed law of God. He used the example of Corban, a practice some

Jews followed which involved giving a gift to the temple in order to be exempt from supporting their parents (Mark 7:9-13). Finally, Jesus explained, "There is nothing that enters a man from outside which can defile him; but the things which come out of him, those are the things that defile a man" (Mark 7:15). The Pharisees were concerned with the externals of their religion when they should not have neglected their internal spiritual life and relationship with God.

The scribes and Pharisees were generally respected members of society. The Pharisees in particular had a degree of popularity and influence over the common people. Jesus' disciples became concerned. "Do You know that the Pharisees were offended when they heard this saying?" they asked Jesus (Matt. 15:12). Perhaps they hoped Jesus might retract His statement that had angered the Pharisees or at least modify His comments so as not to incite their hatred. The disciples may have been willing to begin observing the traditions of the Jews to avoid future controversy. But Jesus was not about to waver in the essence of His teaching. "Every plant which My heavenly Father has not planted will be uprooted," He declared (Matt. 15:13). It did not matter how popular the teacher was, if his message was not accurate, he was not helping people. Jesus reminded His disciples that their inner sin nature, not externals like washing one's hands, was the cause of defilement (Matt. 15:18-20).

Following the dispute with the scribes and Pharisees, Jesus again withdrew to the region of Galilee to concentrate His energies on training the twelve disciples. During this time, they had opportunity to view His glory from three different perspectives. First, they saw His glory as He continued to minister to people in need. Second, they came to a deeper understanding of who He really was and understood His glory when He introduced them to the idea of the forthcoming church. Third, three of the disciples were given the opportunity to see Jesus' transformation into the glory of heaven on the mount of transfiguration.

I. The Glory of His Ministry (Matt. 15:21–16:12; Mark 7:24–8:26)

One of the purposes in the four retreats from Galilee during this part of Jesus' ministry was to get some much needed rest (*first* – Matt. 14:22; Mark 6:31; Luke 9:10; John 6:1; *second* – Matt. 15:21; Mark 7:24; *third* – Matt. 15:29; Mark 7:31; *fourth* – Matt. 16:5; Mark 8:13). He went into the region of Tyre and Sidon located to the north of Galilee on the coast of the Mediterranean Sea. This was a Gentile region where He was not as well known, but His fame preceded Him. "He entered a house and wanted no one to know it, but He could not be hidden" (Mark 7:24). Even though this was to be a period of rest, Jesus continued His ministry of healing.

During His second retreat with His disciples, Jesus was approached for help by a woman who is described as both "a Greek" and "a Syro-Phoenician by birth" (Mark 7:25). The word "Greek" does not necessarily mean she spoke Greek or that she was a citizen of a Greek city-state. Because there is no Greek word for "Gentile" or "non-Jew," the New Testament uses the term *ethnos* meaning "nation" or "people grouping" when referring to a group of Gentiles, and "Greek" when referring to an individual Gentile.

Mark identifies this woman as a Syro-Phoenician to distinguish her background from that of other Phoenicians. A Syro-Phoenician was a member of the Phoenician community in Syria. A well-known Libo-Phoenician community was located in Libya, North Africa. A large group of Phoenician settlers had begun a community there and named their town Carthage which means "new town." In time, Carthage grew to become one of the principle cities of North Africa. The city was so strong that at one time it opposed Rome under the leadership of Hannibal.

When this woman approached Jesus with her need, Jesus appeared to reject her need. Her daughter was under the control of a demon and this mother believed Jesus could help. Therefore, "she kept asking Him to cast the demon out of her daughter" (Mark 7:26). The verb used here occurs in the imperfect tense emphasizing her persistence in asking in the face of apparent rejection.

Jesus responded to these persistent requests with a most unusual statement. "Let the children be filled first, for it is not good to take the children's bread and throw it to the little dogs" (Mark 7:27). Although Jesus did not expressly call the woman a dog, His illustration came very close to doing so. In the Middle East, most dogs were wild and roamed in packs as scavengers. The Jews hated dogs and often referred to non-Jews as "Gentile dogs." However, this woman did not take offense at what Jesus said. Rather, she assumed Jesus was referring to a pet or house dog and used that picture to justify her continued request. "Yes, Lord, yet even the little dogs under the table eat from the children's crumbs," she noted (Mark 7:28).

This incident between Jesus and the Syro-Phoenician woman is difficult to understand. Some critics have used this account to suggest Jesus was a racist or anti-woman. But this passage is better understood when two principles which governed the ministry of Jesus are remembered. The first is the principle of concentrated focus. Because the time was brief in which He would minister on earth, He needed to concentrate the focus of His ministry on His own people, the Jews. While He also had limited ministry to Samaritans and other Gentiles, most of His energy was devoted to reaching the Jews. In the later dispensation of the church, He would commission others who like Paul would concentrate their energies among the Gentiles.

The second principle governing Jesus' ministry was the principle of tested faith. While it would have been easier for both Jesus and the woman involved for Him to immediately respond by casting out the demon, it was better for the woman and His disciples for Jesus to delay His actions to demonstrate the greatness of this woman's faith. It is interesting to note that the two greatest examples of faith identified by Jesus were both exercised by Gentiles (Matt. 8:10; 15:28). Ironically, Matthew chose to emphasize the accounts of both these individuals in a gospel written primarily to a Jewish market. This woman got what she wanted when she demonstrated her faith. In the process of delaying her request, He was able to illustrate to His disciples the principle of persistent faith. A real faith will persist in prayer until it has what it seeks. When the woman got home, she found her daughter lying in bed, probably exhausted from the exorcism of the demon (Mark 7:30). The demon had been cast out of her the very hour her mother had been commended for her faith (Matt. 15:28). It is highly unlikely that the woman or her daughter ever viewed Jesus as a racist or anti-woman.

Jesus left that region and traveled to Decapolis. The name *Decapolis* means "ten cities" and was a region on the east of the Sea of Galilee under the control of Herod Philip. When He got to the area, He chose not to go to one of the cities of the area but rather climbed a mountain to be alone with His disciples. Soon, the people learned where He was and came to Him in mass. "Then great multitudes came to Him, having with them the lame, blind, mute, maimed, and many others; and they laid them down at Jesus' feet, and He healed them" (Matt. 15:30). Among the many who came to be healed was a deaf mute. Jesus took this man aside and performed a rather unusual ritual as He healed Him. First, He placed His fingers in the man's ears. Then He spat and touched the man's tongue. Then, Jesus looked toward heaven and sighed saying, "Ephphatha" which is Aramaic and means "be opened" (Mark 7:33-34). This was the first word that man had ever heard. Instantaneously, he was healed.

Why did Jesus go through this unusual ritual to heal this man? Some Bible teachers believe Jesus may have been attempting to build this man's faith by communicating with him using sign language. If this were the case, Jesus first drew the man's attention to his need, he could not hear or speak. Using spit may have pointed to the inability of medical treatment to help in this case. At that time, saliva was thought to have special curative powers. By looking to heaven and sighing, Jesus was telling the man the miracle could only happen as God intervened.

The multitude continued to come to Jesus in the mountain and remained with Him day after day. When Jesus realized the people had not eaten for three days, He told His disciples He wanted to feed them. As with the earlier feeding of the five thousand, the disciples pointed out a lack of resources to do so. A search for food only yielded seven loaves of bread and a few small fish (Matt. 15:34). As He had done earlier with the five thousand, He performed a miracle to feed this crowd of "four thousand men, besides women and children" (Matt. 15:38).

Because of the similarities between the feeding of the five thousand and the feeding of the four thousand, some critics argue there was only one event reported in two different forms. The problems with this view are many. First, both Matthew and Mark who record the miracle of the feeding of four thousand also record an account of the feeding of five thousand. Matthew was an eyewitness involved in both these miracles. Mark's gospel is thought to be based on Peter's memory of the events of the life of Jesus (Peter was also an eyewitness). Further, both gospels report Jesus referring to both miracles (Matt. 16:9-10; Mark 8:19-20). Also, these miracles involved two different-sized groups, occurred in two different places, began with two different amounts of food, ended with the collection of two different amounts of leftovers, and concluded with two different responses on the part of the crowd that was fed.

II.   The Glory of His Identity (Matt. 16:13-26; Mark 8:27-37; Luke 9:18-25)

Following the feeding of the four thousand, the crowd willingly got into boats and returned to Galilee. Later, Jesus and His disciples also determined to return to Galilee and sailed to Magdala in the region of Dalmanutha. Magdala was located in central Galilee on the west shore of the lake. Although Jesus and His disciples had been out of the region for some time, the Pharisees wasted no time in confronting Him. This time they were accompanied by the Sadducees, a theologically more liberal sect within Judaism to which most of the priests adhered. Among other weaknesses, Sadducees denied the existence of angels or supernatural works. However, there were few things the Pharisees and Sadducees could agree on outside of their opposition to Jesus and later their joint opposition against the early church.

On this occasion, the Pharisees and Sadducees came to Jesus demanding a sign that He was indeed the Messiah. While Jesus did many miraculous signs to help people believe (John 20:30-31), the religious leadership of Israel had already demonstrated they had no intention of believing. He criticized them for their unwillingness to discern the signs that had already been performed. Jesus explained that these signs were much more reliable than the signs they commonly used to discern the weather. Jesus called them a "wicked and adulterous generation" and reminded them again of the coming sign of Jonah (Matt. 16:4). Jesus used the term "adulterous" in the same context of the prophets who rebuked Israel for lusting after false gods rather than remaining faithful to God.

After this confrontation with the Pharisees, Jesus and His disciples left Galilee for the fourth time. This time they sailed back to Bethsaida Julias, the site of the feeding of the five thousand. The decision to leave Galilee so soon after their arrival may have come as a surprise to the disciples. In their haste to get ready for the trip, they forgot to get bread. As they crossed toward their destination, they heard Jesus say, "Take heed and beware of the leaven of the Pharisees and the Sadducees" (Matt. 16:6) "and the leaven of Herod" (Mark 8:15). The Herodians adhered to Judaism but were viewed by many Jews as compromisers because they recognized the rights of Rome and cooperated with Roman authorities. Not until the disciples heard these words of Jesus did they realize they had forgotten to bring bread with them. But Jesus was not talking about bread. He reminded His disciples of two recent miracles in which He fed five thousand and then four thousand men with a total of only a dozen loaves of bread. If He wanted bread, Jesus could find bread. The leaven He was referring to was much more important. It was the moral leaven of legalism, compromise and sin which had permeated these three groups making them unfit. Among the Jewish leaders, these three sects were consistently opposed to Jesus' ministry. Each of them represented a dangerous type of leaven.

THREE KINDS OF DANGEROUS LEAVEN

The leaven of the Pharisees– hypocrisy
The leaven of the Sadducees – false doctrine
The leaven of the Herodians – worldliness

As they neared Bethsaida, a group leading a blind man by the hand came to meet Jesus. When Jesus applied spit to the man's eyes, a measure of sight was restored to him. The healed man noted he could see men, but they looked like walking trees. Some Bible teachers believe the man may have seen a group of men carrying branches. When Jesus touched the man's eyes, "he was restored and saw everyone clearly" (Mark 8:25). Jesus sent the man home asking him not to even go into the nearby city to report the miracle. Jesus was still seeking rest and anonymity because of the ongoing confrontation with the Jewish leaders.

From Bethsaida, Jesus and His disciples turned north toward the city of Caesarea Philippi near Mount Hermon, the tallest mountain that can be seen from all sections of the Holy Land. Some Bible teachers believe Jesus went to the Old Testament city of Laish, an important city belonging to the tribe of Dan. The city was in a resort area of Palestine in those days, but had been the center of two forms of pagan worship. The first and oldest was that of the worshiping Pan, a god thought to be half man and half goat. He was the god of natural joy and was most often portrayed playing an instrument known as "the pan flute." Also, this city had become a center of emperor worship, the unifying faith of the Roman empire. Philip had built a temple in this city devoted to the worship of Augustus Octavius. Jesus first taught His disciples about the church as they approached this city.

Jesus asked His disciples two questions. The first was, "Who do men say that I, the Son of Man, am?" (Matt. 16:13). When He asked this question, Jesus used his human designation, "Son of Man," to ask His disciples how He was being perceived popularly. They responded that he was viewed as being in the same company as the prophets like John the Baptist, Elijah, or Jeremiah. Then He asked a second question. "But who do you say that I am?" Peter responded, "You are the Christ, the Son of the living God" (Matt. 16:16). Peter used the title of deity to describe Jesus, "Son of God." Some critics have questioned why Jesus would have asked these questions when He knew His disciples had expressed their faith·in Him as Messiah much earlier. The answer to this objection may be clearer when it is realized these questions were not designed to produce an initial expression of faith but to confirm the continued existence of faith. John the Baptist had confessed faith in Jesus as the Messiah at the beginning of Jesus' public ministry, but later John had some lingering doubts. In light of Jesus' persistent refusal to lead an armed revolt against Rome as people expected of their Messiah, and the growing hatred to Jesus' ministry among the respected religious leaders of Israel, it would have been natural for the disciples to have second thoughts about Jesus. This has been called their greatest statement of faith. Here at Caesarea Philippi they came to a deeper appreciation of who Jesus was. Jesus noted that Peter's conclusion about His deity was a revelation given him by His Father. Then He added, "And I also say to you that you are Peter, and on this rock I will build My church, and the gates of Hades shall not prevail against it" (Matt. 16:18). This statement that introduces the church has been variously interpreted throughout history. Some monks interpreted it to mean Jesus wanted them to build a large church on the massive rock cliff in that region, and responded by building one. Others claimed Jesus meant the church would be established by Peter whose name meant "a stone" and developed the idea of an apostolic succession in the Papacy. But Peter himself identified Jesus as the rock upon which the church would be built (cf. 1 Peter 2:7).

In this first mention of the church in Scripture, Jesus noted the church would prevail against the gates of Hades. Gates were perceived to be the strength of a city, yet even the strength of the unseen world beyond could not stop the ever-advancing Christian church. As this church faithfully proclaimed the gospel, it was using the keys of the kingdom of heaven to set people free from the bondage of sin both here on earth and in heaven (Matt. 16:19). Failure to share the Good News (the gospel) was to bind people in their sins both now and for eternity.

As Jesus introduced this concept of the church to His disciples, the emphasis of His ministry distinctly changed. "From that time Jesus began to show to His disciples that He must go to Jerusalem, and suffer many things from the elders and chief priests and scribes, and be killed, and be raised the third day" (Matt. 16:21). He had earlier mentioned the cross in His ministry, but not as explicitly nor as often as would now be the case.

Notwithstanding the willingness of the disciples to follow Jesus even though some of the crowds were now deserting Him, the idea of their leader being crucified was revolting. The fact that crucifixion was a common form of execution at that time did not minimize the horror associated with the practice. The disciples naturally would object to the idea of Jesus being crucified – and object is exactly what Peter did. "Far be it from You, Lord; this shall not happen to you!" he argued (Matt. 16:22).

"Get behind Me, Satan!" (Matt. 16:23). Jesus called Peter the name of His ultimate enemy. While Peter's intention may have been noble – to save Jesus from a horrible way to die – it would also accomplish the will of Satan by preventing Jesus from fulfilling the greatest aspect of His messianic work. Only by giving His life on the cross could others obtain eternal life.

III.   The Glory of His Eternity (Matt. 16:27-17:13; Mark 8:38–9:13; Luke 9:26-36)

About a week later (Matt. 17:1), Jesus called aside three of the disciples. Peter, James, and John were about to see the glory of Jesus in a way few people would ever see. As they climbed a high mountain (probably Mount Hermon) with their Master, they had no idea they would soon see Jesus in the glory which had been His for all eternity. A week earlier, they had heard Jesus say, "there are some standing here who shall not taste death till they see the Son of Man coming in His kingdom" (Matt. 16:28). Now they were about to witness something so spectacular they would be unable to share their secret vision with anyone until after Jesus rose from the dead.

While Jesus was praying, He "was transfigured before them. His face shone like the sun, and His clothes became as white as the light" (Matt. 17:2). Moses and Elijah appeared with Jesus and began to talk with Him about the events surrounding His upcoming death in Jerusalem. The disciples had been napping, but the brightness of the light and sound of voices roused them from their sleep. When Peter realized what he was seeing, he understood the meeting of these three men – Jesus, Moses, and Elijah – was indeed significant. "Let us make here three tabernacles: one for You, one for Moses, and one for Elijah," Peter suggested (Matt. 17:4).

God Himself responded to Peter's suggestion by stressing the uniqueness of Jesus. For the second of three times during the public ministry of Jesus, the voice of God was audibly heard. "This is My beloved Son, in whom I am well pleased. Hear Him!" (Matt. 17:6). At the sound of God's voice, the disciples fell on their faces scared. When Jesus told them there was no reason to be afraid, they looked up to find Him alone.

On the way down from the mountain, Jesus asked the three disciples not to report the vision until after His resurrection. While the disciples had gained a deeper understanding of the glory of Jesus from their experience on the mountain, one question still puzzled them. They had always been taught Elijah would reappear in Israel before the coming of the Messiah. Jesus answered their question in two ways. First, he told them Elijah truly is coming first and "will restore all things" (Matt. 17:11). Second, He added "Elijah has come already, and they did not know him but did to him whatever they wished" (Matt. 17:12). The disciples understood this second comment to refer to John the Baptist (Matt. 17:13).

Conclusion

While the glory of His deity was veiled during His days on earth, those who watched Jesus carefully could see and recognize evidences that He was God. Jesus' disciples affirmed this when they worshiped Him as God. Sometimes today, Christians may have difficulty identifying evidences of God's glory around them, but as they ponder the work of God in, through, and around them, they too will respond to God in worship, celebrating both who He is and what He is doing.

CHAPTER 17

THE TWELVE:

IN PURSUIT OF GREATNESS

Matthew 8:19-22; 17:14–18:35; Mark 9:14-50; Luke 9:37-62; John 7:2-52

When Jesus and His three disciples reached the bottom of Mount Hermon, they found a large crowd gathered around the disciples which had remained at the base of the hill. Among those in the crowd, was a group of scribes arguing with the disciples. When the people saw Jesus coming, they began to run toward Him, greeting Him. Jesus, directing His attention to the scribes, asked, "What are you discussing with them?" (Mark 9:16).

Before they could respond to His question, someone in the crowd raised a problem which may have been at the root of the debate (Mark 9:17). A man concerned for his son's welfare had brought him to Jesus' disciples for help. This man's son was possessed by a demon that produced epileptic fits and inhibited the boy's ability to speak. Under the control of the demon, the boy often foamed at the mouth and ground his teeth together. The father had watched his son in torment and wanted to help him. When he learned that Jesus' disciples were in the area, he hoped they could help. Perhaps the father had heard reports of how the disciples had cast out demons on their earlier ministry tour. But when he brought the boy to the disciples, they failed to cast out the demon.

When Jesus learned of their failure, He commented on the disciples' lack of faith and asked that the boy be brought to Him. As soon as Jesus saw the boy, He perceived there was something unusual about this case. Turning to the father, Jesus asked how long his son had been afflicted. The father mentioned there had been many other similar attacks and begged Jesus to help. Jesus agreed suggesting, "If you can believe, all things are possible to him who believes" (Mark 9:23).

In tears the father responded, "Lord, I believe, help my unbelief!" (Mark 9:24). Jesus, seeing a crowd gathering, quickly rebuked the evil spirit. The boy's body went into severe convulsions as the spirit departed, then laid still on the ground. From the crowd, voices began speaking to one another in a stunned whisper. "He is dead," they concluded as they saw the limp body lying on the ground (Mark 9:26). "But Jesus took him by the hand and lifted him up, and he arose" (Mark 9:27). When the crowd saw this miracle, "they were all amazed at the majesty of God" (Luke 9:43).

Later, when they were alone with Jesus, the disciples asked why they had been unsuccessful in casting out the evil spirit. Earlier, Jesus had indicated their lack of faith as reason, also adding something He viewed as "perverse" had been a contributing factor (Luke 9:41). In addition to that earlier response, Jesus added, "This kind can come out by nothing but prayer and fasting" (Mark 9:29).

What had Jesus earlier identified as "perverse" in his disciples' lives? While Jesus did not specifically identify the problem, the context of this event in the life and ministry of Jesus suggests He may have perceived the presence of a proud spirit which hindered the disciples in their ministry. In the days to come, the disciples' actions made it clear that they were caught up in the egotistical pursuit of greatness. Jesus responded to the problem by teaching important principles of humility, both by example and explanation. This teaching emphasis of Jesus climaxed with His visit to Jerusalem for the feast of Tabernacles, a feast celebrating the forty years God humbled Israel in the wilderness before allowing them access to the Promised Land (cf. Lev. 23:33-43).

I.   The Humility of the Master (Matt. 17:22-27; Mark 9:30-32; Luke 9:43-45)

From the mount of the Transfiguration, Jesus and His disciples secretly reentered Galilee. This time they had a degree of success in avoiding the crowds, and Jesus was able to spend some quality time with His disciples. His message to the disciples during those days was, "Let these words sink down into your ears, for the Son of Man is about to be betrayed into the hands of men" (Luke 9:44). But the disciples had difficulty understanding what He meant. That one would know and willingly allow His life to be taken by the hostile authorities in Jerusalem was inconsistent with their concept of greatness.

When they came to Capernaum, Jesus and His disciple once again found themselves dealing with people. When the temple tax collectors saw Peter, they asked, "Does your Teacher not pay the temple tax?" (Matt. 17:24). Perhaps because there had been so much recent hostility directed at Jesus from the religious leaders in Jerusalem, Peter got defensive and quickly claimed Jesus did pay the tax. Later, Jesus raised the issue with Peter.

Jesus led Peter to identify a universal principle of taxation as practiced in that day. Kings taxed only those outside the royal family, but members of the royal family lived tax-free. The consistent application of this principle to the issue of the temple tax meant Jesus was exempt from paying the tax because He was one of the free sons. But for Jesus, there was another principle at stake here. Though he had the right not to pay the tax, he expressed a willingness to lay aside His right so as to not offend others. He directed Peter to go fishing and check the fish's mouth. There he would find a coin which was the exact amount to pay the temple tax for two (Matt. 17:27). This miracle was as close as Jesus ever got to using His miraculous powers for some personal benefit.

II.   The Pride of the Disciples (Matt. 8:19-22; 18:1-35; Mark 9:33-50; Luke 9:45-50, 57-62)

Despite the first example of Jesus in humbly determining to lay down His life, and His second example to pay a tax even though He had a right to tax-exemption, the disciples still did not learn the lesson of humility. "Then a dispute arose among them as to which of them would be the greatest" (Luke 9:46). This contention would be fought among the disciples right up until the night Jesus was arrested. But when Jesus asked them what they had been discussing among themselves, they were too embarrassed to say (Mark 9:34). Jesus knew what the problem was and decided to address it head on.

Jesus called a child over and sat him down in the middle of the group "Assuredly, I say to you, unless you are converted and become as little children, you will by no means enter the kingdom of heaven. Therefore whoever humbles himself as this little child is the greatest in the kingdom of heaven" (Matt. 18:3-4). If the disciples would repeatedly argue over who would be greatest in the kingdom of heaven, Jesus would repeatedly emphasize the concept of servant leadership. The path to greatness begins with humility, and this was going to be one of the hardest lessons the disciples would be required to learn. Jesus raised the issue, and defense mechanisms went up in the disciples.

John spoke on behalf of the group on this occasion. "Master, we saw someone casting out demons in Your name, and we forbade him because he does not follow with us" (Luke 9:49). No doubt the disciples felt Jesus would appreciate their action as it helped preserve the integrity of their ministry. But Jesus realized His integrity was not at stake, but rather His proud disciples had an exclusive outlook on ministry. "Do not forbid him," Jesus responded, "for he who is not against us is on our side" (Luke 9:50).

Jesus continued His painful lesson on humility. At all costs, He wanted His disciples to avoid offending others in any way that would cause them to stumble. While He recognized people inevitably would be offended, in no way did that justify being responsible for the offense (Matt. 18:7). It was better that a man be physically handicapped than to suffer the spiritual consequences of tolerating this or any other sin (Matt. 18:8-9).

Just as a shepherd would leave ninety-nine secure sheep to find one that was lost, the disciples needed to have that kind of concern for the most insignificant people within their sphere of influence. They needed to develop this attitude in ministry for three reasons. First, the "little ones" are represented in heaven by angels who have direct access to God (Matt. 18:10). Second, this was Jesus' attitude. "For the Son of Man has come to save that which was lost" (Matt. 18:11). Finally, this was God's concern. "Even so it is not the will of your Father who is in heaven that one of these little ones should perish" (Matt. 18:14).

When a person has this humble attitude toward others in ministry, it will directly impact his or her relationships with them. Jesus gave His disciples specific guidelines for resolving differences between each other in the context of church discipline. First, they were to deal with the problem one on one, discussing the offense only with the brother involved (Matt. 18:15). If that does not resolve the problem, they were to return to the offending brother with one or two others who would act as witnesses (Matt. 18:16). If the problem still remained unresolved, it was then to be brought to the church (Matt. 18:17). If the offending brother still refused to deal with the offense, the church was to cut him off from their fellowship (Matt. 18:17). Clearly, at each step in this process of discipline, the intent was to persuade the offending brother to change his behavior and be restored to fellowship. But if that objective could not be achieved, cutting the person off from the fellowship may have been the best thing for the offender and the church. Sometimes alienation causes the offender to realize the seriousness of his ways and repent. If he does not repent, it is better that he not be part of the church and continue hindering its reputation.

FOUR STEPS TO PROBLEM SOLVING IN THE CHURCH

1. Deal with the problem one on one.
2. Discuss the problem with one or two witnesses.
3. Bring the matter to the church for resolution.
4. Expel the brother from the church.

This need to be forgiving toward an offending brother was difficult for a proud person to accept. It is not surprising that Peter asked how many times a brother should be forgiven, suggesting seven times might be an adequate number. Peter's offer of forgiving a person seven times was extremely fair compared to the common view of the rabbis that one should be forgiven three times. But Jesus responded to Peter's suggestion, "I do not say to you, up to seven times, but up to seventy times seven" (Matt. 18:22). The numbers seven and seventy are often used in Scripture to suggest completeness or wholeness. Many Bible teachers believe Jesus' reference to "seventy times seven" meant to continually forgive without end, rather than merely four hundred and ninety times.

Jesus told a parable to illustrate this principle of forgiveness (Matt. 18:23-35). In the story, a man was in debt to his king for about ten thousand talents (about $1.2 million). Because he could not pay, the king ordered the sale of all the man's assets, including his family, so that the debt would be paid. But the man begged the king for more time, offering to pay the debt in full, and the king responded by forgiving the mans's debt completely.

Later, that same man found one of his associates that owed him a hundred denarii (about $17.00). The man demanded immediate payment from his associate who could not pay. The associate begged for more time to pay, but the request was denied. The associate was imprisoned until the debt was paid.

Those who witnessed this event reported it to their king. The king was understandably upset with the inconsistent behavior of the man whose debt he had forgiven. He called the man in to be accountable. In anger, the king had the man thrown in prison until his debt had been paid in full.

The message of this parable was applied by Jesus when He said, "So My heavenly Father also will do to you if each of you, from his heart, does not forgive his brother his trespasses" (Matt. 18:35). When we consider how much God forgives in saving our souls, it is inconsistent not to forgive the comparatively minor offenses of others.

One way in which Jesus demonstrated humility before His disciples was by consistently refusing to promote Himself. Jesus yielded to God's timing in

His life. It had been about six months since Jesus fed the five thousand and the Feast of Tabernacles was approaching. Jesus' family urged Him to go to Judea for the feast "that Your disciples also may see the works that You are doing" (John 7:3). These brothers of Jesus did not yet believe He was the Messiah and may have been mocking Jesus, suggesting if His miracles were real, He should welcome the opportunity to go to Jerusalem and have them authenticated by the religious authorities. "If You do these things," they added, "show Yourself to the world" (John 7:4). Jesus responded to their sarcasm by reminding them, "My time has not yet come" (John 7:6). He urged them to go on their way as He was not yet ready to go to Jerusalem.

After they left, Jesus decided to go to Jerusalem, but did so secretly. he must have been aware the religious leaders of that city would be watching for Him, expecting Him to be present at Israel's most colorful celebration (John 7:11). By leaving late for the feast and taking a different route than a Jew would normally take, Jesus was able to arrive at the feast secretly about the midpoint of the week of celebration.

As Jesus and His disciples began the journey to Jerusalem, they took a route through Samaria probably to avoid the crowds of Galileans coming to the feast. As the weary day of trial approached an end, Jesus sent messengers to prepare for His arrival in a particular Samaritan village. When the Samaritans realized Jesus was heading for Jerusalem, they chose not to make their hospitality available to Him. When James and John heard the report from the messengers, they were furious. Once again, their pride had been offended. "Lord, do You want us to command fire to come down from heaven and consume them, just as Elijah did?" they asked (Luke 9:43). Jesus rebuked the two disciples for their wrong spirit. "The son of Man did not come to destroy men's lives but to save them," He reminded them (Luke 9:56). Other villages were nearby, so "they went to another village" (Luke 9:56).

During the trip to Jerusalem, Jesus was approached by a scribe desiring to become one of His disciples. This was unusual because most scribes were decidedly opposed to Jesus' ministry and few others would consider following Him in light of the opposition in Jerusalem. But when the Lord reminded the scribe He and His disciples did not so much as have the security of a place to sleep each night, the scribe apparently chose not to follow Him (Matt. 8:19-20).

This would-be disciple was not the only one who would not count the cost and therefore could not follow Jesus. Another was interested in following Jesus, but wanted to wait out the few remaining years of His father's life before leaving the family (Luke 9:59). Still another was willing to follow after a suitable farewell party had been planned and conducted (Luke 9:61). But Jesus was not eager to get disciples who would not sacrifice for the work of the kingdom. His mission in life was too important to risk it on chasing indecisive followers.

THREE HINDRANCES TO DISCIPLESHIP
Failure to Count the Cost
Conflicting Sense of Duty
Indecisive Commitment

III.   A Celebration of Humbling (Luke 9:51-56; John 7:2-52)

When Jesus arrived in Jerusalem, He found a place in the temple where He could teach the people. As He taught in the temple, the religious leaders were amazed at His insight, even more so in that He was perceived as having not been formally trained as a rabbi (John 7:15). They had difficulty accepting Jesus because He was not an alumnus of one of their two rabbinical schools. Jesus pointed out that His accreditation for ministry was from God. "My doctrine is not Mine, but His who sent me" (John 7:16). If the leaders were willing to do God's will, they would perceive the divine authority associated with Jesus' teaching. "Why do you seek to kill Me?" He asked them (John 7:19).

While the religious leaders in Jerusalem had for some time now been committed to killing Jesus, the people visiting the city apparently did not know their motives. When Jesus asked the leaders to identify their motives, the people were confused and wondered why Jesus thought anyone was out to get Him. Jesus continued pointing out the inconsistency of their official response to His ministry. The Greek word *chelate,* used to identify the anger of the Jewish leaders (John 7:23), was a term used to express the horror one felt toward some monstrous act. But the monstrous act over which they were angered was the healing of a man on the sabbath which had occurred some nineteen months earlier (John 7:23). As Jesus continued teaching, some of the people who lived in Jerusalem realized He was the One their leaders were seeking. But seeing Him boldly teach in the midst of the temple area led them to wonder if the priests had discovered this really was the Messiah (John 7:26). Things just did not seem to make sense one way or another. As the Pharisees heard what was being said, they became concerned and ordered the temple guard to arrest Jesus. But the soldiers were impressed with Jesus' teaching and failed to make the arrest (John 7:46).

As the Feast of Tabernacles came to a close, it was customary for the priests to draw water from the pool of Siloam down near the lower southern wall in Jerusalem. They marched in procession to the temple. The ceremony was meant to commemorate the provision of water from the rock during the wilderness wanderings. That simple religious act was performed with all the pageantry one might associate with religious liturgy. Crowds of worshipers would follow the priest from the pool to the altar. As the priest began pouring the water on the altar, their ecstasy knew no bounds. Many think this is the moment that Jesus shouted, "If anyone thirsts, let him come to Me and drink. He who believes in Me, as the Scripture has said, out of his heart will flow rivers of living water" (John 7:37-38). This shout would have disrupted the ceremony and angered the Jewish leaders.

In this statement Jesus lists four steps in being filled with the Holy Spirit.

HOW TO BE FILLED WITH THE SPIRIT

Thirst – Desire
Come to Me – Repent
Drink – Obey/Receive
He Who Believes – Faith

Because Jesus disrupted their pageantry by yelling His claims of deity, the Pharisees were even more committed to destroying Jesus than before. They were upset that their own guard seemed to be "deceived" by Jesus and that the crowds of people did not seem to know better than to follow Him. But not all Pharisees were opposed to Jesus. As they discussed the matter, Nicodemus who had led a delegation to meet with Jesus at night two and a half years earlier reminded his colleagues the law forbade the judging of a man before he was formerly accused (John 7:51). "Are you also from Galilee?" they chided Nicodemus. "Search and look, for no prophet has arisen out of Galilee" (John 7:52). Ironically, the Jews held that Jonah, Hosea, Nahum, Elijah, Elisha, and Amos were all Galilean prophets, but their hatred for Jesus caused them to ignore this and look for any reason to discredit His claims.

Conclusion

Sometimes Christians today have the same problem with pride with which the disciples of Jesus struggled. Naturally a person should want to strive to achieve greatness in life, but a disciple of Jesus needs to learn that humility is the means by which God grants true greatness. The half-brother of Jesus later summarized this principle of the Christian life when he encouraged first-century Jewish Christians, "Humble yourselves in the sight of the Lord, and He will lift you up" (James 4:10).

CHAPTER 18

JESUS OF NAZARETH: THE LIGHT SHINING IN DARKNESS

John 7:53–10:21

s October settled over Jerusalem, the cool days of autumn made people forget about the unbearable heat of summer. They were willing to spend more time outdoors. During the Feast of Tabernacles on the fifteenth day of the seventh month in the Hebrew calendar (cf. Lev. 23:34), the people lived in booths to commemorate the years Israel lived in tents in the wilderness. A booth was a lean-to of branches (Neh. 8:15) where the people left the comfort of Jerusalem to sleep outdoors. By the conclusion of the week of festivities, they were glad to return to the comforts of their own homes. Many from out of town began the long journey home early the next day, but some stayed in Jerusalem for a few more days before leaving. Jesus and His disciples apparently remained in the Jerusalem area for about a week. During this time, they probably spent their evenings on the mount of Olives and their days in the temple area.

By the end of the Feast of Tabernacles, the Sanhedrin was united in their opposition against Jesus. Prior to this feast, most of the opposition against Jesus came from the scribes and Pharisees. Now the chief priests who were Sadducees, led the majority party in the Sanhedrin to join the opposition against Jesus (John 7:45). During the week following the feast, this opposition became stronger and more pronounced. Only the gospel of John records the events of that week, but it is not always easy to distinguish between the days involved. His account begins with an event staged by a group of scribes and Pharisees early Monday morning and continues without interruption to describe the healing of a blind man on the Sabbath (Saturday). John's purpose in recording the events of this week was apparently not to document the details of Jesus' life, but rather to describe the character of Jesus as the light of the world. He was the light shining to those both in moral and physical darkness. John's account of that week also includes a proverb describing Jesus as a shepherd which is as close as John comes to recording any of Jesus' many parables.

I. The Light of the World Shining in Moral Darkness (John 7:53–8:59)

Although the account of the woman caught in the act of adultery is missing in some early manuscripts (John 7:53–8:11), most Bible teachers agree it is an accurate record of a significant event in the life and ministry of Jesus. The account is referred to in the writings of several church fathers including Jerome, Ambrose, and Augustine. It is also referred to in the third century *Apostolic Constitutions.* According to Augustine, some men objected to this event, fearing their wives would use it to justify immorality and on that basis removed it from the gospel. This may explain why the account is missing in some manuscripts.

Very early on Monday morning after the Feast of Tabernacles, Jesus returned to the temple and began teaching in the court of the women near the temple treasury. As he began, a group of scribes and Pharisees approached the group dragging a panic-stricken woman. When they arrived, they threw the woman in the midst of the group and began to explain the situation to Jesus. This woman had been caught in the act of adultery and was being brought to Jesus so He could pronounce appropriate sentencing. This group of accusers was not likely very large. The Greek word *orthrou* translated "early" (John 8:2) refers to the early dawn hours of the day, just before sunrise. Many of the religious leaders may have chosen to sleep-in that morning because they had just had a busy week of ministry and were sleeping in their own beds after a week of "camping out." The delegation of scribes and Pharisees may have been as small as a half a dozen men. These men had risen early because they had a plan by which they hoped to trap Jesus.

Adultery tended to be a major problem during the Feast of Tabernacles. The large influx of visitors to the city and the "campground" setting of the week contributed to opportunities for immoral behavior. The problem was so severe, the religious leaders tended to overlook it during the week. These men would have had no problem finding a woman committing this act during the week. The absence of her partner in this account has led some to believe the religious leaders may have staged an encounter so as to insure they caught this particular woman in the act. Had these men been serious about their supposed concern for upholding the law, they would have taken this woman to a special court which had been established by the scribes to judge cases of adultery. The presence of scribes in the group suggests this option would have been known by the group and available to them had they desired to take advantage of it. Instead, they brought the woman to Jesus believing they had a situation where they could finally trap Jesus. They reminded Jesus of the biblical penalty for adultery. "Now Moses, in the law, commanded us that such should be stoned. But what do You say?" (John 8:5). The law called for the stoning of a betrothed woman who committed adultery (Deut. 22:22-24) and required some form of execution for other cases of adultery (Lev. 20:10). In both cases, both parties involved in the act were to be treated the same. Because the Romans refused to allow the Jews to stone people, most often adultery was punished by strangulation.

These religious leaders probably asked their question of Jesus in the way they did because of the trap they hoped to set. If Jesus did not uphold the law of Moses and agree the woman should be stoned, then it could be argued Jesus was not committed to the written law of God. If on the other hand, Jesus condemned this woman, He would lose His popular appeal as "a Friend of sinners." In a third instance, Jesus could incur the wrath of Rome. The Romans had banned the practice of stoning and to encourage someone to do so was to challenge the authority of Rome. Jesus' initial response to these accusers was to ignore them. But when they continued to persist in their asking, Jesus responded in such a way as to neither condemn the woman nor condone her sin. "He who is without sin among you, let him throw a stone at her first" (John 8:7). Then He stooped down and continued writing on the ground.

Bible teachers have wondered what Jesus wrote on the ground that day. Some have thought He wrote the names of the men who had brought the woman and listed their individual sins. Others believe He wrote the number seven or wrote out the seventh commandment which banned the practice of adultery. Others believe Jesus may have just been doodling in the sand to pass the time and allow His words time to achieve their desired effect.

One by one, the men who had brought the woman to Him began to leave, "being convicted by their conscience" (John 8:9). The Greek word *eleqchomenoi* translated "convicted" literally means "to bring to the light and expose." In the context of a statement Jesus would make in just a matter of moments about being the light of the world, John's use of this word for conviction demonstrates one of the functions of this light, that of exposing the darkness of sin. A second function of light emphasized in Jesus' statement is that of revealing the way of life (John 8:12).

THE FUNCTIONS OF LIGHT

To expose the darkness of sin.
To reveal the way of life.

When Jesus looked up to the woman standing alone in the center of the crowd, He asked if none of her accusers were present. When she acknowledged they were not present to condemn her, Jesus responded, "Neither do I condemn you; go and sin no more" (John 8:11). Jesus then revealed Himself, "I am the light of the world" (John 8:12). As He made this dramatic statement for the first time, there was a number of contexts in which it could be understood. First, as noted above, He had just demonstrated His power as the light in exposing the darkness of sin even in the heart of those who would have considered themselves most righteous. Second, Jesus probably made the statement just as the bright morning sun rose over the Judean hillside "like a bridegroom coming out of his chamber" (Ps. 19:5). Third, during the feast of Tabernacles, the four large lamps in the temple were lit to commemorate the pillar of fire that led Israel in the wilderness. This light was so bright, it was said to illuminate the entire city of Jerusalem. Also, Jesus may have been using this image of light in the context of a number of messianic prophecies which portrayed the Messiah as a shining light (Isa. 9:1; 42:6; 49:6; 50:1-3; Mal. 4:2).

During the course of that week, Jesus probably engaged in numerous confrontations with the Pharisees. John records the essence of these confrontations in a typical account of that week. If this account is to be understood as having occurred on a single day, that day was the Sabbath (John 9:14). Likely, the antagonism of the Jewish leaders against Jesus continued to grow during the week and climaxed with the healing of the blind man on the Sabbath. During that time, Jesus made a number of pointed charges against the religious leaders, which are listed on the chart below.

JESUS' CHARGES AGAINST THE RELIGIOUS LEADERS
1. They were of this world (John 8:23)
2. They were in their sins (John 8:24)
3. They were not believing (John 8:24, 45)
4. They were slaves to sin (John 8:34)
5. They sought to kill Him (John 8:37)
6. They did Satan's works (John 8:41)
7. They were not of God (John 8:47)
8. They wanted to do Satan's desires (John 8:44)
9. They dishonored Jesus (John 8:49)

In the course of His teaching, Jesus warned these leaders their refusal to believe would have serious eternal consequences. First, they would die in their sin (John 8:21). Second, they would die in their sins (John 8:24). Jesus used the word *sin* in both the singular and plural to emphasize sin in both its essence and expression. These Jewish leaders did not believe in the doctrine of original sin, but it was manifested in both their sinful attitude and their sinful behavior.

Among those who responded positively to His message, two degrees of faith were expressed. First, there were those who "believed in Him" (John 8:30), an expression used by John to indicate saving faith. Second, others simply "believed him" (John 8:31); they believed He spoke the truth. This second group was unwilling to commit their lives to Him and did not express saving faith. Jesus told this group they could experience personal liberty if they became His disciples and abode in His word. This liberty would be the natural result of their personal discovery of "the truth." But the people responded that they were already free and were not in bondage (John 8:33). Seven months before, a crowd of Galileans had wanted to make Jesus king and march against the occupying armies of Rome, but now they ignored the Roman soldiers stationed in the temple area as they claimed to be a free people. Jesus did not address their political realities as He responded to their claim because He was not talking about political bondage, but rather moral bondage. "Whoever commits sin is a slave of sin," He affirmed (John 8:34). One of the reasons the people were reluctant to follow Jesus was due to their strong sense of national pride. They considered themselves the children of Abraham and assumed the righteousness of Abraham had been transferred to them from generation to generation. But as Jesus explained, Abraham was not the only father. They also considered themselves the children of God, but Jesus suggested a more accurate view made them children of Satan (John 8:44). Three fathers of Israel are mentioned in this account.

THREE FATHERS IN JOHN 8

Abraham (John 8:39)
God (John 8:42)
Satan (John 8:44)

The dispute between Jesus and these nominal Jews changed dramatically when Jesus confessed, "Your father Abraham rejoiced to see My day, and he saw it and was glad" (John 8:56). Initially, the Jews had asked, "You are not yet fifty years old, and have You seen Abraham?" (John 8:57). Some Bible teachers use this response of the Jews to suggest Jesus lived to be an old man and was at this time about fifty, but this is inconsistent with many other references to the age of Jesus in the Gospels. Others claim this statement shows the pressures of Jesus' ministry had aged Him so that He looked like He was about fifty years old even though He was only in His early to mid-thirties. More likely these people referred to being fifty years old because that was the age of retirement from active ministry for a Levite (Num. 4:3). They were saying, "You are not yet old enough to retire, and have you seen Abraham?" When did Abraham see the day of Jesus and rejoice? A number of answers to this question may be suggested. First, some thought Abraham knew the Messiah would be among His descendants and rejoiced, seeing Messiah in his seed by faith (Gen. 12:3). Second, some rabbis taught Abraham's vision included a prophetic view of history (Gen. 15:8-21). Abraham saw Jesus in a vision or dream. Third, some interpret Abraham's laugh at the prophetic announcement of Isaac's birth as a laugh of joy based on the realization that the Messiah would come through the line of Isaac (Gen. 17:17). Some rabbis taught the expression "well advanced in age" (Gen. 24:1 - literally "gone into days") referred to a kind of prophetic odyssey in which Abraham traveled to the future history of the nation. Fifth, some may have interpreted the phrase to mean Abraham was now rejoicing as he witnessed the Messiah's days on earth as he viewed it from paradise (cf. Luke 16:22-31). Jesus indicated the key to understanding this claim was not the experience of Abraham but the identity of Jesus. "Most assuredly, I say to you, before Abraham was, I AM," He told the people (John 8:58).

II. The Light of the World Shining in Physical Darkness (John 9:1-41)

The people's response to Jesus' clear revelation of Himself as the "I Am" of the Old Testament was immediate and violent. They began picking up stones and throwing them at Him intending to kill Him by stoning. This was the prescribed penalty for blasphemy under the law of Moses. Jesus managed to escape this attempt on His life and passed through the crowd unrecognized.

As Jesus and His disciples went out the door of the temple, they noticed a blind man begging. This was probably the beautiful gate or the golden gate. This man was known by his reputation as one who had been born blind (John 9:8). He had over the years become almost a permanent fixture in the area as he

. begged from those on their way to worship in the temple. When the disciples saw the man, they asked Jesus a question, "Rabbi, who sinned, this man or his parents, that he was born blind?" (John 9:2).

Based on the interpretation of a number of Old Testament passages (Ex. 20:15; 34:7; Num. 14:18; Deut. 5:9; Jer. 31:29-30; Ezek. 18:2), it was widely believed that children bore the consequences of their parent's sins. This would be the most logical explanation in the minds of many for the birth of a blind son. But some rabbis also taught that because the child was a person from the moment of conception, it was possible for a child to sin prior to its birth (cf. Gen. 25:22; Ps. 51:5). Hellenistic Jews also believed that souls existed prior to birth and that they might be assigned a handicapped body as punishment for their behavior before coming into this world. While God may use sickness or other problems in life to discipline one for his sins, it is wrong to conclude every sickness or problem is the direct consequence of an act of sin. Sometimes God has a higher reason for allowing such events to happen. As Jesus explained on this occasion, "Neither this man nor his parents sinned, but that the works of God should be revealed in him" (John 9:3). Then Jesus "spat on the ground and made clay with the saliva; and He anointed the eyes of the blind man with the clay" (John 9:6). He then sent the man down the valley to wash in the pool of Siloam. When the man washed the clay from his eyes, He could see for the first time in his life. When he returned to the temple area, he was immediately recognized and questioned concerning his ability to see. When he attributed the miracle to "a Man called Jesus" (John 9:11), he was taken to the Pharisees. By healing this man, Jesus once again challenged the traditions of the Jews regarding their sabbath laws. On this occasion, He violated three specific aspects of this law.

THREE VIOLATIONS OF THE SABBATH LAW

1. Spitting on the ground.
2. Making the clay mixture.
3. Healing a man born blind.

The Pharisees questioned the man and were told how Jesus healed this man who had been born blind. Although Jesus had healed others of blindness, this case was unique in that it is the first recorded case of a man healed from blindness with which he was born. As they heard the story of this man, the Pharisees themselves were divided in their conclusions. Some argued Jesus could not be from God because of His constant violations of the Sabbath laws. Others wondered how a "sinner" could perform such miracles. Others doubted the integrity of the man and thought they could disprove the testimony of him who had been born blind. In an apparent attempt to discredit this miracle, the man's parents were cross examined. The parents were asked, "Is this your son, who you say was born blind? How then does he now see?" (John 9:19). The question put to these parents suggested three ways they could help the religious leaders discredit the miracle. First, they could deny the man who was seeing was really their son. Second, they could confess he had really not been blind as they had claimed all these years. Third, they could suggest some other explanation for the miracle. The parents responded, "We know that this is our son, and that he was born blind; but by what means he now sees we do not know" (John 9:20-21). The religious leaders' opposition toward Jesus had grown to the point they had threatened to expel anyone from the synagogue who supported Him. The parents, though happy their son could now see, were afraid of saying anything that could be perceived as supportive of Jesus. They simply reminded the authorities their son had reached the age of maturity and could speak for himself. "Give God the glory!" the Pharisees urged the healed man. This expression was often used in a legal setting to call someone to tell the truth and confess (cf. Josh. 7:19). This entire meeting between the man and the Pharisees continued to be confrontational in nature and resulted in his being formally excommunicated from the synagogue. The Greek word *ekballo* translated "cast out" (John 9:34) was used technically to describe their reaction against this healed man. This practice of excommunication involved a person being removed from the synagogue normally for a period of about sixty days. To be put out of the synagogue meant he would be ostracized by everyone. No person would come within six or seven feet of him during this period of time. Often, the formal casting out involved the blasting of a horn and pronouncement of certain curses.

Although the man was cut off from others during this time, Jesus would not be cut off from the man. When He heard what had happened, Jesus found the man to encourage and strengthen his faith. As the man began to recognize Jesus as the Son of God, "he worshiped him" (John 9:38). The Greek word *prosekunesen* translated "worshiped" is always used by John of the worship of God. Unlike the apostles (Acts 10:25; 11:18) and angels (Rev. 22:9), Jesus made no effort to discourage this man's worship. He was worthy to receive this worship because He is God (cf. Rev. 4:11; 5:9-13).

III.   The Light of the World Shining Like a Shepherd (John 10:1-21)

In a confrontation with the Pharisees following this, Jesus used a series of illustrations from the shepherding industry to teach several biblical principles. First, Jesus portrayed himself as the shepherd of the sheep. Shepherding was an important part of the economy of Israel and was an industry the religious leaders would have known well. Not only did they rely on shepherds for their supply of sacrificial animals, the Lord was often viewed as "the Shepherd of Israel" (Ps. 80:1) and the people of Israel thought of themselves as the sheep of His pasture (Ps. 100:3).

Jesus first told the Pharisees that He, not they, was the true shepherd of the sheep (John 10:2). He used the illustration of the sheepfold to illustrate this point. Shepherds customarily led their sheep into the security of a fold for the evening. These folds had a single entrance and were surrounded by a fence or a heavy hedge of thorns. Sometimes those who tried to steal sheep would try to climb the fence to get into the fold, because the door was guarded at night. The sheep could distinguish between these rustlers and the true shepherd because (1) the shepherd entered through the door, (2) the sheep knew the sound of the shepherd's voice, and (3) the shepherd knew the name of the sheep. Normally a shepherd was responsible for a small flock of up to about one hundred sheep, so a bonding relationship existed between the shepherd and his sheep. This was not true of the stranger who tried to rustle the sheep. Second, Jesus portrayed Himself as the door to the sheepfold (John 10:7). Jesus used this illustration to explain the means by which people could (1) enter into a secure relationship with God, (2) experience personal liberty, and (3) be sustained spiritually as suggested in the following chart.

I AM THE DOOR (John 10:9)

If anyone enters by Me, he will be saved – Salvation
and will go in and out – Liberty
and find pasture— Spiritual Food.

Jesus' third application of this industry at this time portrayed Him as "the good shepherd" (John 10:11). The good shepherd can be distinguished from the hireling (hired hand) in that the shepherd (1) gives His life for the sheep, (2) has a genuine concern for the sheep, (3) knows the sheep, (4) is known by the sheep, and (5) is committed to gathering the whole flock. Once again, the response to Jesus was divided. Some thought He had lost His sanity. Others attributed His miracles and teaching to His being under the control of a demon. But others realized that His works and words could not be written off so easily. They simply wondered, "Can a demon open the eyes of the blind?" (John 10:21)

Conclusion

Many of the names Christians may use to describe Jesus today such as Dayspring, Day Star, Sun of Righteousness, and Bright and Morning Star remind them of Jesus' role as the Light of the World. That light may repel those who are unwilling to deal with the sin in their life, but it should draw the believer into a deeper, more meaningful relationship with the Lord. One of the principles of the abundant Christian life involves walking "in the light as He is in the light" (1 John 1:7). Only then will one's fellowship with Christ be as full and rich as it could be.

CHAPTER 19

THE TWELVE:
RECOVERING THEIR LOST POWER

Luke 10:1–12:59

From the time the disciples returned from their ministry tour, Jesus devoted much of His time and energy to training them and dealing with their growing problem of pride. When He and three of His disciples descended the Mount of Transfiguration, He interrupted an incident which had developed primarily over the inability of His disciples to cast out demons, something He had uniquely empowered them to do earlier. It was becoming increasingly more obvious that the disciples had lost their power with God and it was having a direct impact on their ministry effectiveness.

How did these disciples respond without the power of God for effective ministry? For a period of time, they appeared to continue, apparently unaware of their problem. Still, the absence of that power impacted their life in ministry in a number of ways. One of the evidences of a spiritual problem was reflected in their failure to understand even the most basic principles of the gospel (cf. Luke 9:44-45). In recording an occasion in which Jesus told His disciples about His coming crucifixion, Luke uses four expressions to emphasize the disciples' failure to understand what was being said. "But (1) they did not understand this saying, and (2) it was hidden from them so that (3) they did not perceive it; and (4) they were afraid to ask Him about this saying" (Luke 9:45).

A second evidence of their spiritual problem was reflected in their pursuit of prestige and position rather than looking for opportunities to serve (cf. Luke 9:46-48). Jesus called them to humility that they might again have power with God, but their desire for greatness not only hindered the power of God in their lives, it impacted their attitude toward others who were involved in ministry. They opposed those who were doing what they should have been doing but could not do because they had lost the power of God (Luke 9:49-50). Jesus responded by warning them against carnal sectarianism.

Without God's power in their life and ministry, the disciples became more concerned with getting revenge on those who wronged them than reaching out to others with the gospel (Luke 9:51-56). Again, Jesus had to deal with this consequence of their spiritual problem by reminding them of the fundamental purpose of His ministry, to reach out to others offering salvation. As a result of their loss of spiritual power and the attitudes which had developed within the disciples, they became less effective in ministry. Because Jesus still had an important mission to fulfill, He began collecting and commissioning new followers to accomplish His work. Seventy disciples were recruited and sent out in ministry, but none of the twelve were apparently involved in any sphere of ministry until they recognized their need and asked Jesus to teach them to pray (Luke 11:1). One of the ways Jesus brought the disciples to a place of recognizing their need was to allow them to see others involved in effective ministry.

I.   Three Examples of Effective Ministry (Luke 10:1-42)

The first example of effective ministry witnessed by the disciples was that of seventy young disciples sent out by Jesus. This event is recorded only by Luke. These seventy were sent out in pairs to minister in cities Jesus planned to visit in the remaining twenty weeks of His ministry. This suggests Jesus may have increased His itinerant teaching ministry during the final months of His ministry rather than easing off. Jesus' motivation for sending out these seventy disciples was the same He had when He sent out the twelve. "The harvest truly is great, but the laborers are few," He explained. "Therefore pray the Lord of the harvest to send out laborers into His harvest" (Luke 10:2). Jesus' identification of these disciples as "lambs among wolves" (Luke 10:3) suggests these disciples were younger or less experienced than the twelve who were addressed as more mature sheep. Jesus' instructions to these disciples did not differ substantially from those given earlier to the twelve. There is no specific reference to their being able to cast out demons although they appear to have had some influence over demons during their ministry tour (Luke 10:17) and received this power after they returned (Luke 10:19).

Why did Jesus choose seventy disciples for this ministry? Some Bible teachers see a relationship between Jesus sending twelve disciples then seventy disciples, and Moses recognizing the leaders of the twelve tribes then appointing seventy elders over Israel. Another answer to this question may be related to the Jewish practice of viewing the number seventy in terms of completeness. Seventy nations were thought to represent the whole world (cf. Gen. 10), seventy elders represented the entire nation, and seventy translators translated the entire Hebrew Bible (LXX). Perhaps the real reason was related to the size of the task involved and the availability of suitable candidates for ministry. In His instructions to these disciples, Jesus reminded them "the laborer is worthy of his wages" (Luke 10:7). Later, the apostle Paul quoted these exact words along with a quote from Deuteronomy 25:4 as scriptural authority for paying the pastor (cf. 1 Tim. 5:18). Paul's use of this verse in this way suggests the gospel of Luke had not only been written and circulated among the churches by that time, it was recognized as authoritative as Deuteronomy which was considered one of the most important books of the Old Testament. Many Bible teachers point to this as an argument for the inspiration of the New Testament.

Jesus told these disciples to wipe the dust of a city off them as they left if that city did not receive them. He added, "But I say to you that it will be more tolerable in that Day for Sodom than for that city" (Luke 10:12). Jesus often compared the judgment facing those who rejected Him during His public ministry with that suffered by those judged in the Old Testament. The underlying principle governing these comments is that those who have more spiritual light also have more moral responsibility to respond. Failure to do so means they will face greater consequences in terms of a greater judgment. When these disciples returned from their ministry tour, they rejoiced in that even the demons were subject to them through their use of the name of Jesus (Luke 10:17). Jesus confirmed this conclusion noting "I saw Satan fall like lightning from heaven" (Luke 10:18). The Greek verb *etheoroun* translated "saw" is in the imperfect tense and may be expressed "I was seeing with interest." Different Bible teachers note three times when Jesus may have been seeing Satan fall. First, He may have witnessed Satan's fall during his original rebellion in heaven (Isa. 14:12-14). Second, Jesus may have seen him fall as these disciples ministered with spiritual power. Third, He may have been looking forward to the ultimate fall of Satan at the end of the kingdom age (Rev. 20:1-3, 7-10).

WHEN DID SATAN FALL?

Past – during his rebellion in heaven
Present – when Christians minister with spiritual power
Future – at the end of the kingdom age

While Jesus could appreciate these disciples rejoicing over their influence over evil spirits, they had something even greater to rejoice in. "Nevertheless do not rejoice in this, that the spirits are subject to you, but rather rejoice because your names are written in heaven" (Luke 10:20). The greatest source of joy in the Christian life is not related to ministry success but rather is found the knowledge of personal salvation.

The second example of effective ministry witnessed by the disciples was related by Jesus in a story (Luke 10:25-37). A certain lawyer confronted Jesus hoping to test Him and asked, "Teacher, what shall I do to inherit eternal life?" (Luke 10:25). When Jesus turned the question back to the lawyer, this man responded by reciting the two foundational principles of the law, that of loving God and loving one's neighbor. Jesus agreed with the man's response and urged him to follow those principles. Jesus was not teaching one could earn his way into heaven but recognized that loving God would involve trusting Him for salvation. Attempting to justify himself, the lawyer asked, "And who is my neighbor?" (Luke 10:29). The law was not clear in its definition of what made one a neighbor. It could be interpreted in a rather narrow sense (cf. Lev. 19:18), which is what tended to be the case among the Jews of that day. Jesus broadened that view of a neighbor by relating a story which has become one of His best known and loved by generations of Christians.

Some Bible teachers believe the account of the Good Samaritan is not a parable in the usual sense of the word but rather an account of a real event. Supporting this view is the unusual attention to detail given in the account (i.e., a certain man, a certain priest, a certain Samaritan, etc.) and the fact this story is not expressly identified as a parable in Scripture. Even those who view this account as a parable agree the details given in the story are so accurate it is likely to have been the way it was if these events had really happened.

The story is set on the road to Jericho. This road was known as a place where robbers often attacked people. It was a winding road with large rocks by the side of the road making it an ideal place for them to hide and wait for unsuspecting travelers. Because of this, many travelers journeyed along this road in groups and at all costs tried to avoid using it at night. Sometimes, however, this was not possible and people had to chance making the journey alone. That appears to have been the case with the four individuals involved in this account.

In this story, a man is overcome by thieves and beaten and robbed. After the thieves leave, both a priest and a Levite pass the man on the road and do nothing to help him. Because a priest had to serve in the temple only one month every two years, many lived in Jericho which was something of a resort community. Both the priest and Levite involved in this story may have been returning home from their term of ministry in the temple.

The one who did help turned out to be a Samaritan. The rivalry between the Jews and the Samaritans was so strong that they normally had no dealings with each other. It is noteworthy that the man for whose benefit the story was being told could not bring himself to even say the word Samaritan when Jesus asked him to identify the man who was neighborly (cf. Luke 10:37). This Samaritan used his own provisions to provide first-aid treatment for the man who was beaten, and then paid for his extended care. In the story, Jesus demonstrated what it means to be a neighbor and urged His listeners to follow the example of the Samaritan.

The third example of ministry witnessed by the disciples was that of Martha of Bethany. Martha welcomed Jesus into her home, but then became "distracted with much serving" (Luke 10:40). In her frustration, she became upset with her sister who had joined others listening to Jesus teach. When she asked Jesus to intervene and get Mary to help her, Jesus advised her to concentrate on preparing just one dish for the meal. He noted, "But one thing is needed, and Mary has chosen that good part, which will not be taken away from her" (Luke 10:42). This is one of several biblical expressions urging single-mindedness.

SINGLE-MINDEDNESS

But one thing is needed (Luke 10:42)
You still lack one thing (Luke 18:22)
But one thing I do (Phil. 3:13)
Do not forget this one thing (2 Peter 3:8)
I will also ask you one thing (Luke 20:3)

II. Three Essentials of Effective Prayer (Luke 11:1-13)

Jesus' comment "one thing is needed" (Luke 10:42) could be applied to the disciples concerning the matter of prayer as easily as it could be applied in the original context. After witnessing Jesus praying, the disciples asked Him to teach them to pray. Jesus did so, emphasizing three essentials of effective prayer. He urged His disciples to pray as a disciple using the disciple's prayer He had taught them earlier (Luke 11:2-4; cf. Matt. 6:9-13), as a friend in need approaching another friend who can help (Luke 11:5), and as the child of their heavenly Father knowing He would respond to their request as a loving father responds to his child (Luke 11:13). These three essential attitudes summarize Jesus' teaching on prayer on this occasion and are the basis for a number of important principles of prayer.

THREE ESSENTIALS OF EFFECTIVE PRAYER

Pray as a Disciple
Pray as a Friend
Pray as a Child

Jesus began His instructions on prayer by reciting part of the model prayer He had earlier given His disciples (cf. Matt. 6:9-13). Because He begins with the words, "When you pray, say" (Luke 11:2), some Bible teachers believe this justifies the practice of reciting these very words in prayer. While this may be an acceptable form of prayer, Jesus originally meant this prayer as a model or pattern of developing his petitions to God. A disciple may recite the Lord's prayer as he prays, but he will also use it as a pattern for his prayer life and express his desires to God in his own words.

Effective prayer begins when one comes to God on favorable terms. Jesus urged His disciples to understand God as their Father as they pray. The Greek word *pater* translated Father was the favorite name of God used by Jesus because it emphasized the warm relationship which exists between the Father and His Son. This became the Christian name for God as the early church understood God's love for them as part of the family of God. In this context, Jesus also likens God to a friend who can help another in need (cf. Luke 11:5-8).

The second characteristic of effective prayer involves the recognition of God as heavenly and holy (Luke 11:2). His heavenliness emphasizes His sovereign control over all of life. Recognizing this in prayer supports one's faith in God's ability to respond. The root meaning of the word holy is "to separate." This aspect of the holy nature of God causes one to seek God's glory in prayer. When God is approached in worship, He is more willing to respond to the expressed need.

Third, the disciples needed to pray with an awareness of their own evil nature and desires. Like all people, they were evil by nature (Luke 11:13) and were inclined to practice sin as they had opportunity to do so (Luke 11:4; cf. Mark 7:21-23). Also, they could effectively pray, when they made their needs known to God. Jesus urged His disciples to pray using the first person plural, "Our Father" (Luke 11:2). In this way they could avoid a selfish attitude in prayer because what they wanted for themselves they were also asking for others.

A fifth characteristic of effective prayer is that it involves making specific requests and seeking specific answers. Jesus taught the disciples to pray for present needs (daily bread), past sin (forgiveness), and future trial (lead not . . .

deliver from). In His parables on prayer, the friend seeks three loaves of bread (Luke 11:5), a son asks for bread, a fish, and an egg (Luke 11:11-12), and the disciple is encouraged to ask specifically for the Holy Spirit (Luke 11:13).

Effective prayer is also characterized as growing in intensity in one's desire to get things from God (Luke 11:9). Asking becomes seeking, then seeking becomes knocking as one grows in his commitment to get the power of God. Each of these verbs is given in the sense one should keep on asking until it is given, keep on seeking until it be found, and keep on knocking until it be opened to them. Finally, effective prayer is made when one comes with a deep confidence that his heavenly Father is more eager to answer than the disciple is to ask (Luke 9:13). Every attribute of God demands that He hears and answers prayer. At the very heart of the life of faith is the belief that God exists and is by nature a rewarder of those who diligently seek Him (cf. Heb. 11:6).

III. Three Explanations of Eternal Principles (Luke 11:14–12:59)

Jesus continued ministering to those who came to Him with physical needs and out of that ministry found opportunities to teach the eternal principles of God. Much of the content of Jesus' teaching ministry in Judea was similar to that which He taught in Galilee.

Because of this, some critics argue the gospel writers were confused on some of the details of history in their accounts of the life of Christ. But it would be more accurate to recognize that Jesus taught the unchanging truth of God and that people in Judea needed to hear the same truth as much as those in Galilee. Even today, many itinerant Bible teachers will repeat the same sermon in two different places to two different groups of people. There is no reason to suspect Jesus did not do the same. Luke records three sermons taught by Jesus in which He addressed many of these eternal principles which had been taught in Galilee earlier. Jesus' first sermon came as a result of a familiar criticism of His ministry. During the course of His ministry, He cast a demon out of one who was mute and the man spoke (Luke 11:14). While many of the people were amazed at this evidence of God's power, some suggested the miracle was performed by the power of Beelzebub. In response to these thoughts, Jesus repeated some of the things He had taught in Galilee concerning casting out evil spirits and the evil character of that sign-seeking generation (Luke 11:17-36).

In the midst of His message, a woman in the crowd shouted out, "Blessed is the womb that bore You, and the breasts which nursed You!" (Luke 11:27). This statement is the closest thing to the worship of Mary recorded in the New Testament. Jesus responded to this woman by suggesting there is a better basis for blessedness in life.

"More than that, blessed are those who hear the word of God and keep it!" (Luke 11:28). As Jesus concluded this first sermon, a Pharisee invited Jesus to his home for a meal. The Greek word used by Luke to describe this meal suggests it was probably a breakfast (Luke 11:38). Jesus accepted this invitation but did not perform a ceremonial washing before the meal as was customary among religious teachers of that day. His host's astonishment that Jesus did not wash before eating became the basis of His second sermon (Luke 11:39-52). In the course of this message, Jesus pronounced six woes upon those gathered in that group for seven sins which were characteristic of the scribes, Pharisees, and lawyers of that day. As had occurred on numerous other occasions, Israel's religious leaders were again alienated by Jesus.

THE SEVEN SINS OF THE SCRIBES, PHARISEES, AND LAWYERS

1. They fail to clean the inside (Luke 11:39).
2. They pass by justice and the love of God (Luke 11:42).
3. They love the best seats in the synagogue (Luke 11:43).
4. They are like graves in that others are unaware of their inner man (Luke 11:44).
5. They load men with burdens too heavy to bear (Luke 11:46).
6. They honor the dead prophets whose message they refused to accept (Luke 11:47).
7. They have taken away the key of knowledge and hinder others in their pursuit of it (Luke 11:52).

Jesus' third sermon on this occasion appears to have been preached outside the home of the Pharisee to a larger gathering of people (Luke 12:1-59). During the course of this message, He spoke to different parts of His audience at different times so that this sermon appears as a series of messages. He began by warning the people of "the leaven of the Pharisees, which is hypocrisy" (Luke 12:1). He explained everything hidden would someday be revealed and urged the listeners to place their trust in God. Jesus called on them to confess Himself before men understanding His response before the angels of heaven would be similar to their response before others. Even in the face of opposition from religious and civil authorities, they should continue to trust God, "for the Holy Spirit will teach you in that very hour what you ought to say" (Luke 12:12).

Jesus was interrupted in this message by a man who wanted Him to tell his brother to share an inheritance (Luke 12:13). Jesus responded to this request by first noting He was not the judge or arbitrator in that matter and then warning the individual making that request about the danger of covetousness. To illustrate this principle, Jesus taught the parable of the rich fool. In this story, a rich man had a plentiful harvest. After considering what to do, the man decided to build larger barns to house his wealth. The man's self-centered attitude is evidenced by his abundant use of the first personal pronoun (eleven times in three sentences) and his motto for life expressed in the words "take your ease; eat, drink, and be merry" (Luke 12:19). God's attitude toward this man was to view him as a fool and hold him immediately accountable for his actions.

Then Jesus turned His attention to His own disciples (Luke 12:22). His message to them emphasized their need to have faith in God and be faithful in service. Drawing on a number of illustrations from nature, Jesus stressed His disciples could trust God to provide for them if they first applied principles of biblical stewardship in their lives. Then He told them a series of parables stressing the need to be faithful in serving God and watching for the return of Christ. He again reminded His disciples that division within homes would be one of the consequences of His ministry.

Then turning to the crowd, Jesus urged them to be discerning (Luke 12:54). When the people saw clouds blowing in from the west, they knew it would rain because the sea was to the west. When clouds blew in from the south, they knew it would be a hot dry day because the desert was to the south. How much better it would have been if they had discerned the times as well as they discerned weather patterns and been prepared for the coming of the Messiah.

Jesus concluded this third message with a practical reminder to attempt to settle their disputes out of court. "When you go with your adversary to the magistrate, make every effort along the way to settle with him, lest he drag you to the judge, the judge deliver you to the officer, and the officer throw you into prison" (Luke 12:58). Once the sentence was begun, it would be too late to negotiate a settlement. This was only one of several occasions when Jesus spoke to the very practical matter of resolving differences.

Conclusion

Just as the original disciples of Jesus needed to learn these important lessons concerning spiritual power and effectiveness in ministry, Christians today also need to learn these important lessons. It is possible to become so busy in one's service for God that important things like prayer are allowed to slip. When Christians begin to sense their effectiveness in ministry is beginning to wane, one of the first places they should look is within themselves. Only when Christians have a healthy prayer life can they be effectively used of God in ministry in the lives of other people.

CHAPTER 20

JESUS OF NAZARETH:
HIS MINISTRY IN PEREA

Luke 13:1–17:10; John 10:22-42

lthough Jesus avoided any kind of political liberation of Palestine, the Jews at that time generally expected that the Messiah would free them from the power of Rome. As a result, many incidents occurred involving a group of Jews led by different self-proclaimed messiahs who revolted against Rome. These revolts never secured the widespread involvement of the people although most Jews were probably sympathetic to their cause. Also, these revolts tended to be more likely to occur during significant religious celebrations in the Hebrew calendar such as Passover or the Feast of Dedication. The Romans tended to look at these revolts as minor irritations although they realized they had the potential of growing into civil war if not dealt with swiftly. When an uprising began, a group of soldiers would be assigned to bring it to an end as quickly and efficiently as possible. This usually involved a battle in which the leaders of the revolt were either killed or captured and crucified. When the leaders of the revolt were killed, their followers scattered and the threat to Roman security came to an end (cf. Acts 5:36-37). During a feast that past year, there appears to have been a small revolt of Galileans in the temple area. This revolt was apparently sparked by Pilate's decision to use funds from the temple treasury to repair the lower aqueduct bringing water into the city. To bring an end to this rebellion, Pilate ordered his troops into the temple disguised as pilgrims. At a given signal, these troops attacked the rebels, killing some. Some of those who witnessed this event reported to Jesus "about the Galileans whose blood Pilate had mingled with their sacrifices" (Luke 13:1).

Those who reported the incident to Jesus may have hoped He would speak out against Pilate, but instead He used the event as an opportunity to stress the need for repentance. Recently, a tower in Siloam had collapsed, probably because of a weak foundation, killing eighteen people. Jesus pointed out that neither the martyrs in Jerusalem nor the victims in Siloam were any worse than ordinary people, "but," He added, "unless you repent you will all likewise perish" (Luke 13:5).

Jesus then told a parable about a barren fig tree (Luke 13:6-9). A man planted a fig tree, but for three years running, it did not produce figs. Although the man wanted to uproot the tree right away, the keeper of his vineyard convinced the owner to give the tree one more chance. The gardener would dig around the roots and fertilize the tree hoping to stimulate the tree to bear fruit. If it failed to do so the fourth year, they agreed it could then be cut down. Some Bible teachers see this parable as Israel's last warning from Jesus to repent. He had been involved in public ministry for three years but realized little fruit. During His final year of ministry, He intensified His public ministry, particularly in the southern parts which had been most resistant to His teaching. He would soon return to Jerusalem for His final Passover, then determine the fate of the nation. It is interesting to note one of the first things He would do during His final week in Jerusalem was to curse a barren fig tree (cf. Mark 11:14).

I.   Jesus in the Face of Opposition   (Luke 13:10-35; John 10:22-42)

While teaching in one of the synagogues on a Sabbath, Jesus healed a woman and again drew upon Himself the anger of the religious leaders. This woman is described as having "a spirit of infirmity" which some Bible teachers interpret to refer to a demon which caused a physical disease (Luke 13:11). This disease affected the woman's posture to the extent she could not straighten herself or get up without assistance. When Jesus said, "Woman, you are loosed from your infirmity" (Luke 13:12), and laid His hands on her, she was instantaneously healed. Although she responded to this miracle by glorifying God, the ruler of the synagogue was filled with indignation. This ruler apparently felt the people who sought healing on the Sabbath were responsible for such miracles and claimed them rather than Jesus. "There are six days on which men ought to work; therefore come and be healed on them, and not on the Sabbath day," he told the crowd (Luke 13:14). While his remarks may have sounded pious to others, Jesus saw them as an expression of hypocrisy. Jesus noted it was acceptable to take one's ox or donkey from the stall to be watered on the Sabbath and argued that "a daughter of Abraham, whom Satan has bound – think of it – for eighteen years" should be released from that bondage on the Sabbath (Luke 13:16). Although Luke only records the verbal expression of the ruler of the synagogue, apparently many others who were present opposed Jesus' practice of healing on the Sabbath. They could not refute the logic of Jesus' argument and were embarrassed. Others however rejoiced in His miracles. Jesus taught them the parables of the Mustard Seed (Luke 13:18-19) and the Leaven (Luke 13:20-21). Jesus visited the city of Jerusalem on at least one occasion between the feast of Tabernacles and His final Passover in the city. The feast of Dedication (Hanukkah) is an eight day celebration of lights observed annually in December and is the only feast of the Jews mentioned in the New Testament which does not have biblical roots. This feast was instituted in 165 B.C. to commemorate the rededication of the temple. The temple was defiled under Antiochus Epiphanies when pigs were sacrificed on the altar (Dec. 25, 168 B.C.). The Jews responded by building a new altar and rededicating the temple. One of the principle features of this feast was the lighting of lights both in the temple and in individual homes.

As Jesus walked in Solomon's porch about the time of this feast, the

Jewish leaders recognized and confronted Him (John 10:24). Perhaps because the feast they were observing commemorated an aspect of the Maccabean revolt, they asked Him directly if He were the Messiah. Jesus had on many occasions previously answered that question, but His view of the Messiah differed from theirs. "I told you, and you do not believe," He answered (John 10:25). He explained the reason they did not believe was because they were not His sheep. He had made this claim three to four months previously following the feast of Tabernacles. "My sheep hear My voice, and I know them, and they follow Me," He explained (John 10:27). As He explained this principle, He again referred to God as His Father. This was the name most often used by Jesus to describe God, but in calling God "My Father," He was implying He also was God. The Jewish leaders recognized this and again gathered stones to throw at Him (John 10:31). This time Jesus challenged their actions in an unusual way. When the Jewish leaders accused Him of blasphemy, "because You, being a Man, make Yourself God" (John 10:33), Jesus quoted a psalm which claimed "You are gods" (John 10:34; cf. Psalm 82:6). This statement was probably based on Exodus 21:6 where the judges of Israel are called *elohim* (gods) because they are the representatives of *Elohim* (God). Using a common rabbinical approach to interpreting the text, Jesus argued He could not be accused of blasphemy when the Scriptures call the leaders of Israel "gods." While His argument prevented His stoning, it did not appease the Jewish leaders or change their minds about Him. They tried to arrest Him, but once again "He escaped out of their hand" (John 10:39).

Jesus left Jerusalem and returned to the place where John had begun his ministry across the Jordan River. As He ministered among those who were the first to respond to John's preaching, the people immediately recognized a significant difference in the ministry styles between Jesus and the Jews. The people responded in faith to Jesus. "John performed no sign, but all the things that John spoke about this Man were true," they reasoned (John 10:41). This statement refutes two extreme positions regarding the existence of miracles. First, those who deny the existence of miracles and argue they are little more than parts of a colorful legend have difficulty explaining why there were no miracles ascribed to one of the most significant men in the New Testament. Second, those who claim miracles are a necessary evidence of the power of God at work in a person's ministry have difficulty explaining how John's ministry could be so effectively used by God without the presence of signs. Christians today need to be careful of those advocating both extremes.

The religious leaders of the Jews were not the only ones committed to destroying Jesus at this time. As He was teaching one day, a Pharisee apparently concerned for Jesus' welfare warned Him, "Get out and depart from here, for Herod wants to kill You" (Luke 13:31). Jesus told the Pharisee to tell Herod he could not thwart Him from His appointed ministry. Jesus determined to continue doing what God had called Him to do without Herod's interference "for it cannot be that a prophet should perish outside Jerusalem" (Luke 13:33).

As Jesus contemplated His coming death in Jerusalem, He felt sorry, not for Himself, but for the city which had rejected His constant offers of salvation. As a hen gathers her chicks to protect them, Jesus wanted to protect the city, but they were not willing to accept Him (Luke 13:34). As a result, Jerusalem would not have their Messiah until He came in power and glory.

II. Jesus and His Attitude Toward Sinners   (Luke 14:1–15:32)

Even among those leaders who remained hospitable to Jesus, there was a reluctance to accept Him fully. When He was invited to eat with the Pharisees, He noted and commented upon their tendency to always seek the best places. He suggested they should rather take a lower place and then allow their host to invite them to a higher place if appropriate. He also suggested they use their dinner parties as opportunities to minister to the poor and handicapped rather than as a tool to climb the social ladder. During a meal with the Pharisees Jesus told the parable of the Great Supper. When a man prepared a banquet and invited his friends, they all gave excuses and refused to come. Some said they could not come because of their possessions (a field), others because of employment (the purchase of oxen), and others for family reasons (a new wife). Refusing an invitation to dinner was considered an insult in the Middle East and could lead to a declaration of war in some Arab societies even today. In his anger, the man who had prepared the feast for his friends sent his servants to go into the streets and then into the highways and hedges and compel anyone they could find to come to the dinner. Because of their refusal to come when first invited, the original guests were not permitted to participate. Jesus then warned the crowd to count the cost involved before becoming one of His disciples. Just as a builder will do cost estimates before beginning a building and a ruler will use diplomacy to prevent a battle he does not think he can win, so individuals should consider the cost of both following and not following Jesus before they make their decision.

As Jesus taught the crowd, a growing number of tax collectors and obvious sinners began to gather around Him. The scribes and Pharisees murmured, "This man receives sinners and eats with them" (Luke 15:2). In essence they were accusing Jesus of compromise because He associated with sinners. Although these men were right in their observation (Jesus spent time with sinners), they were wrong in their attitude (Jesus attempted to win them). Jesus told three parables to emphasize the rejoicing which takes place in heaven when sinners repent.

In the first story, a shepherd notices one of his sheep is missing and leaves ninety-nine sheep that are safe to find the one that is lost (Luke 15:4-7). In the second story, a woman who has lost one coin out of her wedding garland cleans her house until it is found (Luke 15:8-10). In the third story, a man with a rebellious son eagerly looks for his return home (Luke 15:11-32). Each of these stories mention something valuable which was lost and the recovery of that lost article as a cause for celebration. Because these parables were taught to stress heaven's rejoicing over repentant sinners, some Bible teachers believe Jesus' choice of "lost things" symbolically represents three kinds of sinners.

> **THREE KINDS OF SINNERS IN LUKE 15**
> *Sheep* – The sinner that strays
> *Coin* – The sinner that falls
> *Son* – The sinner that rebels

III. Jesus and His Teaching about Stewardship (Luke 16:1–17:10)

One of the most unusual stories Jesus ever told was directed to His disciples. In this story, a rich man had a steward who was found to be wasting the man's resources. When the rich man learned of the problem, he confronted the steward, gave him his notice of termination, and called for an accounting of the books. The steward realized the easy lifestyle as a manager would soon be lost, so he contacted the rich man's creditors and agreed to settle outstanding accounts at reduced amounts provided payment be made immediately. Although the rich man lost potential income through his steward's action, the owner commended the steward for his swift action and shrewdness. The steward was out of a job, but he had a number of businessmen who owed him favors and he would probably be able to maintain his lifestyle. When Jesus applied the parable, He said, "make friends for yourselves by unrighteous mammon, that when you fail, they may receive you into an everlasting home" (Luke 16:9).

This parable may have been directed specifically at Judas Iscariot who had dipped into the funds to purchase a field just outside of Jerusalem (Acts 1:18-19). Jesus may have been warning Judas he had been found out even though none of the other disciples suspected anything at that time. His advice to Judas was to correct the error before it became public knowledge and he was branded as a thief. In its broader application, Jesus may have told this parable to urge people to use their financial resources to further the work of God so that at the end of their lives they might be received into everlasting homes by those who benefitted from their stewardship of money on earth. Jesus taught much about stewardship during His ministry and on this occasion also stressed two common themes relating to the stewardship of one's financial resources. First, Jesus noted, "He who is faithful in what is least is faithful also in much" (Luke 16:10). This principle states that the way a person uses a small amount of money is reflective of the way he or she will use larger resources. Second, Jesus taught, "No servant can serve two masters" (Luke 16:13). This principle states there can only be one primary interest in the life of the believer. Jesus taught that it is impossible for a man to serve both God and money without experiencing dysfunction.

When the Pharisees overheard Jesus' teaching on stewardship, "they derided Him" (Luke 16:14). They were offended by His teaching because they loved money. Jesus responded to the Pharisees' opposition by warning them, "You are those who justify yourselves before men" (Luke 16:15). He illustrated this truth by recounting the experience of a rich man and a beggar named Lazarus. Many Bible teachers view the account of the rich man and Lazarus as a true story rather than a parable. One of the reasons for this belief is that no one was ever named in this parable. Sometimes this story is called the story of Dives and Lazarus. The name *Dives* is Latin and means "rich man." This name was probably ascribed originally as a Latin adjective and became the traditional name of this particular rich man. A Greek manuscript discovered in this century suggests the man's real name was Neues, but most New Testament manuscripts do not include the rich man's name.

In the account of the life and afterlife of these men, the rich man lived well in life, but found himself in "the place of torments" when he died. Lazarus, who lived poorly as he begged at the rich man's gate, enjoyed fellowship with Abraham in paradise after death. When the rich man realized his own hopeless estate, he pleaded with Abraham to send Lazarus back from the dead to warn his brothers who were doomed to the same fate. Abraham responded, "If they do not hear Moses and the prophets, neither will they be persuaded though one rise from the dead" (Luke 16:31). Because of the similarity in names between this beggar and Jesus' friend whom He brought back to life, some believe these were the same people. The reference to one rising from the dead is probably better applied to the Lord Himself. In repeating Abraham's words to the rich man, Jesus warned the Pharisees that their refusal to accept Him on the basis of Moses' prophecy meant the Pharisees would reject Him even after Jesus confirmed this message by rising from the dead. Having dealt with the Pharisees, Jesus again turned His attention to His disciples. "It is impossible that no offenses should come," He warned, "but woe to him through whom they do come!" (Luke 17:1). Jesus did not want the inevitability of coming offenses to be used by His disciples to justify their own sin, nor did He want these offenses to destroy relationships which had developed within the group.

Jesus taught three important principles relating to interpersonal relationships (Luke 17:3). First, "take heed to yourselves." This means the disciple's first concern in a case of strained relationships should be to insure he is not responsible for the problem. Second, Jesus taught "if your brother sins against you, rebuke him." Sometimes offenses are caused by those who do not realize they are offensive and they need to be confronted with the problem. Third, "if he repents, forgive him." Forgiveness must be exercised in every human relationship because humans are subject to a sinful nature.

The idea of forgiveness is difficult to apply. People naturally look for excuses to justify their failure to forgive. Recognizing three of the most common excuses individuals use, Jesus noted this forgiveness was not according to the evidence of fruit in the life of the person claiming to repent (Luke 17:4), nor is it something only to be done by spiritual giants who have great faith (Luke 17:5), nor is it to be exercised only when one feels like doing it (Luke 17:6-10). Rather, good interpersonal relationships include forgiveness as a matter of moral duty. Jesus told His disciples, "So likewise you, when you have done all those things which you are commanded, say, 'We are unprofitable servants. We have done what was our duty to do'" (Luke 17:10).

Conclusion

Jesus did not let the intense opposition of political and religious leaders thwart His emphasis on ministering to others. When it became practically impossible to minister in Jerusalem, Jesus reached out to Judea and Perea. He was flexible and creative to accomplish His objective through various means. Also He understood that different kinds of sinners responded in different kinds of ways to different kinds of appeals. In this respect, Christians today can learn much from the ministry model Jesus adopted during His Perean ministry.

CHAPTER 21

LAZARUS:
HIS DEATH AND NEW LIFE

John 11:1–12:11

*J*esus continued ministering in Perea, the region on the other side of the Jordan River. As winter turned to spring, the fields on the hills that overlooked the Jordan River valley began to turn green. New life was evident in nature. Jesus received an urgent communication from a family with whom He had formed a deep relationship. Mary and Martha wrote Jesus to tell Him of a serious illness which threatened the life of their brother Lazarus. The Greek word *asthenon* translated "sick" (John 11:1) literally means "without strength." While the specific illness with which Lazarus was afflicted is not identified in Scripture, its effect was to sap his stamina and energy. In their appeal, the sisters reminded Jesus of His relationship with Lazarus noting, "Lord, behold, he whom You love is sick" (John 11:3). This family was more than just a passing acquaintance to Jesus. When visiting Jerusalem, Jesus often resided in the Bethany area. There may have been many occasions when He and His disciples were entertained in their home, these visits are not mentioned in the Gospels. This family had demonstrated their love for Jesus in a number of ways. Later, Lazarus' sister Mary would anoint Jesus' feet with fragrant oil and wipe His feet with her own hair as an expression of love and worship. When the sisters sent a messenger to Jesus, they had no doubt He would heal their brother as He had healed so many others.

The sisters had every reason to believe Jesus felt toward them as they felt toward Him. In the record of their message to Jesus, the Greek verb *phileo* is used which is the love which bonds brothers or close friends. This verb is sometimes translated "brotherly kindness" (cf. 2 Peter 1:7). Although the use of this word suggests the existence of a strong bond of love between Jesus and Lazarus, John uses the even stronger Greek verb *agapeo* which is described as sacrificial love, the real love Jesus felt toward each of the three members of this family (John 11:5). As the messenger passed the message to Jesus, he probably waited for Jesus' response. Perhaps He anticipated Jesus would immediately cross the Jordan river and make His way to Bethany. Instead, Jesus merely sent back a message of comfort and encouragement to the sisters. "This sickness is not unto death, but for the glory of God, that the Son of God may be glorified through it" (John 11:4). The disciples were no doubt aware of the special relationship that existed between Jesus and the family in Bethany and may have wondered at His response. Still, Jesus had on some other occasions healed people without being present. Perhaps He was going to do so again. As the messenger journeyed back to Bethany with the words of Jesus, he may have wondered if Lazarus was already well or would be healed because of the words Jesus had spoken. Perhaps he eagerly anticipated the response of the sisters concerning the way Jesus would heal their brother.

But Lazarus died. The name Lazarus means "God has helped," but in this battle with this illness, God apparently did not help. Instead of returning to a house of celebration as he had anticipated, the messenger arrived to find a home in deep mourning over the loss of a deeply loved brother. No doubt all the emotional responses to death were present as friends and family gathered in the home together. There was sorrow over the loss of a loved one, but this was accompanied by a wild mix of fear and anxiety, insecurity, anger, guilt, self-accusation, despair and self-punishment. "Why had God allowed this to happen to them?" was no doubt a question repeatedly asked by those in sorrow. And when the messenger arrived to communicate what must have seemed like a very strange message from Jesus, he would constantly hear from the sisters, "If Jesus had been here" (John 11:21, 32, author's translation). The touching story of the events surrounding Lazarus' death and his subsequent resurrection illustrate an important biblical principle in the experience of those whose life had been touched by Lazarus. Earlier Jesus had explained, "The thief does not come except to steal, and to kill, and to destroy. I have come that they may have life, and that they may have it more abundantly" (John 10:10). In this account, death was a thief that destroyed a family, but Jesus would give them life abundantly. Most people are incapable of having a right attitude toward the celebration of life until they are first able to deal with their wrong attitudes toward death.

I.   Attitudes Toward Death and Dying (John 11:7-44)

Two days after sending the messenger back with His message about the glory of God, Jesus announced to His disciples His intention to return to the area around Jerusalem. The disciples perhaps remembered the attempted assassination of Jesus at the last feast they celebrated in Jerusalem. "Rabbi, lately the Jews sought to stone You, and are You going there again?" they asked (John 11:8). Jesus responded, "Are there not twelve hours in the day?" (John 11:9). Some Bible teachers believe Jesus spoke these words as dawn broke that morning and was referring to the trip He and the disciples would take to Bethany. Realizing it would be a full day's journey, Jesus may have been suggesting they would be safer traveling during daylight hours. However, another practical consideration is the spiritual application to believers who are urged to "trust and obey" Jesus as they "walk in the light as He is in the light" (1 John 1:7). Jesus further explained to His disciples, "Our friend Lazarus sleeps, but I go that I may wake him up" (John 11:11). The idea that the body sleeps in death until the resurrection is a common image of death in both the Old and New Testament (cf. 2 Sam. 7:12; 1 Cor. 15:20, 51; 1 Thess. 4:13-14), but the disciples understood Jesus to be referring to the physical sleep of rest which often occurs as the body fights off sickness. The Greek verb *kekoimetai* is a perfect passive indicative meaning "he has fallen asleep and continues to sleep." If this referred to physical sleep as the disciples thought, it was a sign that Lazarus had passed the critical stage of the illness and was on the road to recovery.

The disciples were understandably confused. Why would Jesus remain where He was when He learned Lazarus was on his deathbed, then risk going to Bethany when it was apparent Lazarus was recovering? To resolve this confusion, Jesus plainly told His disciples, "Lazarus is dead" (John 11:14). He indicated that somehow His absence during Lazarus' illness was better because going to him now would strengthen their faith. Even though Lazarus was now dead, Jesus wanted the disciples to accompany Him as He went to him. Addressing his fellow disciples, Thomas said, "Let us also go, that we may die with Him" (John 11:16). Ironically, this disciple who was first to declare his willingness to follow Jesus to the cross was the last disciple to believe in the reality of the resurrection of Jesus from the grave. His attitude toward death may be described as that of doubt and despair. He appears to have been willing to follow Jesus even to death in a somewhat fatalistic way, assuming he was bound to die sooner or later. His attitude at this time, as well as later at the resurrection of Jesus, was anything but faith.

An interesting irony in the account of the raising of Lazarus concerns attitudes toward Jesus' timing. Most people apparently assumed Jesus arrived too late because Lazarus had been dead four days (cf. John 11:21, 32, 37). In reality, Jesus arrived just in time. According to the custom of the Jews, the period of mourning for the dead lasted about a month, but that period was divided into three periods. The first three days of intense mourning was a time for family members to grieve over their loss. After the fourth day, the mourning was less intense and friends of the family were expected to visit and express their condolences. By arriving on the fourth day, Jesus came to His friends on the first opportunity a friend would be expected to express condolences. Bethany was only two miles from Jerusalem and Jesus was well aware of the danger represented in that city. Also, friends of Lazarus and his sisters from Jerusalem were expected to make their way to Bethany that day. Rather than go to His friends' home and encounter people from Jerusalem, including the Jewish leaders, Jesus apparently decided to wait in the cemetery outside of Bethany. He sent a messenger to the sisters to meet with them privately. Martha was the first to receive the message that Jesus was in the area, and she characteristically responded immediately to go out to meet Him. Martha, the more "task-oriented" of the two sisters, may have been the manager of the household (cf. Luke 10:38-42). She may have coped with the loss of her brother best by throwing herself into social duties and waiting on others. Her behavior and conversation with Jesus suggest she may have viewed the death of her brother with disappointment. When Jesus told her Lazarus would live again, she thought He was speaking of a general resurrection from the dead and confessed her belief in that hope. Jesus corrected her limited understanding by speaking His fifth "I am" statement, "I am the resurrection and the life. He who believes in Me, though he may die, he shall live. And whoever lives and believes in Me shall never die" (John 11:25-26). In response to this revelation of Himself to Martha, she confessed, "I believe that You are the Christ, the Son of God, who is to come into the world" (John 11:27). Jesus helped three people face their different attitudes toward death in different ways. He realized that people have different personalities and each respond to the same thing in different ways. He also knew there were ways to help certain types of people that would not work as well with others. Therefore, He led despairing and doubting Thomas into a confrontation with events that were the cause of his despair. Jesus talked with disappointed Martha in an effort to strengthen her faith in God. When He later dealt with a discouraged Mary, Jesus ministered to her through His presence, because He realized His words would not have the impact with her in her condition that they might have with others.

HOW JESUS HELPED THREE HURTING PEOPLE

Despair – He led him to face the cause of despair.
Disappointment – He taught her to strengthen her faith.
Discouragement – He ministered through His encouraging presence.

As noted above, Mary responded to her brother's death with discouragement. The description of Mary in Scripture suggests she was the idealist in the family and tended to be more naturally expressive and emotional. Apparently she had turned her grief inward and cut herself off from others. When Martha went out to meet Jesus, Mary remained in the house. Later, when Martha told Mary Jesus was looking for her, she hurried out of the house toward Jesus in such a way as others in the house thought she was going to the tomb to mourn. When she did see Jesus, she broke down completely weeping uncontrollably. Jesus Himself was affected emotionally by what He witnessed. He experienced His disciples' doubt and the sisters' emotional collapse. All about were the paid professional mourners, perhaps wailing words without meaning. "He groaned in the spirit and was troubled" (John 11:33). The Greek verbs used to describe Jesus in this verse suggest He was deeply agitated, disturbed, and probably angered at the hypocritical mourning of those who accompanied Mary. When Jesus came to Lazarus' tomb, He too wept, but His crying differed from that of others. The Greek verb *edakrusen* refers to quietly weeping or shedding a tear without crying audibly. This shortest verse in the Bible has been paraphrased, "Tears came to Jesus' eyes" (John 11:35, Living Bible). When others saw Jesus weep, they knew His tears were a genuine expression of His deep love for Lazarus. "See how He loved him!" they exclaimed (John 11:36). While others viewed death in exclusively negative terms, it is clear from Jesus' actions on this and other occasions that He viewed death in terms of deliverance. It has been noted Jesus never encountered a dead body that remained dead. His own death would be the means by which believers would be delivered from the bondage of sin. Later, the apostles would teach the importance of death to self as a key to victorious Christian living (cf. Gal. 2:20; Rom. 6).

WHAT BROUGHT TEARS TO JESUS' EYES?

His love for Lazarus (John 11:3)
His compassion for Mary in sorrow (John 11:32-33)
The callousness of the Jews (John 11:33, 37)
His disciples' ignorance concerning His power (John 11:16, 40)
The unbelief of some Jews present (John 11:45)
The indecision of some who professed faith (John 11:46)

Jesus asked to be brought to Lazarus' tomb. When He got there, He made an unusual request. "Take away the stone," He said (John 11:39). It was customary to bury people in caves and place a large stone at the entrance to seal the tomb. When Jesus asked that the stone be removed, Martha immediately objected. Jews widely believed that the soul of an individual hovered around the body of the deceased for three days before departing. After three days, they thought, the spirit of that person made a final decision to never again reenter that body. When that took place, the body would begin to rapidly decompose. According to this view, it was now impossible to reunite the body and soul of the deceased. Opening the grave would only release the offensive odor of the decaying body. Under normal circumstances, there would be nothing unusual about Martha's reluctance to have the tomb reopened. Jesus responded by reminding Martha of the message He had sent them earlier by messenger. "Did I not say to you that if you would believe you would see the glory of God?" (John 11:40). While it is not clear Martha understood the meaning of that glory, she apparently withdrew her objection and allowed the grave to be reopened. When this was done, Jesus prayed. His brief prayer of thanksgiving given on this occasion illustrates three characteristics of "the prayer of faith" (John 11:41-42).

THE PRAYER OF FAITH

Grows out of communion with God.
Effects faith in others who witness it.
Accomplishes exactly what it prays for.

Jesus called out, "'Lazarus, come forth!' And he who had died came out bound hand and foot with graveclothes, and his face was wrapped with a cloth" (John 11:43-44). Some Bible teachers believe Jesus called Lazarus by name because if He had not, all the dead in that cemetery may have come back to life. Those who had gathered by the tomb to mourn one who had died, now witnessed one who was alive again. Just Lazarus' death reflected various attitudes toward death and dying, so Lazarus' life would reflect various attitudes toward life and living.

II.   Attitudes Toward Life and Living (John 11:44–12:11)

The first attitude toward life and living expressed at the resurrection of Lazarus was that of liberty. "Loose him, and let him go," Jesus told those gathered on that occasion (John 11:44). Lazarus had been buried in grave clothes that bound him. Lazarus needed to be liberated from those grave clothes to completely enjoy his new life. Some Bible teachers note a parallel between the physical grave clothes which bound Lazarus and the struggles of a Christian defeated by the sinful habits developed before he became a Christian. In both cases, the person involved is hindered in his new life until the grave clothes are dealt with.

HINDERED BY GRAVE CLOTHES

bound hands – hindered service
bound feet – hindered walk
face cloth – hindered vision

Faith was the second attitude toward life and living expressed at the resurrection of Lazarus. Many of those who came to mourn with Mary left the grave that day believing in Jesus (John 11:45). This was the ultimate objective of every miracle in Jesus' life and ministry.

Indecisiveness was another attitude toward life and living expressed at the resurrection of Lazarus. Some who saw what happened, quickly ran to the Pharisees to report what had happened. Apparently they rejoiced in the benefits of Jesus' miracles, but they were not prepared to do so at the risk of alienating the religious leaders who were opposed to Jesus. They wanted the best of both worlds and were unable to decide which was best for them.

Some who heard of this resurrection expressed their own insecurity and were confused over how to respond. This became evident at an informal meeting of the Sanhedren. They simply did not know what to do. It was obvious that Jesus was an authentic miracle worker and that these miracles contributed to His broad public appeal. They were concerned that if His popularity grew much more, the Romans would be alarmed at the potential threat to their security and remove the Jewish leaders from their positions of influence. Caiaphas, the high priest had a pragmatic and calloused view of the situation and suggested "that one man should die for the people, and not that the whole nation should perish" (John 11:50). Caiaphas probably made the statement intending to mean that if Jesus' death were arranged, the Jewish nation would be saved from the consequences of Roman military action, but God used the statement of the high priest to communicate a prophetic statement concerning the substitutionary nature of Jesus' death (John 11:51-52). The Jewish leaders had for some time agreed Jesus should be killed, but "from that day on they plotted to put Him to death" (John 11:53). The response of the family most directly impacted by this resurrection was that of worship and witness. This became evident some time later at a supper prepared in honor of Jesus. Martha worshiped Jesus through her hospitality (John 12:2) while Mary worshiped Him through the sacrificial gift of the fragrant oil of spikenard (John 12:3). As for Lazarus, his very presence became such a powerful witness that many Jews began to believe in Jesus (John 12:11).

Conclusion

The account of Lazarus' resurrection is a vivid picture of the spiritual experience of every believer. The apostle Paul later explained, "even when we were dead in trespasses, (God) made us alive together with Christ" (Eph. 2:5). But Lazarus' resurrection was only the beginning of his new life of service for Christ. Once he was released from the grave clothes that bound him, he became an effective witness of the power of Jesus to meet needs in the lives of those in his sphere of influence. So Paul also reminded the Ephesians, "For we are His workmanship, created in Christ Jesus for good works, which God prepared beforehand that we should walk in them" (Eph. 2:10).

CHAPTER 22

JESUS OF NAZARETH:
HIS FINAL JOURNEY TO JERUSALEM

Matthew 19:1–20:34; Mark 1:1-52; Luke 17:11–19:28

The Jerusalem area posed a danger to Jesus even before He raised Lazarus from the dead, so it is not surprising that He left Bethany shortly after the miracle. Although He was aware He would die in Jerusalem in only a matter of months, He was concerned about God's timing in His life and knew His hour had not yet come (cf. John 2:4; 12:23). When Caiaphas agreed Jesus would have to die, the Sanhedrin began to make more definite plans to have Him executed. "Therefore Jesus no longer walked openly among the Jews, but went from there into the country near the wilderness, to a city called Ephraim, and there remained with His disciples" (John 11:54). Ephraim was located about five miles northeast of Bethel in what was known in earlier days as the "hill country." Situated high in the mountains, it was possible to see as far away as the Dead Sea from the city gate, so it was unlikely the Jewish leaders could send troops to arrest Jesus in this city because they would be spotted long before they arrived. Jesus apparently determined to spend some time here with His disciples before traveling north through Samaria to join friends in Galilee as they made their way·to Jerusalem for Passover. Abraham's ancient prophecy would be fulfilled at that Passover: "God will provide for Himself the lamb for a burnt offering" (Gen. 22:8).

After a brief stay in Ephraim, Jesus began His final journey to Jerusalem. The most direct route to that city was south, but Jesus still had much to do before He would offer Himself for the sins of the world. In each of the regions He visited on His way to Jerusalem, He found people in need and took time to address their concerns and alleviate their suffering. His journey took Him through Samaria into Galilee, then east over the Jordan to Perea. Jesus passed through the city of Jericho, apparently for the first and last time during His years of public ministry. Even in that city which had long ago been cursed by Joshua (Josh. 6:26) and which was home to so many opposed to Jesus, a couple of individuals found in Jesus a concern for those who longed to meet Him.

I. His Final Days of Ministry in Samaria (Luke 17:11-19)

Before getting to Jericho, Jesus passed through Samaria, and turned into a village probably located very near the border of Samaria and Galilee. Bible teachers are not agreed on the exact location of this village and are divided on whether the village was located in Samaria or Galilee. Some believe the village was in Galilee because it is believed nine of the ten lepers were Jewish. But others claim a Samaritan likely would not be welcomed in the company of nine Jews. Although the one leper who returned is identified as a Samaritan and foreigner, the ethnic identity of the other nine is not specifically identified in the text. They too may have been Samaritans. From a distance, ten men afflicted with leprosy called out to Jesus for mercy. Because there was no known treatment for leprosy, lepers were isolated from others in society. Lepers were required to warn people who were approaching by crying out "unclean, unclean." When these lepers realized Jesus was entering the city, they cried out, "Jesus, Master, have mercy on us" (Luke 17:13). They had no doubt heard of other lepers who had been healed by Jesus and hoped for similar treatment. Jesus responded by telling them, "Go, show yourselves to the priests" (Luke 17:14). According to both Jewish and Samaritan law, a leper could not return to society after being diagnosed a leper until he was reexamined by the priest and declared healed of the disease (cf. Lev. 14:3). Jesus did not heal these lepers right away, but rather called upon them to exercise their faith by going to the priest to be examined. It was only as they made their way to the priest that they actually experienced a healing (Luke 17:14).

As these ten men realized what had happened, they were no doubt excited about being able to return to their families and friends. The examination period for a cleansed leper lasted eight days (Lev. 14:1-32). This may have motivated the men to run even faster toward the nearest priest so as not to spend any longer than necessary away from their homes. One of the ten however determined to first turn back to Jesus to express his gratitude to God for what had happened in his life. He returned "and with a loud voice glorified God, and fell down on his face at His feet, giving Him thanks" (Luke 17:15-16). The man who returned was a Samaritan. Jesus noted the return of only one of the ten lepers who were healed and asked three questions. First, He asked, "Were there not ten cleansed?" (Luke 17:17). In asking this question, Jesus was identifying the state of those who obtain a blessing from God. His second question, "Where are the nine?" This question pointed out those who did not pause to thank Him for it. His third question, "Were there not any found who returned to give glory to God except this foreigner?" (Luke 17:18) identified the state of those who worship God as an expression of what God has done for them. While the other nine would spend the next eight days being examined by the priest, Jesus apparently exempted this Samaritan from that regulation when He told him, "Arise, go your way. Your faith has made you well" (Luke 17:19).

II. His Final Days in the Ministry in Galilee (Luke 17:20–18:14)

Jesus likely did not intend any extended ministry in Galilee as He made His way north. Most Bible teachers agree He went to Galilee primarily to join other pilgrims on their way to Jerusalem for the feast. Many of those who followed Him during His ministry tours probably would travel to Jerusalem for the feast. By traveling in their company Jesus would have added security and prevent the Jewish leaders from taking His life before He was ready to lay it down.

When Jesus came into Galilee, He was recognized by the Pharisees who asked Him when the kingdom of God would come. Some Bible teachers believe this question was asked in a sarcastic way, intended as a ridicule based on Jesus' earlier message, "Repent, for the kingdom of heaven is at hand" (cf. Matt. 4:17). Jesus knew the Pharisees needed to first recognize the King before being overly concerned about the kingdom, so He responded to the question by first stressing that aspect of the kingdom which is the rule of God in the life of the believer. He noted, "The kingdom of God does not come with observation;...For indeed, the kingdom of God is within you" (Luke 17:20-21). To His disciples who had to some degree learned the lesson about the kingdom, Jesus further explained His return to establish His kingdom. First, there would be a time "when you desire to see one of the days of the Son of Man, and you will not see it" (Luke 17:22). During these days following the ascension of Jesus, people at times would suggest the time of the kingdom had arrived. This has occurred on several occasions throughout the history of the church, even in recent years. Jesus warned, "Do not go after them or follow them. For as the lightning that flashes out of one part under heaven shines to the other part of heaven, so also the Son of Man will be in His day" (Luke 17:24). He will return to establish His kingdom, but He will do so suddenly and without warning, much like a flash of lightning. Before Jesus would come in power and in glory with His kingdom, He would first go to the Cross. "But first He must suffer many things and be rejected by this generation" (Luke 17:25).

Throughout His ministry, especially in these latter months, Jesus devoted much of His time preparing His disciples for the Cross. He wanted them to understand this was a preliminary step toward the kingdom which they desired so greatly. He also wanted them to understand that those responsible for the cross would not escape the judgment of God. Jews generally assumed that God would judge the Gentiles and bless them during the kingdom age. Jesus emphasized the Second Coming would be a time of judgment and compared it to the flood during Noah's life and to the destruction of Sodom. When the disciples asked Him when this would happen, Jesus answered, "Wherever the body is, there the eagles will be gathered together" (Luke 17:37). As camel caravans traveled through the desert, occasionally one of the animals died. When that happened, the carcass of the animal was left behind as the caravan moved on. Somehow, the birds of prey could always find the carcass. Jesus used this to illustrate that God's judgment and destruction of those who did not believe would be obvious when it happened. In light of the event surrounding the return of the Lord in power and glory, it was important during that period between the Cross and the kingdom "that men always ought to pray and not lose heart" (Luke 18:1). Jesus told two parables designed to encourage the right kind of prayer. In the first story, Jesus told of a widow who continually pestered a judge concerning her cause until he heard the case. The primary lesson of this parable was that one should express his faith in God through continual praying (Luke 18:7-8). In the second story, Jesus emphasized the character of prayer that is heard by God. He compared the prayers of a proud Pharisee and a humble tax collector. The Pharisee exalted himself in his prayer by reminding God of all the pious things he did, such as fasting and tithing. Pharisees fasted twice a week, every Monday and Thursday, in honor of the traditional view that Moses went up Sinai to receive the law on Thursday and returned with the law on Monday. The tax collector stood off in the distance feeling unworthy to even look toward heaven and simply prayed, "God be merciful to me a sinner!" (Luke 18:13). The Greek word translated "be merciful" literally means "be pleased or satisfied" and is related to the work "propitiation" which is used to describe the Cross as the payment for sin (Rom. 3:24). For this reason, the tax collector's prayer is often referred to as "the sinner's prayer." It was this second prayer which God heard. Jesus summarized this principle of prayer noting, "everyone who exalts himself will be humbled, and he who humbles himself will be exalted" (Luke 18:14).

III.   His Final Days of Ministry in Perea (Matt. 19:1–20:28; Mark 10:1-45; Luke 18:15-34)

As Jesus left Galilee to go to Perea, He was followed by the multitudes on their way to Passover and took time to heal them of their afflictions. Among those in the crowd were a group of Pharisees who determined to test Jesus. They asked Jesus, "is it lawful for a man to divorce his wife for just any reason?" (Matt. 19:3). Most likely these men asked Jesus the question to determine which of the two schools of thought Jesus adhered to concerning the question of divorce. Under the law, Moses had permitted the granting of divorce "for the nakedness of a thing" (literal translation). Among the Jews of that day, there were two views as to what that meant. The more liberal view suggested it referred to any cause including a wife putting too much salt in the soup or a husband finding a more beautiful woman whom he wished to marry. The more conservative view limited grounds for divorce to adultery. Both views agreed that the granting of a divorce freed both parties to remarry, but they were not agreed under what conditions such a divorce should be permitted. Jesus responded to the question of the Pharisees by emphasizing the ideal established by God in the beginning. He noted that marriage was established in the garden and involved three stages. First, "a man shall leave his father and mother." This leaving stage was to be followed by a cleaving stage as he "joined to his wife." Finally, there was a weaving stage as "the two shall become one flesh" (Matt. 19:5). Most Bible teachers agree that becoming one flesh refers to more than physical union and involves the weaving together of two personalities into a healthy marriage, and two separate physical bodies become one in their physical offspring.

> **Three Essentials in a Healthy Marriage**
> Leaving -> Cleaving -> Weaving

The Pharisees were disappointed that Jesus did not address the specific question as to legal grounds for divorce, so they pressed Him further. "Why then did Moses command to give a certificate of divorce, and to put her away?" they asked (Matt. 19:7). Jesus attributed Moses' actions concerning the certificate of divorce to "the hardness of your hearts" (Matt. 19:8). Although divorce was permitted under the law, it was never encouraged nor required. The ideal response to an adulterous spouse was that of Hosea who continually loved his wife and sought to bring her back to himself, but because so few people are that tenderhearted, the law provided limited grounds for divorce. Jesus explained His view regarding the grounds for divorce noting, "whoever divorces his wife, except for sexual immorality and marries another, commits adultery; and whoever marries her who is divorced commits adultery" (Matt. 19:9). When Jesus' disciples heard His position, they reflected their own low view of the family which was probably typical of others who followed a wandering Rabbi of that day, when they said, "If such is the case of the man with his wife, it is better not to marry" (Matt. 19:10). Jesus agreed marriage was not for everyone "but only for those to whom it has been given" (Matt. 19:11). He then identified three kinds of eunuchs. The first were those who were born eunuchs. Second were those who were castrated by men, usually servants in charge of harems or who worked in close proximity to the owner's wife and children. Third were those "who have made themselves eunuchs for the kingdom of heaven's sake" (Matt. 19:12). This refers to those who choose a life of singleness and celibacy in order to serve God without the distractions normally associated with married life. Just as marriage was not for everybody, neither was singleness for everyone, but "he who is able to accept it, let him accept it" (Matt. 19:12).

Marriage was not the only area of family life where Jesus and His disciples apparently differed in their outlook. Jesus also had a greater concern for children who on this occasion were considered a nuisance by His disciples. When a group of little children were brought to Jesus to be prayed for by Him, the disciples tried to discourage the mothers from bringing the children. But Jesus intervened and responded, "Let the little children come to Me, and do not forbid them; for of such is the kingdom of heaven" (Matt. 19:14). Among those who came to Jesus in Perea was a man simply known as the rich young ruler. He had been impressed with Jesus and determined to follow Him. When He came to Jesus, He asked what were the conditions to obtain eternal life. He called Jesus, "Good Teacher" (Luke 18:18). Jesus reminded the young man only God was good and only in keeping His commandments could he enter into eternal life which he sought. This man insisted he had kept all the commandments from his youth and wanted to know what he lacked. Jesus responded, "If you want to be perfect, go, sell what you have and give to the poor, and you will have treasure in heaven; and come, follow Me" (Matt. 19:21). Jesus' advice to this man is puzzling because He did not require others to give up their possessions to become His disciples. Some Bible teachers believe Jesus made this requirement here because He knew this man was committed to his possessions and would not be able to serve both God and his wealth. While this may be the case, there may be another reason why Jesus responded as He did. According to an early tradition of the church, the rich young ruler was a Levite from Cyprus named Joses but was nicknamed Barnabas by the apostles in the early days of the church. If this was the case, the young ruler's possessions were evidence he did not keep the law because a Levite was not to have a possession of land (Josh. 13:14). In his case, coming to Jesus would involve repenting of owning land. Later, when Barnabas was converted, he sold his land and gave the money to the apostles to be distributed as they saw fit (Acts 4:37). But on this occasion, the rich young ruler "went away sorrowful, for he had great possessions" (Matt. 19:22). As the rich young ruler left, Jesus said, "Assuredly, I say to you that it is hard for a rich man to enter the kingdom of heaven. And again I say to you, it is easier for a camel to go through the eye of a needle than for a rich man to enter the kingdom of God" (Matt. 19:23-24). The disciples would no doubt be confused as they considered this statement and reflected on the conversation they had just witnessed between Jesus and the rich young ruler. Jews generally believed that riches were an evidence of God's blessing. Now Jesus seemed to be indicating riches would prevent a person from experiencing the ultimate blessing of God, that of entering into the kingdom. "Who then can be saved?" they wondered. Jesus reminded His disciples, "With men this is impossible, but with God all things are possible" (Matt. 19:26).

Peter asked Jesus what he and the disciples could anticipate by way of reward for having left all to follow Jesus. Jesus promised them they would "sit on twelve thrones, judging the twelve tribes of Israel" (Matt. 19:28). He added others would also be rewarded for their sacrifice for His name's sake. "And everyone who has left houses or brothers or sisters or father or mother or wife or children or lands, for My name's sake, shall receive a hundredfold, and inherit everlasting life" (Matt. 19:29). He illustrated His liberality in rewarding His disciples by telling them a parable of a landowner who hired workers to work in his vineyard (Matt. 20:1-16). Throughout the day, he hired everyone he could find, offering to pay them for working in the vineyard. At the end of the day, the landowner paid everyone for a full day's work, even though some had only worked one hour. When those who had worked all day complained about being treated the same as those who had worked one hour, the landowner noted they were paid the amount for which they had agreed to work, and he would pay others what he chose. The emphasis of this parable was that God rewards as He sees fit and the disciples should not be concerned with how God treats them in comparison to others.

As Jesus made His way toward Jerusalem, the Cross rather than the kingdom was predominant in His mind. Privately He told His disciples, "Behold, we are going up to Jerusalem, and the Son of Man will be betrayed to the chief priests and to the scribes; and they will condemn Him to death, and deliver Him to the Gentiles to mock and to scourge and to crucify. And the third day He will rise again" (Matt. 20:18-19). It was becoming increasingly more clear to the disciples that the end of their time together as a group following Jesus was coming to a close. By this time, James' and John's mother was in some way affiliated with Jesus' ministry. Apparently Alpheus, their father, had died and she was free to follow Jesus with a group of rich ladies. She came to Jesus asking to do something for her sons. When Jesus asked what she wanted, she replied, "Grant that these two sons of mine may sit, one on Your right hand and the other on the left, in Your kingdom" (Matt. 20:21). When Jesus noted the price of death that would be required by the men to achieve that honor, they agreed they were prepared to pay it. Jesus said, "You will indeed drink My cup, and be baptized with the baptism that I am baptized with" (Matt. 20:23). Of the twelve disciples, James became the first to die as a martyr for the cause of Jesus, and John was the last to die. Both shared in the sufferings of Jesus in a unique way, but the decision as to the seating arrangement in the kingdom was left to the Father. When the other disciples heard about the request, they were angry at the two brothers. It is evident from the number of times this topic came up in their discussions that each of them had private ambitions for a special spot of recognition in the kingdom. Recognizing the problem that existed within the band of disciples, Jesus called them together to remind them of the principle of servant leadership. What He wanted His disciples to practice was exactly the way He had been living among them. "The Son of Man did not come to be served, but to serve and to give His life a ransom to many" (Matt. 20:28).

IV. His Final Day of Ministry in Jericho (Matt. 20:20-34; Mark 10:46-52; Luke 19:1-28)

Traveling from Perea to Jerusalem, Jesus crossed the Jordan River and passed through the city of Jericho. This may have been the only time Jesus came to this city during His public ministry. On this day through Jericho, three men were changed as they came into contact with Jesus. The first two men were blind men who yelled out to Jesus asking for mercy despite being told to be quiet by the crowd gathered around Jesus. In recounting this story, Mark and Luke only identify one of the two men. According to Mark, one man was named Bartimaeus, the son of Timaeus. Luke suggests the healing took place as Jesus entered Jericho (Luke 18:35) whereas Matthew and Mark claim it occurred as they left the city (Matt. 20:29; Mark 10:46). Many Bible teachers believe this apparent discrepancy is due to the existence of two Jerichos, the old city and a new city which had been built by Herod. The miracle probably took place as Jesus left the old city and approached the new city which was home to Zacchaeus. Others believe Jesus was approached by the blind men as He entered the city but did not heal them until He was leaving. These men appealed to Jesus calling Him "Rabboni" which was the highest term for Master and "Son of David" which was a common messianic title. After they received their sight, they began to follow Jesus.

The third man whose life changed the day Jesus passed through Jericho was a man named Zacchaeus. Although the name Zacchaeus means "pure," apparently this Zacchaeus was anything but pure. He is described as "a chief tax collector" and one who was "rich." This suggests he had abused his influence to collect more tax than was required and had earned his wealth by extortion (cf. Luke 19:8). Also, as a chief tax collector, he may have been the one to whom Matthew would have reported when he collected taxes in Galilee. Matthew's decision to follow Jesus may explain why Zacchaeus was so eager to see Jesus. When word spread that Jesus was in the area, a crowd quickly formed around him. Because he was short, Zacchaeus climbed one of the many sycamore trees lining the road so he could see Jesus as He passed by. When Jesus came to that point along the road, He looked up to the tree and said, "Zacchaeus, make haste and come down, for today I must stay at your house" (Luke 19:5). Jesus' decision to eat with a tax collector in a city which was home to so many respected Jewish leaders produced a ripple of response in the crowd. But as a result of the day Jesus spent with this man, "salvation" came to his home. This was the only time in Jesus' ministry that He used the word "salvation" which later became the most common expression used to describe conversion. Again Jesus reminded those around Him, "the Son of Man has come to seek and to save that which was lost" (Luke 19:10).

Despite His constant emphasis on the Cross, some of those who followed Jesus still anticipated the immediate establishment of the kingdom of God. Because Jesus sensed a militant attitude prevalent in the crowd, He told a parable to discourage them from attempting to make Him king as they had wanted to do at the feeding of the five thousand a year earlier. In the parable, a nobleman went to a country to receive a kingdom and then return (Luke 19:12-27). He placed his servants in charge of his resources while he was away, but the citizens of the country determined the subordinate would not be their ruler. When the man returned victoriously, he called for an accounting of his servants' faithfulness. Those who had been faithful were rewarded, but those who had not been faithful were disciplined. Also, those who refused to recognize his rulership were ordered executed. This parable was repeated a few days later for a different purpose, but on this occasion, Jesus was apparently concerned with teaching the crowd the kingdom was still a long way off (Luke 19:11). Those who considered themselves His servants should demonstrate their faithfulness during the interim between the Cross and the kingdom.

Conclusion

In the final weeks of His public ministry, Jesus demonstrated His faithfulness to His commission by traveling through the land seeking and saving the lost. He found them among the lepers and Pharisees, among the crowds and tax collectors. Those who found salvation and person fulfillment in Him wanted to celebrate His kingship, but Jesus reminded them of the need to follow His example of faithfulness. Christians today still anticipate the day when they will be able to celebrate the kingship of Christ in its fullness at His return to establish the kingdom, but in the interim they recognize His authority through faithful obedience to His command to continue seeking and saving the lost.

CHAPTER 23

SUNDAY AND MONDAY: DAYS OF CELEBRATION AND DEMONSTRATION

Matthew 21:1-19; Mark 11:1-18; Luke 19:29-48; John 12:12-50

lthough Passover fell on Thursday, April 6, in A.D. 30, by the end of March the city of Jerusalem was already filling up as Jews from all parts of the world arrived to ceremonially purify themselves for the upcoming feast. Although the feast was intended as a time to reflect back to God's deliverance of the nation from Egypt, many of those coming into the city for this feast were looking ahead to the continuing confrontation between Jesus and the Jewish leaders during this week of celebration. As they came to the temple area, many remembered hearing Jesus teach during previous feasts in that very spot. "What do you think," they wondered, "that He will not come to the feast?" (John 11:56). By now, it had become obvious to just about everybody that Jesus was not appreciated by the religious establishment in Jerusalem. In a rare demonstration of solidarity among warring religious factions, "both the chief priests and the Pharisees had given a command, that if anyone knew where He was, he should report it, that they might seize Him" (John 11:57). At both the Feast of Tabernacles and the Feast of Dedication earlier that year, the Jewish leaders' intense hatred toward Jesus erupted when they picked up stones to begin stoning Jesus. He escaped unharmed on both of the previous occasions but He must have been very much aware of the Sanhedrin's intention to destroy Him. The odds were that Jesus simply would not return to Jerusalem for the feast but like many others, celebrate it somewhere else with family and friends.

NINE DAYS IN APRIL THAT CHANGED ALL HUMAN HISTORY
Saturday – A Day of Conversion
Sunday – A Day of Celebration
Monday – A Day of Demonstration
Tuesday – A Day of Instruction
Wednesday – A Day of Anticipation
Thursday – A Day of Preparation
Friday – A Day of Crucifixion
Saturday – A Day of Opposition
Sunday – A Day of Resurrection

But on Friday, March 31, just six days before Passover, Jesus was seen in Bethany, a village a couple of miles east of Jerusalem. Bethany was the home of Lazarus and his sisters, the same Lazarus who had been raised from the dead earlier that year. Quickly the people began making a connection between Jesus and Lazarus being together in Bethany. As people in Jerusalem talked, a rumor spread that Jesus would be honored at a special supper hosted by Lazarus at his home in Bethany. If the rumor was true, it was a rare opportunity to not only see this Jesus whom the Sanhedrin was trying to destroy, but also see a man who had been raised from the dead. "Then a great many of the Jews knew that He was there; and they came, not for Jesus' sake only, but that they might also see Lazarus, whom He had raised from the dead" (John 12:9). As the crowd gathered in Bethany for the dinner that Saturday, it would mark the beginning of the nine days in April that would change all human history.

I.   Saturday, April 1: A Day of Conversion (John 12:1-11)

Perhaps the most common way to honor a guest in the Middle East is to give a banquet in their honor. Hospitality is an important part of the lifestyle of many families in that part of the world. Jesus may have lived in their home during His final week on earth. What is known with some degree of certainty is that He was entertained in Lazarus' home for at least one meal. It was only natural that the family of Lazarus who had recently been raised from the dead would want to express their appreciation to Jesus. Because of the similarities in the accounts of this meal (John 12:2-8) and that in the home of Simon the Leper (Matt. 26:6-13; Mark 14:3-9), many commentators believe both accounts describe the same meal. Some Bible teachers have even suggested Simon the Leper was the father of Lazarus, Mary, and Martha. But while there are many similarities in the two accounts, enough differences exist to suggest these accounts describe two different meals. At each of these meals, Jesus was anointed in a symbolic way. Part of this symbolism related to His role as the Lamb of God. The passover lamb was selected for sacrifice four days before it was finally approved for slaughter. The two anointings of Jesus were separated by four days by Jewish reckoning. Following the second anointing, Judas Iscariot finalized the terms under which he would betray Jesus. Also, the two anointings were symbolic of the two anointings planned for Jesus' body after death. He was anointed at His burial by Joseph of Arimathaea and Nicodemus (John 19:39-40). The women who discovered the empty tomb were coming for the second anointing of Jesus' body (Mark 16:1). At some point during this meal, "Mary took a pound of very costly oil of spikenard, anointed the feet of Jesus, and wiped His feet with her hair" (John 12:3). In describing this ointment, John uses the Greek word *nardou* which is probably derived from the Sanskrit word *nalada* referring to a particular fragrant plant native to India. He also uses the Greek word *pistikes* which means "faithful," "reliable," or "genuine" to describe the perfume, suggesting this ointment was probably imported from India. This conclusion is further supported by Judas Iscariot's estimate of the cost of this ointment at 300 denarii (about 25 denarii per ounce). In a contemporary economy, this ointment would sell for about $800.00 per ounce. Mary used twelve ounces to anoint Jesus' feet. After pouring this ointment over Jesus', Mary wiped them with her own hair. This would have been an extremely humbling act for a woman of Mary's stature. It was generally considered a disgrace for a woman to appear in public with her hair unbound. Mary's response on this occasion may have been prompted by her hearing of another woman in Galilee who similarly wiped Jesus' feet with her hair (Luke 7:36-50).

Judas Iscariot objected to this extravagant worship by Mary and pointed out the funds used on the ointment could have been given to the poor. Judas was not interested in the poor but himself. He was the treasurer of the group and had been dipping into the funds. The disciples later learned he had purchased a field outside of Jerusalem with funds from their purse (Acts 1:18). He may have thought He could better hide his theft if he had a large influx of cash such as that which was spent on the perfume. Jesus responded by coming to Mary's defense. "Let her alone," He said. "She has kept this for the day of My burial. For the poor you have with you always, but Me you do not have always" (John 12:7-8). Some people have interpreted Jesus' statement on this occasion as a justification for their lack of concern for the poor. This conclusion is inconsistent with the emphasis of Jesus' ministry which included preaching the gospel to the poor. Rather, Jesus was commending Mary for her sense of priority. Obviously, one can do everything that ought to be done for others, but one should do something in their service for God. When that person does something for God, they are neglecting other areas of potential ministry. Jesus' response on this occasion suggests He is more likely to commend what we do than to criticize us for what we cannot do. Those present at this banquet honoring Jesus represented two different groups. Probably the larger number of those present were Galileans who were supportive of Jesus and His ministry, but there was also "a great many of the Jews" present (John 12:9). This latter group probably lived in Jerusalem and were there out of curiosity. They may have wondered why their religious leaders were so intent upon destroying Jesus and determined to find out for themselves. Also, others may have come to confirm a rumor they had heard concerning the raising of Lazarus from the dead. By the end of the banquet, the religious leaders believed Lazarus also would have to be killed, "because of account of him many of the Jews went away and believed on Jesus" (John 12:11).

II. Sunday, April 2: A Day of Celebration (Matt. 21:1-11, 14-17; Mark 11:1-11; Luke 19:29-44

According to the calculations of Sir Robert Anderson, the next morning began the final day of Daniel's sixty-ninth week. If his calculations are accurate, there may have been some orthodox rabbis in Jerusalem who awoke that morning in anticipation of some significant event about to take place in their city. As Jesus rode through the city gate later that day, these Jewish leaders could not help but recognize the prophetic significance of His act in the light of messianic prophecy. In a sense, the triumphant entry was a formal challenge to the Jewish leaders to once and for all determine if Jesus was not the Messiah promised by Daniel and other prophets. As Jesus approached the city of Jerusalem that morning, He paused at the Mount of Olives and sent two of His disciples into the village of Bethphage to secure the colt upon which he would ride into the city. Bethphage was a village on the outskirts of Jerusalem which was probably considered part of the metropolitan Jerusalem area. Although only the colt was necessary to fulfill biblical prophecy, Jesus apparently suggested His disciples bring both the colt and its mother (Matt. 21:2). No doubt it would be easier to convince the colt to go with the disciples if its mother were also coming.

In instructing His disciples on securing the colt, Jesus recognized they may be asked why there were taking the animal. If this question was raised, the disciples were told to respond, "The Lord has need of it" (Mark 11:3). This is the only occasion in the Scriptures where a specific "need" is identified with any member of the Trinity, although the principle of God "needing" some part of His creation is often illustrated throughout the Scriptures. On this occasion, it was not possible for Jesus to accomplish what needed to be done without the use of the colt. By way of application, there are many dimensions of Christian ministry today which can only be accomplished as God is free to act in and through His people. When the animal was brought to Jesus, the disciples threw their coats on the colt and Jesus sat on it. Putting coats on the donkey and on the road as it walked along was an expression of celebration. Others cut palm branches which were also placed on the road as Jesus rode by. Palm branches were a symbol of messianic power and the national independence movement of the Maccabees. Because of this symbolic action, today the Sunday before Easter is known as Palm Sunday. As the crowd gathered around Him on His ride into the city, they sang a well known Hebrew hymn celebrating the Messiah (Ps. 118). As this psalm was part of the Great Hallel (Psalms 115–118) used in the observance of the Passover meal and part of the Egyptian Hallel (Pss. 113–118) sung at the feasts of Passover, Pentecost, Tabernacles, and Dedication, it was well known by those gathered on that occasion.

The massive crowd of people who joined this celebration was composed of two groups. First were those who were with Jesus in Bethany and came into the city with Him. Second were those already in the city who heard Jesus was coming and ran out to meet Him. Watching the massive celebration under way, those most opposed to Jesus' ministry became discouraged in their attempts to bring an end to this messianic movement. "You see that you are accomplishing nothing," the Pharisees confessed among themselves. "Look, the world has gone after Him!" (John 12:19). How large was the crowd that celebrated the Messiah on Palm Sunday? The Scriptures do not record the number of people involved but every indication suggests it was a popular movement. According to one census, there were 256,500 lambs sacrificed for Passover in Jerusalem. Normally, there would be at least ten people partaking of a single Passover lamb. This means there were probably 2.6 million people in the city for the feast. In light of the timing of this particular feast, at the end of Daniel's sixty-ninth week, people would be more likely to join such a celebration than at other Passovers. Even if as few as ten percent of those present were involved, it would certainly seem to the Jewish leaders that the whole world had gone after Him. A crowd of that size would still be larger than the normal population of the city.

Some of the Pharisees present in the crowd of people thought the singing of this messianic hymn in a context where it was being obviously applied to Jesus was something that should be brought to an immediate end. They appealed to Jesus to rebuke His disciples, but Jesus responded, "I tell you that if these should keep silent, the stones would immediately cry out" (Luke 19:40). Yet in the midst of this messianic celebration, Jesus realized the city of Jerusalem was still not ready to receive Him. As the city came into clear view, Jesus wept over it. "If you had known, even you, especially in this your day, the things that make for your peace!" He sighed. "But now they are hidden from your eyes" (Luke 19:42).

Many Bible teachers have recognized the significance of Jesus riding a donkey through the city gates on this occasion in contrast to the description of Him coming on a white horse at the Second Coming (Rev. 19:11). A ruler would ride through the city gates on a donkey when he came in peace, but on a horse if he came in war. Even though He knew those in Jerusalem would within a week be responsible for His death, He came to them in peace. When He arrived in the temple area, "all the city was moved" (Matt. 21:10). Some Bible teachers believe this statement refers to a mild earthquake or tremor which may have shaken the city, but others believe the expression is used here as something of a metaphor – that the whole city was impacted by the presence of Jesus. The presence of Jesus in Jerusalem transformed all that was taking place. This is vividly illustrated by Jesus healing the blind and the lame in the temple. The blind and lame were normally banned from the temple, but when Jesus was present, they came into the restricted area to be healed (Matt. 21:14). Also, young children in the temple area began singing the messianic hymn their parents had sung as Jesus rode into town. When the chief priests and scribes saw and heard what was taking place, "they were indignant" (Matt. 21:15). "Do You hear what these are saying?" they asked (Matt. 21:16). Jesus had heard but was not concerned. He responded by reminding the scribes of the rest of they hymn. "Have you never read, 'Out of the mouth of babes and nursing infants You have perfected praise'?" (Matt. 21:16). As the day wore on and evening approached, Jesus left Jerusalem and returned to Bethany for the night.

II. Monday, April 3: A Day of Demonstration (Matt. 21:12-13,18-19; Mark 11:12-18; Luke 19:45-48; John 12:20-50)

As Jesus made His way to Jerusalem from the Mount of Olives the next morning, He was hungry. Off in the distance, He noticed a fig tree covered in leaves. Jesus went to the fig tree hoping he would find something on it to eat. Some Bible teachers believe Jesus was looking for figs on the fig tree even though figs were not normally ripe at this time of year. The name Bethphage literally means "house of unripe figs." Figs in this place tended to ripen early because of the heat from the Jordan valley. These same factors also resulted in the tree dropping its fruit quickly as the hot winds from the east blew. Other Bible teachers believe Jesus may have been looking for Taqsh which was a nut-like substance that grew on fig trees before the figs appeared. But when

Jesus inspected the tree, He found nothing but leaves. Jesus responded to this discovery by cursing the fig tree. "Let no one eat fruit from you ever again" (Mark 11:14).

Some Bible teachers believe there is a parallel between this cursing of the fig tree and the Parable of the Fig Tree which Jesus taught about a year earlier. In the parable, the fig tree did not bear fruit for three consecutive years. It was permitted one more year to bear fruit or be destroyed. By Jewish reckoning, the cursing of this fig tree took place at the close of Jesus' third year of ministry. As Jesus cursed the fig tree, it may have been symbolic of what was happening to the nation as it had rejected Him for three years.

When Jesus came to the temple, He once again asserted His authority as Messiah and cleansed the temple as He had three years earlier. The commercial activity in the temple had again intruded into the place of prayer. As a result, what had been intended to help people worship God was hindering their worship of God. Jesus rebuked those responsible, reminding them of the charge of Isaiah and Jeremiah, "My house is a house of prayer, but you have made it into a den of thieves" (Luke 19:46; cf. Isa. 56:7; Jer. 7:11). This action resulted in the religious establishment being even more committed to destroying Jesus, but they "were unable to do anything; for all the people were very attentive to hear Him" (Luke 19:48).

Among those intent upon hearing Jesus was a group of Gentiles present at the feast. Normally Jesus taught in the court of the women in the temple which was an area open to all Jews but restricted to Gentiles. As a result, a group of Gentiles contacted Philip and expressed their desire to see Jesus. An early tradition of the church claimed these Gentiles had come with a message from the King of Edesa. Accordingly this Gentile king had come to believe Jesus was the Messiah and was prepared to welcome Him to His kingdom even as the Jewish nation rejected Him. According to the tradition, Jesus did not go to the kingdom Himself but rather the napkin of St. Veronica which was supposed to have born the image of Jesus' face was taken to the king and revered by the people as a genuine relic. Some art historians who believe the Shroud of Turin is the actual burial cloth of Jesus argue St. Veronica's napkin was really the shroud folded so as to expose the face of Jesus. The name Veronica literally means "true image." Others believe the Gentiles were philosophers from Greece with questions for Jesus. Perhaps they were Gentiles from Galilee wanting to see Jesus.

Philip discussed the request from the Gentile delegation with Andrew, the only other disciple with a Greek name. They took the request directly to Jesus. The Scriptures are not clear whether Jesus ever actually met with this group of Gentiles, but many Bible teachers believe He probably met with them as He and His disciples left the temple that day and passed through the court of the Gentiles. Several have noticed Jesus' immediate response to these Gentiles and His disciples as the universal significance that His death was near. "The hour has come that the Son of Man should be glorified" (John 12:23). The manner in which He was to be glorified was not by being welcomed into a Jewish kingdom but rather by dying on a Roman cross for the sins of the world. Jesus told them that just as a grain of seed must be planted in the ground and die to produce fruit, so He had to die to produce the fruit of His labors. And what was true in the experience of Jesus was also true in the experience of those who would follow and serve Him. Only then would they be honored by His Father.

This event in the final week of Jesus' ministry began His passion or suffering which was climaxed on the cross. "Now My soul is troubled, and what shall I say?" He acknowledged. "Father, save Me from this hour? But for this purpose I came to this hour. Father, glorify Your name" (John 12:27-28). The Greek word *tetaraktai* translated "troubled" means to be agitated or disturbed. Although Jesus knew the cross was the means by which He would accomplish His greatest work and be glorified by His Father, that did not mean He was not uneasy about the physical, emotional, and spiritual suffering that would be associated with the cross.

Following Jesus' brief prayer to His Father, God again broke the silence of heaven and said, "I have both glorified it and will glorify it again" (John 12:28). Those who heard the voice of God were reluctant to attribute it to God. Some passed it off as thunder while others claimed an angel had spoken. Jesus told the people the voice had been heard for their benefit. Even though the cross would look like a defeat, Jesus knew it represented His ultimate victory. He announced both the world and ruler of the world would soon face judgment, "and I, if I am lifted up from the earth, will draw all peoples to Myself" (John 12:32).

For more than three years now, Jesus had ministered among the Jews, demonstrating through His miracles that He was indeed the Messiah. "But although He had done so many signs before them, they did not believe in Him" (John 12:37). Instead, the prophecies of Isaiah concerning the spiritual blindness of the nation and their reluctance to believe God's message were being fulfilled in that generation (cf. Isa. 6:10; 53:1). When it became clear most of the people were not responding, Jesus left the crowds to themselves. Some were beginning to realize who Jesus was, and even among the Jewish leaders, "many believed in Him" (John 12:42). But those who believed were reluctant to go public because of the Pharisees' influence and the humiliation that would be associated with being excommunicated from the synagogue. "They loved the praise of men more than the praise of God" (John 12:43). Jesus understood what was happening in many lives and sought to minister to their need. He encouraged them not only to believe in Him, but to believe in the One who had sent Him. Again He reminded His listeners that He only spoke the message of His Father. The true believer in Jesus is also a believer in God.

Conclusion

As Jesus began His final week of public ministry on earth, the people celebrated His coming and witnessed great demonstrations of His messianic power. But the crowds that chanted, "Hosanna to the Son of David! Blessed is He who comes in the name of the Lord!" (Matt. 21:9) on Sunday were the same crowds who early Friday morning cried out, "Away with Him, away with Him! Crucify Him!" (John 19:15). Their worship of Christ on Sunday lacked commitment to Him and turned to opposition by Friday. Christians today should be careful to let their worship of God grow out of a deep personal commitment to Jesus. The impact of worship which grows out of a vital relationship with God will last beyond the day in which it is offered.

CHAPTER 24

TUESDAY/WEDNESDAY: LEARNING UNDER THE MESSIAH

Matthew 21:19–16:16; Mark 11:19–14:11; Luke 10:1–22:6

*E*ach evening, Jesus and His disciples left Jerusalem and stayed in Bethany. Jesus had friends in Bethany that were no doubt willing to extend hospitality to the group. Also, with the religious establishment in the city committed to killing Him, Jesus was wise to leave the city until the appointed time of His death. The evening Jesus observed the Passover with His disciples (Thursday) appears to have been the only evening Jesus spent in the city of Jerusalem during His public ministry. It was also the evening of His arrest in a garden just outside the city gate.

As Jesus and His disciples came into Jerusalem on Tuesday, April 4, the disciples noticed the withered fig tree. Only the day before, that same tree had been covered in leaves. When Jesus inspected it for fruit and found none, He had cursed it. Now it was dead. Remembering the events of the previous day, Peter spoke in astonishment. "Rabbi, look! The fig tree which You cursed has withered away," he exclaimed (Mark 11:21).

Jesus took this opportunity to teach Peter and the other disciples some important principles relating to the prayer of faith. This type of prayer is always effective in accomplishing its end whether that end is the healing of the sick (James 5:15), altering climactic conditions (James 5:17-18), raising the dead (John 11:41-42) or overcoming apparently insurmountable problems (Mark 11:23). Sometimes the prayer of faith is called "the faith of miracles" because it effects God's intervention in a miraculous way.

In His instructions on this kind of prayer, Jesus suggested four steps in praying the prayer of faith. First, the one praying must "have the faith of God" (Mark 11:22, author's translation). The second step in praying is the "faith expression" which means to express what God is going to do (Mark 11:23). Third, the praying one needs to continue believing and be careful not to let doubt shake his confidence in God (Mark 11:23-24). Finally, the believer needs to be receptive and responsive to the Lord's leading concerning things brought to his mind as he prays (Mark 11:25-26).

The conversation between Jesus and His disciples on the way into Jerusalem marked the beginning of one of the busiest days in the final week. The synoptic gospels record more detail of Jesus' teaching in the temple and on the Mount of Olives on Tuesday, April 4, than for any other single day in this week. Without question, the final Tuesday of Jesus' ministry was a day of intensive instruction.

I. Tuesday, April 4: A Day of Instruction (Matt. 21:19–25:46; Mark 11:19–13:37; Luke 10:1–21:36)

As Jesus walked into the temple to begin teaching, He was immediately approached by a group which included the chief priests and some scribes. They soon revealed their hidden agenda in approaching Jesus, to challenge Jesus' authority to teach in the temple. While this group was probably antagonistic toward Jesus before they approached Him, it was a common occurrence for the scribes and priests to ask about one's authority, especially when that person was teaching publicly in the temple. The question they asked Jesus were similar to questions a Bible teacher might be asked today regarding where he was ordained or received his theological training.

Jesus realized this group was not prepared to recognize His authority to teach, because they had repeatedly rejected Him in the past. He agreed to answer their question only if the group first answered His own question. Jesus asked them about the authority of John the Baptist to teach. The scribes knew they could not answer that question without having to face the consequences of their answer. They reasoned, "If we say, 'From heaven,' He will say, 'Why then did you not believe him?' But if we say, 'From men' – they feared the people, for all counted John to have been a prophet indeed" (Mark 11:31-32).

Had the scribes answered His question, Jesus could have claimed the same authority as John because He had been accredited by John the Baptist earlier in His ministry. But the Jewish leaders refused to answer the question claiming they did not know. When the leaders refused to answer His question, Jesus refused to answer their question directly. Instead, He remained in the temple teaching parables which made it clear He believed He had a greater right to teach than the priests who normally served in the temple area.

Jesus had immense popular appeal but did not have the endorsement of the religious leaders in Jerusalem. His ministry was oriented toward the common man. Jesus illustrated the thrust of His ministry to the masses by telling the parable of a man with two sons (Matt. 21:28-32). When the man asked the first son to work in the vineyard, he first refused and then changed his mind and went to work in the vineyard. When the second son was asked to work in the vineyard, he agreed he would do so but never got around to doing it. Jesus used this parable to illustrate two kinds of people in Jerusalem. Some were notable sinners who were not doing the will of God but then repented of their sin and followed God. Much of Jesus' public ministry was devoted toward these. The second group appeared righteous because they gave lip service to the concept of obeying God, but they never got around to actually doing what they had committed themselves to do. The religious leaders could not help but realize Jesus was talking about them.

Jesus also told a second parable about an absentee landlord who continually sent servants to collect rent (Matt. 21:33-41). Whenever the servants came to the tenant farmers, the farmers beat, stoned, and finally killed the servants rather than pay the rent due. When this continued to happen, the landlord sent his own son hoping the farmers would respond to him. They responded by killing the man's son. According to Jewish law, if a man died without an heir, his estate could be claimed by anyone, but priority was given to those living on the land. The farmers may have assumed that by killing the heir, they could own the land outright. But killing the heir only sealed the fate of the farmers. Even the Jewish leaders recognized the landlord would "destroy those wicked men miserably, and lease his vineyard to other vinedressers who will render to him the fruits in their seasons" (Matt. 21:41). This parable was based on the history of Israel. One common designation of the nation in the Old Testament is that of the vineyard of God. The servants who repeatedly came to the vineyard and were rejected represented the prophets. Jesus Himself was the son of the landlord who would be soon killed by the tenant farmers. Jesus applied this parable to that situation by reminding the religious leaders of an often repeated messianic psalm. "The stone which the builders rejected has become the chief cornerstone. This is the Lord's doing, and it is marvelous in our eyes" (Matt. 21:42; cf. Ps. 118:22-23).

A number of the names and descriptive titles of Jesus in Scripture are related to rocks or stones. He is described as "the Chief Cornerstone" (Eph. 2:20), "a Cleft of the Rock" (Ex. 33:22), "a Precious Cornerstone" (Isa. 28:16), "a Rock" (Matt. 16:18), "the Rock that is Higher than I" (Ps. 61:2), "the Rock of Israel" (2 Sam. 23:3), "a Rock of Offense" (Rom. 9:33), "the Rock of my Refuge" (Ps. 94:22), "the Rock of Our Salvation" (Ps. 95:1), "the Rock of your Stronghold" (Isa. 17:10), "a Sardius Stone" (Rev. 4:3), "the Shadow of a Great Rock" (Isa. 32:2), "that Spiritual Rock" (1 Cor. 10:4), "a Stone cut out of the Mountain" (Dan. 2:45), "a Stone cut without Hands" (Dan. 2:34), "the Stone of Israel" (Gen. 49:24), "a Stone of Stumbling" (1 Peter 2:8), "the Stone which the builders rejected" (Ps. 118:22), "my Rock of Refuge" (Ps. 31:2), and "a Tried Stone" (Isa. 28:16). This stone is rejected by men but honored by God. Also, this rock is portrayed as destroying those who attempt to destroy it.

The Pharisees easily perceived the meaning of these parables and tried to arrest Jesus. But they had to back off from their plans because of the probable consequences of arresting Jesus in that context. Part of their reasoning for wanting to destroy Jesus was to prevent any kind of public uprising that could be perceived as threatening to Roman control. If they arrested Jesus publicly, they perceived the people may have begun an uprising.

The next parable Jesus taught was the parable of the wedding feast (Matt. 22:1-14). In this account, a king invites his people to the marriage of his son, but the invitation is treated lightly and either ignored or opposed by those invited. The king responds to this by sending his army to destroy the city, then inviting others to come.

In the crowd of those who come to the feast, a man is discovered who is not suitably dressed for the occasion. He is expelled from the feast because he is not dressed right. In interpreting this parable, most Bible teachers suggest the "right dress" to wear at the marriage supper of the Lord is "the garment of salvation." Those who are not saved at the marriage supper will be cast out "into outer darkness; there will be weeping and gnashing of teeth" (Matt. 22:13).

On this, the last day of Jesus' public ministry, various parties of Jewish leaders attempted to break Jesus' power over the people through a series of confrontations. People commonly interrupted a rabbi as he taught, to ask him a question to test his theology and thereby determine to which party he belonged. As Jesus was confronted by the Pharisees, the Herodians, and the Sadducees, He was confronted by the standard types of questions with which they interrogated different rabbis. The difference in Jesus' case was that these issues were raised with malice in an attempt to discredit Him publicly and destroy His popular appeal. But in His answers to each of the questions, Jesus continued to expose the shortcomings of the religious leaders and maintained His personal credibility.

The first of these challenges came from a coalition of Herodians and Pharisees. These two groups could not agree on the issue of tribute being paid to Rome. The Herodians tended to pay the tax and make other concessions to Rome without considering themselves to have in any way compromised. The Pharisees viewed paying the tribute as being contrary to the law. But the question was asked to Jesus for reasons other than to resolve a theological debate. If Jesus sided with the Herodians and argued for paying the unpopular tax, He would alienate those among His followers who tended to be anti-Roman. If however He sided with the Pharisees on this issue, then He could be turned over to the Romans as a law breaker.

Jesus recognized the nature of this test and called for a coin. When the particular coin was brought to Him, He asked, "Whose image and inscription is this?" (Matt. 22:20). The coin bore the image of Tiberius Caesar and the inscription read, "Tiberius Caesar, son of the divine Augustus, himself to be called Augustus or revered emperor." In this title, Caesar claimed to be a god. Jesus responded, "Render therefore to Caesar the things that are Caesar's, and to God the things that are God's" (Matt. 22:21). In this statement, Jesus affirmed the principle of good citizenship, but refused to allow citizenship to be an excuse for not worshiping and/or obeying God.

The next test Jesus confronted came from the Sadducees. The Sadducees did not believe in the resurrection and probably used this case study they presented to Jesus as a stock argument against the Pharisees who believed in the resurrection. In the case in question, a woman survives seven husbands who are also brothers. This practice of a brother marrying the widow of his dead brother was known as levirate marriage and was both part of the law of Israel and common outside Judaism. Assyrian laws (1250-1450) included provision for this arrangement as did other societies. The Sadducees' question coming out of this particular case was, "To whom is she married in the resurrection?"

The Pharisees taught the resurrection life was essentially an extension of the present life and similar to this life in terms of activities and relationships in which people may be engaged. Jesus corrected this common misconception by pointing out there would be no marriage in the resurrection. Then He addresses the larger problem of the Sadducees. He accused them of ignorance of the Scriptures and the power of God. He argued for the resurrection on the basis of a verb tense recorded in Exodus 3:6, 15 ("I am" rather than "I was"). God did not say "I was" the God of Abraham who had been dead four hundred years, but God said "I am" the God of Abraham implying Abraham was still alive in His presence. Jesus' argument in this context illustrates His strong commitment to the verbal inspiration and inerrancy of Scripture.

When the Pharisees heard how Jesus responded to the Sadducees, they were encouraged and regrouped to test Jesus. One of them asked Jesus to identify the greatest command in the law. The Jews taught that Moses had given 613 commands to the nation, 365 expressed as negatives and 248 expressed as positives. In his question, this particular scribe may have been trying to involve Jesus in the controversial task of evaluating the importance of each command and determining which ought to be respected above the others. The Jewish leaders tended to do this with such laws as pertained to the Sabbath and the rite of circumcision. Jesus did not deal with regulatory law in His response but rather called people to the heart of the moral law of God by stressing two closely related commands. First, people should love God with their total being. Second, they should love their neighbor as they loved their own self (Matt. 22:37-40). When the questioner agreed with Jesus' response, he was perceived as not far from the kingdom because he had come to value the moral law higher than the ceremonial law.

Jesus then challenged the Pharisees on their own interpretation of the Scriptures as He had earlier done with the Sadducees. He asked them, "What do you think about the Christ? Whose Son is He?" (Matt. 22:42). When the Pharisees responded with their standard answer to that question and identified the Messiah as the Son of David, Jesus asked them to explain why David called the Messiah "Lord" in Psalm 110 (Ps. 110:1; cf. Matt. 22:43-45). The Jewish leaders recognized the messianic nature of this psalm, but were reluctant to identify the Messiah as more than just a great king. When confronted with this question, the Pharisees were unable to answer Jesus. Having seen Jesus confound three different groups of Jewish leaders who had tried to test Him, no one else dared to question Him further. Jesus concluded His public teaching ministry with a discourse which to this day is viewed by many as the most severe denunciation of anyone or any group recorded in any literature. Jesus' last public discourse was a denunciation of the scribes and Pharisees (Matt. 23). He noted they sat in "the seat of Moses" but they did not practice what they preached. When the Jews built their synagogues, they normally built them so the people would be facing Jerusalem during the service. The speaker sat in a chair with his back to Jerusalem and taught the people out of the law. This chair was "the seat of Moses" and symbolized the idea that he had the support of the temple in Jerusalem as he taught the law. But although they may have had some credibility based on the seat in which they sat, they lacked any credibility based on their own lack of faithfulness to keeping the heart of the law. Jesus told His disciples, "Therefore whatever they tell you to observe, that observe and do, but do not do according to their works; for they say, and do not do" (Matt. 23:3).

After His attack on the hypocrisy of the religious leaders of Israel, Jesus left the temple area to go to the Mount of Olives. As He left, He paused by the treasury and watched how people gave (Mark 12:41-44; Luke 21:1-4). Typically, the wealthier men came in and gave many coins into the temple treasury in such a way as to draw attention to how much they gave. But one of those Jesus watched was a widow who gave two mites to the treasury. Although the widow's mites amounted to a total offering of about one fourth of a cent, that offering was valued greater than the larger gifts of the rich because she gave of her living rather than out of the surplus. Jesus' last lesson to His disciples in the temple was a lesson in stewardship.

From the Mount of Olives, Jesus and His disciples had a good view of the city of Jerusalem and the temple area of that city. The temple covered about twenty acres and could hold a quarter of a million people. Some of the stones used in the construction of this temple were as large as a house (30' x 18' x 12'). From their perspective on the Mount of Olives, the gold and white temple standing against the setting sun must have amplified the beauty of the temple. It was not surprising that the disciples were moved by what they saw and called on Jesus to see the spectacular sight.

"And Jesus said to them, 'Do you not see all these things? Assuredly, I say to you, not one stone shall be left here upon another, that shall not be thrown down'" (Matt. 24:2). In light of the size of some of those stones, Jesus' comment could only refer to a complete destruction of the temple. This prompted four of the disciples, the four who had been in the fishing business together before following Jesus, to come to Him and ask Him three questions (Matt. 24:3) First, they wanted to know when this destruction of the temple would take place. Second, they wondered what if any would be the sign of Jesus coming. Third, they wanted to know what signs might mark the end of the age. In responding to these questions, Jesus gave what has become known as "the Olivette Discourse." Because of the prophetic nature of this discourse, it is discussed later in this book in connection with its historical or anticipated historical fulfillment.

II.   Wednesday, April 5: A Day of Anticipation (Matt. 26:1-16; Mark 14:1-11; Luke 22:1-6)

If Tuesday, April 4, was one of the busiest days in the ministry of Jesus, Wednesday, April 5, has been called "the day of silence" because there is no specific record of anything taught or done by Jesus that day. Actually, because the Jewish day began with the sunset of the previous day, there were three events which took place late on Tuesday which may characterize the nature of that Wednesday. First, Jesus again predicted His death, this time dating it two days later – Friday (Matt. 26:1-5). Second, He was again anointed for His burial, this time at the home of Simon the Leper (Mark 14:3-9; Matt. 26:6-13). Third, Judas Iscariot finalized the terms of a deal with the religious leaders of Jerusalem and agreed to betray Jesus (Matt. 26:14-16; Mark 14:10-11; Luke 22:3-6). These three events characterize the last Wednesday in Jesus' public ministry as a day of anticipation. Prior to the Passover season, the Jewish leaders determined to destroy Jesus, but agreed they would not take Him until after the feast. Jesus demonstrated He was in control of His own destiny by forcing these same leaders to go through with their plans, but to do it in accordance with God's timing rather than their own. "The hour" in which Jesus would finish His messianic work by offering Himself as the ultimate sacrifice for sin was at the beginning of the Feast of Unleavened Bread rather than "after the feast." Two days before He was crucified and hours before Judas agreed to betray Jesus, Jesus told His disciples the exact day He would die (cf. Matt. 26:2).

Jesus apparently revealed the day of His death to His disciples as they made their way to the home of Simon the Leper. Because lepers were cut off from the rest of society and forced to wander outside the city, it is likely this Simon was a leper who had been healed of the condition, perhaps even healed by Jesus. Even though he no longer had the condition that had cut him off from his family and friends, he was still known as "the leper." At his home Jesus was again anointed with an expensive perfume. As was the case just a few days earlier, a comment was made about the cost of the ointment and how the money could have been spent better by meeting the needs of the poor (Matt. 26:9). But once again, Jesus supported the one who had taken her resources and spent it in this way.

As Judas Iscariot watched the expensive ointment being poured over Jesus' head, he must have thought he was beginning to see a new pattern develop. For some time now, Judas had been in charge of the disciples' collective finances and had been using the group's funds for his own personal interests. While others saw Jesus anointed with expensive ointment, Judas saw money that should have gone into the disciples' funds being diverted away from his control. This combined with Jesus' own insistence that His death was very near caused Judas to realize he would soon no longer have access to these funds upon which he had begun to depend. Later that evening, Judas Iscariot met with a group of religious leaders to agree on the terms of his betraying Jesus (Matt. 26:15). He left that meeting with thirty pieces of silver, the price of a slave. Some Bible teachers believe that may have only been a down payment, the rest to come after he had completed his part of the deal. All that remained not was for Judas to find the appropriate opportunity and alert the Jewish leaders when all was ready.

Conclusion

As Jesus concluded His public ministry in Jerusalem, He devoted much of His time to teaching His disciples important principles they needed to know to effectively serve Him in the years to come. Many of the issues which Jesus taught that week were raised by the questions of those He taught. Christians today can learn from the example and emphasis of Jesus. First, contemporary disciples of Jesus need to be effective in teaching biblical principles which speak to the issues concerning the people who are concerned. Second, if Jesus thought it was important that His disciples should learn these truths, it must be just as important for His disciples today to be continually learning the truths of the Scriptures.

CHAPTER 25

THURSDAY, APRIL 6:
A DINNER AND A DISCOURSE

Matthew 26:17-35; Mark 14:12-31; Luke 22:7-38; John 13:1–17:26

*L*ittle is known concerning Jesus' life and ministry between the Tuesday evening meal in the home of Simon the leper and the Thursday evening observance of the Passover meal by Jesus and His disciples. It was no doubt an emotionally draining time for Jesus as He moved toward the conclusion of His ministry, yet it was not a time for Jesus to cut Himself off from those closest to Him. "Now before the feast of the Passover, when Jesus knew that His hour had come that He should depart from this world to the Father, having loved His own who were in the world, He loved them to the end" (John 13:1). On the final night of His life on earth, Jesus gathered with His disciples to observe the Passover. Within twelve hours, He would offer Himself once and for all as God's ultimate sacrifice for sin.

One reason why little is recorded concerning the activities of Jesus and His disciples during the daylight hours of Thursday, April 6, may be due to the fact that little could be done on that day. It was customary in Galilee to do no work on the day of the Passover. Jesus and His disciples likely followed that custom. In Judea, all work had ceased by noon and the preparations for the Passover were already under way. Even in the temple, the daily evening sacrifice was offered at 2:30 in the afternoon to leave the priests time to perform their sacrificial responsibilities as people brought them the Passover lambs to be killed. It was probably late morning when Jesus sent Peter and John to make preparations for observing the Passover that evening. By 11:00, they had probably secured the room and were following the Jewish custom of silently searching the corners of the room with a candle to insure there was no leaven present. Then they would have gone out to purchase a lamb and other supplies for the dinner that evening. By the time of the evening sacrifice which was offered earlier than usual on this day, one of the two disciples was probably lined up with thousands of others outside the temple waiting to present the lamb to be killed. He would have joined the others in singing the "Hallel" (Psalms 113-118) as he waited for his turn to present the lamb.

Jesus and His disciples probably did not come into the city until later in the afternoon, after Peter and John had finished preparing and reported they were ready. As the disciples made their way into Jerusalem, they were no doubt aware the next day was the day Jesus had identified as the day of His death

(Matt. 26:2). Just in case there was trouble, they had secured a couple of swords (Luke 22:38). As they talked along the way, the subject of their conversation was a subject that had become a common theme in their discussions. "There was also rivalry among them, as to which of them should be considered the greatest" (Luke 22:24). This issue may have been raised as the disciples contemplated the seating arrangements at the table. Once again Jesus tried to teach His disciples the principle of servant leadership. "For who is greater," He asked, "he who sits at the table, or he who serves? Is it not he who sits at the table? Yet I am among you as the One who serves" (Luke 22:27).

I.   The Last Passover and the Lord's Supper (Matt. 26:20-29; Mark 14:17-25; Luke 22:14-30; John 13:1-30; 1 Cor. 11:23-34)

As the sun began to set over Jerusalem, people all over the city began the traditional observance of this most ancient feast of Israel. Probably just after 6:00 Thursday evening, Jesus initiated the Passover observance with His disciples. He took the first cup of wine in His hands and gave thanks. After the drinking of this first cup of wine, it was customary to engage in a ceremonial washing of one's hands. Apparently at this point in the evening, Jesus "rose from supper and laid aside His garments, took a towel and girded Himself. After that, He poured water into a basin and began to wash the disciple's feet, and to wipe them with the towel with which He was girded" (John 13:4-5).

When Jesus came to Peter, Peter refused to let Jesus wash his feet. Foot washing was a necessary but undesirable task in the Near East and was usually assigned to the lowest servant in the house. Probably because of Jesus' desire to teach His disciples true humility, He took this job on Himself; but the thought of Jesus washing his feet was too much for Peter to take. When Peter objected, Jesus simply explained, "If I do not wash you, you have no part with Me" (John 13:8). When Peter heard that, he reacted in the opposite extreme and asked Jesus to also wash his hands and head.

While Jesus was washing the disciples' feet to teach humility by example, He also had another teaching objective in mind, that of the necessity of cleansing for fellowship with God. He explained, "He who is bathed needs only to wash his feet, but is completely clean; and you are clean, but not all of you" (John 13:10). People customarily bathed in the public bathhouses before going to a person's home for a meal, but between the bath and the home, his feet would get dirty. When this happened, the person did not need another bath, only a foot washing. By way of application in the Christian life, a Christian is "bathed" at conversion but also needs constant daily cleansing from sin to maintain fellowship with God.

After washing His disciples' feet, Jesus explained His actions to them. They knew who He was and understood the inconsistency of expecting someone as great as Him to wash feet. But Jesus argued, "If I then, your Lord and Teacher, have washed your feet, you also ought to wash one another's feet" (John 13:14). Perhaps on this night the message finally began to sink in. Years later, one of those present would write the epistle in which he urged his readers to "be clothed with humility" (1 Peter 5:5).

That night must have been emotionally wrenching for Jesus as He ate the Passover with His disciples knowing the one He had placed in the seat of honor would be the one who before the sun rose again would betray Him to the Jewish leaders. John uses the Greek word *etarachthe* which is translated "troubled in spirit" (John 13:21) to describe Jesus' emotional state. This word conveys the idea of stirring up, disturbing, troubling or throwing into confusion. Perhaps this word is used here because all of these emotional responses were at work in Jesus that night. "Most assuredly, I say to you, one of you will betray Me," Jesus explained (John 13:21). The very thought that one of the twelve would engage in such an act was outside the realm of credibility for eleven of the disciples present that evening. Even though both Matthew (Matt. 26:25) and John (John 13:26) saw Jesus specifically identify Judas Iscariot as the betrayer, when he left that evening to go out and get the soldiers, none of the disciples realized what was taking place (John 13:28). Most Bible teachers believe that not until Judas Iscariot left did Jesus institute the ordinance of the Lord's Supper, with the cup and the bread (1 Cor. 11:23-34).

After drinking the second cup, it was customary to break one of the two pieces of unleavened bread and then give thanks. At this point, Jesus broke with the rabbinical custom and gave thanks before breaking the bread and explained its significance as representing His broken body (1 Cor. 11:24). Then He took the third cup in the Passover meal, the cup of blessing, and explained its significance as representing His blood (1 Cor. 11:25). Just as Israel observed the Passover to remember God's deliverance of the nation, Jesus was leaving His disciples a memorial meal to remind them constantly of an even greater deliverance from the bondage of sin.

II. The Upper Room Discourse (John 13:31–16:33)

After the conclusion of the Passover service, Jesus and His disciples remained in the Upper Room for some time. During that time, Jesus taught what is known as "The Upper Room Discourse" using the Socratic method of teaching. This method involves the use of leading questions to establish learning readiness before teaching important truths. Many Bible teachers believe this discourse includes all the embryonic teaching of the epistles in seed form. This discourse together with the apostolic epistles form the basis for most of what might be recognized as distinctly Christian doctrine. Jesus began by leaving His disciples what He called "a new commandment." This commandment was expressed "that you love one another; as I have loved you" (John 13:34). Jesus identified this bond of love between the disciples as the distinguishing mark or sign by which others would identify them as His disciples. Most Bible teachers believe the epistle of 1 John is an exposition of this basic responsibility of every Christian to love one another.

Jesus was interrupted by four disciples as He taught them in the Upper Room, but He used these interruptions and the questions that were asked as the basis of the next phase of His message. Jesus explained He was going where the disciples could not at that time follow. The first interruption came from

Peter who wanted to know where Jesus was going (John 13:36). When Peter expressed a willingness to lay down His life for Jesus, Jesus warned Peter "the rooster shall not crow till you have denied Me three times" (John 13:38). Some Bible teachers believe Peter may have received this or a similar warning on at least two occasions that evening. As Jesus explained where He was going to His disciples (John 14:1-3), Thomas became the second disciple to interrupt. He wanted to know the way to the Father's house. Jesus responded, "I am the way, the truth, and the life. No one comes to the Father except through Me" (John 14:6).

Jesus' mention of the Father prompted Philip to ask Jesus to show them the Father. Jesus explained, "He who has seen Me has seen the Father" (John 14:9). In making that statement, Jesus was not denying the existence of a separated personality within the Trinity but rather emphasizing the unity within the Godhead. Because Jesus was God, everything that needed to be known about the Father could be recognized in Him. Jesus went on to explain that His disciples could pray to the Father "in My name" (John 14:12-14) and told the disciples of the coming of the Holy Spirit as their Helper. Even though He was leaving, He was not abandoning them. He and the Father were sending the Holy Spirit and they would also relate to the believer in a special way. Jesus promised, "And he who loves Me will be loved by My Father, and I will love him and manifest Myself to him" (John 14:21).

With the mention of Jesus manifesting Himself to the disciples after He left, Judas (not Iscariot) asked, "Lord, how is it that You will manifest Yourself to us, and not to the world?" (John 14:22). Jesus explained this would be accomplished through fellowship with the believer (John 14:23), by the indwelling Holy Spirit (John 14:24-26) and by the inner peace which He would give His disciples (John 14:27-31). Jesus then went on to explain the relationship between Himself and His disciples in the context of that of the vine and the branches. Just as the branches depend on the vine for life so they can bear fruit, so the disciples would be dependent `on Jesus "for without Me you can do nothing" (John 15:5).

This special relationship between Jesus and His disciples would not exempt them from the problems. In fact, the reverse was going to be true. Because of their relationship with Jesus, the disciples would encounter severe trials they would otherwise have avoided. "They will put you out of the synagogues; yes, the time is coming that whoever kills you will think that he offers God service," Jesus explained (John 16:2). At times the sorrow associated with this rejection and opposition would be intense. John uses the Greek word *thlipseos* translated "anguish" to describe the way the disciples would feel at times (John 16:21). This word describes the sorrow that is sometimes expressed by the phrase "when it hurts too much to cry." Jesus prepared His disciples for those times of sorrow by reminding them of the Comforter whom He would send (John 16:7-15), assuring them God would ultimately turn their sorrow into joy (John 16:20-22), encouraging them to take advantage of their ability to pray (John 16:23-24), and leaving them with His victorious peace (John 16:25-33).

III. Jesus' High Priestly Prayer (John 17:1-26)

Bible teachers are divided as to exactly when Jesus and His disciples actually left the Upper Room that evening. Jesus said, "Arise, let us go from here" (John 14:31) just before comparing His relationship with them to that of a vine and the branches. Some Bible teachers believe the disciples left at that time and that the presence of a vine growing up a wall was the context which prompted His use of that illustration. Others claim Jesus and His disciples began to get ready to leave at that time, but did not leave until some time later.

Most agree that by the time Jesus offered His High-Priestly Prayer (John 17), He had left the Upper Room and made His way to some other place, perhaps the temple area. If Jesus offered this prayer in the temple area, He may have been there as Judas Iscariot was taking the temple guard to the Upper Room to arrest Jesus.

The prayer of Jesus recorded in John 17:1-26 is the greatest example of intercessory prayer found in the Scriptures. In this prayer, Jesus allowed His disciples to witness an example of intercessory prayer and illustrated the nature of intercessory prayer as a unique aspect to the ministry of prayer. When Jesus prayed in the garden, He began with an expression of communion with God, "Father" (John 17:1) and a petition concerning the glorification of the Son (John 17:1-5) before interceding on behalf of His disciples (John 17:6-9) and those who would believe later (John 17:20-26). Although Jesus' High Priestly Prayer was indeed unique, it may also serve as a pattern for intercessory prayer for Christians today. First, no sin hindered Jesus' fellowship with His Father (John 17:1). Second, Jesus began this prayer acknowledging the sovereignty of God in the affairs of His life and ministry, "the hour has come" (John 17:1). Third, Jesus' motive in prayer was the glory of God. Fourth, Jesus recognized the relationship between obedience to the will of God and effective prayer (John 17:6). Fifth, He made specific requests (John 17:9, 15). Each of these principles is important in an effective ministry of intercessory prayer and characterized the final prayer the disciples of Jesus heard Him offer.

"When Jesus had spoken these words, He went out with His disciples over the Brook Kidron, where there was a garden, which He and His disciples entered. And Judas, who betrayed Him, also knew the place; for Jesus often met there with His disciples" (John 18:1-2).

Conclusion

Often someone's final message to his friends and followers is regarded as having special significance. This is especially true when the speaker knows it is his final statement to the group. When Jesus preached His final sermon to His friends and followers, the disciples, He stressed the need for them to love and support one another as they ministered in a hostile environment. He promised to send the Holy Spirit and answer their prayers, but urged them to love one another. He would do what only God could do – send the Holy Spirit and answer prayer, but they had to do what they could do – love one another. God is faithful today in providing His Holy Spirit and responding to our prayers, but in order to achieve maximum effectiveness in the ministry God has for us, we must be faithful to "love one another."

CHAPTER 26

JOHN:
WATCHING JESUS FROM THE GARDEN TO GOLGOTHA

Matthew 26:36-47; Mark 14:32–15:32; Luke 22:39–23:33; John 18:1–19:24; Acts 1:18-19

*J*esus knew He had a long night ahead of Him which would end only as the day of His crucifixion began to dawn. In only a matter of hours, Jesus would be betrayed by Judas Iscariot and arrested by Roman soldiers under the control of the Sanhedrin. Understandably, He was torn inside. Because of His great love for people, He had emptied Himself and become a man so that He could redeem people from the cross. But part of the suffering of the cross included taking the sin of the world upon Himself (2 Cor. 5:21), and in all eternity, Jesus had never experienced sin. In His final hours before His arrest, Jesus chose to spend the time in agonizing prayer to the Father to determine if there might not be another alternative to the cross.

"My soul is exceedingly sorrowful, even unto death," He explained to three of His disciples. "Stay here and watch with Me" (Matt. 26:38). Then a little beyond them in the garden, Jesus prayed one of the most difficult prayers of His life. "O My Father, if it is possible, let this cup pass from Me; nevertheless, not as I will, but as You will" (Matt. 26:39). While the words may be read quickly by the average reader, Jesus took an hour to express this thought to God in prayer. The agony of His soul that evening was so great that "an angel appeared to Him from heaven, strengthening Him" (Luke 22:43).

The inner turmoil felt by Jesus that evening was evidenced not only by the length of time it took Him to pray, but also by a physical condition He experienced as He prayed. "And being in agony, He prayed the more earnestly. And His sweat became like great drops of blood falling down to the ground" (Luke 22:44).

Jesus had asked the inner three disciples to watch with Him, but they were tired and soon fell asleep. When Jesus returned to them an hour later, He found Peter, James, and John asleep and went off to pray again. He checked on them again later and found them still sleeping. After praying a third time, Jesus realized it was time to wake His sleeping disciples. "Are you still sleeping and resting? Behold, the hour is at hand, and the Son of man is being betrayed into the hands of sinners. Rise, let us be going. See, he who betrays Me is at hand" (Matt. 26:45-46).

I.   Friday, April 7: A Day of Crucifixion

By the time Judas Iscariot arrived in the garden with the soldiers, it was very late Thursday evening or, as was probably the case, very early Friday morning. As the Jews began their day at sundown the night before, the betrayal and arrest of Jesus took place on Friday by Jewish reckoning. As the disciples wakened from their sleep in the dark of the evening, they could hear the soldiers as they came toward them, and were confronted with the light of their torches as they arrived in the part of the garden where they were. As they walked and their eyes struggled to adjust, there was no doubt a moment of confusion on the part of the disciples as events began to quickly unfold in the garden.

As the soldiers appeared in the clearing in the garden of Gethsemane, Jesus asked them for whom they were looking. He knew the answer to their question even before they responded, "Jesus of Nazareth" (John 18:5). Then, so that all present would understand clearly what they were doing, Jesus identified Himself as that person using the Old Testament reference to deity "I am." In that statement, Jesus revealed the shekinah glory of God. Those who had come to arrest Him were thrown back instinctively by the power of His revelation and they "fell to the ground" (John 18:6). Were the soldiers and religious leaders aware they had set themselves against God? Jesus demonstrated His ability to avoid arrest should He decide to save Himself from the cross, but did not do so.

Again, Jesus asked the soldiers who they were seeking. When they repeated their former answer, "Jesus of Nazareth," Jesus reminded them He had already identified Himself and appealed that the others with Him be released unharmed. Only then did Judas Iscariot fulfill his agreement made with the Sanhedrin. As Judas approached his master, Jesus turned and asked, "Friend, why have you come?" (Matt. 26:50). Then Jesus asked, "Judas, are you betraying the Son of Man with a kiss?" (Luke 22:48).

By that time the disciples had begun to realize what was happening. One of them, perhaps Simon the Zealot, called out, "Lord, shall we strike with the sword?" (Luke 22:49). Before Jesus could answer, Peter began the attack. In his hand, Peter had one of the two swords the disciples had taken with them earlier that evening. He raised the five-pound sword, approximately eighteen inches of hammered steel, high and brought it down on the head of the closest enemy. His aim was off slightly, and rather than splitting the skull of the High Priest's servant Malchus, he severed the servant's ear from he side of his head. "'Put your sword into the sheath,' Jesus told Peter. 'Shall I not drink the cup which My Father has given Me?' " (John 18:11). Then in the midst of the confusion of that night there was a moment of calm as Jesus paused to heal the ear of Malchus.

As had been previously arranged between Judas Iscariot and the authorities, Jesus was to be identified by a kiss from His disciple. Only then did the soldiers move in and make their arrest. The delay involved in healing

Malchus' ear and arresting Jesus, the disciples were able to escape by running and hiding from the soldiers. In Jerusalem, word leaked out that Jesus was going to be arrested that evening. By the time the committed followers of Jesus heard about the plan, it was late and the soldiers were already on their way to the garden with Judas. Still, at least one young man thought an attempt should be made to warn Jesus of the danger. He had already undressed to retire for the evening, so he grabbed a linen cloth to wrap around himself and made his way to the garden. Despite his noble effort, he arrived late. Jesus had been arrested and rather than warning Jesus to insure His safety, the young man himself was grabbed by some of the soldiers. In a desperate attempt to escape, he managed to work himself free from he grip of his captors and left them holding his bed sheet as he raced away. Although the Bible does not identify the name of this young man, many Bible teachers believe it was John Mark, the one who later recorded this incident in his account of the gospel (Mark 14:51-52).

Jesus was taken into the city of Jerusalem where he was eventually brought before both Jewish and Roman authorities to be tried. In the course of the evening and early morning, Jesus was tried six times. Three of these trials were before Jewish authorities and dealt with the charge of blasphemy. The Jewish authorities had two years earlier decided Jesus should be executed for His violation of their Sabbath laws, but these trials were an attempt to justify their attitude by making it appear Jesus was guilty of a more serious charge. Then, because the Jews did not have authority to execute a person for violating their laws, Jesus was turned over to Roman authorities and charged with treason. The conclusion of the Roman trials was best expressed by Pilate when he confessed, "I find no fault in Him at all" (John 18:38).

THE TRIALS OF JESUS

Before Annas (John 18:12-14, 19-23)
Before Caiaphas (Matt. 26:57-68; Mark 14:53-65; Luke 22:54, 63-65; John 18:24)
Before the Sanhedrin (Matt. 27:1; Mark 15:1; Luke 22:66-71)
Before Pilate (Matt. 27:2, 11-14; Mark 15:1-5; Luke 23:1-5; John 18:28-38)
Before Herod (Luke 23:6-12)
Before Pilate (Matt. 27:15-26; Mark 15:6-15; Luke 23:13-25; John 18:39- 40)

As Jesus' trials began, two of His disciples summoned the courage to go into the city hoping to get information on what was happening to Jesus. Probably as a result of the successful fishing business conducted by Zebedee, he had a second home in Jerusalem according to early church fathers. Because of this, his son John would have had a number of contacts in Jerusalem. Using those contacts, John was able to learn where Jesus was and gain access to the home where he was being tried. Later, John arranged for Peter to have access to the home.

As Peter crossed the threshold to the home, the servant girl responsible for the door asked, "You are not also one of this Man's disciples, are you?" (John 18:17). Her question suggests she knew John was a disciple of Jesus and she may have assumed Peter was also. She probably intended the question to mock or ridicule Peter rather than expose him. But the disciple responded quickly, "I am not" (John 18:17). Peter's denials of Jesus had begun.

On at least two occasions earlier that evening, Jesus warned Peter he would deny Jesus at least three times (Luke 22:61; Mark 14:30). Some Bible teachers believe the reference to the cock crowing referred to a specific hour of the night. The cock was thought to first crow between the third and fourth watch of the night, about 3:00 a.m. The crowing of the cock a second time would then refer to some later hour.

That second cock crowing occurred as Jesus was being moved from one place to another and turned and looked at Peter (Mark 14:72; Luke 22:61). The sound of the cock crowing and the look of Jesus caused Peter to remember the warning Jesus had spoken earlier that evening. Peter retreated to spend the rest of the evening alone weeping over what he had done.

Peter was not the only disciple who sensed remorse for what he had done that evening. Judus Iscariot later felt remorse over betraying Jesus and attempted to return the money he had taken to betray Jesus. In remorse over the consequences of his actions, Judas threw the money to his coconspirators in the temple and went out and hanged himself. He tied a rope around a tree limb extending out over a cliff and fixed the noose around his own neck, but when he jumped out to end his life, his body smashed against the rocks below. As a result, "he burst open in the middle and all his entrails gushed out" (Acts 1:18). The money Judas left behind was used to buy a potters field in which Judas died. That field purchased by the money quickly earned a lasting reputation as "the Field of Blood" (Matt. 27:8; Acts 1:19).

The Jews tried Jesus because they perceived He had violated their laws, but in the course of the trial, they repeatedly violated their own well-defined laws. Observers have suggested there were as few as twenty and as many as one hundred specific illegalities in the proceedings. Many of these illegalities related to Jesus' arrest. Under Jewish law, the binding of a prisoner before he was condemned was unlawful unless resistance was offered or expected. Jesus certainly offered no resistance in His arrest, yet He was bound before being brought to trial (John 18:12, 24). Also, it was illegal for judges to participate in the arrest of the accused (John 18:3). Third, it was a violation of Jewish law to use a traitor and informer to secure the arrest (John 18:5; cf. Ex. 23:6-8). Also, it was illegal to carry weapons on a feast day (John 18:3).

In a Jewish trial, it was the judges' duty to insure the interest of the accused was fully protected (John 18:14). Also, preliminary hearings before a magistrate was foreign to the judicial system of the Jews (John 18:13). Further, the use of violence during the trials was apparently unopposed by the judges (John 18:22-23). Contrary to the laws of evidence, the judges in Jesus' trials sought false witnesses to speak against Jesus (Matt. 26:59; Mark 14:56). In a Jewish court, the accused was to be presumed innocent until his guilt had been confirmed by two or more witnesses (John 11:53). When the false witnesses failed to agree in their testimony, the prisoner should have been released (Mark 14:56-59). Also, the judges found Jesus guilty despite the fact no witness was ever called on behalf of the defense.

Under Jewish law, a number of regulations governed the time, place, and conduct of a trial. No legal transactions including a trial could be conducted at night, yet before morning the Jewish trials were concluded (John 18:28). Also, it was illegal to conduct a trial on a feast day (John 18:28). While an acquittal could be pronounced on the day of a trial, any other verdict required a majority of two and had to come on a subsequent day (Matt. 26:65- 66). The trial should have taken place in the council chamber rather than the home of Caiaphas (John 18:13). Also, it was illegal for the high priest to tear his official robe (Matt. 26:65; cf. Lev. 21:10). If he was not wearing his official robe, he could not place Jesus under oath. Other legal violations took place in Jesus' sentencing.

This court lacked the civil authority to condemn a man to death (John 18:31). Also, no prisoner could be convicted on the basis of his own evidence alone (Matt. 26:63-64). Jesus was found guilty despite the lack of evidence (John 18:30). Further, the balloting which determined Jesus' guilt was illegal. Normally, the roll was called with the youngest voting first. On this occasion, the balloting was simultaneous (Matt. 26:66). When the sentence was pronounced in the palace of the high priest, it was announced in the wrong place. It should have been made in the hall of hewn stone in the temple (John 18:28).

After the Jewish trials, Jesus was surrendered to Roman authorities at the Praetorium, the official residence of the Roman governor, Pontius Pilate. Jesus arrived at the Praetorium in early morning. John uses the Greek word *proi* to describe the time which referred technically to the fourth watch of the evening (3:00 a.m.-6:00 a.m.). If the formal meeting of the Sanhedrin followed the cock crowing at 3:00 a.m., it must have been a very brief meeting. Accounting for all that took place prior to Jesus being surrendered to Roman authorities, it appears Jesus must have been presented to Pilate about 5:00 a.m. Within an hour, He would be condemned to die.

Pontius Pilate was the Procurator of Judea from A.D. 26-36. He was deposed in A.D. 36 by Vitellius and sent to Rome where he was tried and probably executed under Caligula. During his rule in Judea, he used funds from the temple treasury to finance public works projects such as building an aqueduct. Some Bible teachers believe the Sanhedrin permitted this practice in exchange for political favors. When the Sanhedrin presented Jesus to him for execution, they apparently expected Pilate to sentence Him without a trial. Initially, they had not thought of a charge with which to accuse Jesus before Roman authorities. When asked what Jesus was accused of, they could only answer, "If He were not an evil doer, we would not have delivered Him up to you" (John 18:30). Jesus formally charged with at least four violations for Roman law when it become apparent Pilate was going to make up his own mind before condemning Jesus to die (Luke 23:2, 5). While Pilate chose to ignore three of these charges, he could not ignore the charge of treason. Tiberius Caesar was particularly sensitive of treason and every suggestion of its existence was carefully investigated and severely dealt with.

THE ACCUSATIONS IN A ROMAN COURT

Perverting the nation
Failure to pay taxes
Identifying Himself as King
Stirring up the people

It quickly became obvious to Pilate that the charges against Jesus were unfounded, yet he also recognized that Jesus had managed to draw the anger of the Sanhedrin upon Himself. Quickly Pilate determined to avoid, if at all possible, any involvement in condemning Jesus to death. He attempted to return Jesus to be tried by the Sanhedrin. They obviously wanted Him killed, but lacked the civil authority to execute criminals (John 18:31). Then He announced His initial finding and proclaimed Jesus innocent (John 18:39). When that decision was not acceptable to the Jews, Pilate sought to escape responsibility for making a decision and turned Jesus over to Herod. Since Jesus was from Galilee, the area ruled by Herod, Jesus was sent to Herod. Herod had learned about Jesus some time before and hoped to witness a miracle, but Jesus did not perform any miracles during these mock trials. Herod, not wanting to try a prisoner outside his jurisdiction, returned Jesus to Pilate without condemning Him.

Pilate realized the Jewish leaders had delivered Jesus in anger and hoped to resolve the problem by releasing Jesus as a gesture of good will and crucifying a notorious prisoner in His place. Barabbas had been involved in insurrections and had killed people in the process. Pilate was sure if given the choice between releasing Barabbas and Jesus, they would choose the latter. They did not. They called for the release of Barabbas and the crucifixion of Jesus.

As Pilate tried to decide what to do next, he received a strange message from His wife. "Have nothing to do with that just Man, for I have suffered many things today in a dream because of Him," she wrote (Matt. 27:19). The Romans believed the gods would sometimes communicate with mortals through dreams, so the message from his wife must have served to further his resolve to get out of condemning Jesus to death. "You take Him and crucify Him," he told the Jewish leaders, "for I find no fault in Him" (John 19:6). Only then did he learn the real reason the Jews were so intent on having Jesus executed, "because He made Himself the Son of God" (John 19:7). Upon learning of this religious accusation by the Jews and hearing of his wife's dream, "from then on Pilate sought to release Him" (John 19:12).

The Jewish leaders' opposition was so intense, Pilate was unable to set Jesus free. He had Jesus beaten and presented the beaten and bloody Jesus to the crowd which had begun to gather. Pilate hoped to play on their pity, but that did not satisfy those who wanted Him killed. He presented the physically abused Jesus as their king, but they responded, "We have no king but Caesar!" (John 19:15). When it became clear nothing else would work, Pilate condemned Jesus to the cross and symbolically washed his hands claiming he was innocent of Jesus' death.

Jesus was led through Jerusalem to Golgotha carrying the instrument of His execution. This was a custom called "bearing one's cross" and served as a final humiliation of the prisoner before he was crucified. Jesus' accusation was written in Hebrew, Greek, and Latin and read, "This is Jesus of Nazareth, the King of the Jews." But by the time Jesus was led to be crucified, He had been so abused physically that He could not carry His accusation without stumbling. A man named Simon who was visiting the city during the feast from his home in Cyrene, North Africa, was forced to bear the cross. Later, two of this man's sons became prominent leaders in the early church.

"And when they had come to the place called Calvary, there they crucified Him" (Luke 23:33). Crucifixion was the usual form of execution used by Rome to execute those guilty of capital crimes. It involved nailing an individual to a cross in such a way as to maximize the pain involved and suspend the body by the arms. The weakened body of the victim would slump with caved-in chest, normally resulting in death by suffocation. There are records of men who hung on a cross up to nine days before dying. If the soldiers needed to insure that death occurred quickly, they would break the prisoner's legs with a heavy mallet, making it impossible for the prisoner to support himself and prevent himself from suffocating. When the soldiers came to break Jesus' legs, they discovered He was already dead. But prior to dying, Jesus made seven statements from the cross which have had special significance to Christians ever since (see chapter 27).

Conclusion

The Old Testament prophet Zechariah had prophesied concerning that night, "Strike the Shepherd, and the sheep will be scattered" (Zech. 13:7). When Jesus was arrested in the garden, all of the disciples ran. The later actions of three of them are mentioned in Scripture to illustrate how Christians today sometimes deal with failure in the Christian life. Some are like Judas Iscariot who realized the error of his ways but refused to deal with the root problem of sin in his life and headed down the road of self-destruction. Others are like Peter who continued to deny his relationship with Christ until the sound of a crowing rooster and the look of Jesus jarred him into a realization of what he had done and led him down the path of repentance. Still others are like John who also ran when the disciples were scattered but quickly made his way to the place where Jesus was and remained close to Jesus all the way to the Cross.

CHAPTER 27

THE WOMEN AT THE CROSS: FROM GOLGOTHA TO THE GRAVE

Matthew 27:45-66; Mark 15:33-47; Luke 23:39-56; John 19:25-42

The actual crucifixion of Jesus began about 9:00 that morning. The entire trial process under the Roman authorities and the preparations for the crucifixion took about four hours. About noon on the day Jesus was crucified, the sky became dark for three hours. Toward the end of the darkness, Jesus died. "Then the veil of the temple was torn in two from top to bottom" (Mark 15:38). Most Bible teachers believe this veil was torn by God to symbolize that because of Jesus' death, people now could have direct access to God without the mediation of a human priest. When the Roman centurion present at the cross saw the way Jesus died, he could come to only one conclusion. "Truly this Man was the Son of God" (Mark 15:39).

As Jesus hung on the cross and was later placed in a grave, a group of women who witnessed all that happened were nearby (cf. John 19:25; Luke 23:55). These Galilean women not only saw what was taking place on both Golgotha and at the grave, they also heard the final statements of Jesus from the cross and probably reported them to Matthew, Mark, and Luke who later recorded them in the Gospels. Even though they were eyewitnesses of one of the most significant events in all history, it is doubtful they completely understood what Jesus was accomplishing on the cross. Only later did they realize that Jesus had not only died, but that He had died for our sins (1 Cor. 15:3; 1 John 2:2).

I. The Sayings of Jesus from the Cross

People who were being crucified commonly uttered defiant and blasphemous statements at the executioners or crowds which gathered around the cross, but that was not the case with Jesus as He hung on the cross dying. Jesus spoke from His cross seven times. These seven sayings reflect His divine-human nature and His commitment to accomplishing His ultimate purpose in life, providing the salvation of God.

In His first statement from the cross, Jesus prayed a prayer of forgiveness: "Father, forgive them, for they do not know what they do" (Luke 23:34). In the midst of His intense pain and suffering, Jesus paused to pray for those who were the cause of that suffering. In this prayer, He revealed God's immense love for sinners (cf. Rom. 5:8). A very similar prayer to this was later prayed by Stephen, the first martyr of the church, suggesting that Jesus' demonstration of God's love quickly became a model the first Christians strived to reproduce in their life (Acts 7:60).

Jesus' next statement was one of acceptance. Initially, the thieves who were crucified with Jesus joined the antagonistic crowds which had gathered at the cross in taunting and ridiculing Jesus. Then one of the men realized he was not only physically but also spiritually condemned. When this thief expressed his faith in Jesus as the messianic king and asked to be remembered by Jesus when the kingdom was established, Jesus responded, "Assuredly, I say to you, today you will be with Me in Paradise" (Luke 23:43).

THE SEVEN SAYINGS OF JESUS FROM THE CROSS

Father, forgive them, for they do not know what they do. (Luke 23:34)
Assuredly, I say to you, today you will be with Me in Paradise (Luke 23:43)
Woman, behold your son!...Behold your mother! (John 19:26-27)
Eli, Eli, lama sabachthani?– My God, My God, why have You forsaken Me? (Matt. 27:46)
I thirst (John 19:28)
It is finished! (John 19:30)
Father, into Your hands I commit My spirit (Luke 23:46)

Jesus' third statement from the cross recognized a human responsibility that He needed to fulfill. The absence of any reference to Joseph in the Gospels after Jesus' visit to Jerusalem at age 12 has led most Bible teachers to conclude Joseph must have died prior to Jesus beginning His public ministry. As the firstborn son in the family, it was Jesus' responsibility to care for His mother. From the cross, Jesus saw His mother standing next to one of His disciples, John. Looking at His mother He said, "Woman, behold your son!" (John 19:26). Then to John He said, "Behold your mother!" (John 19:27). John immediately accepted Mary and cared for her as he would his own mother.

Jesus' fourth statement from the cross reveals the extent of His anguish over His separation from God as He became the sin-bearer of the world. So haunting were the words as they were uttered from the cross that they were preserved in their original language, "Eli, Eli, lama sabachthani?" which means "My God, My God, why have You forsaken Me?" (Matt. 27:46). At that moment, Jesus experienced alienation from God for the first time in eternity. Although He had never sinned, Jesus experienced this consequence of sin so that those who had sinned could be reconciled to God (2 Cor. 5:18-19).

Jesus' fifth statement from the cross reflected the nature of the physical suffering He was enduring on the cross. As a crucified man reached the human limit of suffering, he experienced intense thirst. When Jesus cried out "I thirst" (John 19:28), it demonstrated He was not exempt from the physical suffering normally experienced in crucifixion. Some might assume Jesus' suffering was less than what others might experience because Jesus was God. Actually, the suffering of Jesus may have been more severe than normal because Jesus was not a hardened sinner who would have been used to the normal consequence of sin. Most Bible teachers believe this statement was made so that Jesus would have the strength to make His next statement of victory.

Jesus' sixth statement, "It is finished!" (John 19:30), was a cry of victory. Several things were "finished" at that moment. First, Jesus accomplished the salvation of God for the human race. Second, He had succeeded in bruising the head of the serpent, fulfilling the first messianic promise in Scripture (Gen. 3:15). Third, Jesus demonstrated God's love (John 3:16). Also, He satisfied the demands of God's holiness (Rom. 5:8).

Fifth, Jesus demonstrated His fulfillment of messianic Scripture by accomplishing the Messiah's greatest work. He also finished the physical suffering of the past several hours.

A seventh thing that was finished was the Old Testament sacrificial system which was intended to foreshadow what had just taken place on the cross. Symbolically, God tore the veil in the temple from top to bottom when Jesus cried out, "It is finished."

Jesus' final statement from the cross was a benediction, "Father, into Your hands I commit My spirit" (Luke 23:46). When He had accomplished all He was meant to accomplish in life, Jesus committed Himself to God in death. Just as Jesus committed His death to God, people today can and should commit their lives to Him.

II.   The Effect of the Cross

The death of Jesus on Golgotha was more than a mere fact of history. While the women witnessed the events of those hours on Golgotha, God saw things happening which were not recognized on earth. The death of Jesus on the cross was viewed from heaven as substitutionary and redemptive. Also, it served as the propitiation by which the world was reconciled to God.

The atonement which Jesus accomplished on the cross was substitutionary in nature. In the context of the Old Testament law, those religious leaders who witnessed the crucifixion understood the need to offer a substitutionary sacrifice for sin. An animal which was slaughtered and placed on the altar in the temple represented the one giving the gift. The death of Jesus was a fulfillment of all the typical sacrifices which had been offered under the law.

There are several aspects of the substitutionary nature of Jesus' death. First, He died for the nation of Israel. Just a matter of weeks before the Crucifixion, Caiaphas had prophesied, "It is expedient for us that one man should die for the people, and not that the whole nation should perish" (John 11:50). Second, Jesus died for Christians. Paul reminded the saints at Rome, "While we were still sinners, Christ died for us" (Rom. 5:8). Third, Jesus died for the church. "Christ also loved the church and gave Himself for her" (Eph. 5:25). Fourth, Jesus' death was adequate for everyone. One of the reasons for the Cross was that Jesus "might taste death for everyone" (Heb. 2:9).

The word "redemptive" also describes the death of Jesus. The word "redeem" means "to purchase." Christians "were not redeemed with corruptible things, like silver or gold...but with the precious blood of Christ" (1 Peter 1:18-19). The nature of this redemption is revealed in three different Greek words that Paul used in Galatians to describe redemption. The first word *agorazo* (Gal. 3:10) means "to purchase in the market." The second word is *ekagorazo*, meaning "to buy and remove from the slave market never to be sold again." The third word, *lutroo* (Gal. 5:1) means "to purchase and give freedom." This means we have been given liberty by Jesus and are no longer slaves but sons.

Another Greek word used to describe Jesus' death is the word *hilasterion* which means "a place of propitiation" (cf. Rom. 3:25; 1 John 2:2; 4:10). In the context of the Old Testament, the place of propitiation was the mercy seat where the priest sprinkled blood on the day of atonement to satisfy the justice of God. Jesus' death was propitious in that it satisfied both the justice of God (1 John 2:2) and the demands of the law (Eph. 2:15; Col. 2:14).

Jesus' death was also the means by which God reconciled the world to Himself (2 Cor. 5:19). In this aspect of Jesus' death, everything was brought into the favorable light of God's mercy. This was accomplished by destroying the cause of the animosity between God and man and changing man himself. Jesus died "that He might reconcile them both to God in one body through the cross, thereby putting to death the enmity" (Eph 2:16). Also, Jesus serves as the mediator between God and man (1 Tim. 2:5) and represents man before God as an advocate (1 John 2:1). When God looks at man, He now sees Him as "crucified with Christ" (Gal. 2:20). When one is converted and therefore "in Christ," there is nothing in man offensive to God.

III.   Saturday, April 8: A Day of Opposition

Because Israel was about to begin observing the Feast of Unleavened Bread, the Jewish leaders felt it was important that the bodies of those crucified not remain on the crosses overnight. When they were certified to be dead, the Roman soldiers took the bodies off the crosses and gave them to anyone who would claim them. Jesus' body was claimed by Joseph of Arimathea, a member of the Sanhedrin who was a follower of Jesus. Along with another member of the Sanhedrin, Nicodemus, he took Jesus' body and buried it in a tomb which had recently been carved out of the rock. By sundown, the beginning of the Jewish Sabbath, Jesus had been buried and the tomb had been sealed by rolling a large stone before the mouth of the cave.

Even though the Jewish leaders were successful in their attempt to execute Jesus, they were still not satisfied. They remembered Jesus had predicted His own resurrection and were afraid His disciples might steal His body to perpetuate their movement. As the Feast of Unleavened Bread began, the Sanhedrin made a formal request for a guard for the tomb of Jesus. Pilate reminded them they had a temple guard which could be used for that purpose and sent them away. The soldiers assigned to police the temple area were Romans and to some extent under the jurisdiction of the Sanhedrin. The tomb was sealed with a Roman seal and a guard was posted to prevent the theft of Jesus' body.

While Jesus' body remained in the tomb, His spirit was engaged in spiritual warfare. Older evangelical Bible teachers called this doctrine "His Descent into Hell." Prior to the resurrection of Jesus, both Paradise and the Place of Torments were located in Hades (cf. Luke 16:19-31). When Jesus died, He went to Paradise as did the thief on the cross who repented of his sins (cf. Luke 23:43). Paradise is also called Abraham's bosom. During the time His body lied in the grave, Jesus was apparently involved in some degree of conflict which resulted in Paradise's release of the captivity of Hades so that "when He ascended on high, He led captivity captive" (Eph. 4:8; Ps. 68:18). The Apostles' Creed describes this event, "He descended into hell."

While the Sanhedrin and evil spirits of Hades continued their opposition to Jesus that Sabbath, those loyal to Jesus rested. They observed the Sabbath, eagerly waiting the morning so that they could return to the tomb and finish the process of anointing Jesus' body for burial. Unknown to all, it would be the last Sabbath of its kind in history. It was the last Sabbath of the Old Testament.

Conclusion

The death of Jesus on Calvary provided the means whereby the world could be saved. Certainly one's first response to this demonstration of God's love is to receive the salvation which God offers (John 3:16). But the Cross was also a demonstration of how believers ought to love one another. As the apostle John, who personally witnessed this demonstration of love, reminded the early church, "Beloved, if God so loved us, we also ought to love one another" (1 John 4:11).

CHAPTER 28

SUNDAY, APRIL 9:
THE END OF THE SABBATHS

Matthew 28:1-15; Mark 16:1-14; Luke 24:1-43; John 20:1-25

When Matthew began his account of the events of Sunday morning, April 9, he wrote, "Now after the Sabbath, as the first day of the week began to dawn" (Matt. 28:1). Similarly, Mark begins his account of the events of that day noting, "Now when the Sabbath was past" (Mark 16:1). Some Bible teachers believe these statements refer to more than the identification of the day of the week, Sunday. In a very real sense, the events of that Sunday marked the end of the observance of the Sabbaths as a Jewish day of rest. Within months, Sunday would be a new day of the week to take special significance in the hearts of many of Jesus' followers. By the end of that century, Sunday would be their day of celebration known as "the Lord's Day" (cf. Rev. 1:10). Also, Sunday was apparently the only day Jesus appeared to His followers in post-resurrection appearances.

Apparently none of Jesus' followers anticipated a resurrection of Jesus despite Jesus' constant teaching on the subject while He was with them (cf. John 2:20; Matt. 16:21; 26:61). The eleven disciples were despondent and had assumed the Cross had marked the end of that special relationship they had experienced with Jesus. Even the group of women who left early that morning to go to Jesus' tomb did not expect to witness a resurrected Savior, but to finish treating a dead corpse. What they discovered when they got there was so unexpected even they themselves did not understand what was taking place at first.

Before the women got to Jesus' grave that morning, "there was a great earthquake; for an angel of the Lord descended from heaven, and came and rolled back the stone from the door, and sat on it" (Matt. 28:2). The angel did not open the tomb so that Jesus could get out, but rather to let others look in and see that Jesus had risen from the dead. The Roman guards who had been charged with guarding the tomb were probably prepared for an attempt on the part of the disciples to steal Jesus' body, but they did not know how to respond to the angel's appearance that looked like brilliant white lightening. They began to shake in fear and fainted. When they recovered, they raced into the city and reported to the chief priests what had happened.

When the priests learned of Jesus' resurrection, their worst fear was realized. They knew they had to respond quickly to the situation. In hurried consultation with other Jewish leaders, they came up with a solution to their problem. The soldiers were paid off and told not to report the angel and Resurrection. Rather, the official story was, "His disciples came at night and stole Him away while we slept" (Matt. 28:13). The soldiers knew they could be executed for sleeping while on duty, but the Jewish leaders assured them they would pull strings to keep them secure in their position should Pilate determine to discipline them. The account seemed plausible, and the soldiers agreed to spread the story among the Jews. Not surprisingly, many believed it. Even some of those closest to Jesus initially believed that the empty tomb meant someone had moved Jesus' body.

I.   The Mystery of the Empty Tomb and Missing Body

As the soldiers hurried into the city, another group was coming toward the tomb from the city. Mary Magdalene deeply loved Jesus as she had loved no other person. She recalled how He had released her from the bondage and torment of the seven demons which had possessed her only a few years earlier. She had been among the women at the foot of the cross who watched Jesus die. It seemed like a part of her died with Jesus that day. The least she could do now was be certain He got a decent burial. Together with several others, she had begun the task as they placed Him in the tomb, but with the Passover approaching they had to leave the task uncompleted. It would not be left unfinished for long. The sun was not even up yet as she was on her way to the tomb. Apparently, she was bolder than the other women, given her background. She walked ahead of the others, thinking Roman soldiers would be there.

But as she arrived at the tomb, things did not seem at all right. The soldiers were not there. She had watched Joseph and Nicodemus lay jesus in the tomb and seal it with a large stone, but the stone had been moved. She had noted the place where the body was placed.

Suddenly, Mary thought she knew what had happened. Obviously the body had been moved, but who moved it? It would have had to have been the Romans, or someone who could have gotten past the Roman soldiers. Who moved Jesus' body? And how were the women going to find it? John! That was her answer! He knew some people close to the high priest. If anyone could find out where the body was it would be John. Leaving the tomb, in her state of mind, she didn't even go back to alert the other women. Instead, she ran back to the city another way to find John and report what had happened.

Quickly she found John's house and banged at the door. As the door opened she found Peter and John. Confused and out of breath she began to gasp out her message. "They have take away the Lord out of the tomb, and we do not know where they have laid him" (John 20:2).

She did not even have a chance to say who "they" were. Because of the impetuous nature of youth, John ran out the door to the garden tomb of Jesus. Peter also wondering at Mary's strange report, began to run after John. Peter was at least ten years older and his age began to show. John easily outran him. As the younger disciple arrived at the tomb, he was reluctant to enter, but stooped down and looked into the tomb.

As John peered into the tomb he saw in the shadows the linen clothes in which the body had been wrapped. He began to understand. As Peter arrived, he was running so hard he couldn't stop and ran past John, into the tomb. He noticed the cloth that had been placed over Jesus' face laying in another part of the tomb, away from the linen grave cloths. John followed his fellow disciple in and gained spiritual insight on what had happened. It had really happened just like Jesus told them it would. He was risen from the dead. John apparently was the first to believe in the resurrection of Jesus, and the only disciple who came to that conclusion without first seeing the resurrected Jesus (John 20:8).

Peter wasn't as easily convinced as John. As he walked away from the tomb, he probably wondered, Why would anyone want to steal a body from a tomb? And why from a tomb so heavily guarded as that of Jesus? And why Jesus' body? The questions probably kept coming, but the answers somehow evaded him. Peter did not like unanswered questions. Things would become more confusing before he would fully understand as the events of the day unfolded.

II.   The Early Post-Resurrection Appearance of Jesus

One of the first reports received by the disciples came from the women who had gone to the tomb with Mary that morning. Apparently Mary had left just before an angel appeared to the other women to explain what had taken place. "Do not be afraid, for I know that you seek Jesus who was crucified," the angel began. "He is not here; for He is risen, as He said. Come, see the place where the Lord lay" (Matt. 28:5-6).

The angel not only explained the mystery of the empty tomb to these women, he gave them a message to share with the disciples. "Go quickly and tell His disciples that He is risen from the dead, and indeed He is going before you into Galilee; there you will see Him" (Matt. 28:7). As the women were returning to the city to tell the disciple what the angel said, they met Jesus Himself. As they reported the story to the disciples, they told how they had actually held Him by the feet and heard Him speak. He too had a message about the upcoming meeting in Galilee. "Go and tell My brethren to go to Galilee, and there they will see Me" (Matt. 28:10).

Next Mary returned to the tomb a second time, later in the morning. She had left the garden hastily, but wanted to return to inspect it more carefully. She too told the disciples how she saw and talked with Jesus. She saw two angels inside the tomb, then met a man she thought was the gardener. The man asked, "Woman, why are you weeping? Whom are you seeking?" (John 20:15). Assuming maybe the gardener had moved the body, or at least knew where it had been moved, she pleaded, "Sir, if You have carried Him away, tell me where You have laid Him, and I will take Him away" (John 20:16).

The gardener responded simply by calling her by name, "Mary!" (John 20:16). Although she was distraught over all that had happened that morning, she immediately recognized the only one who pronounced her name that way. She was not talking to the gardener at all. Turning to Him, she fell at His feet and clung to Him. Knowing at last what had happened, she addressed Jesus by a title which suitably expressed both her reverence and affection for Him, "Rabboni!" (John 20:16).

A third report must have been received by the disciples that morning as they attempted to understand what had taken place at Jesus' tomb. The rumor had begun to circulate around Jerusalem that the disciples had stolen Jesus' body while the guards had fallen asleep on the job. The disciples knew they had not stolen the body, but still the report was confusing. As near as they could determine, the Roman guards were actually admitting they had fallen asleep while on guard duty, but no official disciplinary action was being taken.

A couple, Cleophas and his wife, left Jerusalem to return to Emmaus about seven miles outside of Jerusalem. They were followers of Jesus but nothing was left for them in Jerusalem. Cleophas talked about the unusual events of the morning. How did it all fit together? The body was missing, that at least was a reported fact. But who stole it? That question had still not been answered. Perhaps if they knew who stole it, they might be able to figure out where they had hidden it. And what about the women's reports? Normally they were not given to hysteria, but then again they were not normally witnesses to the crucifixion of a close friend like Jesus.

As Cleophas and his wife walked to Emmaus, the events of that morning and the weekend continued to be the basis of their conversation. It was not surprising that they began feeling worse about things as they contemplated Jesus' death and the death of all the dreams that had begun to form as they anticipated the establishment of His kingdom.

"What kind of conversation is this that you have with one another as you walk and are sad?" someone asked as the couple continued their journey (Luke 24:17). It was not unusual in the East for strangers to talk to one another as they met on the road, but it seemed strange that this individual did not know what had happened in Jerusalem at Passover. The couple assumed everybody knew what had taken place. Before Cleophas could respond, his wife asked, "Are You the only stranger in Jerusalem and have You not known the things which happened there in these days?" (Luke 24:18).

Apparently, they believed, the stranger did not know what had taken place, so they reviewed the events surrounding the Crucifixion. "But we were hoping that it was He who was going to redeem Israel," they confessed with a sign of resignation in their voices (Luke 24:21). Then they mentioned the report of the women who claimed to have seen angels reporting that Jesus was alive. The stranger listened to the account but was not discouraged with what He heard. "Ought not the Christ to have suffered these things and to enter into His glory?" he reasoned (Luke 24:26). As they continued their journey together He began to explain passages from the Old Testament that seemed to indicate all that had taken place was consistent with what should have been expected.

As the stranger explained these Scriptures, the Old Testament seemed to take on new meaning. Something inside the couple began to change as they understood the events of the weekend in a different light. Before long, they were at their home and the stranger began to part company to continue on His journey. He had been such an encouragement to them. The least they could do was have Him into their home for a meal, so they convinced Him to spend the night with them.

Quickly a dinner was prepared and the three came to the table to eat. The stranger "took bread, blessed and broke it, and gave it to them" (Luke 24:30). Suddenly they understood. The Bible says "their eyes were opened." Not until that moment did they realize the stranger was indeed Jesus Himself. And as they come to that realization, Jesus "vanished from their sight" (Luke 24:31).

Although it was late, Cleophas and his wife quickly returned to Jerusalem and found the place where nine of the disciples had gathered for a dinner of broiled fish. They explained what had happened on the road to Emmaus and how Jesus had broken bread with them. They were told, "The Lord is risen indeed, and has appeared to Simon!" (Luke 24:34).

"Now as they said these things, Jesus Himself stood in the midst of them" (Luke 24:36). The disciples had bolted the door expecting the Jewish leaders to come after them at any moment, but Jesus just passed through the door. As He showed them the physical evidence of the Crucifixion, they realized it really was Jesus, and He had risen from the dead.

Jesus ate some of their fish and a piece of honeycomb, then He shared with them a new commission. "Peace to You! As the Father has sent Me. I also send you," He explained (John 20:21). Then He breathed on them and urged them to receive the Holy Spirit. He stressed the importance of their being faithful in fulfilling the new commission they had just received. "If you forgive the sins of any, they are forgiven them; if you retain the sins of any, they are retained" (John 20:23). Whether or not others would come to faith in Jesus as the Messiah and be forgiven for their sins would to some degree depend on the disciples' faithfulness to their commission. Those they told could be forgiven, but if they failed to tell, would remain in the bondage of sin eternally.

Conclusion

Just as the disciples struggled to come to faith in the resurrection of Jesus, so must each individual come to believe today. Some respond to Jesus with faith quickly like John, but others are like Peter who apparently did not come to faith in the resurrected Jesus until several people told him and he had a personal encounter with Jesus. All who came to faith in the Resurrection found in it a cause for celebration. Even today, the resurrection of Jesus remains a cause for celebration on the Lord's Day.

CHAPTER 29

JESUS: HIS FINAL DAYS
AMONG HIS DISCIPLES

Matthew 28:16-20; Mark 16:15-20; Luke 24:44-53; John 20:26–21:25; Acts 1:1-12

*I*n the week following Easter Sunday, the disciples marvelled at the awesome responsibility that was theirs, that of being witnesses of Jesus' resurrection and communicating to others how they could experience the forgiveness of sins. They knew they would soon be returning to Galilee where Jesus had promised to meet them again, but first there were some loose ends to take care of. Thomas had not been with them when they saw Jesus. He was strong-minded, silent, but also skeptical. Thomas was among the first to whom the disciples told that they had seen Jesus. Judas, another disciple was also a absent from that meeting. Probably very early that week they learned of Judas Iscariot's suicide. Judas had been a key member of their group and was responsible for the disciples' finances. It would take some time to sort out the group's finances and appoint another to assume that responsibility.

The disciples may have been surprised at Thomas' reluctance to believe their corporate testimony as they reported to him that they had seen the resurrected Jesus. They may have forgotten how reluctant they also had been to believe the early reports of the women and Mary Magdalene that Sunday morning. Thomas was just as reluctant to believe, and said, "Unless I see in His hands the print of the nails, and put my finger into the print of the nails, and put my hand into His side, I will not believe" (John 20:25). To him, that did not seem an unreasonable request. The disciples themselves claimed they had seen the nail prints before they recognized Jesus and believed in the resurrection from the dead (John 20:20).

Very early in the church's history, Christians began referring to Sunday as "the Lord's Day" (cf. Rev. 1:10). One reason suggested for this title was that Jesus' appearances after His resurrection all occurred on Sundays. While some records of the post-resurrection appearances do not specifically identify the day of the week, those which do include sufficient detail to determine the day of the week Jesus appeared; all agree it was on a Sunday.

I. Sunday, April 16: Jesus and Thomas

A week after the Resurrection, on Sunday, April 16, the disciples were again gathered together in the evening. This time Thomas was with the others.

Once again, the doors of the room had been bolted as the disciples apparently thought they may still be in danger. No one was really sure what the Jewish leaders were going to do about Jesus' disciples as the conflicting accounts of a stolen body and the resurrection of Jesus were continuing to be reported around town. Then, just as had happened a week earlier, Jesus came and stood in their midst. Again, He greeted His disciples with the familiar "Peace to you!" (John 20:26).

Very soon in this visit, it became clear Jesus had come primarily for Thomas' benefit. Turning to the doubting disciple, he said, "Reach your finger here, and look at My hands; and reach your hand here, and put it into My side. Do not be unbelieving, but believing" (John 20:27). Just as He had offered the others a close look at the physical evidence of His crucifixion and resurrection from the dead, Jesus offered Thomas the same opportunity. But Thomas did not need to look. Seeing Jesus in the midst of the disciples and hearing Him speak again was enough to produce a response of faith in his heart. He expressed his faith simply with the confession, "My Lord and my God" (John 20:28).

Jesus responded, "Thomas, because you have seen Me, you have believed. Blessed are those who have not seen and yet believed" (John 20:29). While some Bible teachers believe this was a rebuke to Thomas for his reluctance to believe, others believe Jesus was commending Thomas for his faith and note the difference implied in the two Greek words used to refer to seeing. The first word *eidon* implies the idea of perceiving more than the act of looking with the eyes. The second word *horao* means to perceive with the eyes. Jesus told Thomas, "Because you have seen and understand who I am, you have believed. Blessed are those who like you have not examined me by sight and yet believe" (John 20:29, author's translation).

Sunday, April 23: Jesus and the Seven

Probably during the week following this appearance of Jesus to the disciples is when the disciples realized Judas Iscariot had been pilfering funds from the common purse. The disciples had probably planned to return to Galilee to meet with Jesus anyway, but the realization that funds were missing no doubt convinced them of the need to return to Galilee where they knew they could raise money by fishing. Prior to following Jesus, at least four of the disciples had made their living fishing on the Sea of Galilee. When the group got back to Tiberias, Peter announced his intention to return to fishing. Six other disciples agreed that was a wise decision and got in the boat with Peter that Saturday night (John, James, Thomas, Nathanael, and probably Andrew and Philip [John 21:2]). That night, the disciples did not catch any fish. As it began to dawn over the lake Sunday morning, they began to make their way to shore. Unknown to them, the man they could see standing on the shore was Jesus Himself. "Children, have you any food?" He asked them (John 21:5). The disciples probably assumed He was asking to purchase fresh fish for His family. When they said they had nothing, He responded, "Cast the net on the right side of the boat, and you will find some" (John 21:6).

The disciples knew that from shore you could sometimes see a school of fish that might not be seen from the boat, so they responded to the man's instructions and threw the net in one more time, "and now they were not able to draw it in because of the multitude of fish" (John 21:6). John had spent many years fishing that lake before becoming a disciple of Jesus and recognized this sort of catch had only happened on one other occasion, a time when Jesus had told them to cast in their nets after a previous night of fishing without results. As he came to realize what was happening, he shared his conclusion with Peter. "It is the Lord!" he exclaimed (John 21:7).

In his enthusiasm, Peter grabbed his fishing coat and dove into the water to swim to Jesus. He was not trying to walk on water, nor was he concerned about how he was dressed. Peter was just emotional in his response. By the time everyone got to shore dragging the net full of fish, Jesus already had some broiled fish and toast for them. He encouraged them to bring some of the fish they had caught also and invited them to "Come and eat breakfast" (John 21:12). There were one hundred and fifty-three fish in the net, yet it had not broken. In His invitation to eat, Jesus used the term translated "breakfast" which literally referred to the breaking of the Sabbath fast with a Sunday morning meal (John 21:12). This implied this post-resurrection appearance of Jesus also took place on a Sunday.

After the meal, Jesus and Peter engaged in a brief conversation. Jesus asked Peter, "Simon, son of Jonah, do you love (*agape*) Me more than these?" (John 21:15). Peter responded, "Yes, Lord; You know that I love (*phileo*) You" (John 21:15). Then Jesus directed His disciple, "Keep on feeding my little lambs" (John 21:15, author's translation).

This first conversation was followed by a second similar conversation. Jesus again asked, "Simon, son of Jonah, do you love (*agape*) Me?" and Peter again responded, "Yes, Lord; You know that I love (*phileo*) You" (John 21:16). This second time, Jesus told Peter, "Keep on shepherding the young sheep" (John 21:16, author's translation).

A third time, Jesus spoke to Peter in a similar way. This time Jesus asked, "Simon, son of Jonah, do you love (*phileo*) Me?" (John 21:17). Peter was grieved that Jesus continued to question him concerning his love for his Lord and responded, "Lord, You know (*oida*–to know intuitively) all things; You know (*ginosko*–to know experientially) that I love (*phileo*) You" (John 21:17). This time Jesus responded to Peter's answer with the directive, "Keep on feeding the mature sheep" (John 21:17, author's translation).

That day on the beach, Peter also learned how his own life would end. A few weeks earlier he had told Jesus he was willing to go to the cross with Him (John 13:37), but then later denied even knowing Jesus. Still, the day would come when Peter would go to a cross for Jesus. "Most assuredly, I say to you, when you were younger, you girded yourself and walked where you wished; but when you are old, you will stretch out your hands, and another will gird you and carry you where you do not wish," Jesus explained (John 21:18). Then, knowing Peter knew exactly what he would encounter in a life of discipleship, Jesus repeated two words He had first spoken to this disciple almost four years earlier, "Follow me" (John 21:19).

Sunday, April 30: Jesus and the Five Hundred

The very next Sunday was probably when Jesus again appeared to His disciples in Galilee, this time on the mountain upon which he had earlier told them to meet Him. This appearance apparently included both the disciples (Matt. 28:7) and a larger group known as the brethren (Matt. 28:10). Many Bible teachers identify this as the meeting of over five hundred identified by Paul (1 Cor. 15:6). At this meeting, Jesus was worshipped as God, but some in the group still had their doubts (Matt. 28:17). The Greek word *distazo* used here means to doubt in the sense of hesitating to act on one's faith. It is highly unlikely that any of the disciples doubted the reality of the Resurrection by this point in time, but some of those present may have been Galileans who had not yet heard the other reports of Jesus' post-resurrection appearances.

On this occasion, Jesus again reminded His disciples of their responsibility to communicate the gospel to others. He addressed the group noting, "All authority has been given to Me in heaven and on earth. Go therefore and make disciples of all the nations, baptizing them in the name of the Father and of the Son and of the Holy Spirit, teaching them to observe all things that I have commanded you; and lo, I am with you always, even to the end of the age" (Matt. 28:18-20).

Although the Great Commission is repeated five times in the New Testament, this account of the giving of the commission is usually considered the most significant as it addresses the strategy by which the nations of the world were to be reached, that of "making disciples."

Sunday, May 7: Jesus Meets His Disciples and Family

After meeting with Jesus on the mountain in Galilee, the disciples returned approximately seventy miles to Jerusalem. By this time, they understood the responsibility that would soon be theirs as witnesses of the Resurrection, but they still did not completely understand how the resurrection of Jesus fit into the biblical revelation concerning the Messiah. A week later they again met with Jesus, apparently in the same home in which they had met Him on two previous occasions (cf. John 20:19-29). On this occasion, Jesus took the time to explain the Scriptures to the whole group of disciples as He had explained them to Cleopas and his wife several weeks earlier.

"And He opened their understanding that they might comprehend the Scriptures" (Luke 24:45). But even with this renewed understanding of the Scriptures, they were still not ready to begin their work. Jesus explained, "Behold, I send the Promise of My Father upon you; but tarry in the city of Jerusalem until you are endued with power from on high" (Luke 24:49).

This may also have been the day that Jesus appeared to His own brother James (1 Cor. 15:7). Little is known about this post-resurrection appearance of Jesus except that it took place prior to His final appearance to His disciples as a group. This may have been the means of His brother's conversion as James and the others in the family did not believe in Jesus as the Messiah earlier (cf. John 7:5), but a week later they were among the one hundred and twenty gathered in the Upper Room (Acts 1:14). James quickly rose to a place of prominence in the early church as the senior pastor of the Jerusalem church. Some Bible teachers believe Jesus's meeting with His brother may have included preparing James for the responsibility that would soon be his.

Sunday, May 14: The Ascension of Jesus

The last post-resurrection appearance of Jesus before Pentecost came forty days "after his suffering" (Acts 1:3). While it is common for many Christians to begin counting these forty days from Easter Sunday, Luke seems to indicate they should be counted from the time when Jesus' actual suffering began. This means this appearance and the ascension of Jesus took place on Sunday, May 14, two weeks before Pentecost Sunday in A.D. 30.

On Jesus' final meeting with His disciples as a group, He again instructed the disciples concerning the kingdom of God, reminding them "John truly baptized with water, but you shall be baptized with the Holy Spirit not many days from now" (Acts 1:5). Because the kingdom of God was important in the Jews' expectation, it was not surprising that the disciples would want to learn more about this subject as they walked together toward the Mount of Olives. Five weeks had now passed since Jesus had risen from the dead, and they wondered how much longer they would have to wait for Him to reign over the kingdom of Israel. "Lord, will You at this time restore the kingdom to Israel?" they asked (Act. 1:6).

Jesus told His disciples it was not for them to know the Father's timing regarding the coming of the kingdom or other matters under His authority. He reminded them of the greatness of their commission. "But you shall receive power when the Holy Spirit is come upon you; and you shall be witnesses to Me in Jerusalem, and in all Judea and Samaria, and to the end of the earth" (Acts 1:8). While they might anticipate the coming of the kingdom, they would soon be empowered to be witnesses to the end of the earth. "Now when He had spoken these things, while they watched, He was taken up, and a cloud received Him out of their sight" (Acts 1:9). In their amazement they continued looking to the sky until they heard the voice of two angels who had joined their group. "Men of Galilee, why do you stand gazing up to heaven?" they asked. "This same Jesus, who was taken up from you into heaven, will so come in like manner as you saw Him go into heaven" (Acts 1:11). Jesus was gone, but He would return just as He had left.

In eager anticipation of what lied before them, the disciples returned to Jerusalem. In the past five weeks, their number had grown as a number of Galileans apparently returned to Jerusalem with them. They returned to the Upper Room where they had celebrated their last Passover with Jesus. Others joined them, one hundred and twenty in total, in a prayer meeting that would last two weeks. Jesus had promised the soon coming of the Holy Spirit and urged them to wait in prayer. They did not know how long they would have to wait, but they were now ready for the next development in their pilgrimage of faith. "And there are also many other things that Jesus did, which if they were written one by one, I suppose that even the world itself could not contain the books that would be written...And truly Jesus did many other signs in the presence of His disciples, which are not written in this book; but these are written that you may believe that Jesus is the Christ, the Son of God, and that believing you may have life in His name" (John 21:25; 20:30-31).

Conclusion

The Great Commission Jesus left His disciples during His final days with them is still operative today. Christians today need to prepare themselves and obey that directive to "make disciples" of every person within their sphere of influence. Then as believers are faithful witnesses of the gospel to those within their sphere of influence, God often widens that sphere of influence so that more will be reached by those who faithfully witness to the saving power of the gospel.

CHAPTER 30

PETER:
PENTECOST AND THE CHURCH
AT JERUSALEM

Acts 1:1–4:37

The one hundred and twenty persons continued together in prayer as they anticipated the coming of the Holy Spirit. At some point in the course of their wait, the decision was made to appoint a twelfth disciple to replace Judas Iscariot. Although the Bible does not indicate exactly when during that two week period the decision was made, there is good reason to believe it occurred on Sunday, May 21, or seven days after they began praying in the Upper Room. As the disciples waited for the coming of the Holy Spirit, their sense of anticipation must have heightened as they approached "the Lord's Day." But on that Sunday, there was no coming of the Spirit, nor did Jesus appear to them. This would have been the first time in the six weeks since Passover that Jesus had not appeared on Sunday. That may have been what prompted Peter and the others to look within the group and conclude that the incompleteness of the twelve caused by Judas Iscariot's defection and suicide may have somehow begun to hinder the group spiritually.

Peter rose on that occasion and reminded those present that the activities of Judas Iscariot were consistent with the prophecies concerning the betrayal of the Messiah. He was not trying to justify the actions of the betrayer but rather recognized that his sin should not come as a surprise to the group. Peter also reminded the group of two Psalms which seemed to indicate another should be appointed to take the vacant office (Psalm 109:8). On that basis, Peter proposed that the group appoint a new twelfth disciple.

In appointing a disciple to replace Judas Iscariot, several conditions were quickly established. First, the new disciple would be chosen from the group that had traveled with Jesus from the beginning (after John the Baptist baptized Jesus) even though they had not been commissioned apostles by Him. Second, the new disciple should have been a witness of both the resurrection and ascension of Jesus. Of those present, only two appeared to meet all these qualifications, Joseph Justus who was also known as Barsabas and Matthias. (Many modern Bible teachers believe they should have waited for the apostle Paul to be added as the twelfth disciple.)

With two equally qualified candidates for one office, the disciples were not prepared to make a decision themselves without some sort of divine guidance, yet they may have believed they needed to make this decision before they would again see Jesus or receive the Holy Spirit. Together they prayed, "You, O Lord, who know the hearts of all, show which of these two You have chosen to take part in this ministry and apostleship from which Judas by transgression fell, that he might go to his own place" (Acts 1:24-25). Then relying upon the Old Testament custom of casting lots, they determined Matthias was the one who should serve in Judas Iscariot's place. "And he was numbered with the eleven apostles" (Acts 1:26).

I. Sunday, May 28: When the Day of Pentecost Was Fully Come

During the two weeks of corporate prayer that took place between the ascension of Jesus and the Day of Pentecost, there may have been other times of inner searching and attempts made to correct what was perceived to be wrong. Some Bible teachers suggest various reconciliations would almost have to have been made in a group of that size who for two weeks lived together in anticipation of the Father's promise. By the end of that period of waiting, a spirit of united fellowship governed the corporate attitude of the group as "They were all with one accord in one place" (Acts 2:1).

Quite unexpectedly, a number of strange phenomena began to take place in and around that Upper Room. First, there was a sound similar to that of a strong gust of wind which seemed to echo from the walls of the room in which they were sitting. Then divided tongues began appearing on each of them that looked like flames out of a fire. Third, "they were all filled with the Holy Spirit" (Acts 2:4), an experience that had previously happened on only rare occasions and hardly ever in a group setting. Then each of them began to speak clearly in foreign languages they had never learned. All this happened very early on the Day of Pentecost, before 9:00 in the morning.

Because Jewish males were required to attend the feast, the city was crowded with pious Jewish men from around the Roman empire who had come to Jerusalem to observe the Day of Pentecost in accordance with the Old Testament law. News of what had taken place in the Upper Room quickly spread throughout the crowded city. As a crowd began to form around the disciples, the people were divided as to just what all of this meant. At least sixteen different linguistic groups present heard these Galileans speaking fluently in their native tongue and wondered what was happening. Others, probably unable to understand the language they heard spoken, simply assumed the group was drunk on the new wine they may have brought as part of the harvest sacrifice.

Peter stood in the midst of the group and explained it was too early for anyone to be drunk but rather what they were witnessing was a manifestation of the outpouring of the Holy Spirit as prophesied by the prophet Joel (Acts 2:16-21; cf. Joel 2:18-32). Apparently, what Peter announced to the multitude was repeated by different disciples in the new languages they were now speaking so those who were fluent in that tongue could understand the message. While not all the specific details of that prophecy were fulfilled on the Day of Pentecost, enough were present to confirm that what was being witnessed was similar to that outpouring of the Spirit of which Joel and other prophets wrote – which many Bible teachers believe will also take place at the second coming of Christ.

The outpouring of the Holy Spirit is a phenomenon which has been largely ignored by Christians throughout the centuries, except during times of spiritual revival in the church. While the Holy Spirit is a person, the Scriptures sometimes portray Him being "poured out" like water upon thirsty people in need of God's blessing. It marks a period of spiritual intensity in which the presence of the Holy Spirit is recognized by others and His work of revival is experienced by Christians. An outpouring of the Holy Spirit is also most often accompanied by an awakening of the unsaved to their need for salvation and an eventual reformation of the society in which the outpouring takes place. This outpouring of the Holy Spirit in Jerusalem on the Day of Pentecost, Sunday, May 28, A.D. 30, is the first of many such outpourings recorded in the history of the church. The following chart illustrates the relationship between these aspects of the ministry of the Holy Spirit.

The Outpouring of the Holy Spirit

The Reviving of the Church   The Awakening of the Masses

The Harvest of Souls

The Reformation of Society

As Peter explained the signs of that day in the context of the outpouring of the Holy Spirit, he pointed to an even greater sign which had been accomplished just outside that city seven weeks earlier. He explained, "Jesus of Nazareth, a Man attested by God to you by miracles, wonders, and signs which God did through Him in your midst, as you yourselves also know – Him being delivered by the determined purpose and foreknowledge of God, you have taken by lawless hands, have crucified, and put to death; whom God raised up, having loosed the pains of death, because it was not possible that He should be held by it" (Acts 2:22-24).

Peter preached the Old Testament as Jesus had explained it to him. He explained the meaning of the crucifixion and resurrection of Jesus within the context of two well-known messianic Psalms (cf. Psalm 16:8-11; 110:1). Just as Peter and the other disciples apparently did not understand the real significance of these Psalms until after Jesus opened their understanding, so many of those who heard Peter preach on Pentecost had never before thought of the Messiah as One who would suffer and be raised from the dead. Peter explained these Psalms could not logically be applied to David who first penned these words under the inspiration of the Holy Spirit, because the corrupted remains of David's body were present in David's tomb. Peter concluded the prophecy must be applied to Jesus who rose from the dead. This made Jesus unique. Peter concluded his argument, "Therefore let all the house of Israel know assuredly that God has made this Jesus, whom you crucified, both Lord and Christ" (Acts 2:36).

Many of those who heard Peter's logical explanation of what was taking place were deeply convicted of their sin. The Greek verb *katenugesan* which is translated "to cut" (Acts 2:37) was a term used by classical writers to report on the devastation of a city by an invading army. Peter's words had brought about a conviction so severe that the people stood devastated in their heart before God. Desperately they wanted to do something to appease the inevitable wrath of God. "Men and brethren, what shall we do?" they asked (Acts 2:37).

Peter called them to repent from their sin and have faith in Jesus as their Messiah. The outward evidence of such an inner response to the gospel would be submitting to what has become known as Christian baptism. "Let everyone of you be baptized in the name of Jesus Christ for the remission of sins; and you shall receive the gift of the Holy Spirit" (Acts 2:38). Then Peter seemed to indicate the outpouring of the Spirit being experienced that day would not be limited to that day nor that city. "For the promise is to you and to your chilren, and to all who are afar off, as many as the Lord our God will call" (Acts 2:39).

That day about three thousand people eagerly responded to Peter's message and were baptized, adding to the infant church in Jerusalem. Because of the Jews' tendency to send only the head of the household to Jerusalem during the feasts, most likely the church was a predominantly masculine institution in its early days. Many of those who responded may have been in town only for the feast and within days or weeks left Jerusalem to carry the message of the gospel back to their hometowns and cities. Within only a few years, most of those converted on the Day of Pentecost would be involved in spreading the gospel in other parts of Judea and other provinces of the known world.

II.   The Early Ministry of the Church at Jerusalem

Those who made decisions to identify with Christ and His church on the Day of Pentecost proved to be deeply committed to those decisions. "They continued steadfastly in the apostles' doctrine and fellowship, in the breaking of bread, and in prayers" (Acts 2:42). A spirit of community quickly developed in that group to the point that they freely shared their possessions with others in the group. Because of the size of the group, there were few places where they could meet together. They met daily in the temple as a larger group celebrating their newly found faith, but also met in smaller groups in homes throughout the city to nurture the fellowship which had developed in the group. Others who chose not to identify with the infant church came to think favorably of them "and the Lord added to the church daily those who were being saved" (Acts 2:47).

The evangelistic outreach of the Day of Pentecost was not the only example of mass evangelism in which this first church was engaged. A little later in time, on an afternoon – about 3:00 p.m. – Peter and John were unexpectedly involved in another large evangelistic outreach. They were on their way to the temple to pray when at the gate of the temple known as Beautiful, they were approached by a lame beggar who was begging for alms. Neither of the disciples had funds to give the beggar, but that did not stop Peter from addressing him. Once he had the beggar's attention, Peter explained, "Silver and gold I do not have, but what I do have I give you: In the name of Jesus Christ of Nazareth, rise up and walk" (Acts 3:6). Then Peter took the beggar by the hand and began to lift him up on his feet.

Suddenly the beggar felt strength returning to the bones in his ankles and feet. He not only stood, but jumped and walked around the temple with the two apostles praising God. In his enthusiasm, his worship of God soon attracted a crowd. This beggar was well known at the gate of the temple, and those who gathered around wondered what had happened to enable him to stand in the temple. Peter soon perceived that some in the crowd were beginning to conclude his special power had resulted in this amazing miracle. Eager to correct the record, Peter took this occasion on Solomon's Porch in the temple to once again preach the gospel.

Again, the focus of the message of the early church was tied to the crucifixion and resurrection. And once again, Peter pulled no punches in clearly fixing the blame for Jesus' death. After reminding his listeners that Pilate had attempted to release Jesus, Peter noted, "But you denied the Holy One and the Just, and asked for a murderer to be granted to you, and killed the Prince of life, whom God raised from the dead, of which we are witnesses" (Acts 3:14-15). As in his sermon on the day of Pentecost, Peter again called on those who heard him to repent and "be converted, that your sins may be blotted out" (Acts 3:19). One of the results of this sermon was that many of those who heard it came to faith in Jesus Christ. By the end of that day, about five thousand men were now an active part of the church at Jerusalem.

III.   The Response of the Church to Persecution

There was another response to Peter's preaching. The apostle attracted the attention of the priests and other Sadducees. The Pharisees had been in control of the Sanhedrin when Jesus was crucified, but it was perceived they botched the job so the Sadducees were now in control. These religious leaders tended to deny the supernatural in their concept of religion and were "greatly disturbed that they taught the people and preached in Jesus the resurrection from the dead" (Acts 4:2). Had Peter avoided any reference to the Resurrection in his message, he and John probably would not have been arrested. But the gospel without the resurrection is not the gospel, and the two apostles and the man who had been healed were taken in custody and spent the night in jail.

The next day, the high priests and other leading Jewish religious leaders met together to discuss the matter. They brought the three men before them to inquire concerning the source of their miraculous power to heal the lame. Peter wasted no time getting directly to the heart of the gospel. "Let it be known to you all, and to all the people of Israel, that by the name of Jesus Christ of

Nazareth, whom you crucified, whom God raised from the dead, by Him this man stands here before you whole" (Acts 4:10). He went on to stress that salvation could only be found in the name of that same Jesus.

Those who heard the apostles speak that day were perplexed. Obviously these men were fishermen and had no formal theological education. It was also obvious "that they had been with Jesus" (Acts 4:13). When they were dismissed from the room in which the hearing was being conducted, the Sanhedrin began discussing their options. Obviously a significant miracle had occurred which could not reasonably be denied. They decided their best hope was to convince the apostles not to talk to others about Jesus. When they pronounced their sentence, the apostles were unimpressed. "Whether it is right in the sight of God to listen to you more than to God, you judge. For we cannot but speak the things which we have seen and heard" (Acts 4:19-20). The council threatened them further, but eventually released the apostles without punishing them. They realized the miracle had broad popular support and chose not to alienate the people by punishing the ones through whom the miracle was accomplished.

When they were released, Peter and John reported all that had taken place to others in the church. When they heard what had taken place, they all prayed together for boldness to continue to be faithful in proclaiming the message with which they had been entrusted. "Now, Lord, look on their threats, and grant to Your servants that with all boldness they may speak Your word," they prayed (Acts 4:29).

God granted their request. "And when they had prayed, the place where they were assembled together was shaken; and they were all filled with the Holy Spirit, and they spoke the word of God with boldness" (Acts 4:31).

In the face of opposition, the quality of the fellowship within the church continued to grow. "Now the multitude of those who believed were of one heart and one soul; neither did anyone say that any of the things he possessed was his own, but they had all things in common" (Acts 4:32). In one example of this corporate sharing, a converted Levite named Joses earned the nickname Barnabas, which means "Son of Encouragement," when he sold his land and his home in Cyprus and gave the money to the apostles to be distributed to meet the needs of others. The church continued to move forward in power in the face of external opposition. If the church's ministry was going to be seriously hindered at all, it would be as a result of problems arising on the inside. Before long the church would be faced with that issue.

Conclusion

One of the results of the outpouring of the Holy Spirit on Pentecost was realized in the effectiveness of the early church's evangelistic outreach. Believers today who are eager to see a similar effectiveness in reaching large numbers of people converted to Christ today should pray and work toward encouraging revival so that their evangelical witness will be core productive. The subsequent record of church history reveals many occasions when a revived church effectively changed their society by winning vast numbers of people to Christ during the period of revival. Many Bible teachers believe that is once again what our world needs today.

CHAPTER 31

STEPHEN:
PROBLEM SOLVER AND PREACHER

Acts 5:1–7:60

While Barnabas earned his reputation by willingly and sacrificially giving his possessions to the church, others were more concerned about earning reputations than meeting needs. One such couple was a man named Ananias and his wife Sapphira. Like Barnabas, they too owned some land and decided to sell it to raise funds for the church. But unlike Barnabas, they decided to keep some of the funds for themselves and let others think they had given everything. While there was nothing wrong with keeping that which belonged to them and no one was required to give sacrificially, there was something seriously wrong with attempting to get self-praise the way Ananias and Sapphira conspired to do.

When Ananias brought his offering to the apostles, Peter confronted him with what he was doing. "Ananias, why has Satan filled your heart to lie to the Holy Spirit and keep back part of the price of the land for yourself?...You have not lied to men but to God" (Acts 5:3-4). When Ananias heard these words, he dropped dead on the spot. Those who witnessed the event were impressed with the seriousness of the matter and had a deeper respect for God. Several young men wrapped the body and buried it immediately.

Three hours later, Sapphira became concerned that her husband had not returned and went to investigate for herself. When she arrived, Peter questioned her about the sale of their land to determine her part in the conspiracy to lie to God. When it became clear that she too was involved, Peter said, "How is it that you have agreed together to test the Spirit of the Lord? Look, the feet of those who have buried your husband are at the door, and they will carry you out" (Acts 5:9). Upon hearing those words, Sapphira dropped dead and was buried by the same ones who had just buried her husband.

This and other miraculous signs and wonders performed by the apostles during these early days had a profound impact upon those both in the church and on the outside. Church members' reverence for God deepened and the unity of the church was maintained. "Yet none of the rest dared join them, but the people esteemed them highly" (Acts 5:13). The deaths of Ananias and Sapphira apparently prevented some people from joining the church who did not have a sincere commitment to Jesus as Messiah. Still, "believers were increasingly added to the Lord, multitudes of both men and women" (Acts 5:14).

During this period when the apostles ministered with unusual spiritual power, great crowds of people were healed of disease and delivered from the control of demons. Those impacted by the ministry came from Jerusalem and the surrounding cities. But as the church continued to grow and impact more lives, the Sadducees again became concerned about the success of the church and its message of the supernatural resurrection of Jesus. Once again, they attacked the church, this time arresting the apostles who were the undisputed leaders of the church.

I.   Continued External Opposition to the Church

Although the apostles were put in prison for the night, they were not found in their cell the next morning. During the evening, they were released from prison by an angel. When the officers arrived the next morning to take the prisoners to the Jewish leaders, they found the prison still shut securely and well guarded, but no prisoners were inside. While the leading priests attempted to understand what was going on, they received a report claiming, "Look, the men whom you put in prison are standing in the temple and teaching the people!" (Acts 5:25).

The officers were sent to the temple to make the arrest and did so without incident. When the apostles were brought before the council of the Sanhedrin, they were immediately accused. "Did we not strictly command you not to teach in this name? And look, you have filled Jerusalem with your doctrine, and intend to bring this Man's blood on us!" (Acts 5:28). But the apostles were not intimidated by the council. "We ought to obey God rather than men," they affirmed (Acts 5:29). Then once again they reminded the Sanhedrin of the essence of their message. "The God of our fathers raised up Jesus whom you murdered by hanging on a tree" (Acts 5:30).

When the Sadducees heard this, they were furious and wanted nothing less than to kill the apostles. They may have done so at that time had it not been for the intervention of a respected Pharisee named Gamaliel. He· suggested the apostles be held in another room while they as a council discuss the matter among themselves. When the apostles were gone, Gamaliel called for caution before the council acted to hastily. He reminded them of other messianic movements which had arisen but died off quickly following the death of the supposed messiah. Based upon what had happened to the movements led by Theudas and Judas of Galilee, he thought it was reasonable to expect the same of this movement led by Jesus of Nazareth. As a Pharisee, Gamaliel was not upset over the teaching of the Resurrection and was prepared to believe it was entirely possible. If this was merely the movement of a man, it would soon pass, "but if it is of God, you cannot overthrow it – lest you even be found to fight against God," he warned (Acts 5:39). Gamaliel's caution was considered by the council and they agreed with the logic of his argument. They called for the apostles and again warned them to stop speaking in the name of Jesus. To demonstrate they were serious about this command, they had the apostles beaten before being released. But the beating and repeated warning of the Sanhedrin did not discourage the apostles in their ministry. "So they departed from the presence of the council, rejoicing that they were counted worthy to suffer shame for His name" (Acts 5:41). Following their arrest, they continued their ministry in both the temple and homes throughout the city.

II.   Significant Internal Conflicts in the Church

While the Sanhedrin's continued opposition did not negatively impact the ministry of the early church, another problem arose within the church that threatened the unity and ministry effectiveness of the church. The church had been growing so rapidly that details of the ministry were getting beyond the apostles' ability to adequately and completely supervise the church. They considered their primary functions to be prayer and the ministry of the Word. The harmony of the new church was interrupted by a dispute which arose over feeding the widows.

While the church was predominantly Jewish in its character at this time, it was composed of two different ethnic groups of Jews, the Hebrew or Palestinian Jews and the Hellenists or Jews from a Greek or Gentile community. The Hellenists received second-rate treatment by Palestinian Jews. So it was not surprising that the Hellenists complained when their widows were overlooked as food and other supplies were regularly distributed. As this murmuring came to the apostles' attention, they recognized the severe impact of the schism if left unchecked. They called together the church to resolve the issue. "It is not desirable that we should leave the word of God and serve tables," they explained (Acts 6:2). Some in the church may have felt the solution to the problem would involve greater supervision over this aspect of the ministry by the apostles. Instead, the apostles proposed the church select seven men who could be appointed to supervise the distribution to the widows. While the term "deacon" is not specifically used to describe these men, many Bible teachers look at these seven men as the first deacons of the church. In this context, the apostles stressed four essential qualifications for such a church officer (Acts 6:3, 5).

CHARACTERISTICS OF A DEACON

Good Reputation
Full of the Holy Spirit
Full of Wisdom
Full of Faith

The church agreed with the wisdom of the apostles' proposal and selected seven men who were given the responsibility. It is interesting to note that each of these men have Greek names and therefore probably had a Hellenistic background. One of the seven is specifically identified as "a proselyte from Antioch" (Acts 6:5). This would make Nicolas the first Gentile officer of the church. When the men were chosen, prayers were offered to induct them into this ministry. As a result of this action of the church, a problem which threatened the ministry effectiveness actually resulted in encouraging and strengthening the church. "Then the word of God spread, and the number of the disciples multiplied greatly in Jerusalem, and a great many of the priests were obedient to the faith" (Acts 6:7). The priests who opposed the Christian gospel because of its focus on the resurrection of Jesus embraced it when they realized how the Christian message could change lives and resolve problems, especially money problems.

Probably about this time the first gospel was written and began to be distributed and used by the church. The gospel of Matthew was written at a time when the church was predominantly Jewish in character. Some of the church fathers claim Matthew wrote a gospel in Aramaic for the Jews but this New Testament gospel was written in Greek. Most probably Matthew took extensive notes of Jesus' teachings in the Aramaic language during their time together. These notes were made available to the early church. As the church began reaching people from a Gentile or Hellenistic background who were not familiar with Aramaic, it became necessary to prepare an authoritative account of the life and teachings of Jesus to assist them in gaining a better understanding of their new faith. Matthew's extensive notes in Aramaic probably became the basis of Matthew's gospel in Greek. This explains the strong Jewish character of the gospel with its various Greek versions of Aramaic expressions.

THE GOSPEL OF MATTHEW

Author: Matthew (Levi)
Recipients: Predominantly Jewish Church
Date of Writing: A.D. 35-45
Theme: Jesus, Son of David, Son of Abraham

Two of those selected as deacons by the church in Jerusalem are probably better known today for their preaching ministry than for their work of waiting tables. One of these was Stephen who, like the apostles, "did great wonders and signs among the people" (Acts 6:8). Stephen was an able communicator of the gospel and often disputed with others in Hellenistic synagogues around Jerusalem including the Synagogue of the Freedmen. This synagogue was probably attended by several rabbis and rabbinical students from Asia and other places who came to Jerusalem to study the Law. Some Bible teachers believe this may have been the synagogue in which Saul of Tarsus ministered prior to his conversion to Christianity. It was not unusual in the synagogues to allow others to teach and then debate the subject of their message if it was contrary to what others present believed. But when Stephen preached the gospel in this synagogue, "they were not able to resist the wisdom and the Spirit by which he spoke" (Acts 6:10).

III.   Effective Preaching Before the Council

Because they could not defeat Stephen through the normally effective means of debate in the synagogue, several of the more prominent members of that synagogue secretly arranged to have men report that Stephen was guilty of blasphemy. This was a serious charge and was effective in inciting the people and Jewish leaders against Stephen. He was seized and brought before the council. There the false witnesses accused Stephen claiming, "This man does not cease to speak blasphemous words against this holy place and the law; for we have heard him say that this Jesus of Nazareth will destroy this place and change the customs which Moses delivered to us" (Acts 6:13-14).

After these witnesses were heard, the whole council focused their attention on Stephen as he was called upon to give an account of the charges. As they looked into his face, it was as though they were looking into the face of an angel. As he began his defense, he reviewed the history of the Jews in a manner similar to that of the Old Testament prophets,

"The God of glory appeared to our father Abraham when he was in Mesopotamia," he began (Acts 7:2). Then he led the council in a brief review of the history of Israel through the period of the patriarchs, Moses, Joshua, David, and Solomon. Stephen reminded the council how Joseph, Moses, and David had all at various times been rejected by the nation. Then he concluded with some pointed remarks directed at the council themselves. "You stiff-necked and uncircumcised in hearts and ears! You always resist the Holy Spirit; as your fathers did, so do you. Which of the prophets did your fathers not persecute? And they killed those who foretold the coming of the Just One, of whom you now have become the betrayers and murderers, who have received the law by the direction of angels and have not kept it" (Acts 7:51-53).

The words of Stephen brought deep conviction to the hearts of the Sanhedrin just as Peter's words on Pentecost brought similar conviction to the hearts of those who heard him. But rather than turning to Stephen to ask how they should respond, they turned their anger on Stephen. When Stephen claimed to have a vision of "the Son of Man standing at the right hand of God" (Acts 7:56), "they cried out with a loud voice, stopped their ears, and ran at him with one accord; and they cast him out of the city and stoned him" (Acts 7:57-58).

One of those present at the meeting of the council that day was a successful young Pharisee named Saul of Tarsus. Later he claimed when the balloting was taken to sentence Stephen and others who followed Christ, "I cast my vote against them" (Acts 26:10). As others that day participated in the actual stoning of Stephen by throwing large rocks at the bruised and bleeding body of this deacon, they placed their coats at the feet of Saul. But even as Saul watched the stoning of Stephen from his vantage point, he could hear the condemned man praying his final words. "Lord, do not charge them with this sin" (Acts 7:60).

In his career as a Pharisee and member of the Sanhedrin, Saul had opportunity to witness numerous executions, but he had not seen many people die the way Stephen died. He was probably more accustomed to hearing condemned criminals curse God and the Romans as they hung on a cross than hearing a man pray for his executioners as they hurled large rocks toward him. Most Bible teachers believe Stephen's preaching and death made a profound impact on Saul of Tarsus and was one of the chief contributing factors which resulted in his conversion. But for now, Saul would still resist the conviction of the Holy Spirit which he and his colleagues experienced as Stephen spoke. He determined to do all in his power to destroy those who belonged to this movement. In the days to come, Saul faithfully conducted his affairs with this determination ever before him.

Conclusion

In the early days of the church, Christians were persecuted for their faith in Christ and often imprisoned or killed. But the external opposition of society against the church did little to hinder the progress of the gospel. The greatest threat to the continued effectiveness of the church in reaching others with the gospel was internal dissension. That is still the case today. Christians who are concerned about the effectiveness of their church's witness in the community should strive to preserve the unity and sense of community within their church. In this way they establish a credibility through their practice so that others will then consider the message the church proclaims.

CHAPTER 32

PHILIP THE EVANGELIST: TAKING THE GOSPEL TO SAMARIA

Acts 8:1-40

aul of Tarsus was not the only Jewish leader angered over the apparent success of this new sect of Jesus' followers. Stephen's trial and stoning was the climax of a growing struggle the religious leaders of Israel perceived to exist between their authority and influence and that of Jesus of Nazareth whom they thought they had disposed of when He was crucified. It was now clear that His followers could not be simply discouraged from propagating their beliefs in Jerusalem. From this point on, the Sanhedrin would take a more direct and active role in doing what could be done to insure this movement did not continue to grow. The action chosen by the Sanhedrin was that of intense persecution. Even as men took and buried the Stephen's body, the council made their plans. Whenever the sect of the Nazarene met publicly in the temple or privately in homes, they would have to be stopped. Saul was as supportive of this plan as any member of the council. "He made havoc of the church, entering every house, and dragging off men and women, committing them to prison" (Acts 8:3).

As the persecution of the church intensified, many believers thought it best to leave Jerusalem with their families. An indirect result of the persecution was that the gospel was carried to cities outside of Jerusalem. "At that time a great persecution arose against the church which was at Jerusalem; and they were all scattered throughout the regions of Judea and Samaria, except the apostles" (Acts 8:1). The plan intended to stop the church from growing actually moved it into a greater phase of growth. "Therefore those who were scattered went everywhere preaching the word" (Acts 8:4).

I.   Philip's Ministry in Samaria

Probably the most unlikely place the Jewish leaders would pursue fleeing disciples was the region of Samaria. This may have been one reason Philip, one of the church's deacons, and possibly others chose that as their new home. When Philip arrived in "the city of Samaria" (probably Shechem), he "preached Christ to them" (Acts 8:5). These people had been exposed earlier to the ministry of both John the Baptist and Jesus Himself. In fact the Samaritans first recognized Jesus as the Christ and Savior of the World (cf. John 4:42). It is not surprising therefore that the Samaritans were very receptive as Philip preached the gospel to them.

Philip's preaching was also confirmed by his authenticating signs. On several occasions, unclean spirits were cast out of those who were possessed and many who were lame and had other forms of paralysis were miraculously healed. As the people turned to Christ as Savior and experienced the benefits of these miracles, "there was great joy in that city" (Acts 8:8).

Another of the reasons the Samaritans were ready to accept Philip's message may have been due to the influence of a sorcerer in the city, named Simon. Simon had practiced sorcery for some time and had convinced the people that he was a significant person. The people were clearly impressed by his ability to make incantation or perform other aspects of occult ritual. But when Philip began performing miracles in Samaria, Simon readily confessed, "This man is the great power of God" (Acts 8:10). Simon himself converted to Christianity and was baptized by Philip. The conversion of Simon influenced many in the city to consider Philip's message which resulted in their conversion also.

Ultimately, the success of Philip's Samaritan ministry must be attributed to the work of the Holy Spirit in converting individuals and transforming societies. The Holy Spirit brings about conviction in the life of the unsaved and effects conversion by drawing individuals to Christ. While the above natural phenomena certainly contributed to the success of the mission, only God can save people. Without the Holy Spirit's work in the life of that city, the other factors would have not been enough to effect the revival which took place in Samaria.

**FACTORS CONTRIBUTING TO THE
SAMARITAN CAMPAIGN'S SUCCESS**

1. The Previous Ministry of John the Baptist
2. The Previous Ministry of Jesus
3. The Authenticating Signs Performed by Philip
4. The Dramatic Conversion of Simon
5. The Work of the Holy Spirit in Conversion

Philip's ministry in Samaria marked a new phase in the outreach of the church. To this point, the ministry of the church had been largely restricted to Jews in Jerusalem and Judea, but Jesus had told His disciples they should also be witnesses in Samaria and to the ends of the earth (cf. Acts 1:8). While the plan sounded good and made sense, the ethnic rivalry between the Jews and the Samaritans was so intense apparently no effort had been made to take the good news of the gospel to them prior to the persecution of the church that led Philip to this region. When news of what was taking place in Samaria reached those who remained in Jerusalem, it was initially looked upon with suspicion. Peter and John were sent to investigate matters more carefully.

II.   The Apostolic Confirmation of the Church

When the apostles arrived in Samaria and met with those who had believed as a result of Philip's ministry, they found a church which existed even though they had not yet received the Holy Spirit to assist in their ministry efforts. Peter and John recognized their need and "prayed for them that they might receive the Holy Spirit" (Acts 8:15).

In Samaria, the believers received the Holy Spirit as the apostles laid hands upon them. Apparently the Holy Spirit's reception was evidenced by some sort of sign such as speaking unknown languages like on the day of Pentecost or the ability to perform miracles. As Simon witnessed what took place, he recognized the relationship between the believers' reception of the Holy Spirit and the apostles laying on of hands. He approached the apostles offering them money and requesting, "Give me this power also, that anyone on whom I lay hands may receive the Holy Spirit" (Acts 8:19).

Simon's request led Peter to believe the former sorcerer did not have a complete understanding of the nature of the Christianity which he had embraced. "Your money perish with you, because you thought that the gift of God could be purchased with money!" Peter exclaimed (Acts 8:20). Peter concluded Simon's heart was not right and called upon him to repent "and pray to God if perhaps the thought of your heart may be forgiven you" (Acts 8:22). Simon immediately repented asking Peter, "Pray to the Lord for me, that none of the things which you have spoken may come upon me" (Acts 8:24).

With the growth of the church outside of the city of Jerusalem, the apostle's role became less that of a pastor and more that of a traveling teacher. After their ministry with Philip in Samaria, Peter and John slowly made their way back to Jerusalem "preaching the gospel in many villages of the Samaritans" (Acts 8:25).

Philip is the only individual in Scripture specifically identified as an evangelist (Acts 21:8). Some Bible teachers believe the evangelist was a gift and/or office in the early church similar in nature to the contemporary church-planting foreign missionary. When the evangelist had successfully planted a church in a community, he turned the church over to indigenous leadership and moved on to a new mission. This appears to be the predominant strategy later adopted by the apostle Paul and those who traveled with him. It was also characteristic of Philip and his ministry that once a church was established in one place, he went on to another. With the church established in Samaria, Philip was now ready to take on a new challenge.

III.   Philip and the Ethiopian Eunuch

In the midst of an apparently successful ministry in Samaria, an angel addressed Philip and redirected his ministry, instructing him to "arise and go toward the south along the road which goes down from Jerusalem to Gaza" (Acts 8:26). Although Philip knew this was a desert region with few if any inhabitants, he followed the angel's direction and made his way to the place. Only when he got there did he recognize a unique opportunity for ministry he might not otherwise have experienced.

Traveling along the road as Philip arrived was a prominent Ethiopian official in the government of Queen Candace of Ethiopia. This man was one of the chief financial officers and held an office similar to that of minister of finance of Ethiopia. He had apparently been to Jerusalem on a religious pilgrimage and was reading from the scroll of Isaiah as he and his party traveled home. A large Jewish community in Ethiopia included the royal family itself. The royal family of Ethiopia claimed it descended from the son of Solomon and the Queen of Sheba (cf. 1 Kings 10:1-13). It is therefore not surprising that a leading member of the Ethiopian government should be interested enough in Judaism to travel to Jerusalem to worship God and have in his own possession a copy of the scroll of Isaiah. One would have to be fairly wealthy in order to be able to afford a personal copy of the Scriptures at that time.

As Philip noted the man reading the scroll of Isaiah, the Holy Spirit identified that man as the reason why he had been pulled from an effective ministry in Samaria. "Go near and overtake this chariot," the Holy Spirit instructed Philip (Acts 8:29). Just as he had obeyed the Lord's leading to leave Samaria, so he obeyed now. A prominent official of the Ethiopian government likely traveled with soldiers who would be on alert as strangers approached their caravan, but Philip was not discouraged from obeying God by the soldiers' presence. Philip no doubt had dealings with many other officers as he served with Stephen as a deacon of the church at Jerusalem.

When Philip approached the Ethiopian official, he asked him, "Do you understand what you are reading?" (Acts 8:30). "How can I, unless someone guides me?" the Ethiopian responded (Acts 8:31). Then he invited Philip to join him in the chariot and explain the Scriptures. Philip noted the place from which the man was reading (Isa. 53:7-8) and beginning at that point explained the Scriptures in the context of Jesus the Messiah. While the Scriptures do not record the content of that lesson, it most likely closely resembled other presentations of the gospel in the book of Acts with its focus on Christ's crucifixion and 'subsequent resurrection. At some point, Philip must have stressed the need for a response.

As the two traveled down the road, they came to an oasis in that desert region in which there was a body of water. "See, here is water," the eunuch noted. "What hinders me from being baptized?" he asked (Acts 8:36). Philip pointed out that baptism was an external indication of an internal heart response to Christ. When the Ethiopian confessed faith in Jesus Christ as the Son of God, there was no reason why he should not be baptized. The man ordered his officials to stop the chariot while he and Philip went down into the water together.

When Philip baptized the Ethiopian Eunuch, he baptized the only one in the New Testament who received Christian baptism without becoming a part of a local congregation of believers. However, others in the party also may have been baptized by Philip or the new convert himself. According to an early tradition of the Ethiopian Coptic Church, the conversion and baptism of this Ethiopian official marked their beginning. After the baptism, the Spirit of the Lord took Philip away. His work had been accomplished. Philip was taken by the Holy Spirit west to the city Azotus, just south of the Plain of Sharon near the coast of the Mediterranean Sea. Philip continued his ministry of preaching from town to town, working up the coast until he came to the city of Caesarea. There he apparently settled with his family although he continued to be known as Philip the Evangelist.

Philip's absence did not diminish the enthusiasm of the recently converted Ethiopian official. "He went on his way rejoicing" (Acts 8:39). This final mention of the Ethiopian Eunuch in Scripture makes it very easy to believe he was instrumental in the founding of the Ethiopian Coptic Church upon his return home. But as the gospel spread south to Ethiopia and abroad throughout all the towns and villages of Palestine, the intensity of those opposed to its success did not diminish. Some of those who had been involved in the persecution of the church at the beginning were "still breathing threats and murder against the disciples of the Lord" (Acts 9:1). As they saw the church spread beyond the city limits of Jerusalem, they determined to extend their efforts to destroy the church elsewhere. One of the most zealous of those involved in that project was about to launch a mission that would forever change his life.

Conclusion

It has been estimated that as many as one in ten Christians have been given the spiritual gift of evangelism by God, but comparatively few are engaged in an evangelistic outreach. Those who, like Philip, have the gift of evangelism need to exercise their spiritual gift by telling others the gospel and inviting them to respond to God by faith. But even if one does not have that particular spiritual gift, every Christian can be involved in the ministry of evangelism, telling others what Jesus has done in their life (cf. Acts 8:4). Just as the early church grew as the result of everyone being involved in witnessing, so the church today would experience similar growth if a similar effort were undertaken. Just as the early church grew as the result of everyone being involved in witnessing, so the church today would experience similar growth if a similar effort were undertaken.

CHAPTER 33

SAUL OF TARSUS:
HIS CONVERSION AND MINISTRY
IN DAMASCUS

Acts 9:1-31; Gal. 1:11-24

he early church's explosive growth in the first few years of its existence was a source of continued rejoicing among the disciples, but it became the focus of irritation to the Sanhedrin as they attempted to bring an end to the continued preaching of the gospel. One of the most zealous of those who actively worked to destroy the church was a young rabbi from Tarsus named Saul. Already this Pharisee had proved himself worthy of the honor he had earned because of his zeal to persecute the church.

Saul was proud of his Hebrew heritage and was named in honor of Israel's first king who like the zealous Pharisee was also from the tribe of Benjamin. He had maintained high standards of righteousness and lived one of the most consistent lives in the city. He was just old enough to qualify to sit on the Sanhedrin and had earned that honor rarely given to a 30-year-old man. Saul's father had raised him well in Tarsus of Asia Minor and taught him the trade of tent-making, although judging from his success to this point in his life, it was highly unlikely he would ever use that skill. Saul would keep busy enough as a teacher of the law.

His father had been wealthy enough to purchase Roman citizenship before his birth so Saul was born with all the benefits of Roman citizenship at a time when Roman citizenship gave an individual many advantages in life. When Saul was about age 14, his father had financed his education under Gamaliel in Jerusalem, one of the most respected teachers of the law of that day. Saul did well in his studies and was beginning to earn a reputation that may have someday rivaled his master. Saul was a young man on his way up, and no one questioned he would continue to rise.

Despite the success Saul had already experienced in his chosen profession, he was not prepared to sit back and coast. He had of course heard of Jesus of Nazareth, particularly as that prophet of Galilee had become increasingly popular during the final years of His life. But like his colleagues on the council, Saul had no idea how rapidly Jesus' following would grow after His crucifixion and reported resurrection. Still, now that the problem existed, Saul would continue to prove his zeal for God and work to eliminate those he perceived to be distorting the teaching of the law. He did not have to examine their teaching very carefully to be convinced the movement was all wrong. Some of his fellow Pharisees were still talking about the prophet Jesus and His total disregard for the law of the Sabbath.

Although Saul had not been on the council for long, he knew that the Sanhedrin sometimes ordained men for special tasks that needed to be accomplished. On other occasions he knew the high priest had exercised his authority to commission a person for a special task. The more he considered the growing problem of these disciples of Jesus of Nazareth, the more he became convinced that someone should have the specific responsibility of finding and arresting these disciples not only in Jerusalem but in the other parts of Palestine to which they had moved. As that conviction grew, Saul determined to offer himself for such service.

Saul presented his plan to the high priest. Soon all the paperwork was done and he was on his way to Damascus with documentation authorizing him "so that if he found any who were of the Way, whether men or women, he might bring them bound to Jerusalem" (Acts 9:2). The trip to Damascus would take several days. By the time Saul arrived, he would not be the same man that left Jerusalem.

I.   The Conversion of Saul of Tarsus

Most Bible teachers believe Stephen's death made a profound impact on Saul and may have prompted him to give Christianity a deeper examination. As he traveled north from Jerusalem, he would have passed through many places where Jesus spent a greater part of His ministry. It is difficult to imagine this did not raise questions in Saul's mind concerning the One whom he was so vigorously opposing. But not until he was getting very close to the walls of Damascus was Saul confronted with a decision about Jesus.

"Suddenly a light shone around him from heaven" (Acts 9:3). As this blinding light appeared, Saul and those with him fell to the ground and tried to look away. With the bright light, a thunderous noise was heard. Those with him heard the noise, but only Saul was able to distinguish the words which were spoken. The voice from heaven made three statements directed at him.

First, the voice cried out, "Saul, Saul, why are you persecuting Me?" (Acts 9:4). Later Saul would write epistles to churches reminding them they were "the body of Christ." Although he did not realize it at the time, in persecuting the church which is His body, Saul had been persecuting Jesus Himself. Curious as to the identity of the voice, Saul asked, "Who are You, Lord?" The surprising answer came back, "I am Jesus, whom you are persecuting. It is hard for you to kick against the goads" (Acts 9:5).

Just as suddenly as the light had appeared on the group, Saul realized he had been wrong in his zealous conclusions about this sect of followers of Jesus of Nazareth. Inside, he was filled with conflicting emotions. A part of him was shocked into astonishment that he Saul could have made such a grave miscalculation. But another part of him was terrified and caused him to shake as he contemplated how God would treat him in light of his actions against Stephen and others in the church.

Although he had been wrong in his conclusions about the infant church, Saul's actions had been prompted by his zeal for God. Even in this moment of confusion, Saul was still eager to perform God's will in his life. "Lord, what do You want me to do?" he asked. If he had expected a new goal in life or a new strategy of ministry, he was probably disappointed when he heard the response. "Arise and go into the city, and you will be told what you must do" (Acts 9:6).

As quickly as the light had appeared over the group, it faded away enabling them to continue their journey. The men with Saul were confused, having heard the noise of a voice but they could not distinguish the words nor could they see anyone who may have spoken the words. As Saul rose from the ground and opened his eyes, he discovered he had gone blind during the strange encounter. His traveling companions had to take him by the hand and lead him where he wanted to go. They brought him into the city and arranged lodging for him in the house of Judas which was located on the main street of the city, a long narrow street running straight through the heart of Damascus and appropriately named "Straight."

For the next three days he could not see and chose not to eat. While others around him carried on in the affairs of a normal lifestyle, Saul spent time praying. The voice had told him he would learn more when he arrived in Damascus, and as near as he could tell, he had arrived. As he sought divine direction for his next step, he saw a vision of a man putting his hands on him. Somehow, Saul knew this man's name was Ananias, but he did not at all resemble the high priest who had given him his authority to come Damascus and did not look like anyone he had met before. While he did not understand all that was involved in the meaning of this strange vision, it appeared that this would be the means of his sight being restored.

The church in Damascus had been warned about the coming of Saul and were alert to the danger he posed to their safety. When one of the disciples named Ananias received a vision in which the Lord told him to go to the house of Judas and find Saul of Tarsus, he was sure there was some mistake. "Lord, I have heard from many about this man, how much harm he has done to Your saints in Jerusalem," Ananias explained. "And here he has authority from the chief priests to bind all who call on Your name" (Acts 9:13-14). While all that Ananias had heard was true, the Lord knew something Ananias did not know that made all the difference in the world. "Go, for he is a chosen vessel of Mine to bear My name before Gentiles, kings, and the children of Israel," He explained (Acts 9:15).

Obediently, Ananias made his way to Judas' house and found Saul of Tarsus. "Brother Saul, the Lord Jesus, who appeared to you on the road as you came, has sent me that you may receive your sight and be filled with the Holy Spirit," he explained. As Saul heard those words, he could feel something falling from his eyes and his sight returned. He had come to Damascus to find and arrest disciples of Jesus, but now he wanted to identify with them as a committed part of this sect he had days earlier wanted to destroy. After he was baptized, he ate. His decision to embrace Jesus as Messiah meant he was now in danger from those who had come to Damascus with him to persecute the church. Saul left his temporary residence in the house of Judas and took refuge in the home of some of the disciples who belonged to the church in Damascus.

The transformation within Saul's life during that week had been so dramatic he felt he needed some time to sort out what was happening. A week earlier, he had been in the presence of the high priest presenting a plan he thought would resolve the problem with those of "the Way" once and for all. Now he himself was a part of that group. During his years of study under Gamaliel, he had developed a deep respect and love for the law. As he thought about the change in his own life, he thought about great turning points in the lives of others before him. First, there was Moses who met God in a bush burning on the side of Mount Sinai. Then there was the nation of Israel who returned to that mountain and also heard the voice of God as He gave the nation the Law. Elijah had also heard the voice of God on Mount Sinai at a turning point in his life. The more he thought of it, Saul became convinced he should make the trip into the wilderness to prepare for what would obviously be a new life when he returned.

II.   Saul's Early Ministry in Damascus

The Bible does not indicate how long Saul remained in the wilderness. Some say three years but others think it was only forty days. But afterwards, Saul returned to Damascus rather than Jerusalem. He planned to be as zealous in his ministry in the name of Jesus as he had been in his earlier commitment to destroy that name. The Jewish leaders apparently decided to ignore the conversion of Saul of Tarsus and continued their broader persecution of the church. Saul however, could not ignore what had taken place in his life. He made his way to the synagogues in Damascus and took advantage of every opportunity to teach. His reputation earned prior to his conversion no doubt insured he would be invited to address the synagogue when he attended. On each occasion, the heart of his message was the twofold claim that the Messiah was the Son of God and that Jesus of Nazareth was the Messiah.

Initially, the people were amazed at what they heard being taught by this respected rabbi. "Is this not he who destroyed those who called on this name in Jerusalem, and has come here for that purpose, so that he might bring them bound to the chief priests?" they wondered (Acts 9:21). But as Saul continued to preach this new message, he developed stronger arguments to prove his conclusions and was soon winning debates with those who opposed his messianic emphasis. Then their amazement turned to animosity. As they considered what to do with Saul, they determined he had to die. Carefully they plotted how they would kill this thorn in the flesh.

Word about the plot leaked out and got to Saul. He learned the Jews who opposed him had guards watching the city gate who were prepared to kill him as soon as he left the city. But there was another way out of the city. Many of the homes in Damascus were built along the city wall and actually made up part of the wall itself. A group of disciples lowered Saul from a window in the wall in a large basket. When he reached the ground, Saul was able to leave Damascus undetected. Leaving Damascus, Saul went south to Jerusalem where he hoped to make contact with the disciples in that city.

It had been three years since Saul left Jerusalem, but the apostles had not forgotten he had left with authority from the high priest to persecute the church, nor had they forgotten the enthusiasm with which Saul had invaded homes and dragged off those who met together for worship and fellowship. As a result, when Saul attempted to join the disciples in Jerusalem, they were afraid it might be a trick to expose others in the church "and did not believe that he was a disciple" (Acts 9:26). The fear was an understandable response of those who knew only the Saul who had left for Damascus three years earlier. There was one notable exception among the disciples in response to Saul. Barnabas, a Levite who may have himself been involved with Saul prior to his own conversion, was convinced Saul's conversion was genuine and introduced him to a gathering of the apostles. At that meeting, Saul explained the details of his conversion. He was accepted by them and the church. For the next two weeks, Saul became an active part of church life in Jerusalem. He took advantage of the opportunity to return to the Hellenistic synagogues in Jerusalem where he had been welcomed prior to his conversion and began preaching the same message he had preached in Damascus.

This time, the opposition to Saul and his new doctrines was direct and extreme. The anger toward Christianity which three years earlier had resulted in the death of Stephen again flared up as Saul became one their champions. Again those who at another time identified themselves as Saul's friends initiated a plot to kill him. The church took action to protect Saul as soon as they learned of the danger. Saul was taken to the city of Caesarea and from there put on a boat to Tarsus. They hoped that there he would be safe from the wrath of the Jews and that he may be able to use his influence in his hometown to tell others of Jesus the Messiah.

Much of the church's persecution during the past three years was apparently either directed by or at Saul of Tarsus. With Saul now back in Tarsus, the Jewish leaders were less intense in their opposition to the gospel. Perhaps the dramatic conversion of Saul caused them to hesitate sending out others on similar missions. "Then the churches throughout all Judea, Galilee, and Samaria had peace and were edified. And walking in the fear of the Lord and in the comfort of the Holy Spirit, they were multiplied" (Acts 9:31).

Conclusion

The dramatic change in the life of Saul of Tarsus was one of the evidences of his conversion. In a later epistle he explained, "If anyone is in Christ, he is a new creation; old things have passed away; behold, all things have become new" (2 Cor. 5:17). Those who have placed their faith in Christ as Savior should periodically pause to evaluate the ongoing change being effected in their life as their new nature in Christ continues to become more evident.

CHAPTER 34

CORNELIUS:
THE BEGINNING OF GENTILE
CHRISTIANITY

Acts 9:32–11:18

With the persecution of the church easing, the apostles were again free to travel widely ministering to disciples in various towns and villages throughout Palestine. On one of these tours, Peter came to the town of Lydda where there was a church. A man named Aeneas, who lived in that town, was in the advanced stages of paralysis and had been bedridden for eight years. When Peter met this man, he addressed him in the name of "Jesus the Christ" and the man was instantaneously healed. That miracle gave credibility to Peter's ministry not only in Lydda but in the nearby settlements on the Plain of Sharon. "So all who dwelt at Lydda and Sharon saw him and turned to the Lord" (Acts 9:35).

Just down the road from Lydda was the coastal city of Joppa. A community of believers also existed in that city. They were faithful witnesses to their town. One of the members of that church was a lady named Tabitha who had earned a well-deserved reputation for her good works and charitable deeds. While Peter was ministering in Lydda, Tabitha became sick and died from the illness. While the disciples always felt a since of loss at the death of one of their fellow believers, the death of Tabitha was particularly hard to accept. They had heard about Peter's mission in Lydda and wondered if he could help them in their sorrow. While they washed Tabitha's corpse and laid it in an upper room in her home, two men were sent to Lydda to implore Peter "not to delay in coming to them" (Acts 9:38).

Peter returned to Joppa and with those sent to summon him. By the time they arrived at the home where Tabitha's body was laid, many of the widows whose lives had been impacted by her charitable acts during her lifetime had already gathered to mourn her death. During her lifetime they had appreciated not only the gifts she had given them but also her friendship. Now they had only the various articles of clothing she had made by which to remember her. Many there that day were wearing clothes made by the one whose passing they mourned.

Peter asked everyone to leave in order that he might be alone with the body. Alone in the room, Peter knelt down and prayed. Then turning to the body, Peter said, "Tabitha, arise" (Acts 9:40). Suddenly life was restored to the corpse and she opened her eyes. When she saw the apostle by her bed, she sat up. Then Peter took her by the hand and lifted her up out of the bed and presented her to the others who were waiting outside. Once again, a miracle became the basis of an effective ministry. "And it became known throughout all Joppa, and many believed on the Lord" (Acts 9:42). Peter remained in Joppa for some time finding hospitality with a tanner named Simon who had a large home near the beach.

I.   Peter and His Vision of an Inedible Banquet

The church of Jesus Christ experienced explosive growth during its first decade of existence with congregations in many cities and towns throughout the entire region of Palestine. But these churches were making no real effort to reach Gentiles within their sphere of influence. Many viewed their faith in Jesus as Messiah as something of an extension of the Judaism in which they had been raised. They widely assumed that Gentiles who did not embrace the monotheistic belief of Judaism and become proselytes to that faith would not respond to the gospel. But many Gentiles had come to recognize the futility of the polytheistic belief systems in which they were raised yet were not convinced they should convert to Judaism. Some had already concluded there was only one true God and worshiped Him to the best of their ability, but they knew little of a personal relationship with that God. One such individual was a Roman centurion attached to the Italian Regiment just up the coast in Caesarea.

Cornelius was "a devout man and one who feared God with all his household, who gave alms generously to the people, and prayed to God always" (Acts 10:2). Cornelius appears to have come to the place in his life where he determined to worship the true God to the best of his ability, but had not learned how he could have a personal relationship with God through the Lord Jesus Christ. Although he did not embrace Judaism, he apparently thought some elements of that faith were good and had adopted them into his own worship of God. One of these was the practice of praying at 3:00 each afternoon. During one of these afternoon times of prayer Cornelius received a vision.

In his vision, Cornelius saw an angel coming in and calling him by name. When he responded to the angel he was told, "Your prayers and your alms have come up for a memorial before God" (Acts 10:4). He was then instructed to send men to the home of a tanner named Simon to find Simon Peter. Cornelius was then told Peter would instruct him further as to what he should do. Then the vision faded as the angel departed.

At the conclusion of the vision, Cornelius called two of his household servants and a loyal soldier he knew he could count on. He explained to them the essence of the vision, noting that the angel wanted him to send men to get Simon Peter to tell them what to do. He then sent them on the overnight journey south to Joppa with that mission.

The messengers from Cornelius did not arrive in Joppa until noon the next day. They found the home of Simon just as Peter himself saw a most unusual vision. Peter had skipped breakfast that morning and was getting quite hungry as he went to the roof of Simon's home to pray at noon. While his host went down below to prepare a meal, Peter fell into a trance and saw a sheet coming down from heaven. On that sheet were a wide assortment of edible animals that had been designated unclean by the food laws of the Old Testament. Then Peter heard a voice, "Rise, Peter; kill and eat" (Acts 10:13).

As hungry as Peter was, the invitation was tempting. But Peter had been raised to believe there were certain things a Jew simply did not eat, and he knew his friends were making a kosher meal below so he piously responded, "Not so, Lord! For I have never eaten anything common or unclean" (Acts 10:14). When he responded in this way, the voice answered back, "What God has cleansed you must not call common" (Acts 10:15). Three times this strange vision and conversation was repeated as Peter waited for his noon meal.

WHAT WAS ON PETER'S SHEET?
The Unclean Animals Identified in Leviticus 11

Beasts of the Field: Camel, Rock Hyrax, Hare, Swine
Fish of the Sea: Anything with both fins and scales
Birds of the Air: Eagle, Vulture, Buzzard, Kite, Falcon, Raven, Owls, Ostrich, Seagull, Hawk, Heron, Hoopoe, Jackdaw, Bat
Insects and Creeping Things: All insects and creeping things except locust grasshoppers and crickets

---

The vision left Peter a little confused and unsure as to the significance or meaning. As he sat on the roof trying to figure it out, the messengers from Cornelius came to the gate of Simon's home looking for Peter. The Holy Spirit then told Peter, "Behold, three men are seeking you. Arise therefore, go down and go with them, doubting nothing; for I have sent them" (Acts 10:19-20). Only when Peter went down to meet the men did he learn they had been sent by a Roman centurion. He agreed to return with them but invited them first to spend the night in Joppa. The next morning he and some of the brethren from the church in Joppa accompanied the men back to Caesarea.

II.   The Conversion of Cornelius and His Household

The larger party took longer to return to Caesarea than the men had taken getting to Joppa, but when they arrived the next day, they found an eager host ready to greet them. The centurion was convinced Peter would have something significant to say to him and his friends so he had gathered together a number of his relatives and close personal friends.

When Peter reluctantly entered the home of this Gentile, the centurion bowed down and worshiped him. Peter immediately objected to this course of action and noted he too was only a man like his host.

The decision to enter the home of Cornelius went against everything Peter believed in as a Jew. "You know how unlawful it is for a Jewish man to keep company with or go to one of another nation," he reminded his host. "But God has shown me that I should not call any man common or unclean" (Acts 10:28). He went on to explain that he had come without objection when asked, but indicated he still did not know exactly why he was there.

Cornelius then recounted the vision he had received four days earlier which had prompted his actions in inviting Peter to his home. Only then did Peter realize what was happening. "In truth I perceive that God shows no partiality. But in every nation whoever fears Him and works righteousness is accepted by Him" (Acts 10:34-35). Like many of his fellow Jews, Peter had a restricted view concerning who could and could not win God's favor. Now that he realized God was interested in the salvation of at least some Gentiles, he began to review the highlights of the life, death, and resurrection of Jesus. "To Him all the prophets witness that, through His name, whoever believes in Him will receive remission of sins," he explained (Acts 10:43).

Even as Peter explained the gospel to this group of Gentiles gathered in Cornelius' home, "the Holy Spirit fell upon all those who heard the word" (Acts 10:44). The Jewish believers who had come with Peter were astonished at what they saw. They saw Gentiles speaking in other languages and praising God, not unlike that which had taken place years earlier in Jerusalem at the very birth of the church. "Can anyone forbid water, that these should not be baptized who have received the Holy Spirit just as we have?" Peter asked (Acts 10:47). The answer was obvious. Peter urged Cornelius and his friend and family to be baptized, and a predominantly Gentile church began in the city of Caesarea. Peter was asked to stay a few days with them to help establish them in their newfound faith in Jesus.

III. Defending Preaching the Gospel to Gentiles

After a brief stay in Caesarea, Peter returned to Jerusalem, but not before news of the Gentiles' conversion had reached the Jewish center and created some discomfort among the followers of Jesus Christ. When the apostle arrived in Jerusalem, he was immediately confronted with something which seemed to be terribly wrong in the Jewish capital. "You went in to uncircumcised men and ate with them!" they accused.

Peter tried to explain his actions the best he could by recounting all that had taken place beginning in Joppa. He understood it was only natural for these Jewish Christians to feel a little uncomfortable with his actions. Perhaps he realized that a part of him still felt uncomfortable with what had taken place in that home. He explained the vision of the sheet let down from heaven and his response to it as it was repeated three times. He then told of the meeting in Cornelius' home and how "as I began to speak, the Holy Spirit fell upon them, as upon us at the beginning" (Acts 11:15). Peter reminded his fellow church leaders of Jesus' promise concerning the baptism of the Holy Spirit and explained his conclusion that God was clearly doing something among the Gentiles.

As the church leaders considered what Peter reported, they sat in silent amazement. Who among them would ever have thought that God was interested in the conversion of Gentiles? As what God was doing in the conversion of Cornelius' household began to dawn on them, their silence turned to approval (Acts 11:18).

It was indeed amazing that these leaders in Jerusalem were so willing to recognize the possibility that a Gentile could be saved and become a part of the church. Culturally, Gentiles tended to be so far removed from Jews that few, if any, Gentiles had even been approached by disciples who were otherwise faithful in their witness to the resurrection of Jesus. At this point, their Scriptures consisted entirely of the Jewish Old Testament and perhaps copies of the most Jewish of the four gospels, Matthew.

If they had thought much about their responsibility to make disciples of all nations, they would have probably reasoned that they should reach every Jewish community scattered throughout all of the nations of the world. Now the conversion of Cornelius presented the church with a brand new arena of ministry. The church was now about fifteen years old, but it was only just discovering what would soon become its biggest and most fruitful field of ministry.

Conclusion

An ethnic bias came very close to hindering the progress of the gospel to the Gentiles which has since proven to be a very responsive group to the message of salvation. The struggle experienced by Peter and those involved in the conversion of Cornelius and his household has been experienced by others as they consider sharing their faith with other people who belong to a different race or ethnic group. It is important that believers today overcome any personal biases they may have and, like Peter, be willing to share the gospel with everyone God gives them the opportunity to speak with. When this is done, one may be surprised to see how God blesses that witness.

CHAPTER 35

BARNABAS:
SHAPING THE CHARACTER OF
CHRISTIANS

Acts 11:19–14:28

Although the conversion of Cornelius convinced the leaders of the church at Jerusalem that God was interested in the salvation of Gentiles, they were still not deeply committed to the wholesale evangelization of Gentile communities. The problem hindering such an open approach to ministry was probably not theological but cultural.

The Jews had worked hard for centuries to maintain their distinctiveness as a society and had experienced some degree of success in that objective. As a result, what one group found appealing might be viewed at appalling by the other.

The New Testament church was designed to be "one body" with the middle wall of partition broken down between the two groups, but in the early days it was difficult to overcome hundreds of years of segregation. One of the first men selected as a deacon in the church at Jerusalem was a Gentile who had converted to Judaism prior to coming to faith in Jesus as Messiah. The conversion of other Jewish proselytes to Christianity most likely took place, but these Gentiles had first adopted the culture and religious heritage of the Jews so that they were really not considered Gentiles in the same sense as other Gentiles. The problem whether Gentiles could or should be evangelized was an issue the church had simply not taken time to address. The Jews' response to Christ had been sufficient to keep the church busy in their disciple-making task.

But as the Jewish believers in Jerusalem scattered after the persecution of the church at the death of Stephen (Acts 8:1-4), the issue became a matter of practical concern to some. There were many Jews and few Gentiles in Jerusalem, but that was not the case in cities like Antioch, a cosmopolitan trade city that linked the east and the west. This was the third-largest city in the Roman empire, located near the fertile crescent. Camel caravans coming from the east loaded their burdens on Roman sailing ships to deliver them to the various ports of the Mediterranean.

When a group of Jewish believers from Cyprus and Cyrene settled in Antioch, they found they had more in common with the Gentiles· of that city than they had with the Jews of Palestine. It was natural for them to share their faith in Jesus the Messiah with their Gentile friends and business associates. Soon some of them also came to put their trust in Jesus. "And the hand of the Lord was with them, and a great number believed and turned to the Lord" (Acts 11:21).

I.   The Church at Antioch

If the conversion of Cornelius marked the beginning of Gentile evangelism, the church at Antioch shortly thereafter became the first church to begin making the transition from being predominantly Jewish in character to becoming predominantly Gentile in its outlook. The change did not pass unnoticed by the church in Jerusalem. When they heard what was taking place they determined to send someone to be certain this local church had not gone too far. Also, the church's location in a crucial city meant its influence could be empire-wide. Barnabas was selected for the job, probably because he shared common Cypriot roots with some of those who were instrumental in establishing the church at Antioch.

Barnabas had already earned a reputation for being able to find the potential good in people and build on it. He had been a source of encouragement to the apostles in the early days of the church in Jerusalem and was one of the first to accept Saul of Tarsus after the zealous Pharisee had been converted. As Barnabas traveled north to Antioch, he stopped and ministered in churches in various towns along the way. Arriving in Antioch, he no doubt recognized some things that were being done differently in the predominantly Gentile community, but he rejoiced in the evidences he saw of God's grace at work in their midst "and encouraged them all that with purpose of heart they should continue with the Lord" (Acts 11:23).

Barnabas was a good man who ministered faithfully in the power of the Holy Spirit and had the ability to trust God for great things in his ministry. As he preached in the church at Antioch, "A great many people were added to the Lord" (Acts 11:24). Barnabas quickly realized that one of the problems confronting this church was the people's cultural background. In Jerusalem, most converts understood the Old Testament Scriptures well and had a basis upon which they could build their personal relationship with God. Here in Antioch, most new converts did not have this background. The greatest need of this church was that of a gifted teacher who could instruct these Gentile converts in their new faith. As a Levite, Barnabas was no doubt capable of performing this ministry with some degree of success, but as he thought about the situation, he remembered a young teacher of the law who could do it much better.

Ten years earlier Saul had headed back to Tarsus to escape the murderous plots of some of his former colleagues. Barnabas remembered the zeal with which Saul had taught the Old Testament Scriptures from a messianic perspective. In Barnabas's mind, there was no one more needed in Antioch at that time than Saul of Tarsus, so he made the trip to the Asian city to find him. "And when he had found him, he brought him to Antioch" (Acts 11:26).

Together, Barnabas and Saul faithfully ministered to the disciples at Antioch during the next year (A.D. 43). A great many people were taught the

Scripture. Not only did the disciples of Antioch acquire an understanding of the content of the Old Testament Scriptures, they began to apply the eternal principles of the Scriptures to their daily lifestyle. This resulted in their earning a reputation in their community which was reflected in a new name applied to members of that church, "And the disciples were first called Christians in Antioch" (Acts 11:26).

Toward the end of that year of ministry, a prophet named Agabus received a supernatural revelation from God concerning a worldwide famine that was about to affect the whole world. This famine actually occurred during the reign of Claudius Caesar who ruled Rome from A.D. 41 to 54. Other historical records of that time suggest the entire reign of Claudius was a time of international distress caused by bad harvests and other causes. As a result of the vision received by Agabus, the church at Antioch determined to send relief to their Christian brethren living in Judea. Once the funds were collected, they "sent it to the elders by the hands of Barnabas and Saul" (Acts 11:30).

II.   Herod's Attack on the Church

Claudius assumed the throne of Rome in A.D. 41 following the reign of Caligula. Caligula had taken the Roman belief in emperor worship seriously and promoted it widely throughout the empire. During his reign he had ordered that a statue of himself be raised in the Jewish temple. Some historians believe the struggle the Jewish leaders had with Rome to preserve the integrity of their faith was one of the contributing factors to their withdrawing from the persecution of the Christian church. When Claudius came to power, he backed down from the hard line of Caligula and made conciliations to the Jews and other religious groups throughout the empire. In Palestine, this action meant that Rome became actively involved in the persecution of the church.

Claudius was represented in Jerusalem by Herod who began implementing the new policies by stretching "out his hand to harass some of the church" (Acts 12:1). When he arrested James, the son of Zebedee, one of the original twelve disciples, and had him killed, he realized he had discovered a means by which he could appease the Jewish leaders who had been antagonistic toward Rome during the reign of Caligula. As Passover approached, his soldiers arrested Peter and imprisoned him with the intention of executing him immediately following the Feast of Unleavened Bread. Four squads of soldiers were assigned to keep Peter in custody during the extended feast. "Peter was therefore kept in prison, but constant prayer was offered to God for him by the church" (Acts 12:5).

While the church often met in large public gatherings such as the temple for times of celebration and worship directed toward God, they also met in smaller groups in homes of various members throughout the city. One of the homes in which the church often met belonged to Mary, the sister of Barnabas and the home in which Barnabas and Saul apparently stayed during their visit to Jerusalem. As news that Peter was to be executed the next morning reached Mary and others in the church, prayer meetings were quickly organized throughout the city. Soon Mary's home was filled with others who pled God for Peter's deliverance.

While the church was praying, Peter was asleep in his cell, chained between two soldiers who were locked behind a guarded door. Suddenly Peter was awakened as he felt someone poking him in the side. He heard a voice saying, "Arise quickly!" (Acts 12:7). As he stood up, the chains fell from his hands. The angel who had gotten into his cell then told Peter to dress and follow him. Still in a daze from his deep sleep and thinking he was somehow dreaming the whole thing, Peter dressed and began to follow the angel. They passed through guard posts unnoticed and came to the iron gate that led to the city. The gate seemed to swing open on its own as they passed through and began down one of the streets. Then Peter found himself all alone in the streets of Jerusalem.Only then did Peter realize he was not dreaming and understood what had just happened. "Now I know for certain that the Lord has sent His angel, and has delivered me from the hand of Herod and from all the expectation of the Jewish people," he said to himself (Acts 12:11). Although he was outside the prison, he knew it was not safe for him to spend the night on the streets where he might be apprehended and returned to his cell. He headed toward Mary's home. When he got there, he knocked at the locked gate.

Most of those inside were busy praying for Peter as Rhoda rose to attend to the gate. When she saw Peter standing there, she was so shocked that she ran back into the home to tell the others and left him still locked outside. When the others heard her report, they assumed she was so emotionally upset over Peter's arrest she had hallucinated seeing him at the gate. When she continued to insist she had seen him, they concluded that Herod had already executed the apostle and that it was Peter's ghost or angel at the door.

But "Peter continued knocking; and when they opened the door and saw him, they were astonished" (Acts 12:16). Peter motioned to them to keep quiet and then explained the strange events of that evening to the group. He sent some of the group to report what had taken place to James, Jesus' half-brother who by this time had risen to a place of prominence in the church similar to that of a senior pastor. Then Peter went off to another place to spend the rest of the night.

The next morning there was quite a commotion in the prison and court of Herod when they learned that Peter escaped. The king conducted a brief investigation into the matter and in keeping with the military custom of Rome, he ordered the execution of the soldiers assigned to guard Peter. Also about that time Herod moved his primary place of residence from landlocked Jerusalem to the coastal city of Caesarea.

Herod had other problems which were of a greater concern to him than the growth of the Christian church. Something had happened that made him angry with the population of the cities of Tyre and Sidon, but before he vented that anger upon the two cities, the leaders of the two cities made peace with him. They depended upon food and other supplies from the territory under Herod's control and feared his move to the port city of Caesarea may have been a first step in cutting off exports to them. After resolving their differences, Herod addressed a large delegation from the two cities from his throne. As he spoke, the people repeatedly shouted, "The voice of a god and not of a man!" (Acts 12:22). Herod believed their politically motivated lies. "Then immediately an angel of the Lord struck him, because he did not give glory to God. And he was eaten by worms and died" (Acts 12:23). The reign of Herod ended with his death in A.D. 44.

Herod's death had no negative impact on the continued growth of the early church. Instead, the church continued to grow and multiply. With the relief Barnabas and Saul had brought from Antioch, the church was able to devote more time to ministry and less to securing basic provisions. Their mission accomplished, the two returned to the city and church of Antioch. Barnabas' nephew, John Mark, returned with them and became a part of their ministry team.

III.   The First Missionary Journey

Barnabas's and Saul's experience in Jerusalem only served to accentuate their desire to work hard to take the gospel of Jesus Christ to people in other parts of the world. Both of these men had roots outside of Judea and knew that much of the known world of that time had not heard about Jesus and may be as responsive to the gospel as the Gentiles had been in Antioch. As they contemplated this matter and discussed it together, they felt God might be leading them into a unique ministry of taking the gospel to other cities in which there was no Christian church. As Barnabas and Saul considered this matter, God confirmed their call in the church. At a time when a number of the leaders in Antioch were fasting together, the Holy Spirit told them, "Now separate to Me Barnabas and Saul for the work to which I have called them" (Acts 13:2). After a further period of fasting, the church laid hands on these two men to identify them as their missionary representatives and sent them away for the first missionary journey.

Barnabas and Saul began their missionary journey by heading for the port city of Seleucia and getting on a boat to Cyprus. Barnabas had sold his real estate holdings on the island a number of years before, but likely he still had some contact with old friends and associates on the island whom he may have planned to contact as he and Saul began to evangelize the island. Also, a number of those who had begun the church in Antioch had roots on the Mediterranean island and may have notified their friends and relatives to prepare for the coming of these apostles.

When they arrived at Salamis, they made their way to the synagogues and began to preach the gospel. Wherever there were twelve Jewish families in a Gentile city, likely a synagogue had been built. These buildings served as Jewish community centers in Gentile cities and were the gathering place of Jews. Normally, the gospel was best introduced to a city through the synagogue. Using this approach to ministry, Barnabas and Saul worked their way across the island until they came to the city of Paphos. John Mark went along to look after details.

In the city of Paphos, the missionary team encountered a strange situation. One of the Jews of that city named Elymas Bar-Jesus had embraced the occult religion of that area and become a false prophet, practicing sorcery. This man served as a sort of spiritual adviser to the proconsul of the area, an intelligent man named Sergius Paulus. When the proconsul learned of Barnabas's and

Saul's presence, he requested that these men come and explain God's Word to him more clearly. They agreed, but they were opposed by Elymas who was obviously "seeking to turn the proconsul away from the faith" (Acts 13:8). In the face of this opposition, Saul turned and addressed the sorcerer, pulling no punches, "O full of all deceit and all fraud, you son of the devil, you enemy of all righteousness, will you not cease perverting the straight ways of the Lord? And now, indeed, the hand of the Lord is upon you, and you shall be blind, not seeing the sun for a time" (Acts 13:10-11).

Several things happened as a result of Saul's comments. First, the sorcerer was immediately blinded and had to depend upon others to lead him around. Second, when the proconsul saw this demonstration of the power of God, he came to believe in Jesus as his personal Messiah. Third, this instance appeared to raise Saul into a more prominent role as leader of the missionary party, perhaps alienating John Mark whose more natural allegiance would have been toward his uncle Barnabas. From this point on in the text, the name Paul occurs before Barnabas. Fourth, Saul appears to have at this point abandoned the use of his Hebrew name and begun to be identified by his Gentile name, Paul. Probably he had been named Saulus Paulus at his birth, and because of his commitment to the Pharisees, he had naturally favored using his Hebrew name Saul. Bible teachers have speculated the decision to begin using his Gentile name may have been due to increased ministry among Gentiles or related to this instance involving the proconsul who was also named Paul.

They determined to leave the island of Cyprus and evangelize Asia Minor. From Paphos, the missionary team set sail to Perga in Pamphylia, today located in modern Turkey. When they arrived, John Mark left the group and returned to Jerusalem. After the departure of the youngest member of the team, Paul and Barnabas traveled north to Antioch in Pisidia. On the sabbath, they attended the synagogue in that town and were invited to address those gathered on that occasion. Paul accepted the invitation and preached the gospel. As was apparently the custom of that day, he explained the death and resurrection of Jesus within the context of a historic survey of Israel's history. Then he explained the resurrection as the fulfillment of certain messianic psalms and prophecies. Finally he concluded, "that through this Man is preached to you the forgiveness of sins; and by Him everyone who believes is justified from all things from which you could not be justified by the law of Moses" (Acts 13:38-39).

The response to Paul's message was extremely positive. Many of the most devout Jews and proselytes present came to believe in Jesus as the Messiah. When the Gentiles in town heard what had taken place in the synagogue, they too wanted to hear the apostle speak. When the next sabbath came by, "almost the whole city came together to hear the word of God" (Acts 13:44).

When the leaders of the Jewish community saw the large crowd that had come to the synagogue, they became envious of Paul's apparent success. As he spoke, they rose to contradict his message and were so angered with the apostle they engaged in blasphemy themselves. When it became clear what was taking place, Paul claimed it was necessary to preach first to the Jews, but if they were going to reject the message, it would be taken to the Gentiles. This brought about a great response among the Gentiles and many believed and were converted not only in that city but throughout the region. The receptiveness of the Gentiles to Paul's message served to anger the Jewish leaders in that town further and they began pulling political strings to have the two missionaries expelled from the region. They left, shaking the dust off their feet in typical Jewish fashion, but they left behind a joyous band of Spirit-filled disciples who continued the work they had begun. Among those numbered in that group was a young convert named Timothy who had followed the example of his mother and grandmother and personally come to faith in Jesus (cf. 1 Tim.1:5).

From Antioch, they traveled east to Iconium. Again they preached the gospel in the synagogue and saw a number of both Jews and Gentiles come to faith in Christ. But once again, the Jews who did not believe turned against the two missionaries. This time they worked with other Gentile unbelievers and the city officials in a plot to abuse and stone Paul and Barnabas. When the two men learned of the plot, they escaped the city unharmed and began preaching in Lystra, Derbe, and other parts of the region of Lycaonia.

In Lystra, Paul healed a man who had been a cripple from his birth. When the people saw this miracle, they assumed the two men were incarnations of their gods. They assumed Barnabas was Zeus, the chief of the gods, probably because of his large stature. The crowd called Paul "Hermes, because he was the chief speaker" (Acts 14:12).

As the priests of Zeus came out to present a sacrifice to them, the apostles tore their clothes to reject their actions and spoke to the crowd to restrain them. They claimed they too were men and urged them to turn from their idols to serve the living God. Although there does not appear to have been any converted as a result of that appeal, they did succeed in discouraging the sacrifice that had been planned.

The Jews that had opposed Paul and Barnabas in Antioch and Iconium soon found the pair in Lystra. The opposition came to the city and incited the people to stone Paul and drag him out of the city. If the second epistle to the Corinthians was written about A.D. 60 as many conservative Bible teachers believe, then Paul was caught up into the third heaven at this stoning (2 Cor. 12:1-6). Some Bible teachers believe the apostle actually died on that occasion and was restored to life to continue his ministry.

In his vision, Paul was "caught up into Paradise and heard inexpressible words, which it is not lawful for a man to utter" (2 Cor. 12:4). This experience was so personally significant that he felt uncomfortable sharing it with others until fourteen years after the fact. Paul, who had at least five visions in which he saw Jesus after the resurrection, apparently looked upon this experience as the most significant. He understood this experience could potentially lead him into pride and distract him from the primary focus of his ministry.

Because of this, Paul believed he had been given what he called "a thorn in the flesh . . . a messenger of Satan to buffet me" (1 Cor. 12:7). Nowhere does the Scripture specifically identify the nature of this thorn, but it was apparently irritating enough that Paul "pleaded with the Lord three times that it might depart from me" (2 Cor. 12:8). On each occasion, the Lord's response to that prayer was, "My grace is sufficient for you, for My strength is made perfect in weakness" (2 Cor. 12:9). As a result, Paul not only learned to accept this problem in his life, but came to appreciate it as a means of securing God's grace for ministry.

The next day, Paul and Barnabas headed for Derbe where they again preached the gospel and won a number of converts to the faith. Then they retraced their steps back through the cities of Lystra, Iconium and Antioch "strengthening the souls of the disciples, exhorting them to continue in the faith" and reminding them that tribulations would precede their entering into the kingdom of God (Acts 14:22). In each church, they appointed elders who would serve as the spiritual leaders of the new churches. Then they returned to Perga and Attalia from which they sailed to Antioch. "Now when they had come and gathered the church together, they reported all that God had done with them, and that He had opened the door of faith to the Gentiles" (Acts 14:27).

Conclusion

Paul's and Barnabas's first missionary journey has served as a precedent for contemporary missionary activity. Like the first missionaries of the church, modern missionaries carry the gospel cross-culturally as representatives of their home church which is their sending base. And like those first missionaries, they are likely to encounter problems of discouragement, spiritual opposition, physical assault, misunderstandings, etc. and need to know the members of their supporting churches are faithful not only in their financial aid but also in praying for them and their ministry. As one contemplates the first missionary journey of Paul and Barnabas, one is again reminded of the need to pray for those involved in missionary work today.

CHAPTER 36

JAMES:
LEADING THE CHURCH INTO
LIBERTY

Acts 15:1-35; Galatians; James

⏀fter they returned from their missionary journey to Cyprus, Pamphylia, and Pisidia, Paul and Barnabas remained in Antioch and again took an active role in the ministry in that city. The church which had sent them out naturally rejoiced when they heard how other Gentiles had also come to believe in Jesus. They had the conviction that other Gentiles like themselves would be receptive to the gospel if given an opportunity to hear and believe. This conviction motivated them to send Paul and Barnabas on the first missionary journey. Now they were grateful to God that they had been able to have a part in this project.

However, not everyone viewed the conversion of the Gentiles with the same enthusiasm. Among the Jews in Judea, there was still a strong feeling that the belief that some could become Christians by simply accepting the Jewish Messiah as Savior was somehow inconsistent. These Judean Jews also wanted all new Christians to adopt the Jewish heritage. A group of Jewish Christians began traveling throughout the region where there were many Gentile converts to Christianity in an attempt to correct what they perceived to be a major problem developing in the church. The essence of their message was this, "Unless you are circumcised according to the custom of Moses, you cannot be saved" (Acts 15:1).

The addition of circumcision and Jewish customs to the gospel challenged the essence of the gospel which Paul and Barnabas had preached on their missionary journey. They had taught people could be converted by simply repenting of their sin and placing their faith in Jesus Christ. Also, the gospel preached by the two missionaries promised people a real liberty in Christ that could not be realized under the bondage of the law. These Jewish Christians were now leading the Gentile Christians into a bondage that could only hinder their spiritual progress. Therefore, when this teaching was introduced in Antioch, Paul and Barnabas strongly opposed it. The dissension and dispute was so severe that the church leaders were invited to Jerusalem in an attempt to resolve the issue.

As Paul and Barnabas traveled south to Jerusalem, they stopped in to preach in the churches in many of the cities in Phoenicia and Samaria. As the people learned of the conversion of the Gentiles, they rejoiced greatly. But some of the Pharisees who had converted to Christianity were not convinced these conversions were genuine. "It is necessary to circumcise them, and to command them to keep the law of Moses," they argued (Acts 15:5). The issue was threatening to divide the whole church as the leaders arrived in Jerusalem to discuss the matter.

I.   The Jerusalem Council

The meeting of church leaders in Jerusalem was the first such meeting in the history of the church and became the pattern by which many of the church's doctrinal controversies in the first few centuries were resolved. The Jerusalem Council, as it became known, was concerned primarily with the relationship a Gentile believer should or should not have with the law of Moses. The findings of this council are particularly significant in light of the historical context when they met in Jerusalem and were primarily addressed by men with deep roots in the religious traditions of the Jews.

As the council began, the discussion was by no means unanimous. People on both sides of the issue were deeply committed to the positions they held. For those who had been raised under the law, allowing Gentiles to become Christians without insisting upon something as basic as the rite of circumcision seemed like a denial of their religious heritage. Those opposed to "legalistic Christianity" probably argued out of the experience of the Gentile converts who seemed to be truly converted without adherence to the law. After some time had been spent discussing the matter, Peter, whose ministry base was largely Jewish in cultural background, rose to address the issue.

Peter reminded the group gathered on that occasion that God had chosen him to first preach the gospel to a group of Gentiles – in Cornelius's home. Peter remembered how surprised he and the others had been in Cornelius home as they witnessed the obvious evidence that God had given them the Holy Spirit just as He had done with the Jewish believers. After reminding the church of that event, Peter asked a question which addressed the very heart of the controversy. "Now therefore, why do you test God by putting a yoke on the neck of the disciples which neither our fathers nor we were able to bear? But we believe that through the grace of the Lord Jesus Christ we shall be saved in the same manner as they" (Acts 15:10-11).

Following Peter's remarks, Paul and Barnabas reported on the success of their missionary journey. Because they understood the purpose of miracles as signs to produce credibility for the message of Christianity, they laid special emphasis in their report on the "many miracles and wonders God had worked through them among the Gentiles" (Acts 15:12). Rather than viewing doctrinal orthodoxy and Christian experience as somehow divorced from each other, Paul and Barnabas built on Peter's doctrinal affirmation and used their ministry experience as a practical confirmation of the biblical principle.

At the conclusion of their report, James then addressed the church with a proposed resolution to the problem. He reminded the church that the strategy of presenting the gospel to the Gentiles was consistent with the prophecy of Amos concerning "Gentiles who are called by my name" (cf. Amos 9:11-12). James concluded, "Therefore I judge that we should not trouble those from among the Gentiles who are turning to God" (Acts 15:19). Still, in recognition that there were certain things which the unsaved Jews in Gentile cities found particularly offensive, James strongly suggested that Gentile Christians be urged to avoid such things as food which had been offered to idols, sexual immorality and eating the meat of animals which had been strangled or not bled. These acts did not affect one's standing with God but would raise barriers which might hinder efforts in the Christian evangelization of unsaved Jews.

This proposed solution of the problems met with the support of not only the apostles and elders, but also the Jerusalem church which had initiated the discussions. The council determined that a couple of men from the Jerusalem church should accompany Paul and Barnabas back to Antioch to report on the council's findings. Judas Barsabas and Silas had proven their leadership in the Jerusalem church and were off to Antioch which had become the center of ministry directed toward the Gentiles.

II.   The Two Epistles of James

Many Bible teachers believe the letter prepared by the Jerusalem council summarizing their findings was probably drafted by James who had risen to a place of prominence in Jerusalem as the senior pastor of the church. There are several reasons for this conclusion. First, the wording of this letter closely resembles the wording of James' address to the council. Second, many similarities in style have been noted between this letter and the pastoral epistle later written by James. Also, James appears to be the only significant, prominent leader in the church who would be naturally chosen to write the letter. Although the original twelve apostles were still active in broader ministry among all churches, the elders in the local church were assuming a larger role in leading the church. James lead the elders in Jerusalem.

In the brief letter to the Gentile believers in Antioch, Syria, and Cilicia, those who taught, "You must be circumcised and keep the law" were identified as not having been authorized by the church of Jerusalem (Acts 15:24). This statement destroyed much of the credibility for "Judistic Christianity." Second, the letter reported the official church position that Gentiles did not have to "keep the law" but should avoid certain practices which might offend Jews in their city and hinder the outreach of the gospel. The Gentiles were urged "that you abstain from things offered to idol, from blood, from things strangled, and from sexual immorality" (Acts 15:29).

If the letter reporting the findings of the Jerusalem Council is viewed as "The Epistle of James to Gentile Believers," the New Testament epistle which bears his name may be viewed as his epistle to Jewish believers. This epistle was probably written about the same time as the Jerusalem Council but was obviously directed to a church that was predominantly Jewish in character. At the time in which it was written, the church was still meeting in the synagogue (James 2:2). Its Jewish character is also evidenced by a strong emphasis on such things as wisdom (James 1:5; 3:17) and keeping the law, which is absent in his epistle to the Gentile believers (James 2:8-12). This epistle also identifies Abraham as "our father" in a context which assumes the original readers were Jewish (James 2:21).

THE EPISTLE OF JAMES

Author: James, the half-brother of Jesus
Recipients: Predominantly Jewish Church
Date of Writing: A.D. 45-50
Theme: The Testing of Our Faith

Over the years, some Bible teachers have struggled with the Epistle of James because of its strong emphasis on works as an evidence of genuine faith. Some have mistakenly believed James was in conflict with Paul in his teaching of justification by faith alone. Actually, James's statements which have been taken out of context to teach a work-oriented plan of salvation really teach that a saving faith will demonstrate itself by its works. The theme of the epistle is "the testing of our faith." James suggests at least thirteen ways in which our faith may be tested and verified as genuine.

JAMES: THE TESTING OF OUR FAITH

Faith Tested by Our Trials in Life (1:1-11)
Faith Tested by Our Personal Temptation (1:12-18)
Faith Tested by Our Obedience to the Scripture (1:19-27)
Faith Tested by Our Impartiality Toward Others (2:1-13)
Faith Tested by Our Production of Works (2:14-26)
Faith Tested by Our Expression in Works (3:1-12)
Faith Tested by Our Expression of Wisdom (3:13-18)
Faith Tested by Our Humility in Relationships (4:1-12)
Faith Tested by Our Conduct of Business (4:13-17)
Faith Tested by Our Response to Social Injustice (5:1-6)
Faith Tested by Our Patient Endurance (5:7-12)
Faith Tested by Our Effectiveness in Prayer (5:13-18)
Faith Tested by Our Ministry to Others (5:19-20)

III. Paul's Response to This Problem

When the church at Antioch heard the letter from the Jerusalem conference read, "they rejoiced over its encouragement" (Acts 15:31). Although Judas and Silas accomplished their primary responsibility with the reading of the letter, both stayed on for some time in Antioch and engaged in a ministry which strengthened the church. Some time later, Judas returned to Jerusalem with special greetings from the Antioch church for the apostles, but Silas decided to stay on at the church. Paul and Barnabas also remained at the church, "teaching and preaching the word of the Lord, with many others also" (Acts 15:35).

Although the problem of the Gentile believers' relationship to the law appeared to have been decided once and for all by the Jerusalem Council, that was unfortunately not the case. During a visit of Peter at Antioch following the meeting in Jerusalem, the problem again arose to the point of confrontation between Peter and Paul. When Peter first arrived in the city, he enjoyed fellowship with the Gentile believers and often ate together with them, but when a group of men were sent by James to the church, Peter withdrew from the Gentiles and fellowshiped only with the Jews. James had a reputation for piously observing the law, and although he did not believe Gentiles needed to come under the law, many of the false teachers in the church that held this view associated themselves with James and his example.

This group's intimidation was so strong that most of the Jews involved in the church at Antioch followed Peter's example of withdrawing from fellowship with Gentile believers including Barnabas. When this took place, Paul confronted Peter with his hypocrisy and reminded him "a man is not justified by the works of law but by faith in Jesus Christ, even we have believed in Christ Jesus, that we might be justified by faith in Christ and not by the works of the law; for by the works of the law no flesh shall be justified" (Gal. 2:16).

This revival of the problem in Antioch after the Jerusalem Council was a forerunner of things to come. These Judaisers became an significant influence in the early church. In several of his epistles, the apostle Paul opposed their teachings and warned his readers to beware of the consequences of this teaching, but the first and most direct of these was the epistle to the Galatians. This is the only one of Paul's epistles written to a group of churches and is generally viewed as a draft of the theological position later expanded upon in Romans. Although conservative scholars are divided as to the date of this letter, it was probably written within a decade of the Jerusalem conference, no later than A.D. 48.

> ## THE EPISTLE TO THE GALATIANS
>
> *Author:* Paul
> *Recipients:* The Churches of Galatia
> *Date of Writing:* A.D. 48-57
> *Theme:* The Liberty of the Believer

The epistle to the Galatians is the biblical source of the doctrine of Christian liberty. It was written at a time when the Judaisers threatened the liberty of the believer with their emphasis on keeping the law. In confronting this problem, Paul demonstrated the weakness of their position and argued the principles upon which the doctrine of Christian liberty is built. This brief epistle is tractarian in nature, but Paul's argument can be traced as it is developed. He argues his position from both his personal experience and his understanding of the law itself. He then concludes his epistles calling on the reader to remain free in the liberty he or she has in Christ, continue walking in the Spirit and ministering to one another in the church. In his closing comments, he called on the church to glory in the Cross rather than the flesh.

GALATIANS: THE LIBERTY OF THE BELIEVER

Introduction to the Epistle (1:1-5)
Problem: The Judaisers Teach Another Gospel (1:6-9)
Paul's Gospel Came through Revelation (1:10-24)
Paul's Gospel was Approved by the Apostles (2:1-10)
The Gospel Stands in Contrast with the Law (2:11-21)
Faith as the Consistent Means of Justification (3:1-25)
Faith as the Means by which Christians are Sons (3:26–4:20)
A Contrast between Faith/Sons and Law/Slaves (4:21-31)
Appeal to Remain Free in Christ (5:1-15)
Appeal to Continue Walking in the Spirit (5:16-26)
Appeal to Minister to Others in the Church (6:1-10)
Conclusion: Glory in the Cross not the Flesh (6:11-18)

Conclusion

The liberty which Jesus secured on the cross was too crucial to the essential character of Christianity for the early church to allow it to be eroded through adding a religious tradition to the gospel. But in the years since, Christians have struggled with a natural tendency to add certain things to the gospel and their understanding of the Christian life. The message of Scripture is clear. Salvation is all of grace. While a person probably should do many good things to evidence their faith in Christ and the new life they have received when they are born again, when one begins to do these things to *secure or maintain* a relationship with God, they may hinder continued spiritual progress. Christians today can only experience the liberty provided in Christ when they depend upon Him *alone* for salvation. Then as they experience the liberty they have in Christ, they will want to "use liberty as an opportunity...(to) through love serve one another" (Gal. 5:13).

CHAPTER 37

PAUL:
TAKING THE GOSPEL TO EUROPE

Acts 15:36–17:15; Philippians

ome time after the controversy with Peter over his hypocrisy in segregating himself from the Gentiles, Paul and Barnabas again began to discuss the possibility of a second mission to the churches they had established on the first missionary journey. They wanted to see for themselves how the new believers were doing, especially in light of the growing influence of the Judaisers who were influencing Gentiles to submit to the Jewish law as a means of completing their salvation. As the team began to discuss their plans, they agreed that the idea was worth pursuing and began to organize the details involved with the mission. All went well until Barnabas suggested bringing his nephew John Mark on the mission.

Paul remembered that Mark had left the team in the midst of the first missionary journey and was opposed to their inviting him to join them for this second mission. Mark left about the time Paul assumed a leadership role which had been held by Barnabas. Mark's departure may have been at least in part due to his resentment over that change. Paul viewed the young man as one who could not stand the pressure of the ministry and had quit before engaging in the real work of the missionary trip. Barnabas always took the side of the outcast or underdog. He may have remembered a time when the church was unsure about the reality of Paul's conversion. Barnabas had seen the ministry potential of Paul, a converted Pharisee, and introduced him to the church at Jerusalem. Now he believed Mark had potential and wanted to give his nephew a second chance.

Both men held strong opinions in the debate over Mark, and as the discussion continued, they became increasingly more committed to having their way on the issue. Finally, "the contention became so sharp that they parted from one another" (Acts 15:39). Barnabas took Mark and sailed to Cyprus. While the Bible does not reveal any details concerning this mission, it was apparently a growing experience for Mark. During this missionary trip or shortly following, he came under the influence of Simon Peter and penned the second of the four gospel accounts of Christ's life. Most Bible teachers view the gospel of Mark as the life of Christ viewed through the eye-witness experiences of Peter.

When John Mark left Paul and Barnabas on the first missionary journey, he returned to his mother's home in Jerusalem. Peter was one of those who met regularly in that home for prayer and no doubt spoke often about his time with Jesus. As Mark listened to these stories, the young man must have realized Peter knew things about Jesus that comparatively few Christians knew. He may have traveled to Antioch with Peter and had opportunity to discuss the life of Jesus in a more intimate setting. As he engaged in ministry among the Gentiles with his uncle Barnabas, Mark would have recognized the difficulties involved in using the gospel of Matthew which was written when the church was largely Jewish in background to teach Gentile believers about Jesus. This may have motivated him to write a gospel to Christians strongly influenced by Roman values. Under the inspiration of the Holy Spirit, Mark wrote the second gospel to meet this need in the church.

THE GOSPEL OF MARK

Author: John Mark (Peter's Memoirs)
Recipients: Predominantly Roman Christians
Date of Writing: A.D. 50–60
Theme: Jesus, the Servant of the Lord

I.   The Macedonian Call

Following Barnabas's departure, Paul decided to form a new ministry team and left in a different direction, traveling through Syria and Cilicia. Because Silas had proven himself a capable leader in both Jerusalem and Antioch, Paul chose him as his associate on this journey. The new team was presented to the church at Antioch and "commended by the brethren to the grace of God" as they began their ministry (Acts 15:40). As they began, they had an effective ministry of strengthening believers in the churches they visited.

When Paul came to the cities of Derbe and Lystra, he found a strong well-established church in those communities. One young man who had risen to a place of prominence in the church was Timothy. Both his mother and grandmother were Christians who nurtured and encouraged Timothy. Timothy showed evidence of maturing well in the Christian life. He had a good reputation among the Christians in both Lystra and Iconium. Paul invited him to join his ministry team as they continued traveling. Although Timothy's mother was a Jewess, his father was Greek. Paul was concerned that this may hinder Timothy's ministry among the Jews in their synagogues, so he arranged for Timothy to be circumcised.

During this first phase of the second missionary journey, Paul and his team traveled from church to church and "delivered to them the decrees to keep, which were determined by the apostles and elders at Jerusalem" (Acts 16:4). This resulted in both a deepening of the Christian experience of these believers and a numerical increase in the growth of the church as others were reached for Christ.

After some initial success on this mission, the team entered a more frustrating phase of ministry in which they seemed to lack clear direction concerning what to do next. They sensed the Holy Spirit did not want them to continue preaching in Asia, so they continued traveling west across Asia Minor, looking for other alternative fields of ministry.

"After they had come to Mysia, they tried to go into Bithynia, but the Spirit did not permit them" (Acts 16:7). They made their way to the port city of Troas, really not sure what they would do next. The harbor faced Greece. Two things happened in Troas that impacted the character of this missionary trip and also the rest of Paul's ministry. First, the missionary team was joined by Luke. Although the author of the third gospel and the Acts does not identify himself by name, he changes his writing style at this point in the historical record from the third person ("they") to the first person ("we") (cf. Acts 16:8, 10). This is actually one way in which Bible teachers have determined Luke's authorship of Acts. Among the known associates of Paul mentioned in his epistles, only Titus and Luke are not named in the company of Paul in the Acts accounts of his ministry. Luke is identified as the author of these two books in part because of the technical use of medical and legal language in these books and the knowledge that Luke was a trained doctor. Some Bible teachers believe Titus may have been Luke's brother, which would account for the silence concerning him in this way (cf. as John does not identify himself or his brother by name in his gospel).

The second significant event taking place in Troas was a vision Paul received which has become known as "the Macedonian Call." Some Bible teachers believe Luke may have just come from Europe prior to joining Paul in Troas or that Paul may have heard many stories about life just across the bay in Europe as he arrived in the city. This may have given Paul an interest in preaching the gospel in Europe, but he received a vision from God one night that convinced him the time had come to take that step.

In his vision, Paul saw a man from Macedonia standing and pleading with him. His message to the apostle was summarized in the request, "Come over to Macedonia and help. us" (Acts 16:9). This vision was unique in Paul's experience and everyone on the team agreed on its meaning. Immediately, the focus of the team's efforts was directed toward securing passage from Troas to Macedonia. They boarded a ship that took them on a straight course from Troas to the island of Samothrace. The next day, they sailed on to Neapolis. From there, the team traveled inland to the colony of Philippi.

II.   Paul's Ministry in Philippi

The city of Philippi was located about nine miles inland from the seaport city of Neapolis. The city had been captured and fortified in 358 B.C. by Philip II of Macedon, the father of Alexander the Great and named in his honor. Philip sought control of the city because of the fertile soil in the marshes around the city, the existence of valuable gold mines in the region, and the city's strategic position in the event of an invasion from Asia. Over the next three centuries, the city dwindled in both size and significance as the Greek empire declined and Rome took its place of world superiority. In the fall of 42 B.C., at Philippi, Octavian and Antony defeated Brutus and Cassius, the leaders of the conspirators involved in of Julius Caesar's assassination. Shortly after that month of conflict, Philippi was elevated in status to become a Roman colony. This new status carried a number of benefits including immunity from taxation. As a result, the city once again began to grow, largely as a result of Italian immigration.

There was not a large Jewish community in the city so the Jews which did live there met at the river for prayer rather than in a synagogue. Roman colonies tended to insist upon such things as emperor worship and other practices the Jews found offensive, so Jesus tended not to settle there. Those who did worship by the river appear to have been almost exclusively women. As they met by the river the Sabbath after Paul and his team arrived, the four men met to pray and worship God with them.

Because of the nature of this group, the four men had an immediate opportunity to preach the gospel without interference. One of those present in the group that Sabbath was Lydia, a recent immigrant from the city of Thyatira, who was involved in the fashion industry in that town. She is described as "a seller of purple" which probably means she dealt largely with the upper class citizens of the city in her business (Acts 16:14). She and her household were the first to respond positively to the gospel. Upon her conversion, she immediately invited the men to accept her hospitality as long as they stayed in the city.

The missionary team continued their ministry for some time working primarily with this group which met regularly by the river for prayer. These were not the only religious people in the city. There was also "a certain slave girl possessed with a spirit of divination...who brought her masters much profit by fortune-telling" (Acts 16:16). As she watched the missionary team go to the river, she announced to all who would listen, "These men are the servants of the Most High God, who proclaim to us the way of salvation" (Acts 16:17).

Initially, the men simply ignored her interruptions and carried on their ministry in spite of her interference. This continued for several days and began to annoy Paul. One day he turned to her and said, "I command you in the name of Jesus Christ to come out of her" (Acts 16:18). Immediately, the girl was released from the bondage of the spirit. While this meant she would no longer be an annoyance to the missionaries with her announcements, it also meant she no longer had the ability to predict the future and could therefore no longer profit her owners.

Angry over the loss of their profit, the owners of the slave girl had Paul and Silas arrested and brought before the officials claiming, "These men, being Jews, exceedingly trouble our city; and they teach customs which are not lawful for us, being Romans, to receive or observe" (Acts 16:20). Many Bible teachers believe the men were successful in having Paul and Silas imprisoned because of the anti-Semitic attitude which was at this time sweeping through the Roman empire. It is interesting that neither Timothy nor Luke who had Gentile fathers were arrested even though they too had been actively involved with Paul and Silas in the ministry in Philippi.

A mob was quickly incited against the two men and the city officials immediately ordered the men to be beaten with rods, without making any further inquiries as to their guilt or innocence. After the beating, they were turned over to the jailer who was ordered to keep them secure. Assuming the men were dangerous prisoners, he locked their feet in the stocks located in the inner prison. Although the day had begun like any other, as the sun set they had been beaten and imprisoned for releasing a girl from the bondage of a demon. The two missionaries responded to these circumstances by "praying and singing hymns to God" (Acts 16:25).

The prayers and singing of Paul and Silas were loud enough that others in the prison could hear what they were doing. By midnight, the whole prison was listening to the words of these two Jewish teachers. Then suddenly, the singing was drowned out by another sound. The earth began to shake and the prison walls swung from side to side. By the time the earthquake ended, every lock in the jail had been rendered useless. Every prisoner was free from his chains and all the doors were opened.

The jailor himself had been sleeping when the earthquake began but quickly woke up during the tremor. When he got to the jail to inspect the damage, he recognized his worst nightmare had come to pass. Seeing the open doors of the jail, he assumed the prisoners had all escaped. He knew the penalty for letting prisoners escape and realized the city officials would not accept the earthquake as an excuse. The easiest way out of this situation was to take his own life immediately. The escape would cost him his life eventually.

As he drew his sword to kill himself, the jailor began to hear a voice. "Do yourself no harm, for we are all here," he heard the voice saying. Calling for a light, the jailor went in to see for himself. It was true. None of the prisoners had escaped, including the two who had been delivered to him that afternoon. Obviously shaken from the events which had disturbed his sleep, he brought Paul and Silas out of the jail and into his own home. There he asked them, "Sirs, what must I do to be saved?" (Acts 16:30). The men answered the jailor, "Believe on the Lord Jesus Christ, and you will be saved, you and your household" (Acts 16:31).

The jailor, his family, and servants continued to listen to Paul and Silas explain the gospel as they cleaned the men's wounded backs. By the time the prisoners' wounds had been dressed, the jailor and his household had come to believe what they had been taught. That night they were baptized. When they returned to the jailor's home, the jailor sat the two men at his table and fed them, rejoicing in his newfound faith in Christ.

The next morning, the city officials sent word to the jail that Paul and Silas could be released. When the apostles learned of the decision, they refused to accept the conditions of the release. "They have beaten us openly, uncondemned Romans, and have thrown us into prison. And now do they put us out secretly? No indeed! Let them come themselves and get us out," Paul explained. When the officers carried this message back to the magistrates, they were afraid and immediately came to the jail. Under Roman law, anyone possessing Roman citizenship was given certain rights which could not be refused. One of these rights involved freedom from punishment without due process of law. The magistrates could be in serious trouble if Paul and Silas pressed for an investigation into the abuse of their rights as Romans. The magistrates came and released the men and pleaded with them to leave the city.

Paul and Silas did so, but not before they returned to Lydia's home to encourage the church.

Of all the churches established by Paul, it is doubtful if any were as close to his heart as the church at Philippi. About ten years after coming to this city, Paul wrote an epistle from Rome in appreciation for a financial gift he had received from the church. This church had supported the apostle financially on several of his missions but for some time was unable to maintain their giving. When the giving was reactivated while Paul was imprisoned in Rome, he wrote the church expressing his appreciation for their gift, reminding them of the precious memories they shared, and reminding them of the importance of keeping Christ as central in the focus of the Christian life. Because of the prominent role Timothy played in developing the church over the decade, he was also designated as a coauthor of the epistle (Phil. 1:1).

> **THE EPISTLE TO THE PHILIPPIANS**
> *Author:* Paul and Timothy
> *Recipients:* The Saints at Philippi
> *Date of Writing:* A.D. 60/61
> *Theme:* Christ and the Christian Life

III.   Paul's Ministry in Thessalonica and Berea

As the team left Philippi, Luke was no longer part of the group. He may have stayed in Philippi to work with the church or may have gone to another city. Paul, Silas, and Timothy continued southwest along the Egnation Way through the cities of Amphipolis and Apollonia until they came to the city of Thessalonica. Thessalonica had been one of the more prominent cities in the region since it was enlarged and renamed by the Macedonian King Cassander in 315 B.C. It was named in honor of his wife, Thessalonica, who was also the daughter of Philip II. It rapidly grew in both size and wealth and for a time served as the headquarters of the Macedonian navy. Even after the fall of the Greek empire, Thessalonica remained an important trading center and continued to prosper.

A large Jewish population existed in Thessalonica, so Paul and his team returned to the practice of preaching in the synagogue. For three consecutive Sabbaths, Paul reasoned from the Scriptures "explaining and demonstrating that Christ had to suffer and rise again from the dead, and saying, 'This Jesus whom I preach to you is the Christ'" (Acts 17:3). This approach to ministry yielded results and a number were converted including a large group of Greeks and number of prominent women in the city.

But although many believed, some did not. Some of the Jews who were not persuaded by Paul organized others to incite a riot in the marketplace. The mob attacked Jason's home where the missionary team was thought to be staying. When the mob could not find them, they seized Jason and some of the others and took them to the city officials. They were accused of harboring "these who have turned the world upside down" (Acts 17:6) and of being involved in a movement which taught the existence of "another king – Jesus" (Acts 17:7). When these charges were made, the officials required Jason and the other Christians who had been seized with him to raise a security bond before they released them. Recognizing that a danger still existed for Paul and his companions, the Christians in Thessalonica helped them escape the city that night.

From Thessalonica, the men traveled west to Berea. Once again the men turned to the synagogue as the basis for a new ministry in Berea. These people were less resistant to Paul's preaching and gave careful consideration to his ministry. As a result, there were a number of conversions including both Jews and Gentiles, men and women. But when word reached Thessalonica of Paul's ministry in Berea, a delegation made their way to that city and began stirring up the crowds against Paul. The Berean Christians responded to this problem by sending Paul to Athens by sea. Silas and Timothy remained behind in Berea to continue the work that had been started.

Conclusion

As Paul began the work of bringing the gospel to Europe, he encountered both opportunity and opposition. Rather than be discouraged by the opposition to his preaching, he rejoiced in the opportunities before him and took advantage of the open doors to preach the gospel. Sometimes it is easy to become discouraged in the Christian life when we focus on everything that goes wrong. A better approach is to recognize the opportunities God has given us to serve Him and take full advantage of them. The resulting blessing of God will more than compensate for any problems we may encounter along the way.

CHAPTER 38

THE GREEKS:
THE RESPONSE OF SCHOLARS
AND SINNERS

Acts 17:16-18; 1 Thessalonians; 2 Thessalonians

The Christians in Berea were concerned for Paul's safety when the Jews from Thessalonica arrived, so they not only got him out of their city, they escorted him on his journey to Athens. They probably went down the river on which the city of Berea was located to the coast and caught a ship from that port heading south. The voyage not only got Paul out of Berea, it got him out of Macedonia. When he landed in the city of Athens, he was in the Roman province of Achaia.

As Paul's traveling companions left him in Athens to return to Berea, he sent back word that Silas and Timothy should join him at their earliest convenience. It is not clear if Paul planned a mission to Athens. He apparently had decided to take some time to rest while waiting for the members of his team. But as he saw what was going on around him in Athens, he soon found himself again engaged in ministry.

Paul's ministry in Achaia focused in the two principle cities of that province, Athens and Corinth. These two cities were different in many respects and this impacted the ministry style of the apostle. Paul understood the way one would explain the gospel to an Athenian philosopher was different from the way one might explain it to a sailor passing through Corinth, but the message of the gospel was the same. Although Paul used many different methods of communicating the gospel, he never compromised the essence of the gospel which he preached. On every occasion, he built an argument for the death, burial, and resurrection of Jesus as the heart of his gospel (cf. 1 Cor. 15:3-4).

I. Paul's Ministry in Athens

The city of Athens had existed for over a thousand years before Paul traveled along the road from the harbor into the metropolis. Over the years, Athens had become a center of Greek sciences and arts. During the Roman era Athens became one of the respected intellectual centers in the empire. As a strongly religious center, it was home to a number of temples, altars, and statues to Greek gods and goddesses such as Zeus (Jupiter) and Athena as well as numerous other deities of other regions. There was even an altar devoted to the worship of "The Unknown God" (cf. Acts 17:23).

As Paul carried on the affairs of life while waiting for his team to arrive, he was increasingly concerned about the widespread idolatry which he witnessed. Soon he found himself again involved in the task of communicating the gospel to those who had not yet heard and responded to Christ. In Athens, Paul adopted a two-fold strategy to reach the people. First, because there was a sizable Jewish population in the town, Paul "reasoned in the synagogue with the Jews and with the Gentile worshipers" (Acts 17:17). Second, because the city was essentially Greek in its population, Paul adopted the Greek approach to raising and discussing issues in the aqora or marketplace.

The Greeks prided themselves on their democratic tolerance of new ideas and pluralistic approach to society. One of the ways this was expressed was in the marketplace. It was common for teachers and philosophers to gather in public places to discuss their ideas about a wide variety of issues. Most new ideas were communicated to the population at large in the marketplace. In a city like Athens, anyone could speak in the marketplace provided they had something to say and did not mind their ideas being challenged by others who might have a different perspective on the issue.

As Paul taught the gospel in the marketplace, he encountered a wide variety of people in his discussions. Many people gathered in the Athenian market and the Areopagus (Mars Hill) who "spent their time in nothing else but either to tell or to hear some new thing" (Acts 17:21). Some of the Epicurean and Stoic philosophers who met Paul in the market wondered what he was teaching. They were told by others, "He seems to be a proclaimer of foreign gods" (Acts 17:18). They arrived at this conclusion because of Paul's consistent emphasis on the resurrection of Jesus, something which the Athenians thought only could happen in the experience of one of their mythological gods.

As curiosity about Paul's message grew, arrangements were made to invite Paul to address the Athenians in the more formal setting of the Areopagus. Paul accepted this opportunity to address the group and preached a sermon which some have criticized for its lack of biblical content. Unlike the sermons Paul and others preached in the Jewish synagogues, this address to the philosophers on Mars Hill makes no reference to Old Testament Scriptures that point to the Messiah, and at one point Paul even includes a quote from a pagan poet. The text of the sermon seems to be based on an inscription on an altar which was part of the syncretistic worship of that city. When Paul preached the gospel, he constantly sought to build bridges with his listeners and bring them around to his conclusion. When talking to those who knew the Scriptures, Paul appealed to the Scriptures as the best way to accomplish this objective. But it is doubtful this crowd was familiar with the Scriptures or that appealing to them would have established any credibility in their mind. Instead, Paul used sources with which the people were familiar to argue to the same conclusion.

Those who are especially critical of Paul's sermon on this occasion often attempt to claim he changed his message and therefore got no results. Neither of these claims is consistent with the biblical account or the transcription of the sermon. Paul clearly identified God as the One "who made the world and everything in it" in contrast to the Athenian view of many gods and spoke directly against the practice of idolatry so common in that city (Acts 17:24, 29). Also included in Paul's message was a clear call to repentance and affirmation of the resurrection of Jesus (Acts 17:30-31). If this message does not appear to be as clear or comprehensive as other explanations of the gospel by Paul, this may be due to the interruption of his sermon at this point, rather than an attempt by Paul to change the gospel. Further, while the bulk of popular opinion appears to have rejected the gospel on this occasion, "some men joined him and believed, among them Dionysius the Areopagite, a woman named Damaris, and others with them" (Acts 17:34).

II.   Paul's Ministry in Corinth

Following his address on Mars Hill, Paul made his way to the seaport city of Corinth. The city of Corinth was a cosmopolitan center where people from various parts of the Roman Empire had either settled or visited regularly to conduct their business. The harbor at Corinth was one of the few located along that coast, so the city naturally became a center of trade. Smaller ships were transported across the isthmus between Corinth and Cenchrea over a series of wooden rails. This only added to the amount of trade passing through its port and increased its commercial value as a trading center.

The reputation of Corinth was tied to its extremely loose moral character. The Greeks used an expression to describe an extremely immoral lifestyle which might be literally translated "to live like a Corinthian." In his epistle to this church, Paul reminded his readers that some of them had been involved in activities ranging from idol worship and sodomy to terrorism and extortion prior to their conversion (cf. 1 Cor. 6:9-11).

Soon after arriving in Corinth, Paul met a man named Aquila and his wife Priscilla. Aquila was born in Pontus, a Roman province just north of Galatia, but had most recently lived in Rome until the Jews were expelled from that city. Although Claudius had begun his rule by making concessions to the Jews even to the point that Herod, his representative in Judea, had taken an active role in the persecution of the church, he later adopted a more anti-Semitic attitude toward the Jews expressed in such acts as banning Jews from living in the capital. When this happened, Aquilla and his wife had apparently moved their tent-making business to Corinth which was one of the major trading centers of the empire. Paul was hired by the couple to make tents because he had been trained in the same occupation as a boy in Tarsus.

Although Paul was engaged in business activities during the week, he continued to attend the synagogue and take advantage of every opportunity to reason with both the Jews and Greeks who attended. This was probably not the first time Paul had adopted this approach to funding his ministry. Some Bible teachers believe Paul may have also worked to support himself during the month he spent in Thessalonica beginning that church (cf. 2 Thess. 3:8). While tent-making was one means of funding a mission to a city, it was probably not the most preferred. Had Paul not been working at making tents during the week, he would have more time to devote to preaching the gospel. No doubt he thought of this often as he sewed together pieces of canvas.

While Paul was in Corinth making tents, Timothy and Silas caught up with him from Macedonia. Very likely the men brought with them a financial gift from the church at Philippi (cf. Phil. 4:15). The arrival of the rest of his ministry team with this gift made it possible for Paul to devote more of his energies to preaching the gospel and getting a church established in this strategic city. Paul continued his ministry to the Jews, preaching with an even greater intensity than he had prior to the arrival of his associates.

As Paul pressed his message that Jesus was indeed the Messiah, the Jews in Corinth became increasingly more resistant to the gospel. Finally Paul addressed their rejection noting, "Your blood be upon your own heads; I am clean. From now on I will go to the Gentiles" (Acts 18:6). In the Old Testament, the prophets were viewed as guilty of the blood of those who were judged unless they had made a determined effort to warn them (cf. Ezek. 33:8-9). When the Jews in Corinth rejected Jesus as their Messiah, Paul claimed his responsibility for preaching to them was complete and that he was going to turn his attention from this point primarily to the Gentiles.

Paul's decision to preach to Gentiles rather than Jews meant he would no longer have access to the synagogue. He moved his following into the home of Justus, a Gentile who worshiped God and lived next to the synagogue. This move apparently did not hinder the effectiveness of Paul's preaching to any great extent. A large group of people were converted after the move, including the household of Crispus, the ruler of the synagogue and many of the Corinthians. Still, despite the continued success of his ministry, Paul had inner concerns about the move.

Paul was deeply committed to his new converts, but it was difficult for him to turn his back on his Jewish heritage. Part of that heritage taught him it was wrong to worship God in a place of one's choosing but that God had a designated place of worship (cf. Deut. 12). While that applied specifically to the temple in Jerusalem, there was a sense in which the Jews also applied that idea to the synagogue. Also, Paul knew from past experience that once the Jews had rejected the gospel, it would not be long before they would turn their attack on him and he would have to leave the town. Paul may have been having second thoughts about the wisdom of his actions in leaving the synagogue when the Lord appeared to him one night in a vision. He was told, "Do not be afraid, but speak, and do not keep silent; for I am with you, and no one will attack you to hurt you; for I have many people in this city" (Acts 18:9-10).

Paul remained in Corinth for an additional eighteen months after the vision and continued to teach God's Word. As he had suspected, the Jews directed some degree of opposition toward him. Their opposition toward Paul was so intense that at one point he was arrested and brought before Gallio, the proconsul of Achaia. He was formally charged with persuading "men to worship God contrary to the law" (Acts 18:13), but before Paul could begin his defense, the case was thrown out because Gallio claimed the dispute was a question of Jewish custom which was outside his court's jurisdiction. The Greeks concluded the Jews were creating problems and took Sosthenes who had become the ruler of the synagogue following the conversion of Crispus and beat him publicly outside the court. While Gallio must have realized what was taking place in front of his own judgment hall, he chose not to take any action. Sosthenes later converted to Christianity and became an associate of the apostle Paul (cf. 1 Cor. 1:1).

III.   The Thessalonian Epistles

During Paul's stay in Corinth, he wrote the two epistles to the Thessalonians which are included in the cannon of Scripture. These were probably the first two epistles written by Paul and demonstrate both the maturity of this infant church and the degree to which a well-defined system of theology had been developed by this early point in the history of Christianity. In both of these epistles, Silas and Timothy are identified as coauthors with Paul (1 Thess. 1:1).

THE EPISTLE OF FIRST THESSALONIANS

Author: Paul, Silas, and Timothy
Recipients: Church of the Thessalonians
Date of Writing: A.D. 52/53
Theme: The Return of Christ

Paul's first epistle to the church focused on the return of Christ and considered four aspects of Christian experience in light of the anticipated Second Coming. These include salvation (1:1-10), service (2:1-20), sanctification (3:1–4:12) and sorrow (4:13–5:28). Each chapter of this epistle includes a specific reference to the return of Christ. The entire epistle suggests the church anticipated the return of Christ at any moment. This epistle is important in developing a biblical eschatology in that it includes one of the key passages dealing with the rapture of the church (1 Thess. 4:13-18).

FIRST THESSALONIANS: THE RETURN OF CHRIST

Salvation and the Return of Christ (1:1-10)
Service and the Return of Christ (2:1-20)
Sanctification and the Return of Christ (3:1–4:12)
Sorrow and the Return of Christ (4:13–5:28)

Paul probably wrote his second epistle to this church only a matter of months later. Bible teachers believe this is the case because of the close similarity in conditions which existed in the church in both epistles and because Silas and Timothy are associated with Paul in both cases. This second epistle also has a strong eschatological emphasis and focuses on the common theme of the Old Testament prophets, the Day of the Lord.

THE EPISTLE OF SECOND THESSALONIANS

Author: Paul, Silas, and Timothy
Recipients: Church of the Thessalonians
Date of Writing: A.D. 52/53
Theme: The Day of the Lord

Paul addressed the problem of the suffering the church was experiencing as a direct result of the persecution which was being directed toward them. He encouraged the church by reminding them that those opposed to the gospel would endure an even greater time of tribulation in God's plan. In this epistle, Paul reveals one of the mystery doctrines which form a basis for understanding the age in which we now live (2 Thess. 2:1-12). Again, his emphasis was on the lifestyle and ministry of the believer in the light of the coming Christ.

SECOND THESSALONIANS: THE DAY OF THE LORD

Introduction (1:1-4)
Enduring the Christian Tribulation (1:4-12)
The Mystery of the Man of Sin (2:1-12)
Living the Christian Life (2:13—3:15)
Conclusion (3:16-18)

Paul remained in Corinth for a while after the aborted judicial hearing, but then left for Syria. Aquila and his wife decided to travel with Paul as far as Ephesus. Gallio's refusal to intervene in a public attack on a Jewish leader may have reminded them of the anti-Semitism they experienced in Rome just before being expelled. If this continued, it would soon impact their business and could result in unnecessary risk to their safety and security.

Conclusion

As the apostle Paul reached out to people with the gospel, he used different approaches to reach different people. He understood different people were at different points in their pilgrimage of faith and met people where they were to begin the process of stair-stepping them to a saving faith in Christ. When he preached to a Jewish group with a good knowledge of the Old Testament Scriptures, he used those Scriptures to teach the gospel. But when addressing a more pagan group like the Athenians he dealt with more basic concepts and built a case for the Resurrection. Paul explained this strategy to the Corinthians when he noted, "I have become all things to all men, that I might by all means save some" (1 Cor. 9:22). Those who desire to reach others for Christ today would be wise to understand and apply this principle.

CHAPTER 39

TYRANNUS:
THE REVIVAL AT EPHESUS

Acts 18:18–20:1; 1 Corinthians; 2 Corinthians

When Paul got to Cenchrea, he shaved his head before getting on the boat to Ephesus. This head shaving action was associated with a religious vow which he had taken. It was customary to shave a man's head at the conclusion of this vow and burn his hair on the altar at the temple in Jerusalem. Paul planned to observe an upcoming feast in Jerusalem and probably carried his cut hair in his belongings as he continued toward that city (cf. Acts 18:21). When he arrived in Ephesus, Paul again went to the synagogue and reasoned with the Jews. Some degree of interest was expressed in his message, resulting in his being invited to remain for some time. Paul turned down this opportunity because he wanted to get to Jerusalem in time for the Passover feast. He agreed to return at a later date if such a visit fit into God's plans for his life and ministry. Then he boarded a ship and sailed from Ephesus to Caesarea. From Caesarea, Paul made a brief visit to Jerusalem and greeted the church there before returning to Antioch which had become his home base of ministry.

Later that year (A.D. 54), Paul again determined to take a third missionary trip back through the area of his former trips. Once again he traveled overland through Asia Minor, to the regions of Galatia and Phrygia "strengthening all the disciples" (Acts 18:23). From there, Paul traveled to Ephesus where he would remain as long as he remained in any city on his various missions.

I.   The Conversion of John's Disciples

Although it had been about twenty-five years since Jesus' resurrection, some Jews still had a deep commitment to the messianic emphasis of the Old Testament. They apparently had not come to understand or recognize the death and resurrection of Jesus. Many of these teachers taught "the way of the Lord" in a manner similar to that of John the Baptist, in *anticipation* of a coming Messiah. One of the most eloquent of these teachers was an Alexandrian Jew named Apollos. When Apollos came to Ephesus and taught in the synagogue, Aquila and Priscilla were among those who heard him. After the meeting, this couple spent some time with Apollos "and explained to him the way of God more accurately" (Acts 18:26).

Apollos was receptive to their input and began teaching the gospel in its more complete context. When he left Ephesus to travel to Achaia, the Christians in Ephesus wrote a letter of introduction in which they urged their fellow Christians in that province of the empire to receive him. Apollos had a very effective ministry in Corinth and "greatly helped those who had believed through grace; for he vigorously refuted the Jews publicly, showing from the Scriptures that Jesus is the Christ" (Acts 18:27-28).

While Apollos was preaching in Corinth, Paul arrived in Ephesus. Shortly after arriving in the city, he met a group of disciples who somehow seemed different from the Christians he met in other places. These dozen men were disciples of John the Baptist who must have been reached by John very early in his ministry. When asked about the Holy Spirit, they claimed they did not even know there was a Holy Spirit. About the time John the Baptist identified Jesus as the Lamb of God which takes away sin, he also discussed the baptism of the Holy Spirit (Matt. 3:11; Mark 1:8; Luke 3:16; John 1:33).

As Paul talked further with these men, it became clear that although they were receptive to messianic teaching, they had never entered into a personal relationship with Jesus as their Messiah. Paul explained, "John indeed baptized with a baptism of repentance, saying to the people that they should believe on Him who would come after him, that is, on Christ Jesus" (Acts 19:4). When the men heard this, they accepted Jesus as the Christ and submitted to Christian baptism. Then Paul laid his hands on them and "the Holy Spirit came upon them, and they spoke with tongues and prophesied" (Acts 19:6).

Paul continued ministering in the synagogue in Ephesus for about three months, "reasoning and persuading concerning the things of the kingdom of God" (Acts 19:8). Once again, the Jews' response to this message was mixed. While some believed, others rejected Paul's message and became antagonistic toward the gospel. Paul responded to this challenge by leaving the synagogue and meeting in an alternate location as he had in Corinth. This time, the church moved to the school of Tyrannus.

II.   The Reviving of the Church

The Greek word *schole* translated "school" refers to the lecture hall or room used by a philosopher or orator. These were extremely common. Most Greek cities had at least one such school. Bible teachers are divided as to the nature of this school. Some believe this was the school of the sophist named Tyrannus mentioned by Suidas and that this facility was made available to Paul to teach the gospel. Others believe this was a private synagogue of a Jewish rabbi named Tyrannus who was sympathetic to the preaching of Paul. Still others believe the expression "school of Tyrannus" was the name of a public hall perhaps in honor of the original owner. The church simply rented the facilities.

Paul's ministry at this school continued daily for two years "so that all who dwelt in Asia heard the word of the Lord Jesus, both Jews and Greeks" (Acts 19:10). This approach to ministry marked a departure from previous methodology used by Paul and may be viewed as a new evangelistic strategy. According to an early Syrian text of this passage, Paul taught the Scriptures daily from 11:00 a.m. through 4:00 p.m. The content of Paul's teaching during these sessions was apparently communicated to others in Ephesus and other cities by those who heard him. Some believe these were the classes to which Paul referred when he later urged Timothy to train faithful men (2 Tim. 2:2). Using this method, Paul trained those who in turn went to other cities and established churches in smaller towns and cities which might otherwise have been ignored by the apostle.

Paul's ministry during this period not only included a strong emphasis on teaching but also a number of "unusual miracles" (Acts 19:11). There were occasions when people were healed and demons cast out because they simply came into contact with a piece of cloth that Paul had used. So spectacular were these and other miracles that soon those outside the Christian community attempted to duplicate them.

Many Jews recognized the reality of demon possession but relied upon the Jewish rite of exorcism to cast them out of a possessed person. When a group of itinerant Jewish exorcists came to Ephesus, a situation arose which gave great spiritual impetus to the church. Seven sons of a Jewish chief priest named Sceva attempted to practice their rite of exorcism with near disastrous results. When they addressed the demon "by the Jesus who Paul preaches" (Acts 19:13), the demon responded, "Jesus I know, and Paul I know; but who are you?" (Acts 19:15). The demon-possessed man then turned on the seven exorcists and overpowered them. The men fled from the house naked and wounded, grateful they were still alive.

Naturally, reports of this event spread through the city of Ephesus quickly and the people were overcome with fear "and the name of the Lord Jesus was magnified" (Acts 19:17). This event shocked many believers into renewed understanding of the reality of the spirit world and its influence in the occult religion of the day. Many confessed their own involvement in these practices and as an act of repentance, they brought the books they owned which they had used in these practices "and burned them in the sight of all" (Acts 19:19). The total value of the books destroyed at that time was estimated at fifty thousand pieces of silver. The "pieces of silver" mentioned here probably amounted to a common day's wage. This response among believers resulted in continued spiritual and numerical growth in the church. "So the word of the Lord grew mightily and prevailed" (Acts 19:20).

During his stay in Ephesus, Paul must have received correspondence from many people he had helped in previous missions. Ephesus was a major city of that day located on the coast of the Aegean Sea. If one wanted to send a message by courier to the apostle, it was fairly certain he would receive it without much delay. This is how Paul learned what was happening in the churches and was able to communicate important messages to others without traveling to the churches himself. When Stephanas, Fortunatus, and Achaicus came to Ephesus from Corinth, they may have brought with them a letter alerting the apostle to some problems which had developed in the church (cf. 1 Cor. 16:17).

When Paul first learned of the problems that had developed in Corinth, through correspondence with members of the household of Chloe, Paul found himself in the midst of the revival with many opportunities for effective ministry, so he contacted Apollos and "strongly urged him" to go to Corinth (1 Cor. 16:12). Although there is no record of these two men ever working together in a mission to a particular city, apparently they were each sympathetic to the other's ministry and willing to cooperate when possible. On this occasion, however, Apollos turned Paul down but agreed he would visit Corinth at some point later. Paul therefore wrote the church an epistle in which he addressed them about issues that had arisen in the church and answered some of the questions that had been raised.

THE FIRST EPISTLE TO THE CORINTHIANS

Authors: Paul and Sosthenes (1 Cor. 1:1)
Recipients: Church of God at Corinth
Date of Writing: A.D. 57
Theme: Christian Conduct

Paul's first epistle to the Corinthians addressed seven specific issues relating to the conduct of the Christian life especially in the context of the church. These included the issue of divisions within the church (1:10–4:21), sexual immorality (5:1–7:40), the limitations to Christian liberty (8:1–10:15), conduct at the Lord's Table (10:16–11:34), the nature of true spirituality (12:1–14:40), the resurrection from the dead (15:1-58), and the collection for the saints in Jerusalem (16:1-4).

---

1 CORINTHIANS: CHRISTIAN CONDUCT

Introduction (1:1-9)
The Issue of Division (1:10–4:21)
The Issue of Immorality (5:1–7:40)
The Issue of Christian Liberty (8:1–10:15)
The Issue of the Lord's Table (10:16–11:34)
The Issue of True Spirituality (12:1–14:40)
The Issue of the Resurrection (15:1-58)
The Issue of the Collection (16:1-4)
Concluding Remarks (16:5-24)

At the height of the Ephesian Revival, Paul determined to return to Macedonia and Achaia before going to Jerusalem. Even as he made those plans, Paul had his sight set on a new mission. He began telling others of his plan, always adding, "After I have been there, I must also see Rome" (Acts 19:21). Throughout his missionary career, Paul had consistently sought out the principle cities of the region and made them the objects of his evangelistic efforts. It was only natural that sooner or later he would look to the largest city of the world as a mission field. He knew that if the gospel were preached in Rome, it would quickly be spread throughout the entire empire.

Paul sent Timothy and Erastus on ahead, probably to prepare for his ministry on the Greek peninsula while he himself remained in Ephesus. Paul had already mentioned the possibility of his sending Timothy to Corinth in his epistle to the Corinthians (1 Cor. 16:10). Of the other members of his team, Erastus was probably the most logical choice to accompany Timothy on the trip. Erastus was a native of Corinth and held a civic office there (cf. Rom. 16:23). Together the two worked their way through their route, ministering to the churches and preparing them for Paul's visit.

III.   The Riot at Ephesus

When Paul wrote his first Epistle to Corinth, he intended to remain in Ephesus until Pentecost (1 Cor. 16:8), but a situation arose which may have cut his stay short. The evangelistic efforts of the church were so successful that the silver industry in the city, that earned much of its profits through making silver shrines used in worshiping Diana, was beginning to suffer a financial setback. It did not take them long to recognize a relationship between their drop in sales and Paul's evangelistic zeal. At a meeting of the silversmith guild, one craftsman name Demetrius noted, "This Paul has persuaded and turned away many people, saying that they are not gods which are made with hands, so not only is this trade of ours in danger of falling into disrepute, but also the temple of the great goddess Diana may be despised and her magnificence destroyed, whom all Asia and the world worship" (Acts 19:26-27).

The worship of Diana was the chief religious cult of the city of Ephesus. According to their myths, Diana was "born" in the woods near Ephesus at the site of her temple when her image fell down from the heavens. She was viewed as the mother or nature of God by her followers and was usually portrayed as a multi-breasted goddess. Her temple in Ephesus was not considered her home but rather the chief shrine where she could and should be worshiped. The silver shrines made by Demetrius and his colleagues were probably crude copies of the temple which were normally purchased by pilgrims to the temple and carried home as worship aids in the cult.

Those engaged in the silver trade making these shrines were an integral part of the temple economy. Paul's success in the evangelization of Asia meant they were losing pilgrims to the temple and therefore experiencing dwindling sales. The burning of occult books probably shocked Demetrius and the others into recognizing the decline in their trade as more than a passing phase. If these Christians continued to be successful in their evangelistic efforts, it might well be that the magnificent temple in their city would become obsolete and be destroyed. This touched off what might be considered a kind of motherhood issue in the city. They became incensed and began chanting loudly, "Great is Diana of the Ephesians" (Acts 19:28). In the confusion that followed, most of the city filled the public theater, but they were for the most part confused as to why the meeting had been called. Somewhere in the rush, two of Paul's companions from Macedonia, Gaius and Aristarchus, were seized by the mob and taken into the theater. Paul wanted to join his friends, but his disciples and a number of public officials sympathetic to Paul convinced him to remain outside.

In the midst of the confusion, the Jews appointed Alexander as their spokesman to address the crowd, but when he began to address them, they once again broke out in the chant, "Great is Diana of the Ephesians!" (Acts 20:34). The chanting continued in the theater for about two hours. Only then was the city clerk able to gain control of the meeting and address the crowd. He argued no one was disputing the greatness of the beloved goddess and warned them that such uprisings could result in the unwanted involvement of Rome in their civic affairs. He noted if Demetrius and the other silversmiths had a legitimate concern, the issue could be addressed by open courts and officials. Then he managed to dismiss the assembly quietly.

After the riot had ended in Ephesus, Paul realized he had once again become the center of a controversy that threatened to hinder the continued ministry of the church. He called the Christians together and revealed his plan to leave. After he embraced those with who he had spent so long, he began his journey to and through Macedonia. One of Paul's chief reasons for visiting the churches of Macedonia and Achaia was to raise funds for the relief of the church at Jerusalem. Although the Christians in the Macedonian churches were very poor, Paul was particularly impressed "that in a great trial of affliction the abundance of their joy and their deep poverty abounded in the riches of their liberality" (2 Cor. 8:2). Although Paul had been concerned primarily with raising funds for the financial need in Jerusalem, the Christians of Macedonia recognized stewardship was a spiritual experience and "first gave themselves to the Lord, and then to us by the will of God" (2 Cor. 8:5).

During this part of Paul's journey, Paul wrote 2 Corinthians. This was probably the third epistle Paul wrote the church (cf. 1 Cor. 5:9), but only two were written under the inspiration of the Holy Spirit and preserved in the canon of the New Testament. The nature of this epistle suggests the church had made significant changes since Paul's first correspondence. It is less confrontational and deals more with Christian ministry, rather than their conduct or lifestyle. Timothy is identified as a coauthor of this epistle suggesting he may have waited for Paul in Philippi while Erastus went on to Corinth.

THE SECOND EPISTLE TO THE CORINTHIANS

Author: Paul and Timothy
Recipients: Church of God at Corinth
Date of Writing: A.D. 57
Theme: Christian Ministry

In discussing his theme, Paul addressed the character of true Christian ministry in general, the ministry of giving in particular as exemplified by the Macedonians, and the nature of suffering which may be associated with ministry for Christ. It is doubtful any of his readers had suffered to the degree of the one who wrote this epistle. Interestingly, in this epistle Paul speaks so much about suffering that he reveals his vision in which he was caught up into the third heaven.

> **2 CORINTHIANS: CHRISTIAN MINISTRY**
>
> Introduction (1:1-11)
> The Nature of Christian Ministry (1:12–7:16)
> The Ministry of Giving (8:1–9:15)
> The Ministry of the Apostle (10:1–13:10)
> Conclusion (13:11-14)

Conclusion

Sometimes Christians who care about their fellow believers find it necessary to confront them about something that is wrong in their life. Paul knew this was difficult to do at times but necessary for the other persons involved. Because he loved the church at Corinth, he was prepared to confront them about their sin. He rejoiced when he saw positive behavioral changes in his converts whether in Ephesus or Corinth. Later he urged Titus to confront those under his care "that they may be sound in the faith" (Titus 1:13). Caring Christians today may be called upon at times to confront those they love and point out the destructive tendencies in their life.

CHAPTER 40

PAUL:
TRAVELING TO JERUSALEM IN
THE SPIRIT OF GOD'S WARNINGS

Acts 20:1–22:30; Romans

From Macedonia, Paul traveled south to Greece where he remained for about three months. While there, he continued to minister among the brethren and was a real source of encouragement to them. Paul wrote his epistle to the Romans during this three-month period, probably from the city of Corinth. Most Bible teachers view this epistle as the most systematic presentation of the Gospel ever written by the apostle. The logic and pattern of argument developed in this book demonstrate something of the quality of the apostle's mind. It probably represents the essence of what Paul preached when preaching the gospel to a predominantly Gentile audience.

THE EPISTLE TO THE ROMANS

Author: Paul
Recipients: Saints in Rome
Date of Writing: A.D. 58
Theme: The Righteousness of God

Some critics have disputed the Pauline authorship of this epistle largely on the grounds of the last chapter. They argue that it is highly unlikely that Paul would have known as many people as he mentioned in Rome because he had not yet been to that city. Those who argue in this way fail to recognize the nature of life in that era. Paul spent much of his time in ministry in the major cities of his world. Although he himself had not yet been to Rome, he had met many from the city of Rome and those who visited Rome. These people would have often traveled to and from the cities in which he ministered and some may have been converted through his preaching. The epistle to the Romans was apparently carried to them by Phoebe, a Christian in Cenchrea who may have been going to Rome on business (Rom. 16:1). Also, for some time Paul lived and worked with Aquila and Priscilla just after they had left Rome. No doubt contacts may have been made between Paul and Roman Christians during that time. Actually, the long list of names in the final chapter of this epistle may be a strong argument for Pauline authorship. An impostor would not likely have mentioned so many people who could have exposed him if he were not Paul.

The epistle to the Romans is in many respects foundational to one's understanding of Christian doctrine. In his systematic approach to explaining the gospel and its implications in one's life, Paul begins with the problem of sin. He argues that sin is a universal problem with which the pagan, moral and religious person must deal (1:18–3:8). The seriousness of sin is emphasized in that it has placed everyone under God's condemnation (3:9-20). Then Paul discusses the doctrine of justification by faith as the correct means by which the sin problem may be resolved in one's standing with God (3:21–5:21). While justification may deal with the sin problem in one's relationship with God, Paul realized that Christians may still continue to struggle with their sin nature. He addresses this problem in discussing the principle of sanctification (6:1–8:39). Paul then addresses the problem of God's relationship with the nation Israel (9:1–11:36). Finally, Paul discusses a number of practical applications of his message in the life of the believer (12:1–15:13).

Paul apparently intended to sail out of Cenchrea directly to Antioch, the church that originally sent him as a missionary, but changed his plans when he learned of a plot against his life. Instead, he decided to take an overland route back through Macedonia at least as far as Philippi. On his journey, he was accompanied by perhaps the largest group yet who traveled with Paul (cf. Acts 20:4). Throughout his ministry, various individuals were associated with Paul in ministry and he rarely worked alone in evangelizing a community. The following identifies some of those who were a part of Paul's company and shared together with him in ministry.

THE COMPANY OF PAUL

Achaicus of Corinth (1 Cor. 16:17), Andronicus (Rom. 16:7), Aquila (Acts 18:18), Aristarchus (Acts 20:4; Col. 4:10), Artemas (Titus 3:12), Barnabas (Acts 13:2), Clement (Phil. 4:3), Crescens (2 Tim. 4:10), Demas (Col. 4:14; 2 Tim. 4:10), Epaphras (Col. 4:12), Epaphroditus (Phil. 2:25-30), Erastus (Acts 19:22; 2 Tim. 4:20), Euodia (Phil. 4:2-3), Fortunatus of Corinth (1 Cor. 16:17), Gaius of Corinth (Rom. 16:23), Gaius of Derbe (Acts 20:4), Jason (Rom. 16:21), Jesus Justus (Col. 4:11), John Mark (Acts 12:25; 13:13; Col. 4:10; 2 Tim. 4:11), Junia (Rom. 16:7), Lucius (Rom. 16:21), Luke (Col. 4:14; 2 Tim. 4:11), Mary of Rome (Rom. 16:6), Onesimus of Colossia (Col. 4:9), Priscilla (Acts 18:18), Secundus of Thessalonica (Acts 20:4), Silas (Acts 15:40), Stephanus of Corinth (1 Cor. 16:7), Sopater of Berea (Acts 20:4), Sosipater (Rom. 16:21), Sosthenes (1 Cor. 1:1), Syntyche (Phil. 4:2-3), Tertius (Rom. 16:22), Timothy (Acts 16:1-3), Titus (2 Tim. 4:10), Trophimus of Ephesus (Acts 20:4; 21:29; 2 Tim. 4:20), Tychicus (Acts 20:4; Eph. 6:21; Col. 4:7; 2 Tim. 4:12), Urbanus (Rom. 16:9)

Paul sent seven of his men ahead to Troas while he and others on his team remained in Philippi for Passover and the Feast of Unleavened Bread. Five days later, they were reunited as a team in Troas and spent a week in that city.

When the disciples met that Sunday, they invited Paul to speak, knowing he was planning to leave the next morning. He preached in the three-story room where they were meeting until midnight. About that time, a young man named Eutychus fell asleep while sitting in the window. When he fell three stories to the ground outside, those gathered thought the worse. But Paul went down and called back, "Do not trouble yourselves, for his life is in him" (Acts 20:10). Then Paul continued talking to the believers until daybreak. In the morning, Eutychus was alive and walking about with little more than memories to remind him of his fall.

I. Address to the Ephesian Elders

Most of the team sailed from Troas, but Paul wanted to walk as far as Assos. There he joined the rest of the team and sailed to Mitylene. They sailed for three days past Ephesus to Miletus, "for Paul had decided to sail past Ephesus, so that he would not have to spend time in Asia; for he was hurrying to be at Jerusalem, if possible, on the Day of Pentecost" (Acts 20:16). This Pentecost would have been the thirtieth in the history of the church at Jerusalem (A.D. 59).

At Miletus, Paul met with the elders of the church of Ephesus and reminded them of their responsibility to fulfill their calling. He began by recalling his own ministry among them in Asia, noting the consistency of his appeal "testifying to Jews, and also to Greeks, repentance toward God and faith toward our Lord Jesus Christ" (Acts 20:21). Then he noted he was on his way to Jerusalem aware "that the Holy Spirit testifies in every city, saying that chains and tribulations await me" (Acts 20:23). He then told the elders he suspected some people would try to assume a position of influence in the church and would damage the flock. He called for the elders to be careful to protect the church from this danger. In the course of his address, Paul noted the threefold responsibility of the pastor to lead, feed, and protect the flock of God (Acts 20:28-29).

In addressing the elders at Ephesus, Paul reminded them of what was probably an often-repeated statement in the early church, "It is more blessed to give than to receive" (Acts 20:35). Paul attributes the original source for this statement to Jesus in a way that assumes it was widely known by believers of that time. Despite the fact this was one of Jesus' better known maxims, it does not appear in any of the four gospel accounts of His life and teaching. Had Paul not mentioned it in this discourse, these words would have been lost to future generations of believers.

At the conclusion of this discourse, Paul knelt and prayed for the elders. This was followed by an emotional parting of the group. "Then they all wept freely, and fell on Paul's neck and kissed him, sorrowing most of all for the words which he spoke, that they would see his face no more" (Acts 20:38).

II. Warning of Agabas

From Miletus, Paul and his companions continued to sail around the coast until they came to the port of Patara. There they were able to secure passage on a ship bound for Syria. They sailed past Cyprus and docked at Tyre and spent a week with the disciples in that city.

Once again, the Holy Spirit warned Paul "not to go up to Jerusalem" (Acts 21:4). At the end of the week, Paul led his team to another ship that took them from Tyre to Ptolemais. After spending the night with some Christians there, Paul and the team traveled to Caesarea and stayed with Philip. Paul had made good time on his trip to this point and decided to spend a little extra time with Philip in Caesarea. While they were there, Agabas came to Caesarea from Judea to once again warn Paul not to go to Jerusalem. Through another prophecy of Agabus, the church had been prepared for the famine years during the Claudius's rule. He was apparently a well-respected prophet of the early church whose prophetic revelations were to be taken seriously. When he arrived at the home of Philip, he took Paul's belt and tied his own hands and feet. Then he announced, "Thus says the Holy Spirit, 'So shall the Jews at Jerusalem bind the man who owns this belt, and deliver him into the hands of the Gentiles' " (Acts 21:11).

When Paul's hosts and companions heard that prophecy, they pleaded with Paul to change his plans and not go to Jerusalem. Despite their desperate pleas, Paul would not change his mind. "What do you mean by weeping and breaking my heart? For I am ready not only to be bound, but also to die at Jerusalem for the name of the Lord Jesus" (Acts 21:13). When the others realized Paul was committed to making the trip to Jerusalem, they stopped trying to change his mind, assuming it was God's will that he should go.

Many Bible teachers question this conclusion and argue that the constant warnings of the Holy Spirit "in every city" (Acts 20:23) climaxing with this in Caesarea suggest God did not want Paul going to Jerusalem. Paul's commitment to go to Jerusalem may have been more than his ethnic pride, but may have been direction he otherwise received from God. Paul deeply loved his own people and wanted to do what he could to reach them with the gospel even if it cost him his own life (cf. Rom. 9:3; 10:1). On this occasion, it appears Paul's personal commitments blinded him from the otherwise clear direction of God concerning the planned trip to Jerusalem.

III.   Taking a Vow in the Temple

Paul and his associates packed and made their way to Jerusalem. They were accompanied on their journey by a group of believers from Caesarea and one of the earliest believers Mnason who was originally from Cyprus and would be Paul's host in Jerusalem. Paul's financial gift to the church at Jerusalem was so great it took a wagon to haul it. The day after their arrival, Paul met with James and a group of elders from the Jerusalem church. He reported what had been taking place in his ministry and they rejoiced together. The elders told Paul arrangements would be made so that he could share this report with the whole church.

Since Paul's last visit to Jerusalem, the church had continued to effectively evangelize the Jews of that city. During that time, reports had circulated in the city that Paul's ministry among the Gentiles had taken on a character inconsistent with the Christianity practiced in Jerusalem and that he had taught the Jews to forsake the law of Moses.

The elders knew that Paul's report concerning what was really taking place would go a long way to ending these unfounded rumors. They suggested in the interim that Paul would demonstrate his allegiance to Moses if he would accompany four of their own men who had taken a vow and were about to be purified in the temple.

The next day, Paul made his way to the temple with the four men. Paul was prepared to pay the expenses involved in the sacrifices to be offered for each of them. In taking this vow of purification, Paul was committing himself to offer a blood sacrifice, something he had taught was inconsistent with the Christian understanding of the Cross. Many Bible teachers see this as Paul's compromise with the Judiasers.

Toward the end of their week of waiting, Paul was prevented from actually offering the blood sacrifice when a group of Jews from Asia recognized him and incited the crowd against him. They had seen Paul with Trophimus in the city earlier that week. When they saw Paul in the temple, they assumed he had defiled the temple by bringing Gentiles into it. God allowed circumstances to prevent Paul from violating what he had written in his epistles.

The mob seized Paul and dragged him out of the temple. Then the temple doors were closed as the people continued to beat Paul, intending to kill him. Then the commander of the Jerusalem garrison learned of the riot, he quickly gathered some soldiers and centurions and stopped the beating. Paul was chained and the officials than asked who he was and what he had done. The crowd shouted back so many contradictory answers, the commander was not sure what to believe.

He assumed he had captured the Egyptian leader of some four thousand assassins who had previously led an insurrection against Rome and ordered that Paul be taken back to the barracks. As Paul was about to be led into the barracks, he asked the commander if he could speak to him. The commander was surprised Paul spoke Greek because he thought he had arrested an Egyptian.

Paul explained·he was a Jew and asked to speak to the mob. When permission was granted, he addressed the crowd in Hebrew. When the mob heard him speak in Hebrew, they were caught off guard and listened carefully. Paul took the opportunity to relate his personal testimony as to how he became convinced Jesus was the Messiah on the road to Damascus. When he began to tell them of his ministry among the Gentiles, the crowd again began to yell, "Away with such a fellow from the earth, for he is not fit to live!" (Acts 22:22).

In frustration, the commander determined to beat Paul and find out once and for all what was going on. "Is it lawful for you to scourge a man who is a Roman, and uncondemned?" Paul asked (Acts 22:25). When the soldiers realized they had bound and were about to beat a Roman citizen, they instinctively backed away. Even the commander was intimidated when he realized he had ordered the binding of a Roman. Paul was held for the night for his own security, and brought to trial the next day, unshackled. The commander wanted to know what Paul had done to incite the Jews against him. Therefore, he "commanded the chief priests and all their council to appear, and brought Paul down and set him before them" (Acts 22:30).

Conclusion

One of the guiding principles of Scripture for discerning the will of God in a matter about which there is no other clear direction is expressed in the proverb, "A man's heart plans his way, but the Lord directs his steps" (Prov. 16:9). When Paul wanted to go to Jerusalem with an offering for the church, he made extensive plans assuming they would be acceptable to the Lord. But when God made it clear there was danger awaiting him if he proceeded with those plans, Paul apparently refused to alter his steps in accordance with new directive. Christians today also need to be careful not to allow their own ambitions and plans for their life to hinder their obedience to God's clearly revealed will.

CHAPTER 41

ANANIAS:
HIS FINAL ATTACK ON
CHRISTIANITY

Acts 23:1–26:32

Almost thirty years had passed since Paul sat on the Sanhedrin as a member. Many changes may have taken place in the composition of the council since then, but some things had not changed very much. The last time Paul attended a meeting of this group, they were concerned with stopping the spread of people following Jesus. Now Paul stood before them as one of the accused with the opportunity to explain his position to those most opposed to it. His mind may have wandered back to a prior meeting he attended when Stephen stood before the same group and preached the gospel before they stoned him. Paul could only hope this meeting might produce a different response.

Another who was present on both occasions was the high priest Ananias. As he thought back over the years, Ananias may have vividly remembered the day he had commissioned a promising young Pharisee on a special mission to Damascus to search out and arrest Christians. He could not have imagined on that day that the one so zealous to destroy the church would years later be one of its chief spokesmen. Even when reports of Paul's conversion in Damascus reached Jerusalem, Ananias had viewed it more as an irritation than threat or danger to Judaism. Now, very likely there were more Christians than Jews in the world. If that was true, the one he had sent to Damascus was to a greater extent responsible than any other.

For more than three decades now, Ananias had been trying to destroy Jesus of Nazareth and His followers. He resented the popular following of that untrained prophet who had so great a disregard for the traditions of the Jews. It was hard for Ananias to understand how Paul, whom he remembered as a deeply committed Pharisee, could be a part of that following. Although he had not planned the arrest of Paul as he had arrested Jesus, Ananias did not intend to let this opportunity pass him by. This was his opportunity to once and for all deal a fatal blow to this new religious movement by destroying one of their most prominent leaders outside of Judea. He was about to launch his final attack on Christianity.

I.   The Trial in Jerusalem

Paul began what would turn out to be a very brief defense with the statement, "Men and brethren, I have lived in all good conscience before God until this day" (Acts 23:1). This claim of innocence did not go unchallenged. Immediately, Ananias ordered those who stood close to Paul to strike him in the mouth. Before the order could be carried out, Paul answered back, "God will strike you, you whitewashed wall! For you sit to judge me according to the law, and do you command me to be struck contrary to the law?" (Acts 23:3).

Paul was correct in the point of law on which he challenged Ananias' actions, but in speaking to the high priest in that tone of voice he had turned other members of the Sanhedrin against him. "Do you revile God's high priest?" those close to Paul asked him (Acts 23:4). When he realized what he had done, Paul agreed it was wrong to speak evil against a leader but argued he did not realize he was addressing the high priest when he made his statement. He knew he was in a no-win situation and wondered how he would get out of it. He then remembered that the Sanhedrin was composed of both Sadducees and Pharisees and that the two groups could never agree over the doctrine of the resurrection from the dead.

"Men and brethren, I am a Pharisee, the son of a Pharisee; concerning the hope and resurrection of the dead I am being judged!" he announced (Acts 23:6). This statement was effective in dividing the group against itself and creating confusion among those who would otherwise be his accusers. The Sadducees were not at all impressed by Paul's references to the resurrection and visions of angels but the Pharisees saw both as a confirmation of their own belief system.

Those who, like Paul, belonged to this sect argued, "We find no evil in this man; but if a spirit or an angel has spoken to him, let us not fight against God" (Acts 23:9). The dissension among the members of the Sanhedrin was so great, the commander had his soldiers remove Paul from the meeting and take him back to the barracks for his own security. That night Paul was not sure what the future held for him. Twice in two days he had been rescued from angry Jews by Roman soldiers. He must have wondered how much longer he would survive the attacks. He knew how the power structures in Jerusalem had worked thirty years ago and could only assume he would be eventually turned over to the Sanhedrin. But that was not going to be the case. That night, the Lord appeared to Paul and announced, "Be of good cheer, Paul; for as you have testified for Me in Jerusalem, so you must also bear witness at Rome" (Acts 23:11). While much might happen in the interim, Paul now had God's promise that he would someday preach in the principle city of the world.

Following the confusion at the hearing before the Sanhedrin, some Jews determined to deal with Paul outside the normal judicial channels available to them. At least forty men formed an alliance and took an oath committing themselves to murder Paul. So sure were they of their imminent success that they vowed to neither eat nor drink until the task was done. While this group opted not to operate within the legal framework of that day, their plans were not entirely unknown to the religious hierarchy. They revealed their plan to the leaders of the Sanhedrin and requested their cooperation in murdering Paul. The Jewish leaders agreed they would request Paul be sent to them the next morning for further questioning, knowing this band of conspirators would kill him as he was being transferred.

Paul's nephew who lived in Jerusalem at the time overheard others talking about the plan. When he had heard enough to realize what was taking place, he made his way to the military barracks to warn his uncle. Paul called one of the centurions and asked him to take his nephew to Claudius Lysias, the commander of the garrison at Jerusalem. When Paul's nephew was alone with Lysias, he reported what he had heard in the city. Lysias sent the young man away asking him not to tell anyone he had revealed this information to him.

Immediately, Lysias called two centurions and ordered them to "prepare two hundred soldiers, seventy horsemen, and two hundred spearmen to go to Caesarea at the third hour of the night; and provide mounts to set Paul on and bring him safely to Felix the governor" (Acts 23:23-24). The commander wrote to the governor, briefly explaining the situation as he understood it. He sent the note with Paul and the troops. The soldiers accompanied the horsemen as far as Antipatris. When they were reasonably certain Paul was safe from those who were committed to killing him, they returned to Jerusalem and let the horsemen carry Paul to the governor. When Felix read the letter from Lysias, he determined to hold Paul until his accusers could appear and make formal charges.

II.   The Hearing before Felix

Almost a week later, Ananias arrived in Caesarea with some of the elders and an orator named Tertullus who had been designated to speak on their behalf. Tertullus commended Felix for the peace and prosperity being experienced in the region and attributed that to the foresight exercised by the governor. He then tried to portray Paul as a threat to the continuation of that peace and prosperity. He claimed, "We have found this man a plague, a creator of dissension among the Jews throughout the world, and a ring leader of the sect of the Nazarenes" (Acts 24:5). He claimed the Sanhedrin had wanted to examine Paul according to their own law when Lysias intervened and violently took Paul from their control. The other Jewish leaders present indicated their agreement with the statement made by Tertullus and otherwise allowed him to speak for them.

As Paul began his defense before Felix, he noted he had been in Jerusalem for some time before his arrest. He noted that during that time, "they neither found me in the temple disputing with anyone nor inciting the crowd, either in the synagogues or in the city" (Acts 24:12). He claimed the Jews could not prove the charges of which they had accused him but confessed he was affiliated with "the Way which they call a sect" (Acts 24:14). He claimed this sect was not divisive but that it was consistent with the teachings of the Jewish Scriptures. He noted he was bringing alms to Jerusalem when some Asian Jews saw him in the temple and began wrongly accusing him. Paul suggested it would have been better if those Jews had appeared before Felix if they had specific charges to lay.

Felix was acquainted with "the Way" and understood some of the tensions that existed between the Christians and the Jews who did not believe. Rather than come to an immediate judgment, he announced an adjournment of the proceedings suggesting, "When Lysias the commander comes down, I will make a decision on your case" (Acts 25:22). Paul remained in custody, but had some degree of liberty not normally afforded to prisoners. He was able to receive both friends and provisions without interference.

Some time later, Felix and his wife Drusilla met with Paul privately to discuss the subject of faith in Christ. Drusilla was a Jewess and both of them had some degree of interest in Christianity. "Paul spoke to them about righteousness, self-control, and the judgment to come, until Felix was afraid and answered, 'Go away for now; when I have a convenient time I will call for you'" (Acts 24:25). Felix and Paul talked again on numerous occasions, but Felix's motivation in those meetings was more financial than spiritual. Because Paul had mentioned giving alms in his hearing, Felix hoped he might be offered a bribe.

Paul remained in custody for the remaining two years of Felix's posting in Caesarea. When Felix was transferred elsewhere, he agreed to leave Paul in custody as a parting favor to the Jewish leaders. Felix was replaced in Caesarea by a new governor, Porcius Festus. Festus soon would be confronted with the case against Paul.

III.   The Hearing before Festus and Agrippa

Festus had only been in the province three days when he made his first trip from Caesarea to Jerusalem. While there, Ananias and a delegation from the Sanhedrin informed Festus about the case outstanding against Paul and requested that he be transferred to Jerusalem where he could be tried. Although they made a pretense concerning the judicial process, these Jewish leaders were aware that men were already in position along the road ready to ambush and kill Paul as he was being transferred.

When the request was made to Festus, he suggested he would be back in Caesarea soon and asked the Sanhedrin to authorize individuals to appear before him there to examine Paul and determine if there was any need for proceeding further. The governor remained in Jerusalem for ten days, then returned to Caesarea. The day after getting back, he conducted a hearing in the case of the Jewish leaders versus Paul.

When the Jews made their accusation against Paul, they charged him with a number of complaints for which they had no apparent evidence. Paul maintained his innocence of the charges arguing he had not violated any law of the Jews, the temple, or Caesar. It must have been obvious to Festus that there was little point in proceeding further in the charges against Paul, but he wanted to establish good relations with the Jewish leaders as he began his term of office in the region. He asked if Paul would consent to going to Jerusalem to be examined by the Sanhedrin.

Paul realized the Sanhedrin would be a hostile court and he would not likely have a fair hearing before them. He knew of their earlier plot to kill him and, although he may not have known of the present plot, he may have suspected such a danger if he returned to Jerusalem. He responded, "I stand at

Caesar's judgment seat, where I ought to be judged. To the Jews I have done no wrong, as you very well know. For if I am an offender, or have committed anything worthy of death, I do not object to dying; but if there is nothing in these things of which these men accuse me, no one can deliver me to them. I appeal to Caesar" (Acts 25:10-11).

As a Roman citizen, Paul had a right to due process of law including the right to appeal his case directly to Caesar. Once such an appeal had been made by a Roman citizen, it could not be denied. After discussing the matter with the Sanhedrin, Festus announced his decision. "You have appealed to Caesar? To Caesar you shall go!" (Acts 25:12). Paul would soon be on his way to Rome.

Some time later, King Agrippa and his wife Bernice came to Caesarea to spend some time with Festus. During the course of their extended visit, Festus mentioned the case of Paul which he had inherited from Felix. He summarized the progress of the case to that point and noted he was still holding Paul until a transfer to Rome could be arranged. The case interested Agrippa. He indicated he would like to hear Paul himself. Felix agreed to make the necessary arrangements. The next day Paul was again brought before a Roman official to defend himself of the charges laid by the Sanhedrin.

Festus introduced the hearing by summarizing what had taken place in the previous hearing with the Jews and suggesting a unique problem which now confronted him. He had a prisoner who had appealed to Caesar, but he did not have a charge to write against the prisoner. Then Agrippa invited Paul to speak on his own behalf.

In his defense before Agrippa, Paul again recounted his background as a zealous Pharisee and his former commitment to destroying the church even in foreign cities. He recounted how he was converted to Christianity while on his way to Damascus intending to arrest Christians and return them to Jerusalem. He then claimed he had been obedient to the heavenly vision he received on that occasion and suggested that was why the Jews were so opposed to him. As he had done so many times before in synagogues and other public gatherings, Paul again focused his comments on the death and resurrection of Christ.

Festus interrupted Paul's defense by shouting, "Paul, you are beside yourself! Much learning is driving you mad!" (Acts 26:24). Paul insisted he was not only sane, but that Agrippa knew enough about the Jews to know what he was saying was true. Agrippa responded differently to Paul. "You almost persuade me to become a Christian," he said (Acts 26:28). Paul responded by suggesting such a conversion was exactly what he could wish for the king.

At that point, the Roman officials stood and left, indicating the hearing was ended. By that point, it was more than obvious that there was no grounds for further prosecution and no reason to continue holding him. "This man might have been set free if he had not appealed to Caesar," Agrippa noted to Festus when they were alone (Acts 26:32). The appeal to Caesar had been made, so very soon Paul would be on his way to Rome.

Conclusion

Jesus had warned His disciples, "In the world you will have tribulation; but be of good cheer, I have overcome the world" (John 16:33). Often that tribulation is personified in one who is antagonistic to God and therefore lashes out at a nearby Christian. "These things they will do to you because they have not known the Father nor Me," Jesus explained (John 16:3). When this happens, believers should not be caught by surprise but rather pray for those abusing them (Luke 6:28), rejoice that they are part of a long heritage of those who have suffered for God (Matt. 5:10-12), and remain faithful to the task to which God has called them (Phil. 3:13-14).

CHAPTER 42

LUKE:
THE JOURNEY TO ROME

Acts 27:1–28:31

$\mathcal{S}$ome time after Paul's hearing before Agrippa, the details of Paul's journey to Rome were finally determined. The apostle and a number of other prisoners were to be transferred to Rome under the supervision of a centurion named Julius who was assigned to the Augustan Regiment. Julius may have been involved in guarding Paul during his imprisonment in Caesarea as they appeared to have a better relationship during the voyage than might otherwise be expected between a centurion and his prisoner. They boarded a ship of Adramyttium and began the voyage to Rome.

Throughout his ministry, Paul had struggled with health problems from time to time and apparently they flared up again just prior to the voyage. The only mention of his illness made by Paul during his ministry is found as a passing reference to his condition when he first arrived in Galatia (Gal. 4:13-15). Some believe this "thorn in the flesh" may have been one of several illnesses. Paul may have suffered from extreme Migraine headaches which sapped his strength and at times affected his eyesight. Others believe he had ophthalmia, another disease that would have affected his eyesight and perhaps explain why Paul dictated so many of his epistles to others rather than simply writing them himself. A third possibility suggested by some Bible teachers is that Paul had a chronic case of Malaria which lasted a lifetime. Because of Paul's poor health as the voyage began, he was accompanied on the trip by Luke and Aristarchus. Julius treated Paul well "and gave him liberty to go to his friends and receive care" during the voyage (Acts 27:3).

By the time Paul began his voyage to Rome, Luke had probably completed his gospel account of Christ's life. While Matthew and Mark apparently wrote their gospels to fill a void, Luke wrote his to clarify the accuracy of some of the things being written. As Christianity continued to grow, apparently many others wrote accounts of Christ's life that were not inspired by the Holy Spirit and therefore not preserved in the New Testament. They may have also included stories about Jesus which had no historical basis in fact. Luke carefully researched the details of Jesus' life which he had addressed to Theophilus who may have been a patron who helped fund the project. While the book of Luke is addressed to a single individual, this account of the gospel appears to have been written to Christians with a Greek background and tends to stress the humanity of Jesus more than the others while not denying His deity. This gospel also deals more with Jesus' teaching on and practice of prayer and his ministry to non-Jews. The gospel appears to have been widely circulated quickly and within a few years was recognized as authoritative as the Old Testament Scriptures (cf. 1 Tim. 5:18; Deut. 25:4; Luke 10:7).

THE GOSPEL OF LUKE

Author: Luke
Recipient: Theophilus/Greek Christians
Date of Writing: c. A.D. 60
Theme: The Humanity of Jesus

I.   The Voyage to Malta

As the ship sailed out of the harbor of Caesarea, it headed north along the coast to Sidon. Paul may have been allowed to go ashore and visit with friends in Sidon while the ship remained in port. When they finally did sail out, the winds were rough so they detoured north around the island of Cyprus rather than sail the more direct route to Myra through the open sea. There Julius found an Alexandrian ship sailing to Italy and transferred his prisoners to that vessel.

This new ship probably intended to sail to Cenchrea and be dragged across the wooden rails to the canal at Corinth, but the winds off the Aegean Sea continued to be strong. From Myra, they continued to sail on course keeping close to the coast until they reached Cenidus. The winds of the ship made the decision to sail south around Crete to avoid the brewing storm on the Aegean Sea.

The southern leg of this journey was not without its difficulties. The crew was pushing the end of the normal sailing season on the Mediterranean Sea and encountered rough weather along the journey. When the island of Crete came in sight the crew tried to sail around its southern coast, but by the time they reached the harbor of Fair Havens near Lasea, they determined the best course of action was to pull into the harbor.

By this time, the September Yom Kippur fast was already past and the winter storms had begun. As the crew discussed plans for the rest of the trip, Paul objected to traveling further until the winter was past. "Men," he explained, "I perceive that this voyage will end with disaster and much loss, not only of the cargo and ship, but also our lives" (Acts 27:10). Paul's opinion was not shared by the helmsman of the ship, nor its owner. The harbor of Crete at Phoenix was a much better harbor to winter in than that at Fair Havens, and the owner and most of the crew agreed they could safely sail what would only be another day's sailing to the better harbor.

While Lucius had come to respect Paul's opinion, that of the owner and sailors of the ship prevailed and the decision was made to sail to Phoenix. They waited for the storm to pass before leaving. When the breeze came in softly off the sea one day, the crew concluded they had a break in the weather and should make the trip to Phoenix. But no sooner had they got out of the security of the harbor when they found themselves in the midst of the storm called Euroclydon. The wind was so severe, the crew could do nothing but let the ship be driven.

The wind blew the ship off course and into the open sea. As they passed south of the island of Clauda, they were finally able to secure the skiff on board, although not without great difficulty. Once the small boat had been secured, the sailors began reinforcing the hull of the ship with cables fearing that the ship may be driven into the Syrtis Sandbar off the coast of Clauda. The sails were hoisted as the crew attempted to avoid this danger.

The next day they determined to lighten the ship because of the severity of the storm. Much of the cargo was cast into the sea in an attempt to save the boat. The next day, this procedure continued and some of the tackle on board was forfeited to the waves. Still the storm prevailed. The clouds were so thick that for several days the men could not discern day from night. The sun did not penetrate the clouds during the day and the stars were hidden from view during the night. The ship continued to be blown west through the stormy sea, though it is doubtful anyone on board had any idea where they were. The situation was hopeless in the minds of most.

The one notable exception to this hopeless outlook on the situation was that of Paul. He reminded the crew they should have listened to his caution back on Crete but also assured them they would survive the ordeal. He explained he had seen an angel who assured him of God's promise that he would appear before Caesar, and guaranteed the security of all who traveled with him. He claimed that although the ship would not survive the storm, everybody on board would even though they would run aground on an island.

Fourteen days into the storm, some of the sailors became suspicious they were approaching land. They began taking soundings and determined the sea was about twenty fathoms deep. When they sounded again a short time later, it was only fifteen fathoms deep. Afraid they were about to run aground on the rocks, they dropped four anchors off the stern and began to pray for daylight so they could determine where they were. Some of the crew began to panic and attempted to jump ship in the skiff. They lowered the lifeboat into the water under the pretense of attempting to pull up anchor. Paul warned Julius and his men, "Unless these men stay in the ship, you cannot be saved" (Acts 27:31). The soldiers responded by cutting the lifeboat loose before any of the crew could enter it and in doing so destroyed their only means of escape.

As dawn approached, Paul urged everyone to eat. During the storm of the past two weeks, everyone had been so busy they had not eaten. He reminded them they needed to eat to insure their survival and reminded them they would survive. "And when he had said these things, he took bread and gave thanks to God in the presence of them all; and when he had broken it he began to eat" (Acts 27:35). Paul's public display of calm after two weeks of stormy weather encouraged others on the ship and they too began to eat. When they were full, they threw the rest of their cargo into the sea, including their load of wheat.

When the day came, enough light shone to make out the shore nearby but none on board could identify what they saw. What they could see was a bay with a beach on which they hoped they could run the ship. While the procedure was not without an element of risk, the crew determined they were at a greater risk if they remained at the mercy of the sea much longer. Also, the ship might have a better chance surviving the run empty than if they still had their cargo on board. They loosened the rudder ropes so they could again steer the ship, hoisted the sails on the mast and cut the anchors loose from the ship. Then they began sailing directly for the beach.

On their way to the beach, the ship got caught between two strong currents and ran aground. The bow of the ship was jammed into the sandy bottom and proved "immovable, but the stern was being broken up by the violence of the waves" (Acts 27:41). It quickly became obvious the ship was going down. The soldiers wanted to kill all the prisoners on board knowing they would be held responsible if any escaped by swimming to shore, but the centurion stopped them from doing this in an effort to save Paul's life. Instead, he ordered all who knew how to swim to jump overboard and make their way to shore. The rest grabbed boards and other pieces of the broken ship and floated into the beach. "And so it was that all escaped safely to land" (Acts 27:44).

II.   The Ministry on Malta

When they got on shore, they learned they were on the island of Malta, well over four hundred miles off course from their original destination. The natives of the region were unusually friendly toward those who had just landed on their beach and built a fire where they could warm up and dry out. It was still raining and cooler than usual as the tail end of the storm passed over the island. The fire was a welcomed sight to the soggy crew, soldiers, and prisoners. The prisoners were probably assigned the task of gathering wood for the fire to insure it would continue burning for some time.

Paul gathered a bunch of sticks like the others and threw them on the fire, but the heat of the fire caused a poisonous viper to crawl out of the bundle of sticks and bite Paul. All who witnessed the event knew that in a matter of minutes, the apostle would be dead.

The people of Malta were superstitious and when they saw what happened they assumed it was some kind of judgment. "No doubt this man is a murderer, whom, though he has escaped the sea, yet justice does not allow him to live," they reasoned (Acts 28:4). But Paul merely shook the snake off into the fire and did not appear to suffer any of the usual symptoms associated with the snake bite. When the people realized Paul had survived the attack, they changed their mind about him and concluded he must be one of the gods.

One of the leading citizens of the island was a man named Publius who served as host to the shipwrecked company for the next three days. Publius' father was sick with dysentery and a fever, but as a result of the prayer and laying on of hands by Paul, the man was miraculously healed. When news of this miracle spread throughout the island, others came who were sick and were also healed. By the time arrangements were made to continue the journey, the people of Malta were eager to honor Paul and the others and give them the supplies they needed.

Three months later, the party sailed from Malta on another Alexandrian ship which had wintered on the island. They sailed first to Syracuse on Sicily and stayed for three days, probably while the ship unloaded one cargo and took on another. Then they sailed to Rhegium on the southern tip of Italy. A day later, the wind was suitable for resuming the journey north and they sailed on to Puteoli. They remained there a week. Paul was entertained by a group of Christians living in that city. Word quickly spread that Paul was in Italy. Christians came to greet him along Appian Way as they traveled to Rome. Believers gathered to greet and encourage him at both Appii Forum and Three Inns. Eventually, the journey reached its ultimate destination, Rome.

III.   The Ministry in Rome

In Rome, Julius turned his prisoners over to the captain of the guard, "but Paul was permitted to dwell by himself with the soldier who guarded him" (Acts 28:16). This gave Paul the opportunity to once again become active in ministry after so long in confinement. Three days after they were settled in Rome, Paul called the leaders of the Jews in Rome to meet with him in his home. Paul recounted a highlight of the events that had brought him to Rome under guard and expressed the desire that he and they could discuss the matter in a civil manner. The Jewish leaders in Rome confessed they had not yet received a report from the Sanhedrin concerning him nor had there been any other evil report made in Rome concerning Paul and his ministry. They were however familiar with the growth of the church in other cities of the empire and were very much interested in what Paul could teach them about the new movement.

Paul recognized the Jews' genuine interest in Christianity and agreed to make arrangements so they could discuss the matter at greater length. A date was agreed upon when they could get together. On that day, many arrived at his home. Even though Paul appeared to have a great deal of liberty in his imprisonment, he was still in custody and apparently could not go to the synagogues of Rome to meet with the Jews. Instead, he spent a full day from morning to evening explaining the Old Testament Scriptures in their messianic context. By the end of the day, many were persuaded that Jesus was the Messiah, but others did not believe. The disagreement that arose in the discussion between these two groups of Jews reminded him of the prophecy of Isaiah concerning the blinding of Israel (cf. Isa. 6:9-10). "Therefore let it be known to you that the salvation of God has been sent to the Gentiles, and they will hear it," Paul concluded (Acts 28:28).

Following the meeting in Paul's rented home in Rome, the Jews continued to dispute the subject among themselves. Paul however continued to have a fair degree of liberty in ministry for the next two years, "preaching the kingdom of God and teaching the things which concern the Lord Jesus Christ with all confidence, no one forbidding him" (Acts 28:31).

Conclusion

The British preacher Charles Haddon Spurgeon once said, "A believer is immortal until God is finished with him." By this he meant that God will providentially take care of believers so that no serious harm comes to them that would in any way hinder them in accomplishing God's will for their lives. That comforting thought is illustrated in many biblical accounts including that of Paul's journey to Rome. Christians would do well to remember this principle when they encounter overwhelming problems in their Christian life.

CHAPTER 43

THE PRAETORIUM GUARD: SPREADING THE GOSPEL IN THE EMPIRE

Philemon, Ephesians, Colossians

Although Acts concludes its account of early church history with Paul arriving in Rome and being placed in custody, the New Testament epistles refer to other historical events of the first century. Paul was probably released from prison and was once again free to travel throughout the Roman empire preaching the gospel.

Under Roman law, if one's accusers did not bring formal charges before Caesar within eighteen months of a prisoner being turned over for trial, that prisoner was presumed innocent and released. Many Bible teachers believe that was probably the case with Paul and that shortly after the two-year period mentioned at the conclusion of Acts, Paul may have left Rome. Some teach he traveled as far west as Spain preaching the gospel (cf. Rom. 15:24). Some Bible teachers believe Paul may have also traveled as far north as Britain and preached the gospel there. An English tradition claims St. Paul's Cathedral in London is built on the site where Paul first preached the gospel on that island. Most facts indicate Paul returned to the churches of Greece to minister. Later, he was apparently arrested again and brought to trial in Rome, perhaps during the persecution of the church under Nero. Although he survived his first defense on this occasion (cf. 2 Tim. 4:16-17), the tradition of the early church claims he was eventually martyred for his faith in Christ.

One question which naturally arises out of the above discussion is, "Why did Luke not continue his account of the life and ministry of Paul?" The most obvious answer to this question is that all these events took place after Luke concluded his account of the early history of the church. Many Bible teachers believe Luke wrote this book toward the end of Paul's first Roman imprisonment. He addressed the book to Theophilus and suggested The Acts of the Apostles was a continuation of his gospel (cf. Acts 1:1). Some Bible teachers believe this account may have also been prepared as a document concerning Paul's ministry in preparation for the anticipated hearing before Caesar. This would explain the great detail given to legal decisions and indecisions made by Roman officials in the Acts.

THE ACTS OF THE APOSTLES

Author: Luke
Recipient: Theophilus
Date of Writing: c. A.D. 60
Theme: The Early History of the Church

I. The Imprisonment of Paul

Under the terms of Paul's imprisonment, he had a great deal of liberty to receive visitors but was always in the company of a prison guard. During the two years in which he remained in these conditions, many guards were no doubt assigned the task of watching Paul. Paul took advantage of this opportunity to preach to some whom he otherwise might not have had the opportunity. When he wrote his epistle to the Philippians during this imprisonment, he noted that his custody had "actually turned out for the furtherance of the gospel, so that it has become evident to the whole palace guard, and to all the rest, that my chains are in Christ" (Phil. 1:12-13). He indicated something of the success of his ministry in Rome when he concluded the same epistle with the comment, "All the saints greet you, but especially those who are of Caesar's household" (Phil. 4:22).

The conversions of guards as they protected Paul probably had a significant impact on the gospel's spread throughout the Roman empire. The guard who was converted at Paul's side may have been later transferred elsewhere in the Empire which stretched from Britain to Africa and from Spain to the Caspian Sea. When the converted guard was transferred to another part of the empire, he carried the gospel with him. In this way, Rome's routine transfer of its military personnel insured the continued outreach of the gospel, even during the days of most severe religious persecutions. Within three hundred years, the entire Roman Empire would be Christianized.

During Paul's imprisonment, he not only had opportunity to reach some of the most influential members of society, but also others who were at the opposite end of the social strata. One of these individuals was a runaway slave named Onesimus who had apparently stolen money from his master in Colosse in Asia Minor and fled to Rome. Onesimus was captured in Rome and held until he could be transfered back to Colosse. During that time, he came into contact with Paul and was converted through the apostle's influence (cf. Philem. 10). In this case, it turned out Paul knew Onesimus's master who was a leader in a church near Colosse and wrote him on Onesuimus's behalf. In this the briefest of all his epistles, Paul called for a reconciliation between the Christian master and his recently converted slave. Paul based his appeal on the love Christians were to have toward others in the family of God. Apart from a few introductory and concluding remarks, the entire epistle consists of Paul's intercession on behalf of Onesimus.

> **THE EPISTLE OF PHILEMON**
>
> *Authors:* Paul and Timothy
> *Recipients:* Philemon, Appis, Archippus, and church
> *Date of Writing:* c. A.D. 60
> *Theme:* Reconciliation of Philemon and Onesimus

II.   The Prison Epistles of Paul

During the first imprisonment in Rome, Paul wrote four epistles which are included in the New Testament. These include the epistles to the Colossians, Philemon, the Ephesians, and the Philippians. Paul apparently sent these epistle to their intended recipients with some of his associates in ministry. Philippians was probably carried to Philippi by Epaphroditus (Phil. 2:25). The other three epistles were apparently carried back to the region by Tychicus (Col. 4:7; Eph. 6:21-22) who was accompanied by Onesimus (Col. 4:9; Philem. 12).

These prison epistles reflect the early development of the interdependence of churches in the New Testament. The Philippian epistle reveals that church often helped fund Paul in his ministry of establishing new churches in other cities (Phil. 4:16). In Colossians, Paul urged that church to encourage Archippus, one of the recipients of the epistle to Philemon, to "take heed to the ministry which you have received in the Lord, that you may fulfill it" (Col. 4:17). Also in that epistle, Paul writes, "Now when this epistle is read among you, see that it is read also in the church of the Laodiceans, and that you likewise read the epistle from Laodicea" (Col. 4:16).

The reference to a Pauline epistle "from Laodicea" has puzzled many Bible teachers over the years because there is no canonical Pauline epistle associated with the church of Laodicea. To resolve this problem, some have suggested Philemon many have lived in Laodicea and that epistle is what is referred to. Others note that some early copies of Ephesians are missing the words "at Ephesus" (Eph. 1:1) and speculate that the epistle was originally written to the church in Laodicea. One major problem with that view is that no manuscript exists of the epistle which identifies Ephesians as being associated with any other church than Ephesus. A third view suggests that while the Pauline epistle to Laodicea may have been valuable to the church at that time, it was of a different character than the inspired epistles of Paul and therefore not preserved by the Holy Spirit. Others suggest the clue to understanding this ministry is found in the identification of this epistle as being "from" rather than "to" Laodicea. It appears to have been the normal practice of the church of a particular region to circulate apostolic epistles when they received them and that the epistle from Laodicea may have been any epistle, probably in the immediate context Ephesians, that came to Colosse from Laodicea.

Perhaps the most significant of the prison epistles is the epistle to the Ephesians. As noted above, some Bible teachers suspect the epistle may have originally been addressed to another church or written as a circular epistle. The bulk of the textual evidence, however, suggests Paul wrote the epistle to the church at Ephesus knowing it would be widely circulated throughout the churches of Asia. This is only natural in light of the unique ministry which the apostle had in that province (cf. Acts 19:10). If this were the case, it would also explain why that epistle lacks the many personal references which tend to characterize Pauline epistle (cf. Rom. 16) and why some copies of the epistle dropped the words "at Ephesus" from the first verse.

THE EPISTLE TO THE EPHESIANS

Author: Paul
Recipients: Saints at Ephesus
Date of Writing: c. A.D. 60
Theme: The Church, the Body of Christ

The epistle to the Ephesians represents Paul's most systematic presentation of his doctrine of the church as the body of Christ. Two doctrines closely related to this are also developed in this epistle, that of the union of the believer with Christ (Eph. 2:1-22) and the doctrine of mystery which is part of Paul's doctrine of revelation and out of which his view of the church is developed (Eph. 3:1-13). This epistle also deals with the position of the Christian "in the heavenlies" (Eph. 1:3-14), the unity of the church (Eph. 4:1-16), and the walk (Eph. 5:1-17), and warfare (Eph. 6:10-20) of the Christian. The epistle also includes two of Paul's prayers for the Ephesian Christians (Eph. 1:15-23; 3:14-21).

EPHESIANS: THE CHURCH, THE BODY OF CHRIST

Introduction (1:1-2)
The Christian "in the Heavenlies" (1:3-14)
Paul's First Prayer for the Ephesians (1:15-23)
The Regeneration of the Christian (2:1-10)
The Reconciliation of the Christian (2:11-22)
Paul's Explanation of the Mystery (3:1-13)
Paul's Second Prayer for the Ephesians (3:14-21)
The Unity of the Church (4:1-16)
The New Character of the Christian (4:17-32)
The New Walk of the Christian (5:1-17)
The Fullness of the Holy Spirit and Relationships (5:18–6:9)
The Whole Armor of God for Spiritual Warfare (6:10-20)
Conclusion (6:21-24)

While Ephesians looks at the church as the body of Christ, Colossians which was written at the same time looks at Christ as the head of the church. Together these epistles help us understand the unique relationship which exists between Christ and His church. The city of Colosse was located about a hundred miles east of Ephesus and the church was probably founded by Epaphras during Paul's ministry at the school of Tyrannus (cf. Col. 1:7). Although Paul never visited many of the Asian cities reached by his students, he shared a burden for them and considered them an extension of his ministry (cf. Col. 2:1). Like the epistle to the Romans, this epistle was written to a church which had not yet been visited by the apostle.

> **THE EPISTLE TO THE COLOSSIANS**
>
> *Authors:* Paul and Timothy
> *Recipient:* Saint in Colosse
> *Date of Writing:* c. A.D. 60
> *Theme:* Christ, the Head of the Church

Because both Ephesians and Colossians were written by the same person at the same time to two churches in very similar situations, it is not surprising that there is some similarity between the two epistles. Sometimes Colossians seems to be an abridged version of Ephesians (cf. Col 3:16–4:1; Eph. 5:18–6:9). Although there were similarities, Colossians made its own unique contributions to Christian theology particularly in the Christian view of the person and work of Jesus Christ (Col. 1:15–2:3) and in the practical out working of the doctrine of the believer's union with Christ (Col. 3:1–4:6).

> **COLOSSIANS: CHRIST, THE HEAD OF THE CHURCH**
>
> Introduction (1:1-8)
> Paul's First Prayer for the Colossians (1:9-14)
> The Preeminence of Christ (1:15-29)
> Paul's Second Prayer for the Colossians (2:1-23)
> The Believer's Union with Christ (3:1–4:6)
> Conclusion (4:7-18)

One of the reasons Paul may have written the epistle to the Colossians was to warn them of a doctrinal error which was developing in the early church which came to be known as Gnosticism. Paul warned, "Beware lest any man cheat you through philosophy and empty deceit, according to the tradition of men, according to the basic principles of the world, and not according to Christ" (Col. 2:8). This heresy of the early church included such things as worshiping angels (Col. 2:18) and tended to equate spirituality with a disciplined lifestyle which included the practice of asceticism (Col. 2:20-22). The name "Gnosticism" is related to the Greek verb *gnosis* which this group used to describe the special "knowledge" they claimed to have acquired and upon which their teaching was largely based.

Gnostics held that matter was inherently evil and therefore argued that Christ did not have a physical body but only appeared as a man. Much of the emphasis on the incarnation of Christ in the writings of John was probably included to correct this error as it later became even more popular. The Gnostics claimed such things as Christ did not leave footprints or cast a shadow during His ministry and used such claims to argue that the body of Christ was nonmaterial. Paul confronted this teaching by challenging their *gnosis* (knowledge) with his *epignosis* (full knowledge) concerning God's will (Col. 1:10).

Another claim of the Gnostics was that the spiritual world consisted of a *pleroma* (fullness) which included a host of intermediary spiritual beings between God and man. On this point also Paul dramatically challenged the Gnostic doctrines. He used the same Greek word they used to describe this host of spiritual being to claim that in Christ "dwells all the fullness of the Godhead bodily" (Col. 2:9; cf. 1:19).

Conclusion

The implication of deity's completeness dwelling in Christ was the Christ's completeness dwelling in the believer. This union of the believer with Christ was foundational to everything Paul believed about the Christian life. For Paul, the Christian life was the life of God in the soul of man. Remembering this principle helps many Christians today experience personal victory in their Christian life as they let God live through them.

CHAPTER 44

PHILEMON, TITUS, AND TIMOTHY: A NEW GENERATION OF LEADERS

1 Timothy, 2 Timothy, Titus, Philemon

lthough the apostles played a very prominent role in the early days of the church, it does not appear God ever intended there to be a continuing ecclesiastical office of the apostle in the church. This office was given to the church along with others to fulfill a specific function, but once that function was complete, it was no longer necessary for it to continue (cf. Eph. 4:11). It is most probably that one of the primary functions of the apostles related to the writing and collecting of the New Testament cannon. With the death of John toward the end of the first century, the cannon was complete and office of the apostle came to an end.

Another function of the apostles in the early days of the church was that of providing spiritual leadership for the early church. They were in charge of the distribution of church funds (Acts 4:37) and teaching and preaching of the doctrines of Christianity (Acts 2:42; 6:4). As the church continued to grow and develop, these tasks were assumed by another office in the church, that of the elder which was also called a bishop (overseer) or pastor (shepherd). At the Jerusalem Conference, the office of the elder was well established in the church and the apostles yielded to the leadership of James who was the senior pastor of the Church in Jerusalem. Toward the end of his ministry, Paul addressed four epistles to three younger men who represented the next generation of leadership for the church. Philemon was the leader of a church which met in his home. Titus had been associated with Paul's ministry earlier and had been sent by the apostle to resolve some problems which had developed in the church on the island of Crete. Timothy had also been associated with Paul in his ministry and was sent by Paul to provide leadership for the church at Ephesus which may have been the most influential church of that day. In the epistles of Paul to these three men, one may gain some insight into the character of the church during the last half of the first century.

I. Philemon and the Church in His Home

As noted above, the epistle of Philemon identifies "the church in your house" (Philem. 2). This was not the first time the New Testament mentions a group of believers meeting in the home of a particular believer. As one studies the pattern of church growth in the early church, there appears to be two aspects to church life. First there was the cell, which was the smaller group meeting together, i.e. for fellowship (cf. Acts 4:32). Secondly, there was the celebration which was a gathering of the cells in a larger group for some corporate activity (cf. Acts 5:14).

For many years, Bible teachers failed to understand just how large the early church was because it was assumed there were no church buildings and churches met primarily in home cell groups. However, recent findings suggest this may not have been the case.Some of the synagogues in which the church met could have seated as many as 10,000 people. While there were times when the church met in homes (cells), it is also evident they met in large gathering places such as the temple (celebration cf. Acts 2:46) and later in synagogues. It may have been that the church meeting in Philemon's home met regularly with other churches for celebration events.

This twofold approach to church growth appears to have been widespread in practice. In addition to its use in Jerusalem, there appears to have also been a number of cells in Rome. In his epistle to the Romans, Paul identified at least five groups of believers in that city which may have been cells (Rom. 16:5, 10-11, 14-15).

Cells also existed in the church at Corinth. That church was apparently composed of a number of Gentile cells which were identified as "the churches of the Gentiles" (cf. Rom. 16:4) and a number of Jewish cells identified as "the churches of Christ" (cf. Rom. 16:16). It is significant that in writing to the Romans from Corinth, the apostle sends greetings from "the whole church" in Corinth (Rom. 16:23). Even though this church later developed a problem with factions within the church, Paul did not apparently relate that situation to the existence of cells in the church. In the same epistle where he so vehemently attacked the problem of divisions within the church, he also commended cells associated with Chloe (1 Cor. 1:11) and Stephanus (1 Cor. 16:5). The following chart outlines several things which are best accomplished in large (celebration) or small groups (cells).

CELLS	CELEBRATION
Teaching	Preaching
Explanation	Worship
Involvement	Expressin
Accountability	Testimony
Content	Motivation

II.   Titus and the Church on Crete

Titus found himself in a different position from that of Philemon in that he appears to have been left with the responsibility of organizing several churches in different cities on the island of Crete (Titus 1:5). Paul left Titus on the island when the centurion ordered their boat to sail out from Fair Havens. Paul wrote this epistle to encourage Titus in his difficult work and encourage him to come to Rome at his earliest convenience. Titus apparently did a good job on Crete as Paul later sent him to Dalmatia (Yugoslavia) on the north east coast of the Adriatic Sea with a similar assignment (2 Tim. 4:10).

THE EPISTLE TO TITUS

Author: Paul
Recipient: Titus
Date of Written: c. A.D. 65
Theme: Pastoral Ministry

Finding suitable candidates for leadership in the Cretan church and developing their potential would have been a challenging task for any Christian leader. The Cretans tended to be "liars, evil beasts, lazy gluttons" (Titus 1:12). Within the church on Crete, there were "many insubordinate, both idle talkers and deceivers" (Titus 1:10). This problem existed not only among the Gentile believers but also among those with Jewish roots. Because of this, Paul called on Titus to "rebuke them sharply, that they may be sound in the faith" (Titus 1:13). Although these Christians professed a personal relationship with God, their behavior denied the likelihood that such a relationship actually existed and disqualified them from potential ministry.

Despite the poor quality of people to choose from, Paul did not waver in the minimum standards by which leadership for the church should be determined. The qualifications for bishops on Crete were not unlike those who held the same office in Ephesus (cf. Titus 1:6-9; 1 Tim. 3:2-7). This epistle deals with three issues relating to pastoral ministry including the standards for a pastor (Titus 1:5-16), the speaking of a pastor (Titus 2:1-15), and the service of a pastor (Titus 3:1-11). The second section in this epistle suggests one of the responsibilities of Titus and other church leaders includes teaching various classes of people minimum standards of Christian behavior. It is likely that the values reflected in that chapter were typical of Christians in all the churches of that era.

TITUS: PASTORAL MINISTRY

Introduction (1:1-4)
The Standards for a Pastor (1:5-16)
The Speaking of a Pastor (2:1-15)
The Service of a Pastor (3:1-11)
Conclusion (3:12-15)

III. Timothy and the Church at Ephesus

Timothy was the third of the three pastors of the next generation to receive an epistle from Paul. Paul and Timothy were closely associated in ministry beginning with the second missionary journey. He was with Paul when many of the epistles were written and was often sent by Paul to deal with situations in a variety of churches including both Corinth (1 Cor. 16:10) and Thessalonica (1 Thess. 3:2). At the time Paul wrote his epistles to his young protege, Timothy was serving as the pastor of the church at Ephesus.

THE FIRST EPISTLE TO TIMOTHY

Author: Paul
Recipient: Timothy
Date of Writing: c. A.D. 64
Theme: Church Order

Paul's first epistle to Timothy was probably written just before his epistle to Titus. Although they share some similar material, the problems faced by Timothy were different than those faced by Titus and this epistle deals with issues of church order broader than that of pastoral ministry. In this epistle, Paul deals with the qualifications of those who would serve as pastors and deacons (1 Tim. 3:1-16), but also addresses the problem of heresy (1 Tim. 1:3-20), the role of prayer in ministry (1 Tim. 2:1-15) and a number of other areas of responsibility relating to the ministry (1 Tim. 4:1–6:21).

---

1 TIMOTHY: CHURCH ORDER

Introduction (1:1-2)
The Problem of Heresy (1:3-20)
The Place of Prayer (2:1-15)
The Qualifications of Church Officers (3:1-16)
The Responsibilities of the Ministry (4:1–6:21)
Conclusion (6:21)

Paul's second epistle to Timothy may well be the last epistle he wrote. Some Bible teachers have looked upon this epistle as a kind of last will and testament of the apostle which he intended to leave to the church. Certainly the tone of this epistle at times suggests he was anticipating the end of his life (cf. 2 Tim. 4:6-8). It may have been that Paul completed the epistle to that point during his second imprisonment in Rome while he waited to learn the verdict of his hearing before Nero. Then when he learned he would not be executed at that time, he concluded the epistle on a much more positive note (2 Tim. 4:9-22). It is not clear whether Paul was released again for some time or remained in custody, but his life had for the moment been spared (2 Tim. 4:16-17).

THE SECOND EPISTLE TO TIMOTHY

Author: Paul
Recipient: Timothy
Date of Writing: c. A.D. 67
Theme: Remaining Faithful

The theme of Paul's second epistle to Timothy was that of remaining faithful. It has been suggested the key to interpreting this epistle is found in the Greek expression *su de* which may be translated "but as for you" and occurs three times in the epistle (cf. 2 Tim. 3:10; 3:14; 4:5). While others might be carried along with the spirit of the world, Paul wanted Timothy to be different. Some were unfaithful to their calling to serve God, but Paul called Timothy to faithfulness in the particular ministry for which God had gifted him (2 Tim. 1:3–2:18). While others were abandoning their fundamental commitment to the Scriptures as the final authority in matters of faith and practice, Paul again called Timothy to faithfulness to the inspired Scriptures (2 Tim. 2:19–4:8). At a time when many of Paul's companions had abandoned him in Rome for a variety of reasons, Paul called on Timothy to be a faithful friend (2 Tim. 4:9-21).

---

2 TIMOTHY: REMAINING FAITHFUL

Introduction (1:1-2)
Remaining Faithful to One's Calling (1:3–2:18)
Remaining Faithful to One's Commitment (2:19–4:8)
Remaining Faithful to One's Companion (4:9-21)
Conclusion (4:22)

It is generally agreed that Timothy responded to Paul's second epistle by immediately heading west to Rome. Paul's request that Timothy "come before winter" (2 Tim. 4:21) has led some Bible teachers to believe the epistle was not received by Timothy until late summer or early fall. This means Timothy would have had to make the journey over land to avoid the storms common at sea in the fall. On his way to Rome, he would have to convince Mark to join him (2 Tim. 4:11) and pick up Paul's cloak and books in Troas (2 Tim. 4:13). When Timothy arrived in Rome, both he and Paul were arrested as part of Nero's ongoing persecution of the church. According to a fairly reliable tradition of the church, Paul was condemned and executed just outside Rome in A.D. 66 or 67. Timothy however was eventually released from custody and continued to minister in the churches (Heb. 13:23). According to tradition, Timothy did die for the cause of Christ as one of the martyrs of the church during the reign of Domitian.

Conclusion

Great Christian leaders throughout history like the Apostle Paul have been men and women who invested in their life of others. Paul himself challenged one whom he discipled to invest his life in reproducing reproducers (2 Tim. 2:2). Christian who want their influence for Christ to be multiplied and outlive themselves should be involved in the practice of discipling others helping them grow in their relationship with the Lord.

CHAPTER 45

PETER:
THE APOSTLE TO THE JEWS

1 Peter, 2 Peter

Two men rose to places of prominence as apostles, although the New Testament church apparently did not formally designate apostolic spheres of ministry. Paul was widely recognized as the apostle to the Gentiles and Peter was the primary apostle to the Jews. As the church became increasingly more Gentile in character, Paul's role in the early church became increasingly more significant. In Palestine and other pats of the empire, many churches were predominantly Jewish in character. In these churches in particular, Peter continued to have a significant ministry.

The Acts which traces early church growth throughout the Roman Empire does not mention Peter after his release from Herod's prison apart from his statement to the Jerusalem Conference. We learn from Paul's epistles that Peter and Paul had a confrontation in Antioch following that conference (Gal. 2:11). Apart from that, they appear to have had a good relationship as fellow workers in the gospel (cf. 1 Cor. 1:12; 3:9). Apparently Peter and his wife traveled extensively in the church in an itinerant ministry probably much like Paul's (1 Cor. 9:5).

For some time, John Mark was apparently associated with Peter in ministry, probably in the Jerusalem area during the later pat of the first missionary journey of Paul and Barnabas. During that time, Peter related to Mark many of his experiences with Jesus during His public ministry. Most Bible teachers belie mark later based his gospel on the stories Peter had told him.

I. The Ministry of Peter

Church traditions relating to Peter after his last mention in the Acts identify him as ministering in five regions. First, Peter appears to have settled in Antioch. The Scriptures reveal Peter did visit Antioch on at least one occasion and felt at home among the Gentile Christians there. According to the third century historian of the church Esebeus, Peter served as the bishop of the church at Antioch for seven years. Most bible teachers see no reason to dispute the historical accuracy of this claim.

The second place associated with Peter's ministry is the peninsula surrounded on three sides by the Euxine Sea, the Agean Sea, and the Mediterranean Sea. Peter's first epistle was addressed to the Jewish Christians in the provinces of Pontus, Galatia, Cappadocia, Asia, and Bithynia. If he had spent some time traveling to the churches of this region, this may explain his special burden for the Jews who believed in those provinces. As noted before, when the gospel was preached in the synagogue, the response was often divided. Although many Jews tended to believe, those who did not often became antagonistic toward the gospel and those who were converted to Christianity. Peter's first epistle deals much with the subject of suffering as a Christian. many of those who first received the epistle may have been suffering severely at the hands of those who years earlier they counted among their closest friends.

Some critics argue against the idea that Peter wrote this first epistle, because the quality of the Greek used is far superior to that which might be expected from one with Peter's background. One reason for this apparent discrepancy may be due to the influence of Silvanus who wrote the epistle at Peter's direction (1 Peter 5:12), likely writing down Peter's dictation as he spoke.

THE FIRST EPISTLE OF PETER

Author: Peter
Recipient: Scattered Jewish Christians
Date of Writing: c. A.D. 65
Theme: Suffering as a Christian

In this epistle, Peter looks at suffering from three perspectives. First he considers it in the context of the salvation of the belier (1 Peter 1:3–2:8). Second, Peter compares the suffering of the belier with that which Christ endured (1 Peter 2:9–4:19). Finally, he considers suffering briefly in the context of Christ's return (1 Peter 5:1-11).

---

1 PETER: SUFFERING AS A CHRISTIAN

Introduction (1:1-2)
Suffering and the Salvation of the Believer (1:3-2:8)
Suffering and the Suffering of Christ (2:9-4:19)
Suffering and the Return of Christ 95:1-11)
Conclusion (5:12-14)

In the course of his discussion in the epistle, Peter identifies a number of concepts which have been integrated into the popular theology of contemporary evangelicals. First, it is Peter who describes suffering as a trial of faith by which its authenticity can be demonstrated (1 Peter 1:7). Second, Peter describes the believer as pat of a priesthood which is the foundational concept of the historic evangelical commitment to lay ministry in the church (2 Peter 2:5, 9). Third, Peter's discussion of the ministry of the elders is one of two new Testament passages in which it becomes clear that pastor, bishop, and elder are different titles for the same church office (1 Peter 5:1-4; cf. Acts 20:17, 28).

The third place of ministry identified with Peter is Babylon. Peter's first epistle was apparently written from Babylon although some Bible teachers believe the reference to the church at Babylon is a cryptic reference to the church at Rome (1 Peter 5:13; cf. Rev. 17:5). Actually, Babylon most likely would be the place someone like Peter with his unique commitment as the apostle to the Jews would desire to ministry. At the beginning of the Babylonians captivity, many of the best Jewish families were taken to Babylon ad most stayed when the remnant returned to the land seventy years later Babylon had such a strong Jewish population that the Jewish historian Josephus published the first edition of his history in Aramaic primarily for their benefit. In many respects, the Jews of Babylon were thought to be more orthodox than those of Jerusalem. That Peter may have had opportunity to pursue ministry there is alluded to in the specific listing of Jews from that area being present when he preached the first Christian sermon on the day of Pentecost (Acts 2:9).

Some Bible teachers also belie Peter may have preached in the region north of Rome in what is today France and Britain. Some historians suggest Peter may have gone north to Britain following the edict of Claudius expelling the Jews from Rome. As early as A.D. 179, a church was built in Britain in commemoration of Peter's ministry in that country and named St. Peter's of Cornhill. Some English Bible teachers believe the Abbey of St. Peter in Westminster Cathedral is built on the spot where Peter received the vision of his epistle (2 Peter 1:14). Another commemoration of the possible ministry of Peter in Britain is a four-foot high, fifteen-inch wide, round-hewn stone which has been excavated at Whithorn. This stone is inscribed in Latin with the words LOCVS SANCTI PETRI APVSTOLI which is translated, "the place of Saint Peter the Apostle." While it is difficult to prove with any degree of certainty that Peter ministered in Britain, it is neither impossible nor improbable that he may have preached on British soil.

Peter does not identify where he was when he wrote his second epistle nor does he identify the specific recipients of the letter. Like Paul's second epistle to Timothy, this epistle was written as the write anticipated his soon execution. The persecution of the church was so severe during the reign of Nero that many Christians wondered if the end of the age had come. In this epistle, the central theme of Peter is that of living on the last days of world history.

THE SECOND EPISTLE OF PETER

Author: Peter
Recipient: Christians
Date of Writing: c. A.D. 66
Theme: Life in the Last Days

In his seocnd epistle, Peter stresses the need for consistent Christian living during that period of time designated as the last days. he begins by stressing eight Christian virtues which the believer should endeavor to develop in his life (2 Peter 1:3-14). Then Peter describes the character of this life as that of expectation recounting both his experience on the Mount of Transfiguration (2 Peter 1:15-18) and the testimony of the prophetic Scriptures (2 Peter 1:19-21).

Peter also noted that the last days would be characterized by the rise of false religous teachers who would deny the very heart of the Christian gospel (2 Peter 2:1-22). In the final chapter o this epistle, Peter calls for continued spiritual growth in anticipation of the Lord's return (2 Peter 3:1-18).

---

2 PETER: LIFE IN THE LAST DAYS

Introduction (1:1-2)
The Life of Character (1:3-14)
The Life of Expectation (1:15-21)
The Life of Opposition (2:1-22)
The Life of Anticipation (3:1-18)
Conclusion (3:18)

Peter apparently wrote both his epistles in hopes of effecting a spiritual revival in the heat of his readers (cf. 2 Peter 1:13; 3:1). Also, Peter makes reference to his readers having received an epistle from Paul which was apparently considered as inspired as the Old Testament Scriptures (2 Peter 3:15). Some Bible teachers assume Peter's original readers were Jews and cite this verse as an argument for the Pauline authorship of Hebrews. it is interesting and perhaps encouraging to note that even Peter found "some things hard to understand" in the writings of Paul (2 Peter 3:16).

II. The Martyrdom of Peter

The fifth place associated with Peter's ministry is Rome. According the the unanimous tradition of the church, Peter ended his life as a martyr in Rome. While no specific evidence confirms that he ever served as the first Pope or Bishop of Rome, most Bible teachers agree he probably died in Rome during Nero's persecution of the church. According to the traditional account of his death, he and his wife were crucified. His wife was executed first while Peter was forced to watch. His last recorded words to his wife were, "Remember the Lord."

When Peter was taken to be crucified, he argued he was unworthy to die in the same manner as his Master. Instead he requested to be crucified upside down. After his death. his body was apparently embalmed and buried in a nearby cemetery in keeping iwth Jewish custom. Constantine recovered what he believd was Peter's bones and moved them into St. Peter's in Rome. Today the Roman Catholic Church claims Peter's bones are still preserved in a tomb in that cathedral.

Conclusion

Peter's reported last words to his wife, "Remember the lord," are cetainly consistent with his message to Christians in difficult times (1 Peter 2:21; 2 Peter 3:1). When believers find themselves in the midst of difficult circumstances, taking time to consider the faighfulness of the lord in His uffering is often enough to help one continue to faithfully endure his problem as he completes the task which is his.

CHAPTER 46

HEBREWS:
THE FALL OF JERUSALEM

Hebrews

When the church began in Jerusalem on the Day of Pentecost, A.D. 30, it was largely viewed as a sect of Judaism. That image of the church continued for a number of years and Christians worshipped often in the Temple or Synagogue celebrating their Christian faith. There was of course some antagonism toward the Christians from the Jews. That antagonism came in waves of persecution, but for the most part it was usually and expression of rivalry or competition. But apart from that, they shared many similar cultural experiences. The Roman authorities tended to look at Christians as a Jewish movement even when increasing numbers of Gentiles became a part of the church. What was true generally in the early church, was even more reflected in a city like Jerusalem. Converted Jews who had been raised in the shadow of the temple tended to see their Christian faith as a fulfillment or completion of their Jewish faith. For many, becoming a Christian meant they believed in Christ but they were still very much Jewish. Their faith in Jesus as their Messiah had influenced a few dietary habits, but little else changed in their culture. Many times, their Christian faith gave them a reason to be more conscientious of the traditions of the Jews.

One notable example of this was James, the half-brother of Jesus and senior pastor of the Jerusalem church. James was considered one of the most pious men in Jerusalem even by those Jews who did not share his Christian faith. It is said he spent so much time in prayer that his knees were swollen like those of a camel. James was martyred by a Jewish mob in Jerusalem just before the destruction of that city by the Romans in A.D. 70. Many of the Jewish citizens of that city viewed the destruction of the temple as the judgment of God upon them for killing such a pious man.

As noted before, one problem confronting the early church centered in the desire of some converted Pharisees that Gentiles should come under the law when they become Christians. In a number of his epistles, Paul warned the churches of the dangers of this teaching and taught that Christianity is not dependent upon conformity to Jewish traditions. As the church matured throughout the first century, it began to look less like a Jewish gathering and came to adopt its own distinctiveness. During the years of persecution of the church by Jews who rejected the gospel, the gulf between these two faiths widened.

Though this trend had little impact on Christians in much of the empire, it resulted in unique tensions for those Christians living in and near Jerusalem. Walking away from Judaism was particularly hard when one lived so close to the center of the Jewish faith. A Christian living in Rome or Philippi may have never seen the temple in Jerusalem, let alone offer the sacrifices associate with the various religious festivals; but the Christian Jew raised in Jerusalem or Bethany may have attended as many as seven or eight of these festivals yearly prior to their conversion.

I.   The Failure of Judaism

One of the more difficult lessons these Jews had to learn was that Judaism had failed to be the light to the Gentiles. Instead of being a faithful witness, the religion of Israel had evolved into a legalistic system of traditions which rejected and opposed the very Messiah to whom they should have given witness. By continually sacrificing animals to God, they were practically denying the finished work of Christ on the cross. Yet for the Christians living in Jerusalem who had been raised in the Jewish tradition, going back to their religious roots was a constant temptation.

This temptation to the Jews resulted in the writing of another epistle which emphasized three things: (1) the finished work of Christ as our great High Priest, (2) warning about the dangers of going back to Judaism, and (3) how much better Christianity was over Judaism. Most Bible teachers agree this epistle was probably written to the church at Jerusalem just prior to the destruction of the temple in A.D. 70, but beyond that there is little agreement in the discussion over who wrote the epistle. The author does not identify himself and the scholars have been divided over who may have written this letter to the Hebrews. Some believe it was written by Paul who did not identify himself fearing the Jews who needed the message most would not read it if they knew it was from him. Others claim the epistle may have been written by Luke and represents the essence of what Luke heard Paul teach to Jews on their travels together. Still others have suggested the epistle may have been written by Apollos who was one of the more prominent leaders in the early church and therefore should be considered as one who may have written the epistle.

THE EPISTLE TO THE HEBREWS

Author: Unknown (Paul, Luke, Apollos)
Recipients: Christian Jews at Jerusalem
Date of Writing: c. A.D. 68
Theme: The Better Way of Christ

The key word in this epistle is the word "better." The author uses this word to describe the superiority of Christianity to Judaism. In the epistle to the Hebrews, Jesus is described as better than the angels (Heb. 1:4), the author is persuaded of better things than apostasy in the lives of his readers (Heb. 6:9), Christians have a better hope than the Jews (Heb. 7:19), they are under a better covenant than the Jews (Heb. 7:22) which is founded upon better promises

(Heb. 8:6), Christ offered a better sacrifice than the priests (Heb. 9:23), Christians have a better possession in heaven (Heb. 10:34), the patriarchs of Israel desire a better country (Heb. 11:16), some obtain a better resurrection (Heb. 11:35), God has provided something better for Christians (Heb. 11:40) and the blood of Jesus speaks of better things than that of Abel (Heb. 12:24). Throughout the epistle, Jesus is compared with angels, Moses, Joshua, Aaron and Melchizedek and in each case is found to be superior. His ministry as the mediator of the covenant and the great high priest offering the ultimate sacrifice for sin is compared with the work of temple priests and is also found to be superior. The author therefore concludes that the life of faith of the Christian is a better way of living and results in the Christian having both a better relationship with God and better relationship with others.

HEBREWS: THE BETTER WAY OF CHRIST

Jesus Is a Better Messenger than the Angels (1:1–2:18)
Jesus Is a Better Leader than Moses and Joshua (3:1–4:13)
Jesus Is a Better Priest than Aaron and Melchizedek (4:14–7:28)
Jesus Is the Mediator of a Better Covenant (8:1–9:28)
Jesus Offered a Better Sacrifice for Sin (10:1-31)
The Life of Faith is a Better Way of Life (11:1-40)
Christians have a Better Relationship with God (12:1-29)
Christians have Better Relationships with Others (13:1-25)

The dangers associated with the Christian going back into Judaism were so serious in the mind of the author of this epistle that six times he pauses to warn the reader. Each of these warning passages are more severe than the previous one and stress the radical difference between these two faiths. To go back after beginning the Christian life meant a person denied everything Christ stood for and accomplished in the atonement. In writing this epistle, the author was convinced his readers would heed his warnings and go on to maturity in Christ.

SIX WARNINGS TO THE HEBREWS

The Danger of Neglect (2:1-4)
The Danger of Unbelief (3:7-19)
The Danger of Disobedience (5:11)
The Danger of Regression (6:4-8)
The Danger of Rejection (10:26-31)
The Danger of Refusal (12:25-29)

Perhaps the best known chapter in Hebrews among Christians is chapter eleven which has been called "The Christian Hall of Faith." In this chapter, the author promotes the life of faith by recalling numerous examples of faith out of the pages of the Old Testament Scripture. Faith is affirming what God has said in His Word. Faith effectively secures the intervention of God to change the apparent course of human events, or on other occasions enabled the faithful to endure an apparent defeat. In every case, faith is a human response to a divine revelation and God and His revelation is always the object of effective faith.

II.   The Fall of Jerusalem

Shortly after the writing of the epistle to the Hebrews, the daily sacrifices in the temple came to an end. Perhaps God providentially removed that standing symbol from view. The disappearance of the daily sacrifice was not the result of the influence of that epistle or the church, but rather the Roman army that under Titus laid siege to the city and eventually conquered it, destroying the temple. Jesus had predicted this event forty years before it took place and had warned those living in Judah to escape to the mountains when they saw the armies surrounding Jerusalem (Luke 21:20-24).

The destruction of the temple in Jerusalem was the result of a Roman action to defeat an uprising of the Zealots in Palestine. This group of Jews traced their historic and political roots to the Maccabean revolt and saw themselves as the children of light in the battle with the forces of evil (Rome). Roman actions such as the erecting of a statue of Caesar in the temple area were viewed as attacks on their religious beliefs and prompted their militant reaction. Titus was sent to Jerusalem to capture a leading group of Zealots in the hope that it would bring about the end of hostilities in that part of the empire.

Titus laid siege to the city and literally starved the people into submission. The human suffering in Jerusalem itself was greater than might otherwise have been expected because the city was crowded with those who had come to the city for Passover when the battle for the city began. Although some of the people apparently wanted to surrender to the Romans and end the siege, the Zealots in control of the city under Simon insured that such a course of action was never given serious consideration.

Toward the end of the siege, the Romans attacked and defeated the Zealots who took refuge in the temple. In the course of the battle, a Roman soldier apparently set fire to the temple hoping to burn the Zealots out into the open. One of the results of this fire was that the gold of the temple melted and flowed between the stones of the temple. The Roman army destroyed the temple in an attempt to recover this gold while looting the city. Actually, not one stone was left standing upon another, an actual literal fulfillment of Jesus' prediction (Matt. 24:2). According to the Jewish historian Josephus, the entire city was burned and destroyed with the exception of three towers.

The Zealots continued their battle with Rome retreating to Masada for their final stand. When it became obvious to them that the Romans were likely to capture many of them when they took the city, the Zealots agreed to kill themselves and their families rather than endure the humiliation associated with capture. On the fifteenth of Nisan (April 1), nine hundred and sixty Jews died in this mass suicide which was later described to the Romans by two women and five children who escaped by hiding in an underground cavern.

The temple was the focal point of the worship of God in Judaism and its destruction resulted in major changes in that faith. The temple has never been rebuilt to this date although the Scriptures suggest there will be at least one, perhaps two more temples built in or near

Jerusalem. Since the capture of Jerusalem and destruction of the temple in A.D. 70, Judaism has changed in its emphasis from that of a worshipping religion to that of a teaching religion. Some of that change had taken place prior to the destruction of the temple, but since then there have been no blood sacrifices offered by the Jews which were at the very heart of their worship of God. Instead, the synagogues which stress teaching the law became the exclusive centers of Judaism, no longer viewed as secondary to the temple.

The destruction of the temple challenged the faith of Judaism in that it could no longer offer the sacrifices it had claimed were necessary to appease God. It also resulted in giving greater credibility to Christianity which argued Jesus had fulfilled the type of these sacrifices in his death and therefore eliminated the need for continual burnt offerings. The Christian Scriptures, i.e. the New Testament, also gained credibility as they had accurately prophesied the city's destruction. Within twenty years of Titus victory at Jerusalem, the leading rabbis in Israel were meeting to discuss what should and should not be considered Scripture.

The councils of Jamnai in A.D. 90 and 118 included discussions concerning whether certain books such as Ecclesiastes and the Song of Solomon should be included in the Old Testament. There is abundant evidence that these books had been considered a part of the Old Testament long before these councils met and the rabbis did not add or remove any books from the canon. Some Bible teachers suggest that one of the reasons for the convening of these councils was the development of the New Testament canon. These rabbis may have discussed the canon because they recognized certain Christian writings were being recognized as being as inspired as the Old Testament. By confirming a canon of Scripture which included only the Old Testament, they may have hoped to discredit the New Testament canon which was beginning to develop. While history reveals that such a canon was developed over the course of time in both the eastern and western church, it may be that the collection of New Testament books in a place like Ephesus would have included all the books in our Bible today, long before the conclusion of the council of Jamnia in A.D. 118.

Conclusion

Early in the siege of Jerusalem, Christians living in the city remembered the words of Jesus concerning the destruction of Jerusalem left the city and escaped from the suffering that followed. These Christians recognized the Scriptures as authoritative not only in matters of faith but also as a standard for their behavior. Christians since have also found biblical principles to be a firm foundation upon which they can build their life.

CHAPTER 47

JOHN:

HIS MINISTRY AT EPHESUS

1 John, 2 John, 3 John

As the first century of the early church era came to a close, most of the twelve men who lived with Jesus had fulfilled their appointed ministry and died violent deaths, but the church which they had humanly established (Eph. 2:20) was spread throughout the known world. According to an early church tradition, the twelve apostles divided up the known world and as witnesses took the gospel "to the ends of the earth" (Acts 1:8). Many places were reached with the gospel which are not mentioned in the Acts.

Scholars generally believe that Andrew ministered in Asia Minor, traveling as far north as Scythia near the Black Sea in what is now southern Russia, and that he was eventually crucified in Patras in Achaia. Because Andrew felt unworthy to die on the same kind of cross on which Jesus died, he was apparently bound to an X-shaped cross which has been preserved in the national flag of Scotland as St. Andrew's Cross. When Aegeas, the governor of Achaia, sentenced Andrew, he ordered that Andrew be tied rather than nailed to the cross in order to prolong his agony.

Philip is also said to have ministered in Asia Minor and Scythia, but apparently the major focus of his ministry was in Galatia and perhaps among the Gauls in France. Philip is the only one of the twelve apostles associated with France in any way. The ethnic relationship between the Galatians and Gauls suggests such a ministry may have taken place in France. Philip apparently was stoned and crucified at Hieropolis.

Bartholomew apparently took the gospel to Armenia and gave birth to the church in that nation. Armenia was the first Christian nation in history and a strong Armenian Christian church still exists which claims to be founded by the apostle. He was beaten and crucified in Albania. Some of the legends associated with Bartholomew place him in India; however, the term India was used to describe a wide area including Persia (modern Iran) and most likely his ministry was restricted to that area.

Thomas is the one apostle who may have preached as far east as India. There is a strong Indian tradition that the Mar Thomas Church in India was founded by that apostle in A.D. 52 when he landed at Cranganore and was instrumental in the conversion of several high caste Hindu families in the area. His life and ministry apparently ended in martyrdom in or near Mylapore on the coast of India.

Little can be determined for certain about Matthew's ministry after the writing of his gospel. He apparently ministered in Ethiopia, but two regions may have been identified by that name, Ethiopia in Africa (Cush) and in Persia (Cos). Matthew may have ministered in both regions. He probably died in Egypt and may have been condemned by the Sanhedrin. Scholars do not agree on the reference to the death of Matthew in the Talmud. Some believe it may refer rather to the death of Mathias.

James the son of Alphaeus is said to have ministered in Syria but was eventually martyred in Jerusalem. Another of the minor disciples, Simon the Zealot, apparently preached across North Africa and up the Atlantic coast of Europe as far as Britain. He then apparently traveled to Syria and preached the gospel there until he was captured and sawed in half. Judas Thaddaeus apparently preached the gospel in Edessa and Armenia and was killed with arrows at the foot of Mount Ararat.

I. The Gospel of John

As the first century came to a close, only one of the original twelve remained alive. John spent the last years of his life in Ephesus except for the period of his imprisonment on the island of Patmos. As the Bishop of Ephesus and the only surviving disciple, he no doubt was widely respected in the church at large. Probably while ministering at Ephesus, he wrote the fourth gospel. In light of the fact that it was written about sixty years after the events took place in Jesus' life, the details which John recalled in this book are remarkable and serve as a strong evidence for the inspiration of this gospel. Unlike the other, this gospel does not seek to produce a biographical account of the life of Christ but rather highlights certain events in an effort to convince the reader that Jesus was indeed the Christ, the Son of God, and to cause the reader to express faith in Christ (cf. John 20:30-31).

THE GOSPEL OF JOHN

Author: John
Recipients: Christians at Large
Date of Writing: c. A.D. 85
Theme: Jesus is the Son of God and Savior

John escaped from martyrdom which the other apostles faced, perhaps because he faced death by remaining with Christ during the trials and crucifixion while the other disciples fled for safety. They had to endure the death from which they ran while John was spared the type of death he faced. The early church rumored that John would not die, but rather remain alive until Jesus returned for His church. John knew this conclusion had no basis in the promise of Christ and he may have written the last chapter of gospel to refute this rumor (cf. John 21:22-23). Some Bible teachers believe the elders of the church at Ephesus added their testimony to John's concerning the authentic account of the event out of which this false rumor had begun (cf. John 21:24).

II.   The Epistles of John

In addition to his gospel, John also wrote three epistles which have been preserved in the New Testament. Each of these epistles was probably written about A.D. 90-95 by John from Ephesus. The first is the longest and deals with the subject of Christian fellowship. It is generally viewed as his exposition of Jesus' "new commandment" (John 13:34-35) to his flock at Ephesus.

THE FIRST EPISTLE OF JOHN
Author: John
Recipients: Church of Ephesus
Date of Writing: c. A.D. 90-95
Theme: Christian Fellowship

John discussed his theme of Christian fellowship in a number of contexts in this epistle. First, he reminded his readers that God is light and those in fellowship with God and other believers should walk in the light (1 John 1:1–2:11). Then he emphasized the need to continually abide in Christ to maintain the quality of one's fellowship (1 John 2:12-28). For John, truth and love were so closely related that righteousness was imperative if a believer was to have fellowship with God (1 John 2:29–3:12). Obviously, fellowship was not possible without the consistent expression of genuine love for one another (1 John 3:13–4:21). Finally, John also emphasized the importance of faith as it related to one's fellowship with God and others (1 John 5:1-21).

---

1 JOHN: CHRISTIAN FELLOWSHIP

Fellowship in the Light (1:1–2:11)
Fellowship through Abiding (2:12-28)
Fellowship in Righteousness (2:29–3:12)
Fellowship in Love (3:13–4:21)
Fellowship in Faith (5:1-21)

In his second epistle, John addresses the subject of Christian faithfulness, i.e., walking in the truth. The brief epistle is addressed "to the elect lady and her children, whom I love in truth" (2 John 1).

Some Bible teachers believe the elect lady is the church and conclude the epistle was addressed either to the church at large or to a particular local church, perhaps the one at Ephesus. Others believe the epistle was addressed to an unidentified Christian woman who had been a source of encouragement to the apostle. Still others believe the epistle was addressed to a lady named Eklekte and that the word translated "elect" is really her proper name.

THE SECOND EPISTLE OF JOHN

Author: John
Recipient: The Elect Lady
Date of Writing: c. A. D. 90-95
Theme: Christian Faithfulness

The book of Second John is the briefest of any of the New Testament epistles. After making his introductory comments (2 John 1-3), John commended the lady for the faithfulness he had witnessed in the life of her children (2 John 4-6). He warned of the danger of the spirit of antichrist at work in the world and gave specific instructions relating to avoiding any relationship with it (2 John 7-11). He then concluded the epistle apparently anticipating visiting with the lady in the near future.

JOHN: CHRISTIAN FAITHFULNESS

Introduction (1-3)
Commendation (4-6)
Instruction (7-11)
Conclusion (12-13)

The third of John's three epistles is addressed to a man named Gaius. This was one of the most common names of that era. This Gaius is not likely any other person in the New Testament. Gaius was apparently a person of influence in a church to which John was writing. The church was being hindered by one named Diotrephes. The theme of this brief letter is Christian ministry. It may have been written to introduce a prospective missionary named Demetrius to the church for their consideration and support.

THE THIRD EPISTLE OF JOHN

Author: John
Recipient: Gaius
Date of Writing: A.D. 90-95
Theme: Christian Ministry

Third John contains only one verse more than Second John and discusses its theme of Christian ministry in the context of three individuals. First, Gaius is commended for his faithfulness in caring for itinerant ministers as they came to his community. Second, Diotrephes is condemned for seeking a place of preeminence in the church which belongs only to Christ. The name Diotrephes means "son of Zeus" as was the kind of name usually reserved for the firstborn of a noble family. Apparently this Diotrephes was converted from a noble background, but had a difficult time in submitting himself to the authority of others. Finally John concludes by recommending Demetrius as a person worthy of support.

---

3 JOHN: CHRISTIAN MINISTRY

Introduction (1-4)
The Ministry of Gaius (5-8)
The Ministry of Diotrephes (9-10)
The Ministry of Demetrius (11-12)
Conclusion (13-14)

III. The Revelation of John

John's final contribution to the New Testament was the book of Revelation. Although it is popularly referred to as the Revelation of John because John is the human author of the book, it is better to call it the Revelation of Jesus Christ because Jesus is the subject revealed in the book (Rev. 1:1). This book was revealed to John one Sunday about A.D. 95 and records seven epistles dictated to John by Jesus and the visions John saw that day while imprisoned on the island of Patmos. Throughout history, this last book of the Bible has been neglected by Christians because of its symbolism, except during times of persecution and/or revival in the church.

THE REVELATION OF JESUS CHRIST
Author: John *Recipients:* Seven Churches of Asia *Date of Writing:* c. A.D. 95 *Theme:* The Revelation of Jesus Christ

Much of this book deals with events in the future history of the world. John was told to "write the things which you have seen, and the things which are, and the things which will take place after this" (Rev. 1:19). In the context of that command, the Revelation can be divided in three parts. The first chapter describes the vision of Christ which John had seen. This is followed by two chapters describing the church of Jesus Christ as it was at the end of the first century. The events described beginning in chapter four all relate to the future history of the world.

THE REVELATION OF JESUS CHRIST
The Things Which You Have Seen (1:1-20) The Things Which Are (2:1–3:22) The Things Which Will Take Place after This (4:1–22:21)

Conclusion

An account of John in his later life claims he was brought before the church at Ephesus to deliver a new message to the church, but when he spoke he simply said, "Little children, love one another." When someone reminded the aging apostle he had often before said the same thing, John responded, "It is enough. It is the Lord's command." Although years had passed since John had first heard Jesus give that "new commandment," he never forgot that love for one another was the distinguishing mark of true discipleship (John 13:34-35). Christians today would do well to remember Jesus' words which John never forgot.

CHAPTER 48

JUDE:
THE GROWING APOSTASY OF
THE CHURCH

Jude

As the church entered its second generation, a challenge in the integrity of the Christian faith arose in the form of subtle false religious teachers within the church. The focus of first-generation Christianity was the experience of "our common salvation" (Jude 3), but the presence of false teachers within the church raised the need to "contend earnestly for the faith which was once for all delivered to the saints" (Jude 3). Among those best prepared to address this problem of apostasy in the church was the writer of the second to the last book of the New Testament, a man named Jude. Apostasy was also a problem Jesus Himself would not overlook as He considered the church's condition at the end of the century in which He died.

Jude, one of the twelve disciples, is unique in that he is given three names in Scripture. Jerome once called him "Trionius" meaning "the man with three names." In Matthew, he is called "Lebbaeus, whose surname was Thaddaeus" (Matt. 10:3). Mark merely refers to him as "Thaddaeus" (Mark 3:18). Not until the much later writings of Luke was Jude's real identity revealed as "Judas the son of James" (Luke 6:16; Acts 1:13).

The name Judas comes from the Old Testament "Judah" which means "Praise." Judas is the Hebrew spelling, while Jude is the Greek representation. When James first named his son, Judas, it was among the most popular names given to Hebrew boys. But historically, after Judas Iscariot betrayed Jesus Christ, the name Judas became offensive to believers. The very name was hated and soon ceased to be used at all. Who would want to name a son after the one who betrayed Jesus.

On the only occasion in which this Judas is recorded as making any statement, John very carefully wrote, "Judas (not Iscariot) saith unto him" (John 14:22). There was probably confusion in the early church over the name Judas, especially when a disciple was named Judas. They confused him with Judas Iscariot. Therefore, Judas probably began using another name, and became known widely as Lebbaeus Thaddaeus. Later in his life, he went back to his original name, but not his Hebrew pronunciation. Because he ministered to Gentiles, he was called by it's Greek spelling, Jude.

One can learn a lot about a man from his name, especially when it is a name he chose for himself. The name Lebbaeus means "a man of the heart." Although some Bible teachers believe the name Thaddaeus like the name Judas means "praise," others believe the name is more likely rated the same root as the Hebrew name for El Shaddai, the name for God usually translated "Almighty." It means "All Sufficient." One writer has suggested El Shaddai is "the God who is enough."

Because of Judas Iscariot's apostasy, Judas Thaddaeus had to change his name. He felt the ridicule heaped on Iscariot and felt the results of his apostasy. In selecting a new name, Judas Thaddaeus was making a statement. From his very heart, he had come to experience the all sufficiency of God. This is particularly interesting in that the only recorded question he ever asked was one which probed into the very heart of the deeper Christian life (cf. John 14:22).

It is difficult to identify any other Judas as the author of the book of Jude. Some argue that Judas, the half-brother of Jesus, wrote the epistle based on the record that there was a brother by that name (Matt. 13:55). There are problems with this view however. First, the brothers of Jesus did not follow Jesus or believe in him before the Cross (John 7:3, 5). Further, if that were the Judas referred to, he would be identified as Judas the son of Joseph rather than the son of James.

Another view makes Judas the son of James the grandson of Zebedee. This view has a little more credibility than the other. The name James the Less applied to the other James among the twelve implies the son of Zebedee was older. It is not beyond the realm of possibility that James the son of Zebedee was old enough to have a mature son. Also, this would explain how Judas, not Iscariot, first began to follow Jesus. If this identification of Judas is accurate, he would represent a third generation following Jesus from the same family. Unfortunately, the strongest arguments supporting this view are only presuppositions.

Because Judas Lebbaeus Thaddaeus had to live with a fruit of the apostasy of Judas Iscariot, it is not surprising that many of the truths in this letter deal with apostasy. Judas (Jude) Thaddaeus was faithful in the face of apostasy. When Judas Iscariot betrayed the Lord and turned traitor, Jude Thaddaeus did not quit. He remained faithful. Because he was faithful, others also continued to follow Jesus. Every man named Judas had to live with the stigma of owning the name of betrayal. Yet one of them wrote an epistle probably expressing the desire of all of them. "It was needful for me to write unto you, and exhort you that ye should earnestly contend for the faith" (Jude 3). The book about false teachers and heretics was written by a man named Judas who had lived with the stigma of apostasy and remained faithful in the face of apostasy. To avoid confusion with the apostasy of Judas Iscariot, Judas Thaddeus changed his name. To some, that might not seem like much of a sacrifice, but to Jude it was important. His family roots were important. Years later, when the danger of being confused with Judas Iscariot was minimized, he appears to have reverted to his original name in its Greek form. As often as his real name appears, so does the reference to his father also occur.

One of the traditions of Jude Thaddaeus resulted in an unusual designation of him as a Roman Catholic saint. Jude is said to have carried the burial shroud of Jesus to the King of Edessa shortly after the resurrection of Jesus. Many art historians believe the tradition is historical. They identify the shroud carried by Jude with the shroud of Turin said to bear the image of Christ. The king who had heard of Jesus before he was crucified wanted to meet Him and be healed of his sickness. When Jude arrived, he is said to have showed the image of Christ to the king who was then instantly healed. The miracle resulted in Jude's identification as "the Saint of the Impossible." Even today, Catholics will "pray" to St. Jude if they want an impossible prayer answered even though the Scriptures never teach prayer to the saints or in the name of saints.

If this epistle was written by the Jude who was one of the half-brothers of Jesus, it would be natural for him to want to write an epistle "concerning our common salvation" (Jude 3). Jude and his brothers grew up with Jesus but only believed in Him as their Messiah after the Resurrection (Matt. 13:55). Because of the salvation he had experienced in coming to trust in his brother as Messiah, he would have wanted to write about the theme of salvation, but the condition which had begun to develop within the church demanded he address a different problem. Some had risen to a place of prominence in the early church who did not share a genuine commitment to the fundamental faith "which was once and for all delivered to the saints" (Jude 3). While the problem was not unique in history, it still needed to be addressed by the church.

THE EPISTLE OF JUDE

Author: Jude (disciple/brother of Jesus)
Recipients: To the Called, Sanctified and Preserved
Date of Writing: c. A.D. 66
Theme: Earnestly Contending for the Faith

In addressing the problem which had arisen, Jude began with a balanced analysis of the situation which existed at that time. First, he noted this problem was not as widespread as one might at first imagine, but was restricted to "certain men" in prominent places (Jude 4).

Second, this problem had arisen as these individuals "have crept in unnoticed." The Greek word *pareisduein* was used to describe the subtle appeal of a pleader influencing the minds of a judge, an exile slipping back into a country secretly to slowly erode the laws upon which that society is built. In every case, it implies something essentially evil influencing a society or situation. Although these individuals apparently professed some degree of faith, Jude describes them as "ungodly" because they lacked a personal faith in God as Savior. These false teachers perverted the biblical faith in God as Savior. These false teachers perverted the biblical teaching concerning the grace of God and used it to justify their loose moral lifestyles (licentiousness). Also, they denied the unique deity of "our Lord Jesus Christ" and in doing so rejected His full and final authority over their life.

Jude reminded his readers this was not the first time apostasy had been a problem in the history of the world. Three specific examples are noted and commented on briefly. First, there were those who left Egypt with Israel in unbelief and were later destroyed in the wilderness (Jude 5). The second case presented was that of the angels who joined Lucifer in rebellion in heaven and have since been chained awaiting judgment (Jude 6). The destruction of Sodom and Gomorrah by God because they gave themselves over to sexual immorality was the third example cited (Jude 7). In each of these cases, God was faithful to judge those guilty of rebellion against Him and His revelation.

Much of this epistle is devoted to alerting the reader how to identify these false religious teachers that were beginning to lead the church into apostasy. Jude suggests some nineteen characteristics of them and their movements. He describes them as dream merchants who build their movements around a personal dream or vision (Jude 8). He adds they engage in immoral activities which "defile the flesh" (Jude 8). They opposed civil authority, rejecting their divinely established authority and speaking evil of individual dignitaries (Jude 8). According to Jude, they speak out of their ignorance of spiritual realities and base their religious beliefs on natural theology (Jude 10).

These false teachers had corrupted themselves and practiced a sinful lifestyle because they are predominantly evil in nature (Jude 10-11; cf. 1 John 3:12). They were primarily motivated by money and were governed in their religious activities by the bottom line and the profit margin (Jude 11). They took on for themselves more than they should or were capable of handling, often making themselves God's personal representative on earth or God incarnate (Jude 11). Like hidden rocks beneath the water's surface, they posed a real danger in the fellowship of the church and may have caused others to be shipwrecked in their faith (Jude 12). They were self-centered, concerned only with "shepherding themselves" rather than shepherding others in their sphere of influence (Jude 12). Like "clouds without water" they held forth the hope of help and blessing but failed to deliver and meet the real needs of their followers (Jude 12).

These false teachers failed to produce the spiritual fruit which ought to be characteristic of "late autumn trees" and thereby evidenced themselves to be spiritually dead without any indication of life remaining (Jude 12; cf. Ps. 1:3; 92:12-14). They were restless and evidenced their personal lack of the peace of God like raging waves of the sea, foaming up their own shame" (Jude 13; cf. Isa. 57:20-21). They continued to remain in spiritual darkness like the "wandering stars for whom is reserved the blackness of darkness forever" (Jude 13). As a result, Jude notes they were destined to be judged by the Lord when He returns to this earth (Jude 14-15). They were unquestionably ungodly in their character and activities (Jude 15). Also, they were given to murmuring and were so discontented in life they had no difficulty at all finding something to complain about (Jude 16). These false teachers were given over to grumbling about their situation in life, often suggesting a source which may be blamed for their fate in life (Jude 16). They were governed in their personal lifestyle by their own desires, lacking accountability to others (Jude 16). Also, they had mastered the art of communication and masked their true identity through the use of "great swelling words, flattering people to gain advantage" (Jude 16).

Not only did Jude describe these men and movements vividly, he also suggested a strategic response to their presence and influence. First, he urged his readers not to be surprised to see the fulfillment of biblical warnings concerning the coming of false teachers (Jude 17-18). Second, he wanted the readers to recognize the true nature of this leadership as sensual, divisive, and nonspiritual (Jude 19). He urged them to continue growing in a deeper understanding of biblical doctrine that would impact their life (Jude 20). Also, he called on them to maintain a vital relationship with God through Spirit-guided prayer (Jude 20). It is interesting to note that the forms of the Greek verb translated "contend earnestly" (Jude 3) are twice used in the New Testament in the context of intensity in prayer (cf. Rom. 15:30; Col. 4:12). To combat these false teachers, true Christians needed to keep themselves in the love of God through consistent obedience to the known will of God (Jude 21). They could avoid becoming discouraged by anticipating the culmination of God's work in human history in the imminent return of our Lord Jesus Christ (Jude 21). Regardless of what was taking place, they needed to continue loving people back to God, including those being influenced by false teachers (Jude 22). Others would have to be rescued from their destructive beliefs and lifestyles through a loving confrontation (Jude 23). In all that was done, Jude wanted his readers to keep their focus on God "who is able to keep you from stumbling and to present you faultless before the presence of His glory" (Jude 24; cf. Rom. 16:25; Eph. 3:20).

JUDE: EARNESTLY CONTENDING FOR THE FAITH

Introduction (1-2)
Identification of the Problem (3-4)
The History of Heresy (5-7)
Description of the False Teachers (8-16)
A Christian Response to False Teachers (17-25)
Conclusion (24-25)

Conclusion

Sometimes Christians today also find themselves having to live with the reputation earned by another. While it is unfair of others to assume all believers are as hypocritical or wrong as a few may be, it nevertheless often happens. Many Christians find it difficult to live with these unjust reputations. But like Judas, not Iscariot, one can discover in these situations a deeper relationship with El Shaddai, "the God who is enough!"

CHAPTER 49

JESUS:
THE COURSE OF
THE CHURCH AGE

Matthew 13, 24–25; Revelation 2–3

Although the New Testament was concluded by the end of the first century, the history recorded in its pages covers a period of time extending more than three millennia. This is because much of the New Testament was prophetic when written and describes a time which even in the context of today appears to be future. In addition to the discussion of events which may be identified over the past 1,900 years since the closing of the canon, the New Testament also describes a period of tribulation on the earth which Bible teachers call "the Great Tribulation" and the establishment of a thousand-year kingdom of God upon the earth.

As we read the pages of the New Testament, we see evidence that the early church anticipated the soon return of Christ to establish His kingdom. The disciples asked Jesus about the timing of His return just prior to His ascension (Acts 1:6). In his epistles to the Thessalonians, the return of Christ was a major theme in Paul's understanding of what it meant to be a Christian. Even at the end of the century, John was writing of Jesus' return as the climax of the Revelation.

While it always seemed possible that Jesus could return at any moment throughout history, looking back from the context of this present day, it now appears the course of this present age was described in some detail for our edification. The contemporary Christian should not be surprised that the Lord has delayed His return, but rather realize that the time fixed by the Father has not yet come (Matt. 24:36). The events of these last eighteen centuries have not come as a surprise to God. He described certain trends which would take place during that period.

Three times in the New Testament, Jesus made prophetic statements which dealt with the trends and events of that period between His ascension and the rapture of the church. These discourses include part of the Olivet Discourse (Matt. 24:4-8), His parables teaching the mystery of the kingdom of heaven (Matt. 13:1-52), and His seven epistles to the seven churches of Asia.

I.   The Olivet Discourse

While much of the Olivet Discourse deals with a time following the rapture of the church, Jesus identified a number of trends and events which would take place prior to His return in His introductory comments. Throughout the course of this age, Jesus taught His disciples to anticipate others who would appear and falsely claim to be the Messiah. He told them messianic movements would continue to arise and deceive many who lack spiritual discernment (Matt. 24:5). There had been such movements prior to the first coming of Christ. History has since demonstrated the accuracy that other false christs came after He left earth.

War was a second thing His disciples were warned that they could anticipate throughout the age. He told them mankind would continue to experience wars and these wars would be widely reported (Matt. 24:6). Also, Jesus claimed these wars would be fought not only as conflicts between nations, but as conflicts between kingdoms or alliances of nations (Matt. 24:7). Some Bible teachers believe that only in this century have "kingdom wars" been fought as distinct from historic international conflicts and note this is the first of the signs marking "the beginning of sorrows" (Matt. 24:8).

Jesus also noted that natural calamities such as famines, epidemic disease, and earthquakes would be experienced in a variety of places (Matt. 24:7). Throughout the years since then, this too has proved to be true. World hunger organizations report that vast multitudes around the world die of starvation every day. While medical research has in the past generation discovered vaccines, cures, and treatments for a vast number of diseases, there remain numerous epidemics in various parts of the world today.

Within the context of the rest of His discourse, Jesus identified two additional trends and events which appear to take place prior to the days of tribulation which lie ahead. The first of these is a consequence of the growing lawlessness which will characterize this age and which is discussed in other prophetic passages (cf. 2 Tim. 3:2-5; 2 Thess. 2:3). Jesus taught that growing apostasy in the world would result in a general callousness in human relationships. "Because lawlessness will abound, the love of many will grow cold" (Matt. 24:12).

The other event mentioned relates to the return of Israel to the land which God gave to Abraham. Jesus told His disciples, "Now learn this parable from the fig tree: When its branch has already become tender and puts forth leaves, you know that summer is near" (Matt. 24:32). Many Bible teachers believe the reference to the fig tree is a reference to Israel returning to the land. This recalls a number of Old Testament prophecies concerning the future history of Israel. The Scriptures teach the people of Israel would someday begin returning to the land of Palestine (Lev. 26:42; Ezek. 36:24), that the nation of Israel would once again be established as political entity (Isa. 44:5), and that the city of Jerusalem would once again serve as the capital of Israel (Isa. 59:20-21). Each of these things have occurred since the Second World War and in the minds of some Bible teachers are signs that the return of Christ for His church may be very close at hand.

II.   The Mystery of the Kingdom of Heaven

Jesus often used stories (parables) to communicate important principles of truth to the common people. In this way, He could teach those who wanted to learn while others who were not prepared to consider His message were blinded to the meaning of His parables. Seven of these parables were taught during one busy day of ministry and recorded by Matthew in a unique collection referred to by Jesus as "the mysteries of the kingdom of heaven" (Matt. 13:11).

The word "mystery" is used in a rather unique way in Scripture to identify areas of truth which were hidden in the past but are now revealed by the Holy Spirit (cf. Rom. 16:25-26; Eph. 3:1-12). Whenever this word is used in the New Testament, it describes some aspect of the period of time between the incarnation and the return of Christ which was not clearly revealed in the Old Testament Scriptures. The mysteries of the kingdom of heaven and the mystery of the seven churches are two areas of the mysteries of God which, when properly understood, enhance one's understanding of this present age.

As we study the seven parables of the kingdom of heaven, we learn a number of things concerning the progress of Christianity throughout the age. First, Jesus taught there would be a continuous sowing of the gospel which would produce a wide variety of results despite various obstacles to its success (Matt. 13:1-23). Second, He noted there would be a counter-sowing by the Enemy throughout the church age (Matt. 13:24-30, 36-43). Third, it appears Christendom would experience significant growth and become a dominant force in the world (Matt. 13:31-33). The time would come when Christendom would be viewed as more of an asset than a liability (Matt. 13:44-46). This must have been a difficult prophecy for the early church to understand as they contemplated it in the midst of severe persecution. Ultimately, Jesus told them, the Christian church would tend to attract both the good and bad to its ranks (Matt. 13:47-51). As has proved the case with the statements made by Jesus in the Olivet Discourse, His revelations concerning the course of this age in the kingdom parables have proven extremely accurate.

THE MYSTERIES OF THE KINGDOM OF HEAVEN

The Sower – There will be a sowing of the gospel
The Tares – There will be a counter-sowing by Satan
The Mustard Seed – Christendom will grow outwardly
The Leaven – The gospel will permeate all of life
The Hidden Treasure – God will gather to Himself
The Pearl of Great Price – A peculiar people
The Dragnet – God will end the age in judgment

II.   The Mystery of the Seven Churches

The growing apostasy in the church by the end of the first century was also addressed by Jesus in seven epistles which he dictated to John on the island of Patmos. While there are bright spots in the descriptions of these seven churches, it is significant that Jesus called five of the seven to repent or risk being subject to His judgment upon their ministry. Two of these epistles mention a heretical movement of the first century known as the Nicolaitons (Rev. 2:6, 15). Some Bible teachers believe this movement was begun by Nicolas of Antioch, one of the first deacons of the church who later came to be influenced by some of the heretical teachers of that era (cf. Acts 6:5). Other false doctrines which arose in the church and were identified by Jesus included "the doctrine of Balaam" (Rev. 2:14) and the teaching of a self-proclaimed prophetess named Jezebel (Rev. 2:20). Each of these movements apparently taught that a person could be a Christian and adopt a loose moral lifestyle.

In addressing the pastors of these seven churches, Jesus began by identifying some characteristics of Himself. In each case, that aspect of who Jesus was offered hope to the church and/or confronted them with the very aspect of God which was being offended by their failure. Even though strong language is used by Jesus to describe some of these churches, He is pictured as being in the midst of the churches (cf. Rev. 1:13). This was true of the church he called dead (Rev. 3:1) and the other he wanted to vomit out of His mouth (Rev. 3:16) as well as those which He commended as faithful (Rev. 2:8-11; 3:7-13). Jesus' message to the churches in danger of apostatizing seems to have been twofold. First, He made it clear their sin was offensive and would be judged severely if they did not repent. He called them to do so.

Second, He wanted to remind them He was as close to them as He had ever been and was within reach when they did repent and reach out to Him once again.

THE SEVEN CHURCHES OF ASIA

Ephesus: The Church That Wandered in its Love
Smyrna: The Church That Remained Faithful in Trials
Pergamos: The Church That Compromised with the World
Thyatira: The Church That Was Entirely Corrupted
Sardis: The Church that Died and Kept Its Reputation
Philadelphia: The Church That Experienced Revival
Laodicea: The Church That Stopped Caring

When Jesus revealed Himself to John on the Island of Patmos, part of that revelation included a description of Himself in His relationship with the seven churches of Asia. Each of these churches had a significant ministry in the province, but they were not the only churches in that region. Churches were also in Hieropolis, Colossae, Troas, Miletus, and perhaps other cities which were not addressed by Jesus. This has caused some Bible teachers to wonder if there might be a special reason why the epistles were addressed only to these churches and not the others. One of the indications that such a reason may exist is the designation of these particular churches as found in the use of the word "mystery" to describe the churches (cf. Rev. 1:20).

Bible teachers in this century began to recognize a parallel between the condition of these seven Asian churches and the general condition of the Christian church in the seven ages of church history. While every church has its own unique character often distinct from others in its community or denomination, certain characteristics have tended to characterize most churches during particular eras. This interpretation of the seven churches is sometimes referred to as the seven church ages.

THE SEVEN CHURCH AGES OF REVELATION

Ephesus – The Apostolic Church (A.D. 30-100)
Smyrna – The Persecuted Church (A.D. 100-316)
Pergamos – The State Church (A.D. 316-500)
Thyatira – The Development of the Papacy (A.D. 500-1500)
Sardis – The Dead Church of the Reformation Era
Philadelphia – The Revived Church of the 18th & 19th Century
Laodicea – The Apathetic Church since the 1905 Revival

Although the dates on the above charts may be open to some discussion, it appears Jesus accurately described the general trends which would characterize the church in the seven church ages. First, He indicated the revived apostolic church would grow cold and wander from its first love (Rev. 2:1-7). Then some churches would endure intense persecution and remain faithful to the Lord as reflected in the second age (Rev. 2:8-11). This would be followed by a third era that states some churches would make wide ranging compromises in their ministries that would place themselves against Christ (Rev. 2:12-17). This would lead to the fourth age of the church in which some churches became so corrupted by false teaching they engaged in practices completely foreign to Christianity and therefore came under the severe judgment of Christ (Rev. 2:18-29). By the time the church entered its fifth age, some churches would achieve great reputations but lack genuine spiritual life (Rev. 3:1-6). Still there was hope. In the sixth age of the church, some churches would experience the continued blessing of God in times of revival even though they were small and apparently lacked the influence of the church in other ages (Rev. 3:7-13). Ultimately, the seventh Laodicean age of the church would be a time in which some churches become apathetic in their relationship to Christ and to ministry (Rev. 3:14-22).

In both cases of the kingdom parables and the church epistles, one could argue there is some overlap in the trends and events alluded to, but the major theme of these mysteries illustrates prophetically the course of this present age. Looking back across the history of the last two millennia, it is possible to see how these prophetic allusions may have been fulfilled. One sign of the soon return of Jesus for His church is the fact that the church appears to be in her last age. Many Bible teachers believe the voice which called to John, "Come up here, and I will show you things which must take place after this" (Rev. 4:1) is symbolic of the rapture of the church. They argue that the rapture of the church will take place as the final age of the church comes to a close .

Conclusion

While many things are happening in our world today that Christians do not understand, it is comforting to know that nothing is taking God by surprise. In

His self-revelation in Scripture, He not only recorded significant historical persons and events of the past, but He outlined the major trends and events of the future history of the world. From today's context, Christians can recognize the apparent fulfillment of some of these trends and events in the "future history of the world" and can therefore be assured God is still in control of His universe.

CHAPTER 50

THE ANTICHRIST: BRINGING PEACE TO A WORLD IN CONFUSION

1 Thessalonians 4, 2 Thessalonians 2, Revelation 4–7

*M*any Bible teachers believe the day in which we live could be very close to the end of this age of grace. They note the many Old Testament prophecies which are repeated in the New Testament concerning a coming time of sorrow and tribulation upon this earth like never before experienced. In light of the severity of periods of tribulation in which some cities, nations, and cultures have gone through in the past, it is not surprising that the most common name used to describe this seven-year period is "the Great Tribulation." Although it is still future, much is known about the future history of this period.

Ironically the period in which this world will endure more tribulation than at any other time will begin with the promise of a new age of peace and prosperity. The Great Tribulation is divided into two periods of three and a half years each. During the first three and a half years of this period, the Antichrist rises to a place of authority and influence in the world, largely because of his effectiveness in bringing peace to a world in the midst of confusion. Only after he is firmly in place does he feel confident enough to break a treaty with Israel and turn against them. That marks the turning point in the history of that era and the peace which Antichrist had apparently established falls apart as the world goes to war against the Jews.

No other period in the history of the world other than this present time could have been the setting for the events described in the prophetic Scriptures concerning the end of the age. The prophet Daniel made two interesting observations about that time which many Bible teachers believe describe the end of the twentieth century. First, these things would take place in a time when people are more accustomed to travel on a larger scale than ever before (Dan. 12:4). In the same verse, Daniel describes a second characteristic of that period, a time when there is a significant increase in the sum total of the world's knowledge. The realization of these things in recent years suggests the next event on God's prophetic timetable may be very soon.

I. The Rapture of the Church

The Great Tribulation will not begin until another event Bible teachers call "the Rapture of the church" takes place. While the Latin word "rapture" which means "caught up" does not occur in the English Bible (very few Latin words do occur in the English Bible), the expression "caught up" does (1 Thess. 4:17). Before God judges the world, He intends to remove His church from the earth because their sins have already been judged on the cross. This decision is not without precedent in the history of God and His people. Before God judged the world of Noah's day with the Flood, He first insured Noah and his family were secure within the ark so they would not be subject to God's judgment upon sin. This is only one of several biblical parallels between the days of Noah and the time of the return of Christ. The Rapture of the church will come suddenly, apparently at a time when it is not generally expected. Without any warning, Jesus will appear momentarily in the clouds as He descends with a shout and blast of a trumpet (1 Thess. 4:16). Then there will be a resurrection of all those who have died in Christ up to the time of that resurrection (1 Thess. 4:16). This will be followed by the actual rapture itself as all living true Christians will be caught up to meet the Lord in the air and are instantaneously changed (1 Thess. 4:17). At this point, God's restraining influence will be taken out of the way (2 Thess. 2:6-7). This restraint may be the salting influence of genuine Christianity, but it may also include that ministry of the Holy Spirit which will to some degree be limited during the tribulation period.

While many things take place at the Rapture, they will happen in an extremely brief period of time. When Paul explained this truth to the Christians at Corinth, he suggested some indication of the total time involved in the above actions in the expression "in a moment, in the twinkling of an eye" (1 Cor. 15:52). These things will happen so fast that some Bible teachers have spoken of a secret rapture. There does not appear to be any attempt to hide the actual event from those who are left behind, but all that takes place will happen so quickly that it is doubtful anybody will see it happen. They will be left with only memories of what things were like and the reality of what exists moments after the Rapture. Some degree of effort will be expended as the unsaved not included in the Rapture attempt to understand what has taken place.

II. The Rise of the Antichrist

One thing that is reasonably certain is that those left behind will not recognize or understand the meaning of the Rapture. Paul reminded the Thessalonians that the people remaining behind would be blinded spiritually so they would believe the lie (2 Thess. 2:11). The confusion left behind by the mysterious disappearance of millions of born-again Christians around the world may be explained in a variety of ways in different parts of the world. The Antichrist will have a believable explanation for their disappearance. In light of the nature of the world at present, it is unlikely the Rapture will be much more than what journalists sometimes call "a one-day wonder." The Rapture will be a story which seems to be extremely important as it breaks, but is soon eclipsed by other fast-breaking major news stories of the day.

Some of the news stories which will tend to be covered by the news media following the rapture of the church will relate to the rise of the Antichrist. While some Bible teachers believe the Antichrist may be alive on earth today, his identity will not be revealed until after the Rapture occurs (2 Thess. 2:3). In the Scriptures, this individual's character is revealed in a number of names and titles used to describe him. Paul described him as the man of sin, the son of perdition, and the lawless one (2 Thess. 2:3, 8). The term Antichrist used by John (1 John 2:22) is perhaps the best-known title of this person because it describes his role as one who seeks to take the place of Christ. He is a false Christ or a pseudo-Christ.

The Antichrist will achieve credibility through performing signs and wonders (2 Thess. 2:9-10). He will also make great speeches which will draw the world into his orbit and give him greater control over world affairs (Rev. 13:5). About this time, ten nations will form a confederacy which will resemble a revival of the old Roman empire (Rev. 13:1). This world body will recognize the Antichrist as unique and describe him as one who has been raised from the dead (Rev. 13:3). It is not clear whether the death wound refers to the resurrection of the antichrist, or the resurrection of the ten-nation empire from the former Roman nations.

While the Antichrist will be a significant person capable of drawing people to himself, at least some of his success will be due to the influence of a false prophet. The false prophet will convince the world to worship the Antichrist because of his apparent resurrection (Rev. 13:12). The Antichrist will cooperate with the false prophet and accept the worship of the people (Rev. 13:4). This false prophet will build personal credibility through exercising signs and wonders including calling fire down from heaven, a substitute satanic Pentecost (Rev. 13:13). He will successfully convince people to make images of the Antichrist which will apparently be used as worship aids (Rev. 13:14).

As he secures greater power in the world, the Antichrist will oppose and overcome the saints who refuse to worship him (Rev. 13:7). At the peak of his power, he will have successfully secured some power over all ethnic and linguistic people groups in the world (Rev. 13:7). His ally the false prophet will convince the world population to receive the mark of the beast, probably for commercial reasons (Rev. 13:16-17). This mark will somehow be related to the number "666." He will also establish what is described in Scripture as the harlot church or an apostate church (Rev. 17). This church is described by the image of sexual immorality, often used in Scripture to describe a group of people who worship other than the true God. Sometimes Bible teachers describe this church as "the apostate church."

One of the most significant events at the beginning of the Tribulation will be an agreement between the Antichrist and Israel in which they come to terms and sign a peace treaty (Dan. 9:27). Perhaps as a part of this treaty, Israel will secure the temple site in Jerusalem and rebuild their temple at the traditional center of Judaism (Rev. 11:1-2). The influence of Antichrist will be great because the site of the temple is presently occupied with a Moslem mosque. To get them to move in deference to Israel will be significant. The completion of this tribulation temple will mark the resumption of the historic temple worship of Israel including offering sacrifices. These sacrifices will not be for salvation, but typical witnesses to the atoning work of Christ will be supplemented with the witness of God from two other sources. First, two witnesses will begin preaching in the streets of Jerusalem (Rev. 11:3). Bible teachers have speculated that these witnesses may be Enoch or Moses and Elijah. Second, 144,000 Hebrew evangelists will preach the gospel through all the world for a witness, perhaps using existing Jewish centers such as temples, synagogues and community centers (Rev. 7:1-8).

During this time, there will be a massive outpouring of the Holy Spirit resulting in the salvation of much of Israel (Joel 2:28-32). Also, a vast number of people from every ethnic and linguistic group will respond positively to the preaching of these evangelists (Rev. 7:9-17). This revival probably will be greater than that experienced during the first century of the church or at any other time since then. There will be a second more intense wave of revival toward the end of these seven years just prior to the return of Christ which will last throughout the thousand-year kingdom of God on earth. This first outpouring will produce significant results.

While the Antichrist secures his power on earth, it appears Christians will appear in heaven before the Bema Judgment Seat of Christ to be rewarded for their faithfulness (2 Tim. 4:8). These rewards will then be tested by a purifying fire to determine their real worth (1 Cor. 3:12-15). Christians will probably then lay their rewards at Jesus' feet as an act of worship in heaven (Rev. 4:10). At that point, it appears the church which is the Bride of Christ will prepare for her marriage to the Lamb (Rev. 21:2, implied).

One other significant event takes place in heaven shortly after the Rapture. A scroll is presented and a call goes out to find one worthy to open the scroll. Although initially nobody appears worthy to open the scroll, it then becomes apparent that Jesus can and will open the scroll (Rev. 5:5). Bible teachers are divided over the identity of this scroll. Some claim it is the title deed to the world noting the only other sealed scroll in Scripture is a title deed for a field purchased by Jeremiah (Jer. 32:14) and that the breaking of the seventh seal is followed by seven trumpets and the announcement, "The kingdoms of this world have become the kingdoms of our Lord and of His Christ, and He shall reign forever and ever!" (Rev. 11:15). Others believe the scroll is a blueprint for the future noting that with the breaking of each seal, some significant event takes place on earth.

III.   The First Half of the Great Tribulation

As the seals of this scroll take place in heaven, parallel events take place on the earth. As the first seal is broken, a rider on a white horse appears and brings war to the earth (Rev. 6:1-2). When the second seal is broken, a rider on a red horse removes peace from human relationships (Rev. 6:3-4). A rider on a black horse will bring extreme famine to the earth as the third seal is broken (Rev. 6:5-6). At the breaking of the fourth seal on the scroll, a rider on a pale horse will bring violent death to a quarter of the world's population (Rev. 6:7-8).

While some Christians believe they will have complete understanding of all things when they die, the breaking of the fifth seal suggests that is not the case. As this seal is opened, the martyrs of the church in heaven will ask God how long it will be before their blood is avenged (Rev. 6:9-11). The timing of such a request is ironic. At the opening of the sixth seal, there will be a variety of unnatural cosmic disturbances including a major earthquake, a darkened sun, the moon appearing bloodlike and falling stars (Rev. 6:12-14). This will be widely recognized as the judgment of God (Rev. 6:16). The people of the earth including leaders in politics, commerce and the military will wish they could die at this point, but many will survive (Rev. 6:15-17).

THE SEVEN SEALS OF THE SCROLL

1. The White Horse Conquering
2. The Red Horse Taking Peace
3. The Pale Horse Bringing Famine
4. The Black Horse Bringing Death
5. The Prayer of the Martyrs
6. The Cosmic Chaos Begins
7. Preparations for the Announcement

Upon opening the seventh seal, heaven is in silence for about a half hour as preparations are made for a major announcement (Rev. 8:1). This announcement will be preceded with the blasts of seven trumpets and parallel events on earth. Before the trumpets are sounded, several things will have probably taken place on earth establishing the conditions which are described in the trumpet judgments.

During the first half of the Tribulation, one of the historic results of the Jewish revival is an improvement in the social and economic conditions of the society in which it exists. Although such conditions have not been established, the Antichrist will accept the credit for having taken a world in chaos and confusion and establishing a sense of stability and security. The people will tend to look to him as a political savior and depend upon his leadership in a broad range of issues. At his peak of power in what appears to be a new age of prosperity, the Antichrist will break his peace treaty with Israel (Dan. 9:27). This treaty was for seven years, but the antichrist will break it after three and a half years. Under the terms of God's covenant with Abraham, this mistreatment of Israel will have serious consequences. The violation of this treaty occurs in the midst of the seven years and probably marks the beginning of what the Old Testament prophets called "the time of Jacob's trouble." This is the tribulation part of the Great Tribulation.

Conclusion

The events discussed in this chapter are still future but could begin occurring at any moment. Christians anticipate the imminent return of Christ for His church (the Rapture) which will mark the beginning of the Great Tribulation. Because no one knows when the Rapture will occur, contemporary

Christians should live every day as consistently as they would live if they knew it was the very day they would be meeting Jesus in the air. Someday, perhaps someday soon, will be that day.

CHAPTER 51

THE ANTICHRIST:
THE TIME OF JACOB'S TROUBLE

Revelation 8–18

$\mathscr{I}$n breaking his treaty with Israel, the Antichrist will immediately adopt a program of antisemitism apparently designed to liquidate Israel. Jesus told his disciples "the abomination of desolation" would appear in the Jerusalem temple. Many Bible teachers believe this means a pig will be offered on the altar (Matt. 24:15). In frustration over his failure to completely destroy the influence of Christianity, the Antichrist will persecute Israel which he views as the mother of Christianity and she will seek refuge in the wilderness (Rev. 12:11-17).

Although many Jews will escape this attack, the two witnesses will continue their preaching ministry until they are killed and their bodies are left in the streets of Jerusalem (Rev. 11:7-9). The deaths of these witnesses will be widely celebrated in the world for three and a half days (Rev. 11:10). Then both witnesses will be restored to life causing those who witness this resurrection to be overcome with fear (Rev. 11:11). The two witnesses will then be caught up to heaven in the presence of their enemies (Rev. 11:12).

Within an hour of this rapture, a massive earthquake will hit Jerusalem destroying about ten percent of the city and killing seven thousand men (Rev. 11:13). The relationship between the rapture of the witnesses and the earthquake is not likely to be noticed by the world leaders of that day. In a kind of retaliation for the deaths of these seven thousand men, an intense persecution of those who have been converted through the ministry of the two witnesses or the 144,000 Hebrew evangelists will probably be launched. A vast number of believers will be martyred for their faith in Christ during the remaining years of the Tribulation (Rev. 7:14).

Just as God has designated Jerusalem as the center for His rule in the world, so the Antichrist will designate Babylon as the center from which his influence goes out to the world. The actual city on the Euphrates in Iraq may be rebuilt to its former glory when it was one of the most beautiful and cultured cities in the world with its hanging gardens. The Babylon mentioned in Revelation is more than the city, it is the total social/cultural nation of the original Babylon including Iraq, Iran, Syria, Turkey, and other surrounding nations. Babylon will be the center of the apostate church. Religious power will give the Antichrist the ability to influence the nations of the world.

The world government administered from Babylon will be publicly portrayed by an image of being religious, scientific, cultured, elegant, prosperous and peaceful; but in reality it will be overrun with greed, selfishness, pleasure, rivalries, force, and other abominations (Rev. 17:1-6). All this will become more apparent as the public facade of the Antichrist's kingdom begins to crack in the face of three series of judgments of God.

I.   The Trumpet Judgments of God (Rev. 8:7–9:21; 11:15-19)

In the drama John witnessed in heaven, he saw seven angels blowing seven trumpets in preparation for a significant announcement. As each of these trumpets were sounded, John witnessed significant events taking place on earth. At the blowing of the first trumpet, one third of the vegetation on the earth was destroyed with fire as a result of hail and lightning storms (Rev. 8:7). At the sounding of the second trumpet, a large mass of burning fire landed in the ocean destroying a third of the water, life, and commercial navigation in the seas (Rev. 8:8-9). As the third trumpet was sounded in heaven, "a great star" collided with the earth destroying a third of the world's fresh water supply and contributing to the deaths of many people (Rev. 8:10-11).

As the fourth trumpet was blown, John witnessed a reduction in the available light in the world by a third as parts of the sun and moon were darkened and a third of the stars ceased shining. One of the several consequences of this phenomena was the existence of total darkness in the world for about eight hours daily (Rev. 8:12). He then saw a flying angel hovering over the earth and announcing three more woes upon the earth which are related to the sounding of three more trumpets (Rev. 8:13).

At the sounding of the fifth trumpet, John witnessed the release of the locust/scorpion-like demons of the bottomless pit. They are apparently released to torment those who are not sealed by God (Rev. 9:1-5). As a result of the pain they inflict, there is a significant increase in the numbers of those who attempt to take their own life, but most will be unsuccessful (Rev. 9:6). These locust/scorpion-like demons will eventually devote their energies to the battlefield for about five months as the world approaches a major international conflict (Rev. 9:7-10).

Much that is known about this conflict is actually recorded in the Old Testament rather that the New Testament as it deals more with the survival of Israel than the church. An alliance of nations in eastern Europe, Russia, the Middle East and North Africa will be formed to attack and destroy Israel (Ezek. 38:1-13). This alliance will attack Israel in mass at a moment when the nation believes itself to be secure from the threat of attack (Ezek. 38:14-17). During this attack on Israel, there will be a massive earthquake in the land altering the relief of the land and causing these armies to attack each other in their confusion (Ezek. 38:18-21). The attacking army will encounter epidemic sickness, rain, hail, fire and brimstone as they begin their attack (Ezek. 38:22). Their carefully developed military strategy will fail as Israel soundly defeats the invading army through God's intervention. The nation will use what the invaders leave behind as an energy source for the nation (Ezek. 39:1-10).

The loss of life in this conflict will be so severe, it will take seven months to bury the dead that remain in the battlefield at the end of this war (Ezek. 39:11-13). At one point, a group of men will be employed and charged with the responsibility of finding and marking the burial sites of any human remains not already buried (Ezek. 39:14-16). The people of Israel will celebrate their victory over the invading alliance and attribute their success in battle to God (Ezek. 39:17-29).

At the sounding of the sixth trumpet, John witnessed death and destruction beyond that in the battle of Gog and Magog. Four angels bound at the Euphrates river were released and destroyed about one-third of the world population An army of some two hundred million people were involved in this battle.. But despite the suffering associated with this trumpet, there was still no evidence of repentance on the part of those living on the earth in those days (Rev. 9:13-21).

At the sounding of a seventh trumpet in heaven, John heard an announcement made that "the kingdoms of this world have become the kingdoms of our Lord and of His Christ, and He shall reign forever and ever!" (Rev. 11:15). As John watched the celebration of this announcement in heaven, he also saw the lost ark of the covenant as it was revealed in the temple of God in heaven (Rev. 11:16-19). While much had already happened on the earth in terms of God's judgment, there was more to follow.

THE SEVEN TRUMPET JUDGMENTS OF GOD

The Partial Destruction of Vegetation
The Partial Destruction of the Seas
The Partial Destruction of the Fresh Waters
The Partial Darkening of Solar Light
The Release of the Locust/Scorpion-like Demons
The Release of Four Angels of Destruction
The Great Announcement Concerning the Kingdom

II. The Warnings of the Seven Angels (A Heavenly View)

Following the announcement in heaven, John continued to watch the temple and saw seven angels coming out of that temple with a special mission on the earth. The first angel flew over the earth preaching the everlasting gospel and calling on people to fear God and worship Him (Rev. 14:6-7). Later, a second angel made a similar flight and announced the imminent doom of Babylon (Rev. 14:8). This was followed by a third angel who flew the same route warning the people on the earth of God's coming judgment upon those who continue worshiping the beast and/or accept his mark on their hand and forehead (Rev. 14:9-11). Apparently there was no positive response to the ministry of these three angels.

After this, John saw "one like the Son of Man" appear in heaven in regal glory sitting on a white cloud as he apparently prepared to return to the earth in judgment (Rev. 14:14). This may have been a fourth angel who had taken upon himself certain characteristics to reveal something of Christ's nature. About that time, a fifth angel came out of the temple and announced the time of harvest had come (Rev. 14:15). When that announcement was made, the angel on the cloud swept over the earth with a sickle and began reaping the earth (Rev. 14:16). Then a sixth angel appeared from the temple with a sharp sickle (Rev. 14:17). When a seventh angel with special power over fire called on the sixth angel to harvest the earth further (Rev. 14:18), the sixth angel responded causing an immense flood of blood outside the city of Jerusalem (Rev. 14:19-20).

In heaven, John watched those present continue their worship of God. At this point, they worshiped God by singing the song of Moses and the song of the Lamb (Rev. 15:1-4). Some time after the phase of worshiping God began, John noted, "I looked, and behold, the temple of the tabernacle of the testimony in heaven was opened" (Rev. 15:5). He was about to witness another phase of God's coming judgment upon the world.

III. The Bowl Judgments of God

As John focused his attention on this tabernacle, seven angels appeared in heaven and were given seven bowls of the wrath of God by the four living creatures (Rev. 15:6-8). Then a loud voice out of the temple announced, "Go and pour out the bowls of the wrath of God on the earth" (Rev. 16:1). This voice apparently authorized this aspect of God's judgment on the earth as the angels began doing so shortly after the announcement was made. John watched in amazement as he witnessed the results of God's unrestrained judgment upon the earth.

The first bowl of judgment was poured out on the earth and all that possessed the mark of the beast and worshiped the Antichrist, both man and beast were plagued with sores (Rev. 16:2). The second bowl of judgment was poured out on the sea and the rest of the sea which had survived God's previous judgments in this period turned to blood and everything dependent upon the sea for its survival died (Rev. 16:3). The third bowl of judgment was poured out on the rivers and springs of the earth and all the fresh water rivers and springs were also turned to blood (Rev. 16:4). The fourth angel poured out his bowl of wrath on the sun and the heat of the sun was intensified to scorch the population of the earth (Rev. 16:8-9). Those who were scorched by the sun did not repent but rather continued to blaspheme the name of God (Rev. 16:9).

As the fifth bowl of judgment was poured out on the throne of the Antichrist, his kingdom fell into a darkness which served to further aggravate their suffering (Rev. 16:10-11). As the sixth bowl of judgment was poured out on the Euphrates River, the river was dried up completely, enabling the armies of the east to march to Israel (Rev. 16:12). At this point, three froglike demons were released to influence the nations of the world to once again attempt an invasion of Israel (Rev. 16:13-14). While they were engaged in this effort, the seventh bowl of judgment was poured out into the air and there was a massive worldwide earthquake destroying most of the world's major cities and radically altering the world relief map (Rev. 16:17-21).

SEVEN BOWLS OF THE JUDGMENT OF GOD
The Plague of Sores
The Sea Turns to Blood
The Fresh Water Turns to Blood
The Sun Scorches the Earth
The Antichrist's Kingdom Is Darkened
The Euphrates Is Dried
The Massive International Earthquake

Perhaps the most significant city destroyed in this earthquake is the capital of the new Babylon. Responses are mixed to the news of the sudden and completely unexpected development. The city is apparently completely destroyed within a single hour, but that destruction was mourned by the other leaders and nations of the world for some time (Rev. 18:9-19). In heaven, the response to the fall of Babylon was totally different. John watched as the residents of heaven celebrated the destruction of that city as a judgment of God upon her for her murders of the saints (Rev. 18:20-24).

Conclusion

The future prospects of the world appear terrifying at times, but Christians rest in the assurance that God has prepared for them a rapture rather than His wrath. God's wrath was satisfied by the death of Christ on Calvary, but those who refuse His Son will remain on this earth to endure the judgment of God in the Great Tribulation. Christians need to warn others of this danger and lead them to receive Jesus as Savior.

CHAPTER 52

OUR LORD JESUS CHRIST: HIS COMING IN POWER AND GLORY

Revelation 19–22

The impact of Babylon's fall on the rest of the world is difficult to measure. Throughout the tribulation period, Babylon was a key player in the world economy. In the aftermath of the collapse, "the merchants of the earth will weep and mourn over her, for no one buys their merchandise anymore" (Rev. 18:11). The Bible's listing of the products traded because of Babylon and lamented over by businessmen and those involved in the shipping industry suggests much of the world depended on her for their revenue, perhaps the source of oil (Rev. 18:12-19).

Babylon was not only a commercial center, but many Bible teachers also believe it was a religious and political center during the years of the tribulation. Babylon is closely identified with the Antichrist and is probably his international capital (Rev. 17:13). Although the city is devastated and burned with fire, the Antichrist will be successful in escaping the city's destruction and will maintain his influence over the nations of the world. The Antichrist may recognize the destruction of his former power base as a judgment of God. This would explain his actions in once again lashing out at the one nation which has remained distinctive throughout the tribulation period by refusing to worship him.

I. The Final Hours of the Antichrist

In the final hours of the Antichrist's reign of terror, Israel is once again invaded by the hostile armies of the world. Most Bible teachers believe the alliance set against Israel on this occasion will include the armies of the Far East (Rev. 16:12, implied). This second alliance will appear to have greater success in battle at least initially than the former alliance. They will capture the city of Jerusalem and take about half the city into captivity (Zech. 14:2). Then the antichrist will be startled by the sign of the Son of Man in heaven and apparently retreat to Megiddo (Matt. 24:30).

John pictured Jesus returning to the earth on a white horse leading the army of heaven into battle (Rev. 19:11-16). In the custom of that day, a military leader would approach on a mule if he came in peace and rode a horse if he were coming to war. Jesus had ridden into a Roman occupied Jerusalem on a mule the week in which he was betrayed and crucified. This time he approaches the same city occupied by a different army, riding on a horse. When Jesus' feet touch earth at the Mount of Olives, the mount will split in two creating an immense valley which will join two seas (Zech. 14:4). Geologists have confirmed the existence of a major fault running through the Mount of Olives which means this is a region subject to earthquakes.

II.   The Return of Jesus

In the battle that surrounds the return of Christ, both the Antichrist and his false prophet are quickly captured and thrown into the lake of fire (Rev. 19:20). The others involved in the attack on Jerusalem apparently are killed in battle (Rev. 19:21). There does not appear to be any survivors among the soldiers who march against Jerusalem.

When Jesus returns, there will be a resurrection of Israel (Dan. 12:1-2). This will be followed by a judgment of the sheep and goat nations in which they will be evaluated in accordance with their treatment of the brethren of Jesus (Matt. 25:31). The Bible also describes a time when the earth will be purged with fire. Some Bible teachers believe this may take place at this point (2 Peter 3:10). At least two other things will take place as Jesus begins His thousand-year reign on the earth. First, Satan will be bound and cast into the bottomless pit (Rev. 20:1-3). Second, the marriage feast of the lamb will be celebrated (Rev. 19:7-9).

III.   The Thousand-Year Reign of Christ

One of the dreams of political leaders throughout the ages has been that of establishing a kingdom on earth that would be governed by peace and prosperity. That dream will never be realized in the history of mankind until the final millennium of time. When Jesus returns to this world in power and great glory, He will establish His kingdom. In doing this, Jesus will remove the curse from the earth (Isa. 11:6-9; Rom. 8:18-22). Also, all sickness will be removed from the earth (Jer. 30:7; Ezek. 34:16).

This is the kingdom of which the apostles asked during their final meeting with Jesus immediately prior to His ascension. Israel will become the head of the nations of the world (Deut. 28:13) and the Lord will dwell in Jerusalem which is again recognized as the capital city of Israel (Zech. 8:3). The Gentile (sheep) nations will enjoy the blessing of the Lord (Matt. 25:33-34; Isa. 11:10; Zech. 8:23) and recognize and value Israel as never before (Isa. 2:2-3). The Throne of David will be once more established in Jerusalem (Luke 1:31). The One described as the King of Kings will receive His kingdom (Dan. 7:9-10) and sit on the throne of David (Luke 1:33). David himself will be raised from the dead and will rule as a vice regent (Ezek. 37:22-24). The apostles will rule the twelve tribes of Israel under David (Matt. 19:28). Other believers will also be appointed to positions of authority and influence to a lesser degree than David and the apostles (Zech. 3:7). This will help maintain order in the kingdom which will last a thousand years (Rev. 20:4-6). Also, the church will reign with Christ during this period (2 Tim. 2:12; Rev. 5:10, 20:6).

No one will die throughout the duration of this kingdom (Zech. 8:4-6; Isa. 65:20). Children will be born but aging appears to take place at a much slower rate during the kingdom age (Ezek. 47:22). People will be engaged in meaningful work and live much as people today live, only without the influence of sin (Isa. 62:8-9; 65:21-23; Ezek. 48:18-19). There will be an increase in solar light which will apparently result in increased prosperity (Isa. 4:5; 60:19-20). The entire world will speak a single universal language (Zech. 3:9). The religious calendar of Israel will once again be observed and the feasts of Israel will be kept (Ezek. 45:18-25).

The topography of Israel will be changed to include a new river (Ezek. 47:1-12), a new land (Ezek. 47:13-14), and a new city (Ezek. 48:15-20). A new much larger temple will be built during the millennium (Ezek. 43:1-17). Memorial sacrifices will be offered in the temple as part of worshiping God (Ezek. 43:18-27; 46:1-15). This temple will be unique from all other temples built since the exile in that the shekinah cloud will return to this temple (Ezek. 43:1-5). A river will flow out from the new temple (Ezek. 47:1-5; Zech. 14:8).

At the end of the thousand years, Satan will be loosed briefly (Rev. 20:7). Satan will deceive the nations once again and gather them together for a final battle of Gog and Magog (Rev. 20:8). The immense army which challenges the peace of the kingdom will be destroyed by the fire of God (Rev. 20:9). Satan will be captured and thrown into the lake of fire (Rev. 20:10). Following this battle, all the peoples of the world will be brought before the Great White Throne to be judged (Rev. 20:11). There will be a resurrection of the unsaved dead so they too can appear before the throne of judgment (Rev. 20:12-13). At this judgment, Death and Hades will be cast into the lake of fire (Rev. 20:14). All whose names are not recorded in the Book of Life will be cast into the lake of fire (Rev. 20:15). This age, like all those before it will end in an evidence of mankind's failure and an appropriate judgment of sin.

IV.   The Eternal Kingdom

Only four chapters in Scripture describe the world God created as it should be, free from the influence of sin. In the final two chapters of the Revelation, John describes "a new heaven and a new earth" (Rev. 21:1). This may be the world which Isaiah called Beulah meaning married as John describes this world in terms of the Bride of Christ being presented to the Lamb. It is a totally new world made by the One who sat on the throne who claims, "Behold, I make all things new" (Rev. 21:5).

Ironically, one of the angels who poured out one of the bowls of God's wrath showed John the city. The wall of the city is described as being made of twelve pure and transparent gems with twelve gates each made out of a single giant pearl. The gates of this city are constantly open and are guarded by a dozen angels. The city is described as being as high as it is long and wide (Rev. 21:16). Some Bible teachers interpret this to mean the city is a cube, while others believe it may look similar to a giant pyramid.

A number of things will be missing in this new and eternal kingdom. First, there is "no temple in it, for the Lord God Almighty and the Lamb are its temple" (Rev. 21:22). Second, there is no sun or moon as the city is constantly illuminated by the light of the Lamb (Rev. 21:23). Also absent from this city is any hint of evil or defilement (Rev. 21:27). This city will also lack the curse (Rev. 22:3) and night (Rev. 22:5). The city will be a center in which "the kings of the earth bring their glory and honor into it" (Rev. 21:24).

Through the heart of this city a river flowed originating in the throne of God. The water of this river was pure and crystal clear. On either side of the river, the tree of life grew once again. It had remained hidden from humanity since the day Adam and Eve ate of the fruit of the Tree of the Knowledge of Good and Evil. Now it once again bore twelve different kinds of fruit which were enjoyed by the residents of the city every month of the year. "And the leaves of the tree were for the healing of the nations" (Rev. 22:2).

Conclusion

As John sat on that hot, dry, and dusty island of Patmos contemplating all that God had in store for His people in the future history of the world, his heart longed for heaven to quickly become a reality. "Even so, come, Lord Jesus," he prayed (Rev. 22:20). Today, Christians are 1,900 years closer to that day than when John first saw this vision. Still, the heart cry of God's people remains the same, "Even so, come, Lord Jesus."

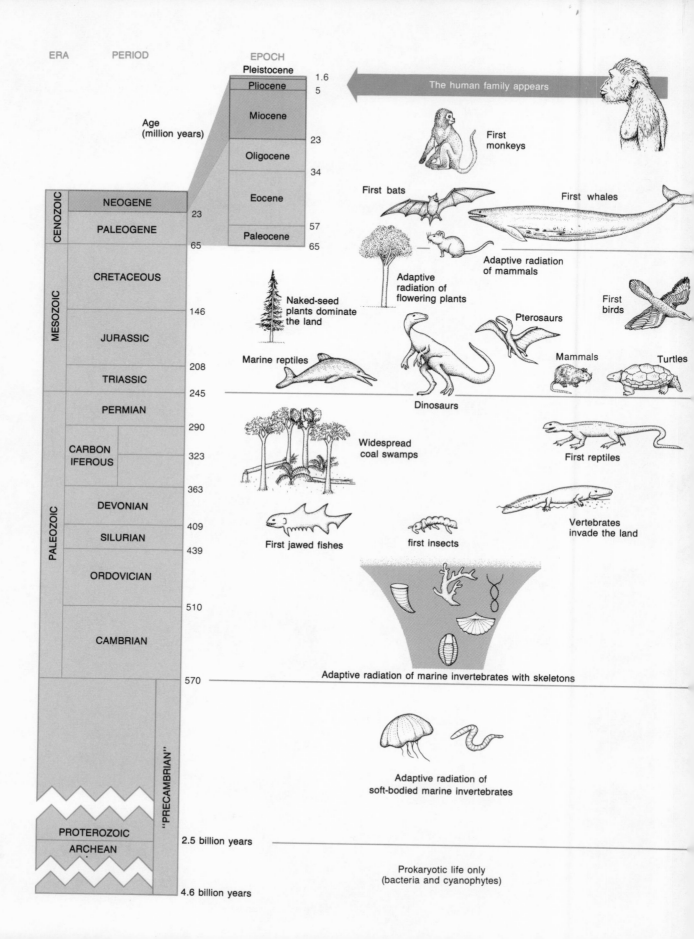

ERA	PERIOD	EPOCH	Age (million years)

Pleistocene — 1.6
Pliocene — 5
Miocene — 23
Oligocene — 34
Eocene — 57
Paleocene — 65

CENOZOIC
NEOGENE — 23
PALEOGENE — 65

MESOZOIC
CRETACEOUS — 146
JURASSIC — 208
TRIASSIC — 245

PALEOZOIC
PERMIAN — 290
CARBONIFEROUS — 323
— 363
DEVONIAN — 409
SILURIAN — 439
ORDOVICIAN — 510
CAMBRIAN — 570

"PRECAMBRIAN"
2.5 billion years
PROTEROZOIC
ARCHEAN
4.6 billion years

The human family appears

First monkeys

First bats

First whales

Adaptive radiation of mammals

Adaptive radiation of flowering plants

Naked-seed plants dominate the land

First birds

Pterosaurs

Mammals

Turtles

Marine reptiles

Dinosaurs

Widespread coal swamps

First reptiles

First jawed fishes

first insects

Vertebrates invade the land

Adaptive radiation of marine invertebrates with skeletons

Adaptive radiation of soft-bodied marine invertebrates

Prokaryotic life only (bacteria and cyanophytes)

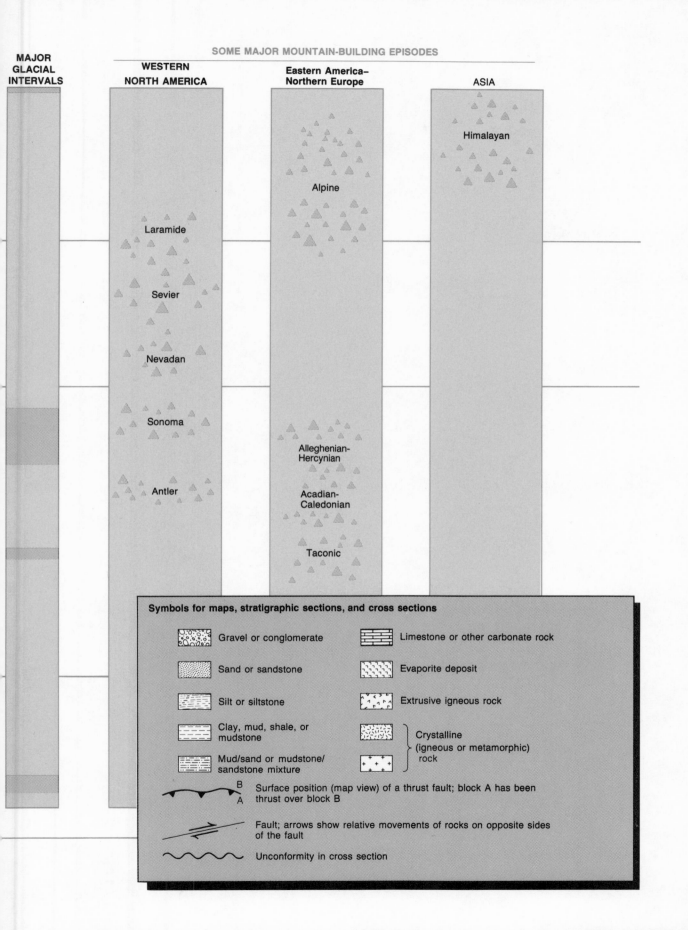

SOME MAJOR MOUNTAIN-BUILDING EPISODES

MAJOR GLACIAL INTERVALS

WESTERN NORTH AMERICA

Eastern America–Northern Europe

ASIA

Himalayan

Alpine

Laramide

Sevier

Nevadan

Sonoma

Alleghenian-Hercynian

Acadian-Caledonian

Antler

Taconic

Symbols for maps, stratigraphic sections, and cross sections

Gravel or conglomerate

Limestone or other carbonate rock

Sand or sandstone

Evaporite deposit

Silt or siltstone

Extrusive igneous rock

Clay, mud, shale, or mudstone

Crystalline (igneous or metamorphic) rock

Mud/sand or mudstone/sandstone mixture

B
A
Surface position (map view) of a thrust fault; block A has been thrust over block B

Fault; arrows show relative movements of rocks on opposite sides of the fault

Unconformity in cross section